"Ernest Renan famously claimed that Islam emerged in the 'full light of history.' Spencer's startling non-biography biography finds quite the reverse. When it comes to Muhammad's life, 'we appear to have precise and detailed historical information, but what we actually have is myth, fable, folk tales, sermonizing, factionalism, and guesswork.' This fascinating book by an accomplished scholar establishes that, in place of Muhammad's supposedly minutely detailed biography, from birth to death 'what he said and did, and who he really was, is... thoroughly lost in the mists of time.' This has immense implications for Islam—and the world."

—**Daniel Pipes**, Middle East Forum

"Robert Spencer's *Muhammad: A Critical Biography* offers not just an overview of the singular life of the founder of the Islamic religion; it is also a unique evaluation of the historical value of the traditions regarding Muhammad's life that most historians take for granted as being historically accurate. Spencer demonstrates that virtually every aspect of what Islamic tradition teaches about Muhammad, including the circumstances of his first revelation, the identity of the being who appeared to him, and even the Islamic prophet's very name, is controverted by other Islamic traditions. He proves definitively that the accounts of Muhammad's life, which he examines in detail, are not historical records, but the product of mythical and legendary development, with the renowned aspects of Muhammad's biography being the result of selection from a great mass of material rather than of remembrance by his contemporaries. This is a groundbreaking work that will revolutionize the popular understanding of the figure of Muhammad and the circumstances of Islam's origins."

—**Ibn Warraq**, Author, *The Quest for the Historical Muhammad*

"The always brave Robert Spencer offers his readers once again an amazing opportunity to look at the history of Muhammad—and the stories that have been told about him—in a thought-provoking manner. Spencer is a genius and this book historical. What is simply accepted by many as the historical truth, deserves further consideration. How trustworthy can a narrative be that was written decades and sometimes even centuries later? This paragon of critical literature shows that not everything always has to be accepted at face value, especially when the consequences of what is said and written can be disastrous. This book a must read for anyone interested in the truth."

—**Geert Wilders**

"What an amazing book! This was such a joy to read, and with all the 'marking-up' I've done with it, I'll be using it for decades to come. This book studies the biography of Muhammad's life through the prism of historical criticism, something which has never really been done adequately before, possibly due to the controversy such an endeavor will cause any author who dares take on such a task (something Spencer is well accustomed to and refers to in his closing statements). Yet because this book is so unique, it will, I believe, be foundational for anyone who wants to really understand who this man Muhammad was (or was not), and why so many millions in the world today choose to follow him. This is certainly a 'must have' book for your library, not only because it is so interesting and readable, but because Spencer has taken the time to amalgamate the best research by the best scholars, and put them all into one book."

—**Dr. Jay Smith**, Pfander Films

"Robert Spencer has once again produced a scholarly tour de force. *Muhammad: A Critical Biography* is a searching enquiry of the earliest Islamic texts pertaining to the ostensible prophet of Islam, demonstrating that these are not and cannot be viewed as firsthand historical sources, but at best as posterior apocryphal hagiography. He perspicuously shows their many contradictions, disparities, and sundry inconsistencies. This book is an accessible yet thorough and comprehensive introduction to the overwhelming difficulties that the early Islamic literary traditions present to those wishing to discover the authentic words and deeds of this towering yet mysterious persona who even so remains firmly enshrouded in the shadows of lore.

—**Prof. Robert M. Kerr**, Research Director, Inârah Institute for Research on Early Islamic History and the Qur'an, Saarbrücken, Germany

Also by Robert Spencer

Confessions of an Islamophobe

The History of Jihad: From Muhammad to ISIS

The Palestine Delusion: The Catastrophic History of the Middle East Peace Process

Rating America's Presidents: An America-First Look at Who Is Best, Who Is Overrated, and Who Was An Absolute Disaster

Obama and Trump: Who Was Better For America?

Did Muhammad Exist?: An Inquiry into Islam's Obscure Origins— Revised and Expanded Edition

The Critical Qur'an: Explained from Key Islamic Commentaries and Contemporary Historical Research

The Sumter Gambit: How the Left Is Trying to Foment a Civil War

Empire of God: How the Byzantines Saved Civilization

MUHAMMAD

A CRITICAL BIOGRAPHY

ROBERT SPENCER

BOMBARDIER
BOOKS

Published by Bombardier Books
An Imprint of Post Hill Press

Muhammad:
A Critical Biography
© 2024 by Robert Spencer
All Rights Reserved

ISBN: 979-8-88845-308-7
ISBN (eBook): 979-8-88845-309-4

Cover design by Jim Villaflores

This is a work of nonfiction. All people, locations, events, and situations are portrayed to the best of the author's memory.

Post Hill Press
New York • Nashville
posthillpress.com

Published in the United States of America
1 2 3 4 5 6 7 8 9 10

*Dedicated with love to all those who love Muhammad,
with hope for our mutual enlightenment.*

Contents

Author's Note

The repetitions of "peace be upon him" in hadiths after every mention of Muhammad's name have been removed for ease of reading. Language in some quotations has been modernized and spelling standardized, in all cases with strict adherence to the sense of the text. The apostrophes signifying elements of the Arabic forms of words and names that have no meaning for the English language have also often been removed for ease of reading. The transliterations of various names are not systematic and are dictated more by what is the common form in English than by adherence to the rules of one system of transliteration or another.

An Imprecise Timeline

As will become clear as this book progresses, there is very little certainty about when the principal events of Muhammad's life took place, or if they even took place at all. This timeline, therefore, is offered as a reference to the general traditional understanding of the timing of these events. The historical facts regarding when they may actually have taken place, if they did take place, are lost in the mists of time.

569 or 570	*Muhammad is born.*
595	*Muhammad marries Khadija.*
610	*Muhammad receives his first visitation from the angel and his first revelation of a portion of the Qur'an.*
619	*Death of Khadija.*
620	*Muhammad marries the six-year-old Aisha; the marriage is "consummated" in 623.*
620	*Muhammad's night journey to Jerusalem.*
622	*The hijrah from Mecca to Medina.*
624	*Battle of Badr.*
624	*Muhammad expels the Banu Qaynuqa and later the Banu Nadir from Medina.*
625	*Battle of Uhud.*
627	*Muhammad marries his daughter-in-law and cousin Zaynab bint Jahsh.*
627	*Battle of the Trench.*
628	*Khaybar raid.*
628	*Treaty of Hudaybiyya.*
630	*Muslim conquest of Mecca.*
630	*Expedition to Tabuk.*
632	*Muhammad dies.*

Who Is This Man?
Is There Even Anyone Here at All?

"I have fabricated things against God and have imputed to Him words which he has not spoken." —Muhammad[1]

It was narrated that Abdur-Rahman bin Abi Laila said: We said to Zaid bin Arqam: 'Tell us a Hadith from the Messenger of Allah.' He said: 'We have grown old and have forgotten, and (narrating) Ahadith [hadiths] from the Messenger of Allah is difficult.'" [2]

Muhammad, the prophet of Islam, is without any doubt one of the most significant personalities in history. He is revered as a prophet by well over a billion people today. Those who are devoted to his teachings insist that they regard him as a mere human being. Yet they accord Muhammad a status that no other human being has ever enjoyed: he is even not to be pictured, as the mere depiction of so wondrous a man could tempt lesser human beings to idolatry. The religion he founded has now spread to every corner of the globe and is aggressively and confidently expanding in a confused and demoralized post-Christian West. Even some who

---

1 Abu Ja'far Muhammad bin Jarir al-Tabari, *The History of al-Tabari*, Volume VI, *Muhammad at Mecca*, W. Montgomery Watt and M. V. McDonald, trans. (Albany: State University of New York Press, 1988), 111.

2 Sunan Ibn Majah, no. 25. Hadith quotations are mostly taken from the anonymously translated compendium at the Islamic website Sunnah.com: "Our goal is to make authentic, comprehensive, and beneficial information pertaining to the sunnah of the Prophet Muhammad (saws) accessible to as many people around the world as possible in order to facilitate research and promote its mainstream and broadly accepted understanding." https://sunnah.com/about. Sunnah.com revises its translations frequently, often to bring them in line with Western sensibilities, so the cited texts in this book may not in all cases correspond with the English version posted at Sunnah.com. They do, however, conform to the Arabic original.

1

do not accept that he was the last and greatest prophet of the one true God readily avow that he was an extraordinary individual.

Islamic scholars state that the reason for this is simple: Muhammad and his Qur'an shine forth with such magnificence and wisdom that any unbiased observer will notice their radiance. The contemporary Islamic scholar Tariq Ramadan states that "the Prophet came to human-kind with a message of faith, ethics, and hope.... Though Muhammad came with this message, throughout his life he kept listening to women, children, men, slaves, rich, and poor, as well as outcasts. He listened to, welcomed, and comforted them."[3]

Another modern-day scholar of Muhammad, Yahiya Emerick, says that "regardless of whether one agrees with the applicability of Islam in politics or society, Muhammad did transform the warring Arab tribes into a new kind of civilization, one based on faith in God and the essential brotherhood of all people."[4]

It is easy to find non-Muslims who have shared in this admiration. The nineteenth-century American writer Washington Irving, who gave us Rip Van Winkle and Ichabod Crane, was not uncritical of Muham-mad, but he did assert that "his intellectual qualities were undoubtedly of an extraordinary kind. He had a quick apprehension, a retentive memory, a vivid imagination, and an inventive genius. Owing but little to education, he had quickened and informed his mind by close obser-vation, and stored it with a great variety of knowledge concerning the systems of religion current in his day, or handed down by tradition from antiquity. His ordinary discourse was grave and sententious, abounding with those aphorisms and apologues so popular among the Arabs; at times he was excited and eloquent, and his eloquence was aided by a voice musical and sonorous."[5] Irving is not alone in making this assess-ment based upon Muhammad as he is depicted in early Islamic sources and presenting it as if it were simple historical fact.

In a similar vein, the twentieth-century English historian W. Mont-gomery Watt rejects the possibility that Muhammad was fabricating his claim to prophethood and asserts that there is "a good case to be made out for believing in Muhammad's sincerity. His readiness to undergo

---

3 Tariq Ramadan, In the Footsteps of the Prophet: Lessons from the Life of Muhammad (Oxford University Press, 2007), 212.

4 Yahiya Emerick, The Life and Work of Muhammad (Alpha Books, 2002), vi.

5 Washington Irving, Life of Mahomet (E. P. Dutton & Co. Inc., 1911), 230.

persecutions for his beliefs, the high moral character of the men who believed in him and looked up to him as leader, and the greatness of his ultimate achievement—all argue his fundamental integrity. To suppose Muhammad an impostor raises more problems than it solves. Moreover, none of the great figures of history is so poorly appreciated in the West as Muhammad."[6]

Early in the twenty-first century, the ex-nun and Islamic apologist Karen Armstrong asserted that the jihad attacks of September 11, 2001 in New York and Washington would have horrified Muhammad, for he "spent most of his life trying to stop that kind of indiscriminate slaughter." She even claimed that Muhammad "eventually abjured violence and pursued a daring, inspired policy of non-violence that was worthy of Gandhi."[7]

Respected for his message, admired for his integrity, revered for his connection to the divine: Muhammad is all that and more. And in mainstream academic circles, few entertain any serious doubts about the historical reliability of the early Islamic accounts of his life. It was in 1851 that the French historian Ernest Renan made his oft-quoted assertion that Islam "was born in the full light of history," yet nearly two centuries later, most historians still take that view for granted, albeit without examining in any depth the issues involved.[8]

Much more recently, the novelist Salman Rushdie, who spent years in hiding and ultimately was critically injured for the crime of mocking Muhammad, likewise confidently asserted that "for the life of Muhammad, we know everything more or less. We know where he lived, what his economic situation was, who he fell in love with."[9] Rushdie's statement would have been more accurate if he had said that there are Islamic sources that give us all this information about Muhammad. Renan's claim, likewise, would be closer to the truth had he said that "the earliest Islamic sources purport to show us Islam being born in the full light of history." Yet that light was not, in fact, switched on until well over a century after Muhammad lived. There was a tremendous proliferation

---

6 W. Montgomery Watt, *Muhammad at Mecca* (Oxford University Press, 1953), 52.

7 Karen Armstrong, *Muhammad: A Biography of the Prophet* (Harper San Francisco, 1992), 5.

8 Quoted in Ibn Warraq, ed., *The Quest for the Historical Muhammad* (Amherst, NY: Prometheus, 2000), 15.

9 Ibid., 15–16.

of material about his life in the ninth century, but that was fully two centuries after the traditionally accepted date of his death.

This is now my third book about Muhammad and my second biography of him. Yet while there is overlap among the three books, their scope and perspectives are vastly different from one another. The first, *The Truth about Muhammad* (2006), was a summary of what the earliest Islamic sources say, and what Muslims believe, about the prophet of Islam. It was designed to give the non-Muslim reader a basic familiarity with the basic facts about Muhammad's life as Muslims understand those facts and to clarify the question of why so many violent jihadis look to Muhammad as their guiding light and inspiration, even as so many others see him as "a gentle man, sensitive, faithful, free from rancor and hatred," as Renan put it.[10]

In *The Truth about Muhammad*, I was not asserting that the Islamic accounts of Muhammad were historically accurate, but only that they were believed by the great majority of Muslims. Then, in *Did Muhammad Exist?* (2012, revised and expanded edition 2021), I examined the historical value of those early Islamic narratives about Muhammad and highlighted the historical problems that prevent many people from taking them at face value.

The present volume is a combination and extension of both approaches and a kind of sequel to both books (although it is not necessary to have read either before reading this one). It presents the life of Muhammad from Islamic sources, as did *The Truth about Muhammad*, although, in this book, I am examining this material with different questions in mind and including a great deal of material that I had to leave out of that volume for reasons of space. It also extends the investigations begun in *Did Muhammad Exist?* by evaluating the material about Muhammad from the standpoint of historical reliability in search of the answer to the question of whether we can know anything at all with any degree of certainty about Muhammad and if so, what exactly we can know.

Also, as was the case with *The Critical Qur'an*, the word "critical" in the title of this book has two distinct meanings. This book, like my edition of the Qur'an, is one small attempt to make up for the general failure of the academic world in the West to conduct any kind of critical

---

10 Ibid., 17.

examination of Islam's origins or of the life of Muhammad, as it has done exhaustively with the origins of Judaism and Christianity and the lives of Moses and Jesus. Western academics have no fear of denying that either Moses or Jesus or both even existed at all or of asserting that if they did, they didn't do anything like what they are depicted as doing in the Hebrew and Christian scriptures. Radically revisionist reconstructions of the origins of Judaism and Christianity have become widely popular in the West.

Whether for fear of incurring a death fatwa and a life-threatening attack like Rushdie or the opprobrium of their peers for being "Islamophobic," however, Western academics have been far less eager to examine the historicity of Muhammad or the reliability of the Islamic accounts of Islam's origins. This book stands, therefore, as one of the first, if not the first, critical biography of Muhammad. Like *The Critical Qur'an*, it is intended to make up for a gap in the study of Islam that compromised and groupthinking academics have not dared to close.

This book is also unapologetically critical in the other sense of the term. I am not a Muslim and believe that a great deal of what Muhammad is depicted as saying and doing is wrong by any moral standard other than the one created by his own words and deeds. In this book, I'll also examine how some of the words and deeds attributed to Muhammad have had devastating effects on the world, precisely because of the reverence in which Muslims hold him. Muhammad is indeed one of the most consequential figures in history, and his teachings have not brought the peace, tolerance, and kindness to the world that one might have expected from the words of Ramadan, Emerick, Watt, and others. That will also be part of our investigations here.

CHAPTER ONE

The Prophet Armed with the Sword

The Creation of Muhammad

The myth of Muhammad may have been born in the Bible.

Contemporary Islamic apologists like to point to various biblical passages and claim that properly understood, these refer to Muhammad.[1] This is not entirely a flight of fancy or feat of wishful thinking, although that is not to say that these apologists are remotely correct. The passages in question are not prophecies or foreshadowings of a coming Arabian prophet. They certainly do not refer to and have never been understood in Jewish or Christian tradition as referring to Muhammad, the prophet of Islam. Nevertheless, they may have been the kernel of the idea that eventually developed into the full-blown myth of the prophet of Islam.

In Psalm 68:16 and Proverbs 12:12, there is found the Hebrew word *hamad*, which means "desired." Song of Songs 5:16 says: "His speech is most sweet, and he is altogether desirable. This is my beloved and this is my friend, O daughters of Jerusalem."[2] In this passage, as the modern-day Qur'an scholar Dr. Robert Kerr has pointed out, "desirable" is *mahamadim*, making this a passage that is particularly favored among Islamic apologists. The claim that this verse actually refers to Muhammad the prophet of Islam is absurd and anachronistic, as it would require the verse to be saying that "he is altogether Muhammad."[3]

1 See, for example, "Who Is 'Muhammadim' in the Song of Solomon?," Islam Compass, n.d., https://islamcompass.com/who-is-muhammadim-in-the-song-of-solomon/.

2 Biblical quotations are generally taken from the Revised Standard Version, National Council of the Churches of Christ in the USA, revised New Testament, 1971.

3 "The evolution of 'mhmd': a secret long hidden in plain sight," Islamic Origins, YouTube, September 4, 2023, https://www.youtube.com/watch?v=OP0j5dUIk6A. I am indebted to this lecture for much of the material in this section.

The Islamic apologist claim also runs into trouble in Hosea 9:16: "Ephraim is stricken, their root is dried up, they shall bear no fruit. Even though they bring forth, I will slay their beloved children." The word used here for "beloved" is *mahamadim*; if Muhammad is meant, the passage would be saying, "I will slay their Muhammad," which would take the wind out of the sails of those who would see Song of Songs 5:16 as a prophecy about the coming of Muhammad. If it were, Hosea 9:16 would necessarily also be a prophecy about Muhammad being killed.

The passage from the Song of Songs, however, does lend itself to a messianic interpretation, with the beloved who is awaited being not just an earthly lover, but the savior figure. Jews and then Christians began to use the same word that is used in Song of Songs, *mhmd*, the desirable one or the praiseworthy one, as a term for God or Christ. We see this in an inscription dating from 518 AD in the Yemeni city of Najran, from which, according to ninth-century Islamic tradition, a Christian delegation later journeyed to meet with the prophet of Islam. The Jewish king Yusuf Asar Yathar, also known as Dhu Nuwas, defeated Christian forces from Abyssinia in battle and celebrated his victory with a rock inscription that concludes with this: "O Lord of the Jews! By the praiseworthy one."[4] In the inscription itself, this is *rbhd b-mhmd*.[5] *Rb* is Lord, as in the Arabic *rab* and related to the word *rabbi*, master or teacher. *Mhmd*, the praiseworthy one, is an early appearance of what would become the name of a prophet, but here refers to God himself.

Over a century later, this title would appear again, but whether or not it was the name of a particular person was by no means clear.

The First We Hear

According to the standard Islamic account, Muhammad was born in 570 and died in 632 AD, and he exercised his prophetic ministry for the last twenty-three years of his life, from 610 to 632.

In the course of those twenty-three years, he produced the Qur'an in piecemeal fashion; he and his followers maintained that it was the record of his revelations from Allah, while his detractors dismissed it as his own imaginings and forgeries.

---

4 A. F. L. Beeston, "Two Bi'r Hima Inscriptions Re-examined," *Bulletin of the School of Oriental and African Studies, University of London*, Vol. 48, No. 1 (1985), 46.

5 Ibid., 45.

The believers, armed with this holy book and the teachings and example of Muhammad, streamed out of Arabia shortly after his death and embarked upon a breathtaking series of conquests, spreading the new religion from Spain to India within one hundred years after Muhammad's death. Muhammad's third successor, Uthman, collected and codified the various sections of the Qur'an and distributed it to the growing Muslim community just over twenty years after Muhammad's death, in the year 653. After that, the conquered peoples accepted Islam more quickly than ever.

All those assertions, however, despite being taken for granted almost universally today, rest on much later writings, writings that are so late that the accuracy of this canonical account cannot be taken for granted.

Going through the available historical records one by one in chronological order, we go for a considerable period before encountering anyone who corresponds fully to the now-familiar figure of the prophet of Islam. Of course, some of the documents of the earliest period of Islam have undoubtedly been lost. Nevertheless, the absence of Muhammad from all of the earliest texts relating to the seventh-century Arab conquests of the Middle East, North Africa, Persia, and India is striking.

According to the available documents, the first time the world heard about a prophet arising in Arabia was in the 630s, from a Greek Christian whose work is known as the *Doctrina Jacobi*, or Teaching of Jacob. This document dates from shortly after the traditional date of Muhammad's death in 632; for all the period of Muhammad's life, and all of his dealings with the world outside of Arabia that are recorded in later Islamic traditions, there seems to have been no notice of Muhammad anywhere, either by Muslims or non-Muslims, that was committed to writing during his lifetime. Muslims insist that the Qur'an constitutes such notice, as it mentions Muhammad by name four times, but there is likewise no independent attestation of the existence of the Qur'an until nearly a century after Muhammad is supposed to have died.

In the passage that is often cited as being an early non-Muslim reference to Muhammad, a Jew recounts the coming of this Saracen prophet. "Saracen" was a term that was in common use at the time to refer to the people of Arabia.

When the *candidatus* [a member of the Roman imperial guard] was killed by the Saracens [*Sarakenoi*], I was at Caesarea and I set off by boat to Sykamina. People were saying "the candidatus has been killed," and we Jews were overjoyed. And they were saying that the prophet had appeared, coming with the Saracens, and that he was proclaiming the advent of the anointed one, the Christ who was to come. I, having arrived at Sykamina, stopped by a certain old man well-versed in scriptures, and I said to him: "What can you tell me about the prophet who has appeared with the Saracens?" He replied, groaning deeply: "He is false, for the prophets do not come armed with a sword. Truly they are works of anarchy being committed today and I fear that the first Christ to come, whom the Christians worship, was the one sent by God and we instead are preparing to receive the Antichrist. Indeed, Isaiah said that the Jews would retain a perverted and hardened heart until all the earth should be devastated. But you go, master Abraham, and find out about the prophet who has appeared." So I, Abraham, inquired and heard from those who had met him that there was no truth to be found in the so-called prophet, only the shedding of men's blood. He says also that he has the keys of paradise, which is incredible.[6]

This does indeed tell us about a prophet among the Saracens and immediately resembles Muhammad because of the telling detail that he was "armed with a sword" and was busy shedding men's blood. Caesarea and Sykamina, however, were in Palestine, and while the Arabs did indeed conquer them just a few years after the traditional date of Muhammad's death, the *Doctrina Jacobi* has him appearing there with the Saracens. This prophet is also proclaiming that the Messiah is to come and that he has the keys to Paradise, neither of which were part of Muhammad's message as depicted in the accounts that Muslims accept as reliable. The reference to the "keys to paradise" could conceivably be a reference to the Qur'an's guarantee of paradise to those who "kill and are killed" (9:111), and Islam does teach that Jesus the Muslim prophet will return at the end of the world and break all crosses, but neither of these are the central or most salient aspects of Islam's message.

Nevertheless, the Islamic apologetic site Islamic Awareness lists the *Doctrina Jacobi* first among "dated and datable Muslim and non-Muslim

6 Doctrina *Jacobi*, vol. 16, 209 (quoted in Robert G. Hoyland, *Seeing Islam as Others Saw It: A Survey and Evaluation of Christian, Jewish, and Zoroastrian Writings on Early Islam* [Princeton: Darwin Press, 1997], 57).

sources mentioning Prophet Muhammad."[7] Yet it simply cannot be asserted with any confidence that this violent Saracen prophet is certainly the same person as Muhammad, the prophet of Islam. While he is a sword-bearing, murderous Arab prophet, the *Doctrina Jacobi* doesn't demonstrate any awareness that he has delivered a new holy book, and his message is sharply divergent from the message of Islam as we know it. Consequently, we must journey on; this nameless prophet is clearly not Muhammad.

It is possible, however, that this Arabian prophet did end up becoming part of the story of Muhammad as it has come down to us. That is, the legends of a sword-bearing prophet arising among the Arabs became an element of the myth of Muhammad, the prophet of Islam, as it was being formed. It is possible that the *Doctrina Jacobi* is based on accounts of a warrior prophet that were circulating at the time that the legend of Muhammad was being formulated, and were eventually incorporated into that legend.

At this point, then—that is, the late 630s—we have a warrior prophet among the Arabs. A document that was written in the flyleaf of a copy of the gospels according to Matthew and Mark around the same time allows us to add more (note that the material in brackets was added by the translator to make the document, which is in an extremely fragmentary condition, more understandable):

> In January {the people of} Homs took the word for their lives and many villages were ravaged by the killing of {the Arabs of} Muhmd and many people were slain and {taken} prisoner from Galilee as far as Beth....[8]

Here we have an actual mention of Muhammad, but there is no reason to assume, as so many do today, that this is a reference to Muhammad, the prophet of Islam, as he appears in the ninth-century literature. Like the Muhammad of Islam, however, this Muhammad does seem to be both an Arab and a warrior, for his Arabs are killing people and ravaging villages, but there is no indication in this passage that he is a prophet. And in light of the fact that the phrase "the Arabs of" was added by the

7 "Dated and Datable Texts Mentioning Prophet Muhammad from 1–100 AH / 622–719 CE," *Islamic Awareness*, January 26, 2008, https://www.islamic-awareness.org/history/islam/inscriptions/earlysaw.

8 *Fragment on the Arab Conquests* (quoted in Hoyland, 116–117).

translator in order to help make sense of this fragmentary writing, we cannot even be completely certain that this was the correct addition or that the original document referred to Arabs at all. This warlord may have been the Arab prophet referred to in the *Doctrina Jacobi*, but he may also have been neither a warrior nor a prophet. In the final analysis, this is an indication that there may have been a warrior named Muhammad operating in Palestine in the 630s, but that was something that the Muhammad of Islam did not do. It may be that when the story of Muhammad was finally being formulated, the various traditions that both of these odd references represent were incorporated into it.

A Christian priest known as Thomas the Presbyter also may have written of Muhammad around the same time, although his writings were revised in the mid-eighth century, and thus the possibility that the reference to Muhammad was added at that time cannot be ruled out.[9] Thomas writes in Syriac of "a battle between the Romans and the *tayyaye d-Mhmt*" in 634.[10] The word *tayyaye*, or *Taiyaye*, means "nomads," although other ancient writers use it in reference to the conquerors of the region. This led the historian Robert G. Hoyland to translate *tayyaye d-Mhmt* as "the Arabs of Muhammad," but he was taking some liberties with the text, since Syriac has both a *t* and a *d*. Thus *Mhmt* may mean "Muhammad," but it may not. If it is indeed a reference to Muhammad, we have here again Muhammad as a warlord, but there is no mention here of him being a prophet or having a new religion or holy book.

The paucity of this evidence, and the complete absence of any sign of the actual figure of Muhammad the Islamic prophet, has not prevented these references from being used to support the claim that the Muhammad of Islam is well-attested in the seventh century, just a few years after his death. Yet these references actually contain nothing that compels one to acknowledge that the Muhammad of Islam is the one who is being spoken about.

In 639, the Patriarch of Antioch, John I, engaged in a discussion with the Arab commander Amr ibn al-As. No contemporary record of

---

9 Historian Robert G. Hoyland notes that "a mid-seventh century Jacobite author had written a continuation of Eusebius and that this had been revised almost a century later when the lists of synods and caliphs and so on were added" (Hoyland, 119).

10 Thomas the Presbyter, *Chronicle*, 147–148 (quoted in Hoyland, 120).

it survives, but it does still exist in a manuscript from the year 874.[11] The author of that manuscript refers to the Arab conquerors as "Hagarians" (*mhaggraye*), referring to Abraham's concubine and Ishmael's mother Hagar. No one on either side of this discussion makes the slightest reference to the Qur'an, Islam, or Muhammad.[12]

In a similar vein, the Patriarch of Seleucia, Ishoyahb III, wrote in 647 about the "Tayyaye" and "Arab Hagarians" who "do not help those who attribute sufferings and death to God, the Lord of everything."[13] In other words, these Tayyaye rejected the crucifixion and divinity of Christ, as does the Qur'an. But once again, Ishoyahb says nothing at all about Muslims, Islam, the Qur'an, or Muhammad.

The Islamic Awareness website provides several examples of how these sparse early records are confidently, and misleadingly, presented as historical evidence for the Islamic Muhammad. Among its list of early references to Muhammad, it includes what appears to be a legal document carved in Arabic on a stone tablet and dating from around twenty years after the traditional date of Muhammad's death. The inscription reads: "In the name of God, the Beneficent, the Merciful…the protection of God and the guarantee of His Messenger…. And witnessed it Abd al-Rahman bin Awf, al-Zuhri, and Abu Ubaydah bin al-Jarrah and its writer—Mu'awiya…the year thirty-two."[14]

The year 32 of the Islamic calendar, which is a lunar calendar, corresponds to 652 AD, which is indeed twenty years after Muhammad is supposed to have died in 632. Islamic Awareness notes that the inscription was discovered on the Temple Mount during archaeological excavations in 1968 and emphasizes that it refers to "the protection of God and His Messenger" (*dhimmat Allah wa daman rasulih*." This is, we're told, "the earliest mention of this phrase in a dated document."

---

11 Patriarch John/Arab Emir, *Colloquy*, 248/257, Nau, Francois, ed./tr. "Un colloque de patriarche Jean avec l'emir des Agareens et fait divers des annees 712 a 716," JA ser. xi, 5 (1915), 225–279 (quoted in Hoyland, 459).

12 Alphonse Mingana, "The Transmission of the Koran," in Ibn Warraq, ed., *The Origins of the Koran* (Amherst, New York: Prometheus, 1998), 105.

13 Edit. Duval, *Corp. Script. Christ. Orient*, tomus LXIV, 97 (quoted in Mingana, "The Transmission of the Koran," 106).

14 "Jerusalem 32 - An Inscription Witnessed by Three Companions of Prophet Muḥammad, 32 AH / 652 CE," Islamic Awareness, July 14, 2018, https://www.islamic-awareness.org/history/islam/inscriptions/jerus32.html.

Allah, his messenger, and the contract of "protection" (*dhimma*) offered to non-Muslims under the hegemony of the Islamic state did indeed become central elements of Islam, but here again, while it's remotely possible that "his messenger" is indeed Muhammad and the "*dhimmat Allah*" is a reference to the entire system of dhimmitude that existed after the ninth century, there is nothing in the text itself that compels this identification. The messenger of Allah could be someone else, and his protection something entirely different from the Sharia system of dhimmitude.

Islamic Awareness also points out that the text refers to "prominent companions of Prophet Muḥammad, namely, Abd al-Rahman bin Awf al-Zuhri, Abu Ubaydah bin al-Jarrah, and a certain Mu'awiya, presumably Mu'awiya bin Abu Sufyan. The first two persons are two of the ten companions of the Prophet who were promised Paradise. Thirdly, Mu'awiya was a well-known scribe of Prophet Muhammad which this inscription also confirms." Very well. But how do we know that Abd al-Rahman bin Awf al-Zuhri, Abu Ubaydah bin al-Jarrah, and Mu'awiya bin Abu Sufyan were prominent companions of Muhammad? We know this, or think we do, because their names appear in the biographical material about Muhammad that dates from the ninth century. Is it possible that their names were taken from this inscription, or from something that served as its source, rather than that this inscription is an early attestation of the presence and reality of Muhammad, the prophet of Islam? Most certainly.

Nevertheless, Islamic Awareness asserts that this document could be "the earliest mention of Prophet Muhammad in an Arabic text, preceding the next earliest mention of him by some three decades." Maybe. But Muhammad isn't actually mentioned at all in this text; Islamic Awareness's conclusion would require us to make a great many assumptions for which there is no compelling evidence.

A Prophet of the God of Abraham

A decade or two later, however, we seem to be on firmer ground. An Armenian bishop named Sebeos writes in the 660s or 670s that "there was an Ishmaelite called Mahmet, a merchant; he presented himself to them as though at God's command, as a preacher, as the way of truth, and taught them to know the God of Abraham, for he was very well-informed, and very well-acquainted with the story of Moses. As the command came from on high, they all united under the authority of a single man, under a single law, and, abandoning vain cults, returned to the living God who had revealed Himself to their father Abraham."[15]

At last, we appear to have encountered the prophet of Islam, whom the Islamic sources from the ninth century onward portray as an Ishmaelite, a merchant, and a prophet of the God of Abraham. The Muhammad of Islam, if we accept the traditional account, was certainly "very well-acquainted with the story of Moses," for the Qur'an retells the story of Moses, Pharaoh, and the Exodus in whole or part again and again (see 2:49, 3:11, 7:103, 8:52, 10:75, 14:6, 17:101, 20:24, 23:46, 26:11, 27:12, 28:3, 29:39, 38:12, 40:24, 44:17, 50:13, 51:38, 54:41, 66:11, 69:9, 73:15, 79:15, 85:18, and 89:10). Islamic tradition records that Muhammad did indeed unite the warring Arab tribes.

Thus within thirty or forty years after Muhammad's death, we finally have undisputable historical attestation of his existence—or so we have been led to believe. For all the correspondences of his Muhammad with the Islamic prophet, however, Sebeos also presents a portrait of Muhammad that differs sharply from the canonical Islamic version. He continues:

> Mahmet forbade them to eat the flesh of any dead animal, to drink wine, to lie or to fornicate. He added: "God has promised this land to Abraham and his posterity after him forever; he acted according to His promise while he loved Israel. Now you, you are the sons of Abraham and God fulfills in you the promise made to Abraham and his posterity. Only love the God of Abraham, go and take possession of your country which God gave to your father Abraham, and none will be able to resist you in the struggle, for God is with you."[16]

The Qur'an does depict Moses saying to the Children of Israel: "O my people, go into the holy land that Allah has ordained for you. Do not turn back, for then you will turn back as losers" (5:21). The Qur'an also depicts Allah saying: "And we caused the people who were despised to inherit the eastern parts of the land and the western parts which we had blessed" (7:137). This also is stated in the context of Moses and the

---

15 Sebeos, *Histoire*, 94–96 (quoted in Crone and Cook, *Hagarism*, 6–7).
16 Ibid.

Exodus from Egypt. The emphasis in Sebeos's quote of Mahmet, however, is on God's promise to Abraham.

This is no mere quibble; the Mahmet of Sebeos is presenting himself as a spokesman for the God of Abraham and expressing love for Israel, while the Allah of the Qur'an, while also presented as the God of Abraham, is quite angry with and hostile toward Israel. Most Islamic commentators identify those who have earned Allah's anger in the Fatihah (Opening), the first sura and most common prayer of Islam, with the Jews. It may, therefore, be that the Mahmet of Sebeos, who seems so favorable toward Israel, represents an earlier stage in the development of the religion that became Islam, while the Qur'an (which, according to Islamic tradition, predates Sebeos's writing by fifty to sixty years) represents a later stage, after there has been a break with the Jews.

As Sebeos continues, the divergences from the Muhammad of Islamic tradition only increase:

> Then they all gathered together from Havilah unto Shur and before Egypt [Genesis 25:18]; they came out of the desert of Pharan divided into twelve tribes according to the lineages of their patriarchs. They divided among their tribes the twelve thousand Israelites, a thousand per tribe, to guide them into the land of Israel. They set out, camp by camp, in the order of their patriarchs: Nebajoth, Kedar, Abdeel, Mibsam, Mishma, Dumah, Massa, Hadar, Tema, Jetur, Naphish and Kedemah [Genesis 25:13–15]. These are the tribes of Ishmael…. All that remained of the peoples of the children of Israel came to join them, and they constituted a mighty army. Then they sent an embassy to the emperor of the Greeks, saying: "God has given this land as a heritage to our father Abraham and his posterity after him; we are the children of Abraham; you have held our country long enough; give it up peacefully, and we will not invade your territory; otherwise we will retake with interest what you have taken."[17]

This is a description that one might expect of a Jewish prophet, not of the prophet of Islam. There is no trace in Islamic tradition of Muhammad leading the twelve tribes of Israel into their ancestral homeland. Nor is there the slightest hint that he was ever the leader of the twelve tribes of Israel at all, or that an army Jews aided the Muslims (who are

---

17 Ibid.

not called that name by Sebeos or anyone else from this period) in conquering Egypt. Ninth-century Islamic tradition does contain the claim that Muhammad wrote a letter to Heraclius, the Roman emperor in Constantinople, or "emperor of the Greeks," but in the Islamic version, he is calling upon the monarch to accept the new religion of Islam. In Sebeos's version, he is lecturing the emperor about the right of the people of Israel to dwell in the land of their fathers.

Muhammad is likewise absent from Sebeos's account of a letter that Muawiya, who became the fifth caliph in 661, sent to the Roman Emperor Constans II while Muawiya was the Arab governor of Syria in 651. Even as Muawiya calls on Constans to renounce Christianity, he says nothing about the Qur'an, Islam, or Muhammad:

> If you wish to live in peace…renounce your vain religion, in which you have been brought up since infancy. Renounce this Jesus and convert to the great God whom I serve, the God of our father Abraham…. If not, how will this Jesus whom you call Christ, who was not even able to save himself from the Jews, be able to save you from my hands?[18]

This arrogant missive reveals a contempt for the crucifixion of Christ that would carry over into Islam and is apparently monotheistic and Abrahamic. But that's as close to Islam as it gets. Muawiya apparently says nothing about the Ishmaelite Mahmet, whom Sebeos had mentioned elsewhere, much less about Muhammad. Nor does he say anything about being a scribe or a messenger of Allah, as noted in the Temple Mount inscription. Sebeos, meanwhile, doesn't say anything about Mahmet in connection with Muawiya.

A Nestorian chronicler who also wrote in the 660s gives us another glimpse of someone who may have been or may later have become, by means of legendary embroidery, the prophet of Islam:

> Then God raised up against them the sons of Ishmael, [numerous] as the sand on the sea shore, whose leader (*mdabbrānā*) was Muḥammad (*mḥmd*). Neither walls nor gates, armor or shield, withstood them, and they gained control over the entire land of the Persians.

---

18 Quoted in Frederic Macler, trans. and ed., *Histoire d'Héraclius par l'Évêque Sebeos* (Paris: Imprimerie Nationale, 1904), 139–140 (translated into English and quoted in Yehuda D. Nevo and Judith Koren, *Crossroads to Islam* (Amherst, New York: Prometheus, 2003, 229).

Yazdgird sent against them countless troops, but the Arabs routed them all and even killed Rustam. Yazdgird shut himself up in the walls of Mahoze and finally escaped by flight. He reached the country of the Huzaye and *Mrwnaye*, where he ended his life. The Arabs gained control of Mahoze and all the territory. They also came to Byzantine territory, plundering and ravaging the entire region of Syria. Heraclius, the Byzantine king, sent armies against them, but the Arabs killed more than 100,000 of them.[19]

This has the Ishmaelites conquering Persia, which the Arabs did indeed do in the 650s. It gives the impression, however, that Muhammad was leading their armies, when Islamic tradition holds that he died before the Arab invasion of Persia even began. There is also no hint here that this Muhammad is a prophet; he is depicted solely as a warlord. The early references to Muhammad generally identify him as either a warrior or a prophet; while the *Doctrina Jacobi* speaks of a warrior prophet, it doesn't name him.

Around the same time, a Maronite chronicler records that in the year 661, "many Arabs gathered at Jerusalem and made Muḥawiya king and he went up and sat down on Golgotha and prayed there. He went to Gethsemane and went down to the tomb of the blessed Mary and prayed in it."[20] It's odd that nearly thirty years after the death of the prophet of Islam, when one of his faithful scribes became caliph of the Muslims, he was made caliph in Jerusalem, not in Mecca, and chose after becoming caliph to pray at Christian sites, when there surely must have been some mosques in which he could have prayed, as this was nearly a quarter-century after the Arab conquest of Jerusalem. In visiting Gethsemane, Mu'awiya is also veering perilously close to acknowledging the crucifixion of Christ, which Islam rejects (cf. Qur'an 4:157). One would expect the accession of a caliph to be accompanied by readings of the Qur'an and declarations that Muhammad is the prophet of Allah. Instead, Mu'awiya takes the throne in a notably Christian ambiance.

The Maronite chronicler later adds:

---

19 *Chron. Khuzistan*, Theodor Nöldeke, translator, "Syrische Chronik," 5–48; Sebastian Brock, translator (quoted in Hoyland, 186).
20 *Chron. Maronite*, E. W. Brooks, ed., J. B. Chabot, trans., *Chronicon Maroniticum* (CSCO 3–4 scr. Syri 3–4; Paris, 1904, 43–74/37–57. Theodor Nöldeke, trans. (quoted in Hoyland, 136).

In July of the same year the emirs and many Arabs gathered and gave their allegiance to Mu'awiya. Then an order went out that he should be proclaimed king in all the villages and cities of his domin-ion and that they should make acclamations and invocations to him. He also minted gold and silver, but it was not accepted because it had no cross on it. Furthermore, Mu'awiya did not wear a crown like other kings in the world. He placed his throne in Damascus and refused to go to the seat of Muhammad.[21]

Where was this seat of Muhammad? Why did Mu'awiya rule from Damascus rather than going there? We are not told. Nor does the chronicler offer any information about who exactly this Muhammad was. Meanwhile, the fact that the cities Mu'awiya ruled over wouldn't accept his coins because they bore no cross is not surprising, as the Arabs by this time had conquered the Middle East and North Africa, and most of the people in those regions at that time were still Chris-tian. The coins of the early Arab empire bear the legend *bismallah*, "In the name of Allah." Others feature variations of this, including *bism Allah rabbi* ("In the name of Allah my Lord"), *rabbi Allah* ("My Lord is Allah"), and *bism Allah al-malik* ("In the name of Allah the King").[22] No early Arab coins say *Muhammad rasul Allah* ("Muhammad is the messenger of Allah").

Mu'awiya and other early Arab rulers apparently acceded to the desire of their people for coins featuring crosses. One coin that was apparently struck in Palestine in the late 640s or 650s, before Mu'awiya became caliph, features a standing figure holding a cross, along with the legend "Muhammad."[23] Other coins dating from this period also feature the word "Muhammad" and a cross.[24] Once Islamic orthodoxy became entrenched, there would be no sign of the cross, as the Qur'an declares that Jesus was not crucified (4:157), and a hadith depicts Muhammad saying that in the end times, Jesus will return to the earth and "break

---

21 Ibid.

22 Nevo and Koren, 250.

23 Clive Foss, *Arab-Byzantine Coins: An Introduction, with a Catalogue of the Dumbarton Oaks Collection* (Washington, DC: Dumbarton Oaks Research Library and Collection, 2008), 34.

24 Volker Popp, "The Early History of Islam, Following Inscriptional and Numismatic Testimony," in Karl-Heinz Ohlig and Gerd-R. Puin, eds., *The Hidden Origins of Islam* (Amherst, New York: Prometheus, 2010), 55.

the cross."[25] There is, however, no sign of that orthodoxy at this point. Another coin, which was apparently minted during Mu'awiya's reign, features the sovereign, who may or may not be Mu'awiya, holding a cross topped by a crescent, a double symbol that did not survive in either Christianity or Islam.[26]

The prospect of coins of the Arab empire, which is universally assumed to have been fervently Islamic, bearing the cross is both shocking and inexplicable in terms of the conventional understanding of Islam's origins. By way of comparison, consider the *History of the Patriarchs*, a Coptic Christian account of the leaders of the Church of Alexandria. This history was originally collected from earlier writings about the various patriarchs around the year 1100 and continued over centuries by many writers; the earliest extant version dates from the middle of the thirteenth century.[27]

By that time, Islamic doctrine had been fully formulated, and in its account of the actions of the Egyptian emir Abd al-Aziz toward the end of the seventh century, the *History of the Patriarchs* reflects that. It records that Abd al-Aziz "commanded to destroy all the crosses which were in the land of Egypt, even the crosses of gold and silver. So the Christians in the land of Egypt were troubled. Moreover he wrote certain inscriptions, and placed them on the doors of the churches at Misr and in the Delta, saying in them: 'Muhammad is the great Apostle of God, and Jesus also is the Apostle of God: But verily God is not begotten and does not beget.'"[28]

This was supposed to have happened only around ten years after the death of Mu'awiya, who had placed crosses on coins and public buildings. The historical value of the *History of the Patriarchs* is severely limited, as it comes down to us only in versions dating from centuries after the events it was recording. Nonetheless, it is indeed possible that Islam's hostility to the cross began to be asserted around the time of Abd al-Aziz, who was Umayyad governor of Egypt from 685 to 705. It was

---

25 Muhammed Ibn Ismail al-Bukhari, *Sahih al-Bukhari: The Translation of the Meanings*, translated by Muhammad M. Khan, Darussalam, 1997, vol. 3, book 46, no. 2476.
26 Foss, 47.
27 Hoyland, 446.
28 History of the Patriarchs of the Coptic Church of Alexandria III: Agathon to Michael I (766), B. Evetts, ed. and trans. (Paris: Firmin-Didot et Cie., 1947), 25.

around this time that we began to get references to Muhammad that are more clearly referring to the now-familiar figure of the prophet of Islam.

The Messenger of Allah

In 685, Abd al-Malik became caliph, and we begin to see references to Muhammad that appear to bring us closer to the prophet of Islam. Abd al-Malik possessed a seal that read: "There is no god but God alone without partner and Muhammad is the Messenger of God."[29] This is not identical to the common Islamic statement of faith, "There is no god but Allah and Muhammad is his prophet," but it's close. If that Islamic statement of faith had existed as such at the time of Abd al-Malik, one would expect him, as caliph of the Muslims, to use it on his official seals. The fact that Abd al-Malik's formulation differs is another indication that the teachings of Islam were still in the process of being formulated. Around this time, we also begin to see coins that assert that "Muhammad is the messenger of Allah."[30]

Also during the reign of Abd al-Malik, a half-Syrian *ratl*, a weight that was used for measuring quantities, bore the inscription: "In the name of God. There is not but God He is one, Muhammad is the Messenger of God, the servant of God Abd al-Malik Commander of the Faithful. Ordered by the amir al-Walid."[31] Here at last is a formulation that could have been stated by any modern-day Muslim, or any Muslim throughout the fourteen centuries between the time of Abd al-Malik and today. We still do not have, however, any reference to the Qur'an or to the voluminous accounts of Muhammad that begin appearing decades later.

A Nestorian Christian chronicler, John bar Penkaye, writes in 690 of Muhammad and the Arabs:

> The Arabs...had a certain order from the one who was their leader, in favor of the Christian people and the monks; they held also, under his leadership, the worship of one God, according to the customs of

29 "A Lead Seal in the Name of Caliph 'Abd al-Malik Ibn Marwān, 65–86 AH / 685–705 CE," Islamic Awareness, March 31, 2014, https://www.islamic-awareness.org/history/islam/inscriptions/seal2.html.

30 "Dated and Datable Texts," Islamic Awareness, op. cit.

31 "A Half Syrian *Raṭl* in the Name of Caliph 'Abd al-Malik Ibn Marwan, 65–86 AH / 685–705 CE," Islamic Awareness, June 22, 2019, https://www.islamic-awareness.org/history/islam/coins/weight7.

the Old Covenant; at the outset they were so attached to the traditions of Muhammad who was their teacher, that they inflicted the
pain of death upon any one who seemed to contradict his tradition.... Among them there were many Christians, some from the
Heretics, and some from us.[32]

Yet even despite Abd al-Malik's movement toward Islam as it has
been known through the centuries, what these traditions of Muhammad consisted of is completely unclear and unrecorded in the literature
of the time.

A tombstone dating from the following year, however, appears to
assume a full-blown Islam and gives us an early usage of that word itself:
"In the name of God, the Merciful, the Compassionate. The greatest
calamity of the people of Islam (ahl al-Islam) is that which has fallen
them on the death of Muhammad the Prophet; may God grant him
peace. This is the tomb of Abassa daughter of Juraij (?), son of (?). May
clemency, forgiveness and satisfaction of God be on her. She died on
Monday, fourteen days having elapsed from Dhul-Qa'dah of the year
one and seventy, confessing that there is no god but God alone without
partner and that Muhammad is His servant and His apostle, may God
grant him peace."[33]

"The year one and seventy," or 71, was the year 691; according to
the lunar Islamic calendar, which is still in use to this day, it was sev-
enty-one years after the hijrah, Muhammad's move from Mecca to
Medina, which marks the beginning of the Islamic calendar. The tombstone also contains the same approximation of the Islamic confession of
faith that we saw on Abd al-Malik's seal and professions of monotheism
and Muhammad's prophethood that would not seem out of place from
any modern-day Muslim.

In that same year of 691, the Dome of the Rock was completed on
the Temple Mount in Jerusalem. On its inner walls are written inscriptions that include quotations from the Qur'an and declarations of
Muhammad's prophetic status. One states: "Muhammad is the servant

---

32 Quoted in Alphonse Mingana, Sources Syriaques, vol. I, pt. 2, 146f (quoted in Mingana, "The
    Transmission of the Koran," 107).
33 "Tombstone of 'Abāssa Bint Juraij, 71 AH / 691 CE," Islamic Awareness, September 11, 2000,
    https://www.islamic-awareness.org/history/islam/inscriptions/abasa.

of God and His messenger."[34] Other inscriptions repeat five times that "Muhammad is the Messenger of God."[35]

However, even this cannot be taken as a clear acknowledgment of the prophethood of Muhammad as we know him. He is not otherwise mentioned in the Dome of the Rock inscriptions, which then go on at great length about how Jesus is not divine but is solely a messenger of Allah. The philologist Christoph Luxenberg points out that since the word *muhammad* means "praising" or "being praised," and hence also "the one who is being praised," the inscription, the phrase "Muhammad is the servant of God and His messenger" is more correctly translated as "Praised be the servant of God and His messenger." Luxenberg explains: "Therefore, by using this gerundive, the text here is not speaking of a person named *Muhammad*, which was made only later metaphorically into a personal name attributed analogically to the prophet of Islam."[36]

The following year, the chronicler Jacob, bishop of Edessa, recorded for the year 618 that "Muhammad goes down on commercial businesses to the lands of Palestine and of the Arabias and of Phoenicia of the Tyrians."[37] Then, for 622, he writes that "Muhammad, the first king of the Arabs, began to reign, 7 years."[38] Corresponding to this is a list of caliphs that was compiled a bit later, sometime after 705: "Muhammad came upon the earth in 932 of Alexander the son of Philip the Macedonian; he reigned for seven years."[39]

The 932nd year according to the Anno Graecorum numbering system that begins during the reign of Alexander the Great is the year 621, which is close to the traditional date of Muhammad's hijrah, or emigration, from Mecca to Medina. The Islamic calendar marks the hijrah as the beginning of Islam, and hence of Muhammad's "reign." Nevertheless, the seven-year period doesn't correspond to any Islamic tradition about the length of Muhammad's rule, although there may be a trace of

---

34 Estelle Whelan, "Forgotten Witness: Evidence for the Early Codification of the Qur'an," *Journal of the American Oriental Society*, 118 (1998), 1–14, reprinted at http://www.islamic-awareness. org/History/Islam/Dome_Of_The_Rock/Estwitness.html.

35 Ibid.

36 Christoph Luxenberg, "A New Interpretation of the Arabic Inscription in Jerusalem's Dome of the Rock," in Karl-Heinz Ohlig and Gerd-R. Puin, eds., *The Hidden Origins of Islam* (Amherst, New York: Prometheus, 2010), 130.

37 Andrew Palmer, *The Seventh Century in the West-Syrian Chronicles* (Liverpool: Liverpool University Press, 1993), 39.

38 Ibid., 37.

39 Ibid., 43.

it in a ninth-century tradition that states of Muhammad in Mecca that "for seven years he perceived effulgence and (divine) light and heard sounds; and for eight years he received revelations."[40] The seven-year period mentioned in the chronicle could be meant to refer to Muhammad's time in Medina after the hijrah and before his conquest of Mecca, but the list then continues: "After him Abu Bakr reigned for two years."[41] There is no hint of the existence of the final two years of Muhammad's life after the conquest of Mecca, about which Islamic tradition has a great deal to say.

Also dating from 692, meanwhile, is an inscription found near the Sea of Galilee and reading: "In the name of Allah, [the Compassionate], the Merciful. There is no god but Allah alone; He has no companion. Muhammad is the Apostle of Allah."[42] Once again, however, no information is given about who this Muhammad, or even if the apostle of Allah is being referred to by his name, or by a title.

Jacob of Edessa also refers to a group he calls the Mahgrayé, which means "emigrants" in Syriac.[43] These people, he says, acknowledge Jesus, but not as the Son of God. The corresponding Arabic word muhajirun refers in Islam to those who accompanied Muhammad from Mecca to Medina in 622. In Medina, according to the traditional story, Muhammad became a political and military leader for the first time, and it is this that is marked as the first year of the Islamic calendar.

Abd al-Malik, who reigned as caliph from 685 to 705, minted coins that read: "Muhammad is the messenger of God whom He sent with guidance and the religion of truth that He might make it prevail over all religions even if the associators are averse."[44] An inscription dating to the year 698 contains the Islamic profession of faith as it stands today and mentions the building of the Great Mosque (al-Masjid al-Haram, or forbidden mosque) in Mecca: "Al-Rayyan b. Abdullah testifies that

---

40 Ibn Sa'd, Kitab al-Tabaqat al-Kabir, S. Moinul Haq, trans. (New Delhi: Kitab Bhavan, n.d.), I, 260.

41 Palmer, The Seventh Century in the West-Syrian Chronicles, op. cit.

42 "The 'Aqabah Inscription from the Time of 'Abd al-Malik, 73 AH / 692–693 CE," Islamic Awareness, September 10, 2000, https://www.islamic-awareness.org/history/islam/inscriptions/malik5.html.

43 F. Nau, "Lettre de Jacques d'Edesse sur la généalogie de la Sainte Vierge," Revue de l'Orient Chrétien (1901), 518–523f (quoted in Nevo and Koren, 235).

44 "Aniconic Silver Coins ("Reformed Coinage"), Minted by the Umayyad Caliph 'Abd al-Malik, From 77 AH / 696 CE," Islamic Awareness, January 22, 2007, https://www.islamic-awareness.org/history/islam/coins/drachm6.

there is no god but God, and he testifies that Muhammad is the Messenger of God. Then reiterates to those to come to testify to that, God
have mercy on al-Rayyan. May He forgive him and cause him to be
guided to the path of Paradise, and I ask him for marytrdom in his path.
Amen. This was written in the year the Masjid al-Haram was built in the
seventy-eighth year."[45] Here again, as on the tombstone of Abassa, we
have a reference to the date as it is counted on the Islamic calendar, as
well as an acknowledgment of Muhammad as a prophet.

We see the first mention of "Muslims" in the writings of John of
Nikiou, a Coptic Christian bishop, in the 690s:

> And now many of the Egyptians who had been false Christians
> denied the holy orthodox faith and lifegiving baptism, and embraced
> the religion of the Muslims, the enemies of God, and accepted the
> detestable doctrine of the beast, that is, Mohammed, and they erred
> together with those idolaters, and took arms in their hands and
> fought against the Christians, And one of them…embraced the faith
> of Islam…and persecuted the Christians.[46]

This text, however, comes down to us only in an Ethiopic version
from 1602, nearly a thousand years after Jacob wrote it. It could have
been altered.[47]

The Qur'an

Meanwhile, there is the Qur'an itself, which mentions the name Muhammad four times (3:144; 33:40; 47:2; and 48:29). None of these mentions
include any biographical information about the prophet of Islam; all
could be using "Muhammad" as a title, "the praised one," rather than as
a proper name. One of these states: "And those who believe and do good
works and believe in what is revealed to Muhammad, and it is the truth
from their Lord, he rids them of their sins and improves their condition"
(47:2). This is a curious statement to make about Muhammad, as he
does not claim to forgive sins; he is, in the words of the Qur'an, only a

---

45 "An Inscription Mentioning the Rebuilding of al-Masjid al-Ḥarām, 78 AH / 697–698 CE,"
   Islamic Awareness, March 1, 2015. https://www.islamic-awareness.org/history/islam/inscrip-
   tions/haram1.html

46 *The Chronicle of John (c. 690 A.D.) Coptic Bishop of Nikiu,* trans. and ed. Robert H. Church
   (London, 1916; reprinted Philo Press), ch. 121:10–11, 201 (quoted in Nevo and Koren, 233).

47 Nevo and Koren, 234.

"warner" (79:45). In the Christian tradition, however, Jesus, does offer forgiveness of sin; was this Qur'anic passage originally a reference to Jesus as "the praised one" forgiving the sins of those who follow him?[48]

A similar question can be asked of 48:29: "Muhammad is the messenger of Allah. And those with him are ruthless against the unbelievers and merciful among themselves. You see them bowing and falling prostrate, seeking bounty from Allah and acceptance. The mark of them is on their foreheads from the traces of prostration. That is their comparison in the Torah and their comparison in the Gospel, like sown corn that sends forth its shoot and strengthens it and rises firm upon its stalk, delighting the sowers, so that he may enrage the unbelievers with them."

This is reminiscent of the words of Jesus: "The kingdom of heaven is like a grain of mustard seed which a man took and sowed in his field; it is the smallest of all seeds, but when it has grown it is the greatest of shrubs and becomes a tree, so that the birds of the air come and make nests in its branches" (Matthew 13:31–33). It also recalls Jesus' parable of the sower (Matthew 13:3–23). Could this Qur'anic passage also have been originally a reference to Jesus, not to the prophet of Islam?

What's more, contrary to the idea that the Qur'an was finalized long before the traditions about Muhammad were committed to writing, there is evidence that at least some elements of the holy book of Islam were still in flux even two hundred years after Muhammad was supposed to have lived. One such tradition concerns Hajjaj ibn Yusuf, the Umayyad governor of Iraq from 694 to 714. An elderly Muslim recounts: "I heard Hajjaj b. Yusuf saying as he was delivering sermon on the pulpit: Observe the order of the (Holy) Qur'an which has been observed by Gabriel. (Thus state the surahs in this manner), one in which mention has been made of al-Baqara, one in which mention has been made of women (Surah al-Nisa), and then the surah in which mention has been made of the Family of Imran."[49] Yet in the Qur'an today, al-Baqara is chapter two of the Qur'an, followed by the Family of Imran, which is chapter three, and then al-Nisa, which is chapter four. Yet apparently the idea that the angel Gabriel favored a different order of the chapters

---

48 "The evolution of 'mhmd': a secret long hidden in plain sight," Islamic Origins, op. cit. I am indebted to this lecture for much of the material in this section.
49 Sahih Muslim, book 15, no. 1296b.

persisted even two centuries after the Qur'anic text was supposed to have been standardized.

Another tradition has Muhammad being reminded of sections of the Qur'an he had forgotten. This would have been a handy tradition to have at hand if one had been called upon, even as late as the ninth century, to explain discrepancies in the text of different versions of the Qur'an. Muhammad's child bride Aisha is depicted as recounting: "Allah's Messenger heard a man reciting the Qur'an at night, and said, 'May Allah bestow His Mercy on him, as he has reminded me of such-and-such Verses of such-and-such Suras, which I was caused to forget.'"[50] The Muslim need not worry: Allah guided even the forgetting (or discarding?) of passages of the Quran. In another hadith, Muhammad says: "Why does anyone of the people say, 'I have forgotten such-and-such Verses (of the Qur'an)?' He, in fact, is caused (by Allah) to forget."[51]

Oral Traditions?

And so, at the close of the seventh century, there are increasing mentions, emanating primarily from the caliph of the Arab empire, of Muhammad as a prophet of Allah. We also have testimony of his being a warrior and some indication that something momentous happened around the year 622, such that the followers of this prophet calculate the date from that event. We know he is an Arab prophet who taught that there is only one God and who rejected the divinity of Christ while professing to hold to the faith of Abraham.

Some would say that this is enough to compel us to accept the historical reliability of the massive body of immensely detailed biographical data about Muhammad that becomes available over the next two hundred years. Yet the very fact that what is asserted about Muhammad in these various seventh-century mentions of him, aside from material that has no correspondence to the Muhammad of Islamic tradition, can be summed up in a brief paragraph leads to the inevitable question: if the massive corpus of material about Muhammad was being preserved orally at this time, why is there no reference to it?

When oral traditions exist, it is not uncommon to find those who know them making reference to them. One example of this comes in the

---

50 Sahih Bukhari, vol. 6, book 66, no. 5038.
51 Sahih Bukhari, vol. 6, book 66, no. 5039.

New Testament. In the Acts of the Apostles, Paul of Tarsus is depicted as quoting Jesus: "It is more blessed to give than to receive" (Acts 20:35). This quotation does not appear in any of the four canonical gospels (or, for that matter, in any of the apocryphal and heretical gospels that circulated in the early centuries of Christianity, either). It is an example of an oral tradition that, as it was known to the early Christians, made its way into Acts.

In a similar way, we would expect that if the Muslims of the seventh century were going through their lives having memorized, in whole or part, the immense corpus of the words and deeds of Muhammad (which, once they were written down, filled dozens of volumes), that someone somewhere would have referred to it. There might be quotes of the revered prophet here and there. There might be references to his deeds. Instead, however, there is just a scattering of affirmations of faith in him, some non-Muslims making assertions about him that are largely inaccurate from the standpoint of Islamic tradition, and a handful of details: He was an Arab. He was a warrior. He was a prophet.

It is noteworthy also that in all the available records regarding Islam in the seventh century, there is virtually no sign of Muhammad's book, the Qur'an, either. The Qur'an, as it stands today, only mentions Muhammad by name four times and contains no biographical information about him at all; still, it is supposed to be the centerpiece of his prophetic claim. Yet if Uthman really codified the text, burned the variants, and distributed copies of the newly standardized book to all the Muslim provinces in 653, Muslims remained notably silent about its existence. There are no quotations of Muhammad in seventh-century literature comparable to the quote of Jesus in Acts 20:35. Nor are there quotations from the Qur'an. If the seventh-century Muslims had the Qur'an, they didn't make a habit of referring to it, which is all the more curious in light of the reverence in which they are supposed to have held it.

Some may contend that their silence about it is immaterial, as there are manuscripts of portions of the Qur'an that date from the seventh century. However, in the absence of other indications that the religion of Muhammad as we know it today was up and running, it would be unwise to take for granted the proposition that these are actually and definitively manuscripts of the Qur'an rather than of source material that was used to construct the Qur'an. One reason for this caution is encapsulated in a curious Islamic tradition that Malik ibn Anas, a jurist who died in 796, records: "Reading from the *mushaf*"—that is, a copy of the Qur'an—"at the Mosque was not done by people in the past. It was Hajjaj b. Yusuf who first instituted it."[52] Those who accept the traditional Islamic account of Muhammad's life and the Qur'an's origins simply dismiss this as an inauthentic tradition, but that presents a new problem: why was it invented?

If Muhammad had really presented the Qur'an as a revelation from Allah during his lifetime, and if Uthman had really codified and distributed it in 653, then why would anyone make up a story about how it only began to be read out in mosques decades later? It is much more plausible that the Qur'an did indeed only begin to be read in mosques in the time of Hajjaj and was projected back into the past to give it a patina of authenticity.

The mosques themselves present yet another series of problems. The Mosque of Amr ibn al-As, the seventh-century conqueror of Egypt, was built in Cairo in 641.[53] If the canonical account of Muhammad and the origins of Islam were true, we would expect this mosque to be constructed so that the worshippers would face toward Mecca as they prayed, in accord with the Qur'an's directive to "turn your face toward the sacred mosque, and you, wherever you may be, turn your faces toward it" (2:144).

However, historian Dan Gibson points out that although the mosque has "undergone numerous restorations so that the original foundation is no longer evident," it is still clear that it was not initially constructed so that the believers would face Mecca for prayer: "a description of the original ground-plan of the mosque shows that the qibla [the direction for prayer] pointed east and had to be corrected towards Mecca later under the governorship of Qurra ibn Sharik," the governor of Egypt from 709

52 Ali al-Samhudi, *Wafa al-Wafa bi-akhbar dar al-Mustafa*, Muhammad Muhyi I-Din Abd al-Hamid, ed. Cairo, 1955, repr. Beyrouth, 4 parts in III vols., Dar al-Kutub al-Ilmiyya, 1984. Quoted in Alfred-Louis de Prémare, "Abd al-Malik b. Marwan and the Process of the Qur'an's Composition," in Karl-Heinz Ohlig and Gerd-R. Puin, eds., *The Hidden Origins of Islam* (Amherst, New York: Prometheus, 2010), 205.
53 Griffithes Wheeler Thatcher, "Maqrizi," *Encyclopedia Britannica*, eleventh edition (New York: Encyclopedia Britannica Company, 1911), 665.

to 715, during which time Hajjaj ibn Yusuf was governor of Iraq.[54] Gibson also discovered that eight of the twenty-one mosques built between 622 and 708 faced Petra, and none at all clearly faced Mecca; two others faced both Petra and Jerusalem, and one was constructed so as to face between Petra and Mecca.[55]

Yet in Islamic tradition, there is no trace of any idea that the Muslims were to face Petra for prayer. What these mosques taught is unclear, but it cannot conclusively be said to have been the Qur'an and the words and deeds of Muhammad. And so we seem to have mosques but no Islamic holy book and no prophet, or at least very little of either one.

54 Dan Gibson, Early Islamic Qiblas: A Survey of Mosques Built between 1AH/622 C.E. and 263 AH/876 C.E. (Vancouver: Independent Scholars Press, 2017), 30.
55 Ibid., 6.

CHAPTER TWO

Creating Muhammad

A Scripture Brought Down to Him from Heaven

The picture seems to become clearer by 730, when John of Damascus, a renowned Christian theologian, wrote of a "false prophet" named *Mamed* who "having happened upon the Old and the New Testament and apparently having conversed, in like manner, with an Arian monk, put together his own heresy. And after ingratiating himself with the people by a pretense of piety, he spread rumors of a scripture (*graphe*) brought down to him from heaven. So, having drafted some ludicrous doctrines in his book, he handed over to them this form of worship."[1] Arianism was a Christian heresy that originated early in the fourth century and was condemned at the first ecumenical council, the Council of Nicaea, in 325. Arius, a priest in Alexandria, taught that Christ was not divine, but had been created by God.

The council, on the other hand, maintained that he was "God from God, light from light, true God from true God." Islam likewise rejects the divinity of Christ, and John may have been suggesting as much by noting that this Mamed had spoken with an Arian. John makes this clear when he notes that the followers of Mamed "call us associators (*hetairiastas*) because, they say, we introduce to God an associate by saying Christ is the Son of God and God.... They misrepresent us as idolaters because we prostrate ourselves before the cross, which they loathe." This corresponds to Islam's rejection of the crucifixion, as well as of Christ's divinity. And John knows some details about Islamic belief as well: "And

---

1 John of Damascus, *De haeresibus* C/CI, 60–61 (*Patrologia Greca* 94, 764A–765A) (quoted in Hoyland, 486).

we say to them: 'How then do you rub yourselves on a stone at your Ka'ba (*Chabatha*) and hail the stone with fond kisses?'"[2]

John also shows some familiarity with the Qur'an. He says that Muhammad "composed many frivolous tales, to each of which he assigned a name, like the text (*graphe*) of the Woman, in which he clearly prescribes the taking of four wives and one thousand concubines, if it is possible." The fourth chapter of the Qur'an is called "Women," and it does allow a man to have four wives as well as "captives of the right hand," who could be called concubines (4:3), but the number of concubines is not specified in the text as we have it. John adds that "Muhammad mentions the text of the Table," and "the text of the Cow"; "The Table" and "The Cow" are chapters five and two of the Qur'an as we have it, respectively. John says that Muhammad's book also contains "the text of the Camel of God, about which he [Muhammad] says that there was a camel from God." There is no chapter by this title in the Qur'an as we have it, but there is a story about a camel of God in the Qur'an, although it is never told fully or clearly (7:77; 11:64–65; 91:11–14).[3]

John goes into immense detail about what the Qur'an teaches about Christ:

> He [that is, Muhammad] says that Christ is the Word of God and His Spirit [cf. Qur'an 9:171], created [3:59] and a servant [4:172, 9:30, 43:59], and that he was born from Mary [3:45 and cf. Isa ibn Maryam], the sister of Moses and Aaron [19:28], without seed [3:47, 19:20, 21:91, 66:12]. For, he says, the Word of God and His Spirit entered Mary [19:17, 21:91, 66:12], and she gave birth to Jesus, a prophet [9:30, 33:7] and a servant of God. And [he says] that the Jews, acting unlawfully, wanted to crucify him, but, on seizing [him], they crucified [only] his shadow; Christ himself was not crucified, he says, nor did he die [4:157]. For God took him up to heaven to Himself.... And God questioned him saying: "Jesus, did you say that 'I am son of God and God'"? And, he says, Jesus answered, 'Mercy me, Lord, you know that I did not say so" [5:116].[4]

2 John of Damascus, *De haeresibus* C/CI, 63–64 (*Patrologia Greca* 94, 765C–769B) (quoted in Hoyland, 486–487).

3 John of Damascus, *De haeresibus* C/CI, 64–67 (*Patrologia Greca* 94, 769B–772D) (quoted in Hoyland, 487).

4 John of Damascus, *De haeresibus* C/CI, 61 (*Patrologia Greca* 94, 765A–B) (quoted in Hoyland, 488–489).

Writing around a century after the date that is generally given for Muhammad's death, John gives us the fullest picture yet of the Islamic prophet's teachings. Although there are still some discrepancies, John's presentation of the Qur'an's statements about Jesus and other matters is closer to the actual message of Islam as we know it than any earlier explanation of what this warrior prophet actually said. Yet John still tells us hardly anything about who exactly this man was, and Islamic sources of the time are largely silent as to the details of his life. That, however, was soon to change.

The Biography of the Messenger of Allah

At the time John of Damascus was writing, the extant information about Muhammad at the time of John would still fill only a page or two. Then, in the middle of the eighth century, there appears to have come a veritable explosion of detailed material about the new prophet. A Muslim named Muhammad Ibn Ishaq Ibn Yasar, commonly known as Ibn Ishaq (704–767), compiled a massive work known as the *Sirat Rasul Allah* (*Biography of the Messenger of Allah*). Ibn Ishaq presents an extraordinarily detailed picture of Muhammad, in which we suddenly know what he said and did at virtually every moment, from his birth to his death.

Islamic tradition tells us that Ibn Ishaq was not Muhammad's first biographer. That distinction belongs to Urwa ibn al-Zubayr (644–713), although he apparently confined himself to passing on traditions orally. Then there was Wahb ibn Munabbih (654–737), who did commit some traditions of Muhammad to writing, but his works are now lost. Ibn Shihab al-Zuhri (677–741) is likewise remembered as preserving traditions of Muhammad, but if he wrote anything, it has not come down to us.

Musa ibn Uqba (675–758) is said to have written a history of Muhammad's battles, but it also was lost until several years ago, when a copy was rediscovered and published. According to the Islamic scholar Robert Kerr of the Inarah Institute for Research on Early Islamic History and the Qur'an, however, the great historian of the hadiths, Joseph Schacht, "cast serious doubt on the reliability of this Kitab al-Maghazi [book of military expeditions], showing that such only emerged in the second century after the Hijra, furthermore that the Isnad were improved and/

or invented at a later date, which he terms as spreading. I doubt that we are dealing with a seventh or eighth century text—those who advocate such will need to prove such."[5]

Sulayman ibn Tarkhan (d. 761) is supposed to have been another early biographer of Muhammad; however, Kerr notes that "a book entitled *Sira* which he is supposed to have authored circulated in the eleventh century AD in al-Andalus. He is claimed to be the author, but this is not the case, it is apocryphal. The Kitab al-Maghazi-genre are all clustered in the ninth century."[6]

Another author of a book of Muhammad's battles was Ma'mar ibn Rashid (714–770), who is credited with another eighth-century *Kitab al-Maghazi*. The Islamic scholar Sean Anthony has stated that this is the earlier extant biographical material on Muhammad. Robert Kerr, however, provides information that dampens the enthusiasm of those who believe that in this work, they have found the earliest records of Muhammad's career. He points out that Ma'mar ibn Rashid's *Kitab al-Maghazi* "is extracted from a much larger book called the *Musannaf* by Abd ar-Razzaq," who was Ma'mar ibn Rashid's "most prominent student after he moved to the Yemen." Kerr notes that the work as it has come to us is more likely the work of Abd ar-Razzaq than of his teacher: "The argument that ibn Rashid was mainly responsible for the extant *Kitab al-Maghazi*'s organization, while not outright preposterous, remains undemonstrated."[7]

Kerr adds that "the assertion that this *Kitab al-Maghazi* may be something very close to a final product as ibn Rashid imagined has no evidence whatsoever to support it; it is, however, certainly not a book authored by ibn Rashid. At the most, if we were to be exceedingly charitable toward Islamic Tradition(s), what we have at best is a later redaction of ibn Rashid's material, a considerable amount of which seems to have been altered for any number of reasons."[8] He notes that "the work clearly does not include everything taught by ibn Rashid on material related to Muhammad's career and expeditions, and even includes three reports—admittedly a tiny number proportionally—not

5 Robert Kerr, email to the author, September 27, 2023.
6 Ibid.
7 Ibid.
8 Ibid.

transmitted by ibn Rashid: a very clear indication of some level of later redaction."[9]

The work in its current form may date from even later: "The jury is still out on whether or not Abd ar-Razzaq was the principal organiser of the extant *Musannaf* which goes by his name—it has certainly been edited after Abd ar-Razzaq, when the current form of the work took shape."[10] Kerr concludes that "it has the feel of a collection of material of later compilers who already had a basic idea of the overarching framework of the career of the Prophet (i.e. it presumes an already established Islamic narrative framework of who Muhammad was supposed to have been) and the first caliphs (it ends with the first Fitna, not with the death of Muhammad) which these compilers could dip in and out of as they suited their needs—and then attribute to earlier authorities (as was frequent at the time)."[11]

Kerr also enunciates the problem with all the early Islamic biographical literature of Muhammad:

> Even if we were to actually have Ma'mar ibn Rashid's *Kitab al-Maghazi* (which we don't), then the same problem applies as with his contemporary Ibn Ishaq (of whom we have nothing preserved either): they are indeed "early," but according to Tradition were nonetheless born several generations after the events they purport to narrate; what sources did they have available and use? Was Arabic at this time a literary enough language to be able to be the linguistic vehicle in which such accounts could be written?
>
> Based on the evidence as it stands: what we have in the *Musannaf* attributed to Abd ar-Razzaq does not contain strictly speaking a work entitled *Kitab al-Maghazi* written by Ma'mar ibn Rashid. With this work, as commendable as Anthony's translation is from a philological point of view, it brings us no closer to the "historical Muhammad" who continues to lurk in darkness beyond the "pale" of history's probing searchlights...[12]

Ibn Ishaq's work, like that of Urwa ibn al-Zubayr, Wahb ibn Munabbih, and Ibn Shihab al-Zuhri, is likewise lost, at least in its original form.

---

9 Ibid.
10 Ibid.
11 Ibid.
12 Ibid.

One of Ibn Ishaq's students, however, al-Bakka'i, passed on a substantial portion of it to a later Muslim scholar, Ibn Hisham, who died in 833. Portions of it are also preserved in lengthy quotations by Muhammad Ibn Jarir al-Tabari (839–923). Ibn Hisham, however, makes no secret of the fact that he revised Ibn Ishaq's work and that al-Bakka'i didn't even give him exactly what Ibn Ishaq had written. Ibn Hisham admits that in his own version, he omitted "things which it is disgraceful to discuss; matters which would distress certain people; and such reports as al-Bakka'i told me he could not accept as trustworthy."[13]

"Reliable" Reports

Thus, it is only two hundred years after the generally accepted date of the death of Muhammad that we begin to get substantial biographical information about him. Yet the biography that Ibn Ishaq, Ibn Hisham, and Tabari have left us is extraordinarily large. The British Islamic scholar Alfred Guillaume's 1955 reconstruction of Ibn Ishaq's work from what Ibn Hisham and Tabari preserve runs to eight hundred pages. Around the same time that Ibn Hisham published his version of Ibn Ishaq's biography, the primary hadith collections began to appear. *Hadith* means "report" or "news," and is the record of Muhammad's words and deeds. Those that are considered authentic form the foundation of Islamic theology and law. The hadith collections also generally contain a section focusing on biographical material about Muhammad. To this day, the information about Muhammad that forms the basis of the canonical Islamic understanding of who he was and what he did comes from the ninth-century biographical material about him.

The primary hadith collections were compiled by several imams. Foremost is that of Muhammad Ibn Ismail al-Bukhari (810–870), whose collection, *Sahih Bukhari* ("Reliable Bukhari"), is generally considered among Muslims to be the soundest and most trustworthy of all hadith collections. According to Islamic tradition, Bukhari traversed the Islamic world collecting no fewer than 600,000 hadiths, 593,000 of which he rejected as inauthentic.[14] The other seven thousand he published in his

---

13 "Ibn Hisham's Notes," in Ibn Ishaq, *The Life of Muhammad: A Translation of Ibn Ishaq's Sirat Rasul Allah*, A. Guillaume, trans. (Oxford: Oxford University Press, 1955), 691.

14 Emad Blake, "Who Was Imam al-Bukhari, the Most Famous Muslim to Document Islamic Hadiths?," Al Arabiya, May 27, 2017, https://english.alarabiya.net/features/2017/05/27/Who-was-Imam-Al-Bukhari-the-most-famous-Muslim-to-documented-Islamic-hadiths-.

massive, multi-volume collection. Second only to Bukhari in terms of trustworthiness, at least in the traditional estimation of Islamic scholars, is Sahih Muslim ("Reliable Muslim"), which was the work of another imam, Muslim ibn al-Hajjaj al-Qushayri (821–875). Other key hadith collections include Sunan Abi Dawud by Abu Dawud as-Sijistani (d. 888); Sunan Ibn Majah by Muhammad ibn Majah (824–888), Sunan Al-Tirmidhi by Abi Eesaa Muhammad At-Tirmidhi (824–893), and Sunan Al-Nasai by Ahmad ibn Shu'ayb an-Nasai (829–915).

Once all this material was published, the amount of information we have about Muhammad is truly breathtaking. Few figures of history from any time or place have been so extensively and meticulously documented. It is because of the sheer abundance of this material that Renan issued his famous assessment that Islam "was born in the full light of history."[15] And while the abundance of material is impressive indeed, there are good reasons to approach it with a certain reserve, at least if one is trying to determine what Muhammad actually did say and do.

If the standard Islamic account is to be believed, all this material was preserved for two hundred years as oral tradition. While the modern mind boggles at such a feat, as people today can't manage to remember even something the length of a phone number without writing it down, in the milieu in which Islam was born and developed, this was not so unusual. In the ancient world, after all, poets would memorize Homer's *Iliad* and *Odyssey* in their entirety and recite them with scrupulous accuracy, so it is not outside the realm of possibility that early Muslims could have had all this biographical information about Muhammad committed to memory for lengthy periods.

Nevertheless, questions about the accuracy of the transmission are inevitable and obvious. How can we be sure that everyone involved in passing along these traditions orally for fully two centuries did so flawlessly, without alteration of any kind? This would require consistently prodigious feats of memory from a large number of people. What's more, the fact that even Islamic tradition notes that Bukhari and the other collectors of hadiths rejected large numbers of hadiths attests to the fact that many were forged. While the science of hadith evaluation within Islamic tradition presents certain formulas by which the authenticity of various hadiths can be determined, can these methods be taken

---

15 Quoted in Ibn Warraq, ed., *The Quest for the Historical Muhammad*, op. cit.

as entirely trustworthy? Is it possible that orthodox Islam considers some forged hadiths to be authentic, and is it likewise within the realm of possibility that some of those that have been dismissed as fabrications are actually authentic?

Even the Muslim and non-Muslim scholars who take for granted the general historical reliability of the hadith and sira literature are aware of these questions and related issues. In his book *The Sunnah and Its Role in Islamic Legislation*, the twentieth-century Syrian Islamic jurist and Muslim Brotherhood leader Mustafa al-Siba'i (1915–1964) attempted to explain why the biographical material about Muhammad appeared so late and yet nonetheless conveyed reliable information. Yet virtually from the outset of his argument, al-Siba'i entangles himself in difficulties. He states that while Muhammad's companions made careful and extensive efforts to preserve the Qur'an, similar efforts were not made for the Sunnah, that is, the traditions of Muhammad's words and actions. This is difficult to square with the foundational claim for the reliability of the biographical material about Muhammad—that those who recorded it had prodigious memories of seemingly unlimited capacity—but al-Siba'i does his best.

"Despite it being an important source of legislation," al-Siba'i explains, "the Sunnah was not recorded during the life of the Prophet in the official manner that the Qur'an was recorded, a fact that is agreed upon. The reason behind that, perhaps, lies in the fact that the Prophet lived for twenty-three years with the Companions, and it was a great task indeed to write all of his sayings, deeds, and transactions on the materials that were available for writing. Many of the Companions would have had to free themselves completely from all other duties, so that they could have dedicated themselves to recording the Sunnah."[16]

The weaknesses of this argument are glaring, and yet it is a staple of the traditional account of Islam's origins. Apparently al-Siba'i expected his readers to accept the idea that while it was beyond the capabilities of Muhammad's companions to write down what he had taught and record what he had done, it was not beyond them to remember it all with scrupulous accuracy and pass it on with 100 percent exactitude to later generations. Yet he adds that while "the Arabs had always

---

16 Mustafa as-Siba'ee, *The Sunnah and Its Role in Islamic Legislation*, Faisal Ibn Muhammad Shafeeq, trans. (Riyadh: International Islamic Publishing House, 2008), 91.

depended greatly on their ability to memorize" and "so they were able to memorize the Qur'an," they did not commit the entirety of the Sunnah to memory: Had the Sunnah been recorded during the Prophet's life as the Qur'an was recorded—and remember that the Sunnah comprised twenty-three years' worth of sayings, deeds, and legislations—the Companions would have had to occupy themselves with memorizing the Sunnah as they memorized the Qur'an, and that would have indeed been difficult for them."[17]

Al-Siba'i even admits the possibility that they might not have been able to memorize this great mass of material perfectly: "Not to mention the fear of mistakenly mixing up some of the concise and poignant words of the Prophet with the Qur'an; this constituted a danger for Allah's Book, a danger that would open the door for suspicion and doubt, which the enemies of Islam would have assuredly taken advantage of. Scholars mentioned in detail these and many other reasons why the Sunnah was not recorded during the lifetime of the Prophet. With the preceding points in mind, one can perhaps better understand the Prophet's saying, 'Do not write down what I say, and whoever writes from me other than the Qur'an, then let him erase it.'"[18]

The Islamic ambivalence about the hadith is represented in some of the hadiths themselves. One says: "It was narrated that Abdullah bin Abu Safar said: 'I heard Ash-Shabi saying: "I sat with Ibn Umar for a year and I did not hear him narrate anything from the Messenger of Allah.""'[19] A variant of this story ascribes it to a different follower of Muhammad: "It was narrated that Saib bin Yazid said: 'I accompanied Sa'd bin Malik from Al-Madinah to Makkah and I did not hear him narrate a single Hadith from the Prophet.'"[20]

Another tradition adds: "It was narrated from Ibn Tawus that his father said: 'I heard Ibn Abbas saying: "We used to memorize Ahadith, and Ahadith were memorized from the Messenger of Allah. But if you go to the extremes of either exaggeration or negligence (in narrating Ahadith), there is no way we can trust your Ahadith.""'[21]

---

17 Ibid., 92.
18 Ibid.
19 Sunan Ibn Majah, no. 26.
20 Sunan Ibn Majah, no. 29.
21 Sunan Ibn Majah, no. 27.

Yet how could one know if one was going to the extremes of exaggeration or negligence? The existence of such traditions and that saying of Muhammad about erasing traditions presents yet another problem: Is the entirety of the Sunnah illegitimate and contrary to the wishes of the prophet of Islam himself? Or was this saying itself fabricated in order to provide an explanation for why the hadith and sira literature began appearing so many years after the death of the man whose actions and sayings are so meticulously recorded in it? Al-Siba'i explains: "I believe that there is no real contradiction between the prohibition and the license to record the Sunnah; the prohibition was limited to the official recording of the Sunnah, while the license to record it was either for special circumstances or individual compilations by specific Companions."[22]

Al-Siba'i also asserts that although "the Sunnah was not officially recorded during the life of the Prophet," this "does not mean that parts of it were not recorded; actually, certain authentic narrations indicate that some of the Sunnah was recorded during the Prophet's lifetime."[23] In support of this claim, al-Siba'i invokes a tradition in which Muhammad issues a series of directives regarding how the Muslims are to behave during the conquest of Mecca; one of those listening asks him to write the rules down, and he commands that they be duly written. Al-Siba'i duly notes in a footnote the sources of this tradition: the hadith collections of Bukhari, al-Darimi, al-Tirmidhi, and Ahmad ibn Hanbal, all of whom wrote not in the seventh century, but in the ninth. Al-Siba'i asserts that "it is even established that some of the Companions had scrolls in which they would record what they heard from the Messenger of Allah," but this also we know only from ninth-century sources.[24]

Fabricated Reports

Further complicating matters is the large number of fabricated hadiths, which even Muslim scholars acknowledge. They couldn't plausibly deny their existence in any case, since it is a well-established aspect of Islamic tradition that Bukhari, Muslim, and the others collected many false hadiths along with the true ones and took immense care to winnow the true from the false. According to al-Siba'i, the trouble began when Ali

---

22 As-Siba'ee, op. cit., 94.
23 Ibid., 92–3.
24 Ibid., 93.

ibn Abi Talib became caliph in 656, after having been passed over for the job three times before, and was immediately challenged by Mu'awiya. Al-Siba'i explains that "each group tried to give credence to their position with proofs from the Qur'an and the Sunnah, and obviously, those two sources did not support every group in all of their claims. Some groups began to interpret the Qur'an falsely and to give implausible meanings to the Sunnah. Some went so far as to lie about the Prophet, inventing hadiths that would support their cause; it was difficult for them to do the same with the Qur'an, for a great number of Muslims had already memorized it, recited it, and related it. From this point on, hadith fabrications began to spread."[25]

This explanation, although it is generally accepted among Muslims, is implausible on its face. Bukhari, who is just one of many collectors of hadiths, is said to have rejected fully 593,000 inauthentic hadiths. So these pious Muslims not only felt free to lie about the Prophet, but apparently did so extremely freely and copiously. One early Islamic scholar, Asim al-Nabil (d. 827), exclaimed in frustration: "I have come to the conclusion that a pious man is never so ready to lie as in matters of the hadith."[26] Al-Zuhri agreed, stating: "A hadith would go forth from us the span of a hand and would return to us from Iraq the span of an arm."[27] Al-Siba'i adds that "Malik referred to Iraq as the house of minting, for hadiths would be minted there and then spread among the people just as coins are minted and then are spread for usage in dealings."[28]

To be sure, biblical scholars have frequently explained the phenomenon of pious fabrication, in which the believer, convinced of certain dogmas, feels free to take liberties with an existing text in order to "correct" it by bringing it in line with established orthodoxy, or even to invent a story outright to illustrate the proper belief. The sheer scale of fabrication, however, involved in the hadith and sira material, even if one accepts the standard Islamic account of Muhammad's life, is staggering. There was, evidently, far more forging and prevaricating going on than there was truth-telling, despite the fact that one hadith has Muhammad himself issuing an unequivocal warning: "Indeed, lying about me is not

---

25 Ibid., 109–10.

26 Al-Khatib al-Baghdadi, fol. 25b, ed. Hyderabad, 84 (quoted in Ignaz Goldziher, *Muslim Studies*, C. R. Barber and S. M. Stern, trans. (New York: George Allen & Unwin Ltd., 1971), II, 55.

27 Al-Siba'i, op. cit., 113.

28 Ibid., 113–4.

like lying about anyone else. And whoever lies about me on purpose, then let him take his seat in the Hellfire."[29]

This warning was not heeded. Islamic scholars, therefore, from the ninth century onward, began to develop methods to distinguish the true accounts from the false. These methods, which are the cornerstone of the "science" of hadith, are still in use today, primarily in the form of a grading system that alerts the reader to how historically reliable a given story about Muhammad is. But then, yet another question arises: how reliable is this grading system?

Its reliability is immediately called into question by the fact that Islamic tradition generally regards hadiths as reliable if they have a sound *isnad* chain, that is, a chain of transmitters from the original source to the point at which the hadith was written down. If all the people who passed on a particular tradition were deemed trustworthy, then Bukhari and the others would grade the tradition *sahih*, or reliable.

While this may seem reasonable on its face, there are a number of problems with it. Muhammad ibn Sirin, an early Muslim scholar who is said to have died in 729, stated the collectors of hadiths "were not used to inquiring after the *isnad*, but when the *fitna* occurred they said: 'Name us your informants.'"[30] The *fitna* refers to the war between Ali and Mu'awiya, which began around 656. This is an acknowledgment from Islamic tradition itself that the oral traditions were circulating for at least a quarter-century after Muhammad's death in 632 without any chain of transmitters at all. Then, when forgeries started to proliferate, it became important to establish that the sources of a given story were reliable.

Yet that also could be fabricated. Al-Siba'i notes that the reliability of the transmitters of various hadiths was, in fact, the first thing to have been faked: "The first topic about which fabricators began to invent their lies was regarding the virtues of individuals; they invented many hadiths that discussed the superiority of their Imams and of the leaders of their sects. It is said that the first to do that were the *Shi'ah*," that is,

---

29 Ibid., 110; cf. Sunan Ibn Majah, nos. 30–41.

30 Quoted in G. H. A. Juynboll, trans., "Muslim's Introduction to His Sahih Translated and Annotated with an Excursus on the Chronology of *fitna* and *bid'a*," *Jerusalem Studies in Arabic and Islam*, 5 (1984), 277, quoted in quoted in Herbert Berg, *The Development of Exegesis in Early Islam* (London: Routledge, 2000), 7.

the followers of Ali.[31] Al-Siba'i quotes early foes of the party of Ali (*shiat Ali*) impugning the honesty of that party: "Take from all whom you meet, except for the Rafidah [Shi'a], for they fabricate hadiths and then take it to be their Religion."[32] And: "One of the Shaykhs of the Rafidah said, 'When we used to gather and find something to be good, we would make it a hadith.'"[33]

Al-Siba'i is a Sunni, and so he makes no mention of the fact that the Sunnis fabricated stories of Muhammad as well. The twentieth-century scholar Joseph Schacht points out that different versions of the same tradition sometimes have different chains of transmitters, with one chain being more reliable than the other. He notes the ninth-century Sunni jurist al-Shafii's dismissal of one hadith as "*mursal*," that is, hurried, and "generally not acted upon." Schacht explains that this means it was "not confirmed by any version with a complete *isnad*." Yet the very same tradition "appears with a different, full *isnad* in Ibn Hanbal...and Ibn Maja," both of whom were also in the Sunni camp.[34]

In light of all this, basing one's estimation of the reliability, or lack thereof, of a particular tradition on the *isnad* chain would be unwise in the extreme. Al-Siba'i points out that there were numerous reasons for the early Muslims to fabricate stories of Muhammad. The primary reason was factionalism. Al-Siba'i insists that accounts of Muhammad appointing Ali as his successor are "without a doubt a fabrication invented by the Rafidah."[35] This was not a matter of one or two stories. Al-Siba'i states that the Shi'ites "went to extremes, inventing hadiths that corresponded to their desires. A good number of narrations they fabricated, for in *al-Irshad*, Al-Khaleeli said, 'The Rafidah made up approximately 300,000 hadiths in which Ali and the Prophet's family were praised.'"[36] Al-Siba'i concedes that "perhaps this is an exaggeration, yet the fact remains that they invented a great number of hadiths."[37]

Yet the Sunnis could not maintain the moral high ground. "Unfortunately," says al-Siba'i, "these were rivaled by some of the people of

31 Al-Siba'i, op. cit., 110.
32 Ibid., 114.
33 Ibid.
34 Joseph Schacht, *The Origins of Muhammadan Jurisprudence* (Oxford: Oxford University Press, 1950), 166.
35 Al-Siba'i, op. cit., 115.
36 Ibid., 115–6.
37 Ibid., 116.

the Sunnah, the ignorant ones among them. They refuted lies with lies, though their lies were considerably fewer. For example, the narration, 'Upon the leaves of all the trees in Paradise is written: None has the right to be worshipped but Allah, Muhammad is the Messenger of Allah, Abu Bakr as-Siddeeq, Umar al-Farooq, and Uthman Dhun-Noorayn."[38] Abu Bakr, Umar, and Uthman were the first three caliphs, all of whom were chosen over Ali.

Besides the political rivalry between Sunnis and Shi'a, al-Siba'i lists other reasons why hadiths were fabricated as well. He claims that the *Zanadiqah*, whom he defines as those who had "hate for Islam as a Religion and a Nation," posed as Shi'ites, or Sufis, or "as a philosopher or wise man" and succeeded in fabricating hadiths that were designed to make Muhammad and Islam look bad.[39] Al-Siba'i offers several examples of what he considers to be ridiculous hadiths that nevertheless somehow made their way into hadith collections that Muslims preserved:

> "Our Lord descends on the night of Arafah upon a camel...shakes hands with the riders, and embraces the walkers."
> "Allah created the Angels from the hair of His anus and chest."
> "Indeed, Allah felt pain in His two eyes and the Angels visited Him."
> "Looking at a beautiful face is worship."
> "Eggplant is a cure for every disease."[40]

While these are undeniably silly things to say and belie the picture of Muhammad that Muslims present to the world of a man who was incomparably insightful and wise, al-Siba'i's argument founders on the fact that, as we shall see, there are numerous hadiths that are generally accepted as *sahih* (reliable) that are just as ridiculous. In al-Siba'i's view, these, too, may be attributable to the malign influence of enemies of Islam. These enemies, he says, "introduced thousands of fabricated hadiths in beliefs, manners, medicine, the halal [permitted], and the haram [forbidden]."[41] He claims that one of these enemies admitted to fabricating a hundred hadiths and that another confessed to creating no fewer

---

38 Ibid.
39 Ibid., 119–20.
40 Ibid.
41 Ibid., 120–1.

than four thousand false hadiths, "in which he would make haram that which is halal and make halal that which is haram."[42]

The Zanadiqah during the Abbasid caliphate, which supplanted that of the Umayyads in the middle of the eighth century, were a loosely defined group of Muslim heretics, as well as atheists and others. Al-Siba'i does not explain how this group achieved such wonderful success in launching its forgeries into the corpus of biographical material that was circulating about Muhammad. Either their forgeries had a remarkable air of plausibility, such that they were readily accepted among at least some Muslims, and preserved for later generations along with authentic hadiths, or there were no significant gatekeepers, and virtually anyone could freely compose sayings or deeds of Muhammad without fear of encountering resistance from those who would point out the inauthenticity of the traditions in question. Either way, it seems as if the environment in the Islamic world of the ninth century was one in which false traditions of Muhammad could proliferate with little difficulty. For succeeding generations, this only compounds the difficulty of trying to determine what, if anything, we can know with historical certainty about the prophet of Islam.

Al-Siba'i further notes that some hadiths were fabricated by the partisans of not just various political factions but the ethnic groups among the Muslims as well. "Certain nationalists," he explains, "invented the hadith, 'Indeed, if Allah is angry, he sends down revelation in the Arabic language, but if He is pleased, He sends down revelation in Persian (Farsi).' Those who were ignorant among the Arabs vied with them, making up the hadith, 'Indeed, if Allah is angry, He sends down revelation in Farsi, and if He is pleased, He sends down revelation in Arabic.'"[43] The hadith and sira literature is indeed full of contradictions, clearly demonstrating that factions within the early Muslim community felt free to fabricate sayings of Muhammad to boost themselves and support their point of view on various issues. Then, the rival party would do the same, and the prophet of Islam would end up on both sides of an issue.

Some hadiths were fabricated, al-Siba'i continues, by storytellers who simply wanted to entertain their audiences. They "were responsible for admonishing and sermonizing, yet most of them did not fear Allah;

---

42 Ibid., 121.
43 Ibid.

what was important to them was only to make people cry in gatherings or to impress people with their sayings."[44] He does not explain how it came to be that so many of those who were responsible for giving sermons in the early Muslim communities had no fear of Allah or any hesitation regarding making up false stories about Muhammad. They were just playing, al-Siba'i says, to crowds who were "expecting wonderful words or words that would make them cry."[45] Pandering to their desires, these preachers would "invent lies, for instance, about Paradise and Hell, in order to make people weep."[46] He offers an example of these fabrications: "Whoever says, None has the right to be worshipped but Allah, Allah creates from every word a bird, whose beak is made from gold and whose feather is made from corals," and comments: "The impudence and temerity of those storytellers is bewildering."[47]

Here again, likewise bewildering is their success. Al-Siba'i once again leaves unanswered the question of why the Islamic community was unable to prevent the flights of fancy of imaginative preachers from being mixed with the authentic sayings of Muhammad. He does, however, relate a story that sheds light on the unreliability of the *isnad* chains and demonstrates clearly why they cannot be taken as establishing anything regarding the reliability or unreliability of various hadiths:

A storyteller stood among the people gathered in the Mosque and said, "Ahmad ibn Hanbal and Yahya ibn Mu'een related to me from Abdur-Razzaq from Qatadah from Anas, that the Messenger of Allah said..." And he related the previous narration. He continued to relate twenty or so pages worth of narrations, while Ahmad stared in amazement at Yahya and Yahya stared in amazement at Ahmad. Each asked the other, "Did you relate this?" And each of them answered, "By Allah, until this hour, I had not heard this." When the storyteller was finished, Yahya asked, "And who related this to you?" He said, "Ahmad ibn Hanbal and Yahya ibn Mu'een." Yahya said, "I am Yahya and this is Ahmad, and we have never heard of this to be among the sayings of the Messenger of Allah..." The storyteller said, "I used to always hear that Yahya ibn Mu'een was an imbecile, but

---

44 Ibid., 122.
45 Ibid.
46 Ibid.
47 Ibid.

that fact has not dawned upon me until now." Yahya asked, "And how is that?" He said, "Is there not any Yahya ibn Mu'een and Ahmad ibn Hanbal in the world other than you two? I have indeed written from seventeen Ahmad ibn Hanbals and Yahya ibn Mu'eens.[48]

This preacher appears to have been caught in the act of fabricating a sound *isnad* chain to give the appearance of authenticity to his story. This highlights the futility of the efforts of some contemporary scholars who try to find authentic hadiths by isolating narratives that have a weak or broken chain of transmitters on the theory that, as Islamic orthodoxy solidified and its trusted authorities were identified and generally agreed upon, no one would fabricate a hadith that depended upon transmitters who were considered untrustworthy. Thus, a hadith that survived with such a chain of transmitters would likely be one from an earlier date that was no longer useful to later generations of Muslims. While this is possible, it pays insufficient attention to the fact that the *isnad* chains were revised wholesale over the years and that the reputations of the people named in them may have been regarded differently among various groups even after the content of Islamic doctrine became a settled matter. Ultimately, there was so much forgery going on, as even Islamic tradition acknowledges, that efforts to isolate authentic narrations from the mass of fabrications are inevitably arbitrary and based on a series of assumptions that are essentially and inescapably speculative.

Al-Siba'i, meanwhile, suggests other reasons why hadiths were fabricated. He asserts that "some ignorant followers of the fiqh schools tried to strengthen their schools by fabricating hadiths."[49] The "fiqh schools" are the schools of Islamic jurisprudence. Thus, presumably, some early Islamic jurists, not finding support among the existing words and deeds of Muhammad for the position they had staked out on a given issue, simply made up a new account of something Muhammad said or did. Here again, this is an oddly unscrupulous way for pious believers to behave, but there is an analogy to it in the proliferation of Gnostic gospels and literature of other heretical Christian sects during the second century and beyond. The people who created that material were apparently sincere believers in the teachings of their group, yet they did not

---

48 Ibid., 122–3.
49 Ibid., 123.

hesitate to put words into the mouths of Jesus and the apostles in order to support their particular perspective.

Such people may have had the best of intentions. Al-Siba'i adds that some people fabricated hadiths out of "ignorance of the religion, yet with a desire to do good."[50] These were "pious people and people who were steadfast in their worship."[51] He asserts that they actually thought that making up stories about Muhammad was a service to Allah and the Muslim community: "By fabricating hadiths regarding the virtues of doing good deeds, these people thought that they were getting closer to Allah and that they were serving Islam."[52] It certainly appears as if some of those who fabricated hadiths were trying to do exactly that; al-Siba'i recounts that "from this category of fabrications are many narrations that enumerate the virtues of different chapters of the Qur'an. Nooh ibn Abee Maryam admitted to having fabricated these narrations. He excused himself by arguing that the people were turning away from the Qur'an."[53]

Al-Siba'i concludes by suggesting several other reasons why Muslims fabricated accounts of Muhammad's sayings and actions: to please a ruler, to "promote a certain Islamic ruling," or to "exact revenge upon an enemy or a specific group," or even out of "the desire to present a unique hadith in terms of either its text or chain" of transmitters. The last item once again presents us with the fact that it is even acknowledged among the community of believers that both *isnads* and *matns*, that is, the contents of particular hadiths, were manufactured wholesale and altered at will. Thus, it would be impossible to try to sort out more reliable from less reliable ones. The traditional Islamic practice of considering a hadith reliable if the chain of transmitters is sound completely ignores the fact that those chains could be falsified as easily as the stories themselves could be invented.

What Is Left?

In the hadith literature, therefore, while some of the accounts may be historically accurate or may at very least record some details that may

---

50 Ibid., 124.
51 Ibid.
52 Ibid.
53 Ibid.

be historically accurate, the historical accuracy of any given story cannot be taken for granted. It also cannot be taken for granted that the story originally referred to Muhammad, the prophet of Islam, at all. The proliferation of forged material was just too great, and extensive use was made of preexisting material. Meanwhile, the criteria that Islamic scholars have used to separate the true from the false are unreliable on their face.

Another indication of the fictional character of the great bulk of the Islamic traditions about Muhammad is that its contents contradict the Qur'an, which, even if it arose later than that same Islamic tradition claims, does predate the biographical data about Muhammad. As we shall see, Islamic tradition records Muhammad performing numerous miracles. Yet the Qur'an repeatedly depicts the unbelievers complaining about the fact that the prophet is not a miracle-worker.

This is a repeated preoccupation of the Qur'an: "They say, Why has no sign been sent down upon him from his Lord? Say, Indeed, Allah is able to send down a sign. But most of them do not know" (6:37). "And they will say, If only a sign were sent down upon him from his Lord! Then say, The unseen belongs to Allah. So wait. Indeed, I am waiting with you" (10:20). "Those who disbelieve say, If only some sign were sent down upon him from his Lord. You are only a warner, and for every people a guide" (13:7). "Those who disbelieve say, If only a sign were sent down upon him from his Lord! Say, Indeed, Allah leads astray those whom he wills, and guides to himself all who turn" (13:27). "Indeed we have made all kinds of comparisons for mankind in this Qur'an, and indeed if you came to them with a miracle, those who disbelieve would indeed exclaim, You are just tricksters" (30:58).

Yet the ninth-century Muhammad of the hadith and sira material performs miracles left and right, rendering it inconceivable that any onlooker would exclaim, "If only a sign were sent down upon him from his Lord!"

Patricia Crone and Michael Cook sum up the situation in their groundbreaking 1977 book *Hagarism: The Making of the Islamic World*:

> There is no hard evidence for the existence of the Koran in any form before the last decade of the seventh century, and the tradition which places this rather opaque revelation in its historical context is not attested before the middle of the eighth. The historicity of the

Islamic tradition is thus to some degree problematic: while there are no cogent internal grounds for rejecting it, there are equally no cogent external grounds for accepting it.[54]

It also must be emphasized that this applies to Islamic tradition as a whole. Because the texts are all so late and bereft of earlier attestation, they stand or fall as a unit. Efforts to isolate a historical core within the larger body of hadith and sira literature are necessarily so speculative as to be essentially worthless and thus foredoomed to failure, as the specifics of a chain of transmitters or some other detail that might lead historians to try to put a general date on a tradition is just as liable to have been faked as the tradition itself. Crone and Cook continue:

> In the circumstances it is not unreasonable to proceed in the usual fashion by presenting a sensibly edited version of the tradition as historical fact. But equally, it makes some sense to regard the tradition as without determinate historical content, and to insist that what purport to be accounts of religious events in the seventh century are utilisable only for the study of religious ideas in the eighth. The Islamic sources provide plenty of scope for the implementation of these different approaches, but offer little that can be used in any decisive way to arbitrate between them. The only way out of the dilemma is thus to step outside the Islamic tradition altogether and start again.[55]

The tradition may not have historical value, but it is nevertheless of cardinal importance, as hundreds of millions of Muslims regard it as absolute fact and as instructions for how they should live today. Accordingly, as the Muslim population swiftly increases in Western Europe and North America, it is increasingly crucial for non-Muslims to develop a thorough familiarity with the sayings and doings that Islamic tradition attributes to Muhammad. At the same time, no one should have, or need have, any illusions about the historical value of this material.

However, despite the lack of any information that would allow some of the material about Muhammad to be determined to be more historically reliable than the rest, or at the very least, earlier, some Western

---

54 Patricia Crone and Michael Cook, *Hagarism: The Making of the Islamic World* (Cambridge: Cambridge University Press, 1977), 3.
55 Ibid.

academics are making attempts to isolate a historical core in the hadith and sira literature. These efforts are generally apologetic in intent. American colleges and universities today receive lavish funding from Islamic entities and individuals in Saudi Arabia and Qatar, and this funding has been the impetus for the degeneration of Middle East Studies departments into platforms for anti-Israel political agitation and Islamic proselytizing.[56]

As academia in the US has moved farther to the left, it has grown increasingly hostile to all opposing points of view. And since Muslims are, in the Left's mythology, a victimized class in need of special protection, this has led to views that are even remotely critical of Islam being driven out of the professional academic world altogether. This has included historical-critical investigations; while they've been taken for granted in academic studies of Judaism and Christianity for over two centuries now, historical examination of the origins of Islam is still largely carried on outside the academic establishment.

When it does enter into American academia, it is generally as part of efforts to exonerate Islam from crimes done in its name and in accord with its teachings by establishing that Muhammad did not actually say or do something that is universally attributed to him and well attested in Islamic tradition. The pseudo-academic Islamic apologists, who are both Muslims and non-Muslims, engaged in such efforts so far have shown no indication of being aware that by engaging in historical criticism of the traditions about Muhammad, they're undercutting the traditional Islamic faith altogether. Their focus is narrowly on the saying or practice that they want to establish is unhistorical.

Some of these academic apologists even admit that the hadiths are inauthentic. They note that such fabrication was common in the ancient world as well as readily acknowledged and discussed in the Islamic sources themselves, and even admit that the hadith literature is full of contradictions, and that the material is quite late in relation to the events

---

56 See, for example, Karen W. Arenson, "Saudi Prince Gives Millions to Harvard and Georgetown," *New York Times*, December 13, 2005, https://www.nytimes.com/2005/12/13/education/saudi-prince-gives-millions-to-harvard-and-georgetown.html; Luke Rosiak, "Foreign Meddling: Department of Education Going After Elite Colleges For Allegedly Taking And Hiding Foreign Cash," *Daily Caller*, June 15, 2019, https://dailycaller.com/2019/06/15/education-universities-foreign-cash/; "Documents Show Texas A&M Appeared to Receive Almost $500 Million in Grants from Qatar Regime," *Judicial Watch*, May 3, 2023, https://www.judicialwatch.org/texas-am-grants/.

it purports to describe. Yet at the same time, they insist that earlier traditions can be isolated by means of criteria including confirmation in an early non-Muslim source, as presumably this means that the practice or saying was so well known that both Muslims and non-Muslims were aware of it.

Another sign that these scholars take as an indication that a tradition is early tradition is that it contains material that contradicts established Islamic orthodoxy. The assumption here is that the community would not have invented material that contradicts its own doctrines, and so accounts of heretical statements or obsolete practices are evidence that a tradition is earlier. This, however, ignores the fact that heretical groups often persisted for centuries alongside the orthodox and may have continued to compose their own material that was no earlier than the traditions that the orthodox party fabricated.

The apologists also turn Islamic tradition on its head by asserting that a weak hadith, particularly one with a broken chain of transmitters or a chain that includes people who are considered untrustworthy, is more likely to be an authentic tradition than one with an impeccable *isnad*. The idea here is that no one would invent a chain of transmitters that included skipped links or unreliable narrators, and so the apologists claim that such stories record earlier traditions. If the tradition survived to a time when Islamic orthodoxy was more settled, the chain of transmitters would have been adjusted. This argument, however, depends upon those who were passing on these traditions being able to gain a comprehensive knowledge of who the most trustworthy hadith transmitters were and adjust the *isnads* accordingly. They seem to forget that those who were inventing and disseminating stories of Muhammad did not have access to Google and may have presented a chain of transmitters in good faith without realizing that the people listed in the chain were denigrated outside of the circle of their community.

Some academics claim that hadiths can also be ruled out as being early if they are not cited amid a controversy in which they might have been helpful for one side or the other. But here again, this assumes that the people involved had a comprehensive knowledge at all times of what hadiths were circulating. Likewise, they suggest that a hadith is likely to have been invented in order to settle a controversy if it addresses that controversy directly, and in this, at last, the scholars are almost certainly correct.

The flimsy, tenuous nature of these arguments only testifies to the impossibility of sifting through the hadith and sira literature to find a historical core. If such a core ever existed, it is not recoverable now. The biographical material about Muhammad must be approached with the understanding that, in terms of historical value, it is all on the same level—and that level is that its historicity is nonexistent.

CHAPTER THREE

Becoming a Prophet

Where was Muhammad Born?

Islamic tradition is unanimous in stating that Muhammad was born in Mecca, became a prophet not far from Mecca, first preached Islam in Mecca, and spent the first part of his prophetic career in Mecca. Toward the end of that career, he returned to Mecca as a conqueror and Islamized that city's central shrine, the Kaʻba. Yet despite its key place in Islam, the Qur'an mentions Mecca by name only once: "And it is he who has kept men's hands from you, and has kept your hands from them, in the valley of Mecca, after he had made you conquerors over them. Allah is the seer of what you do" (48:24).

Yet there is no historical evidence that Mecca was the center of pilgrimage and trade that the ninth-century Islamic literature depicts it as being during the life of Muhammad. As Crone puts it, "It is obvious that if the Meccans had been middlemen in a long-distance trade of the kind described in the secondary literature, there ought to have been some mention of them in the writings of their customers. Greek and Latin authors had, after all, written extensively about the south Arabians who supplied them with aromatics in the past, offering information about their cities, tribes, political organization, and caravan trade."[1]

Yet as with Muhammad himself, the contemporary sources record virtually nothing about this supposedly thriving city. Crone adds: "It is not clear why some scholars believe the overland route"—that is, a well-traveled trade route that had merchants regularly passing through Mecca—"to have continued into the fourth century CE, or even later

---

1 Patricia Crone, *Meccan Trade and the Rise of Islam* (Princeton: Princeton University Press, 1987), 134.

[e.g., the seventh century], or why Islamicists generally assume it to have retained its importance until the time of Mecca's rise to commercial prominence, or to have recovered it by then."[2]

Mecca apparently did exist, but it was nothing like how the hadith and sira literature portray it. In the second century, Ptolemy mentions an Arabian town called Macoraba, which many have identified with Mecca. This, however, establishes nothing regarding the authenticity of the biographical material about Muhammad, for Ptolemy died over four hundred years before Muhammad was supposedly born. Crone also notes that "if Ptolemy mentions Mecca at all, he calls it Moka, a town in Arabia Petraea," that is, in modern-day northern Arabia or southern Jordan, near Petra, the city to which many early mosques point for their direction for prayer, rather than to Mecca.[3]

Mecca goes unmentioned in the surviving accounts of sixth- and seventh-century merchants. Nor does it appear in other writings, as Crone explains: "The political and ecclesiastical importance of Arabia in the sixth century was such that considerable attention was paid to Arabian affairs, too; but of Quraysh and their trading center there is no mention at all, be it in the Greek, Latin, Syriac, Aramaic, Coptic, or other literature composed outside Arabia before the conquests. This silence is striking and significant."[4] She adds: "Nowhere is it stated that Quraysh, or the 'Arab kings,' were the people who used to supply such-and-such regions with such-and-such goods: it was only Muhammad himself who was known to have been a trader."[5]

Only a century after Muhammad's lifetime is there specific mention of Mecca, in the *Byzantine-Arab Chronicle*, an account of Islam's origins that cannot be dated earlier than 741 AD, as it mentions the Roman Emperor Leo III, who died in that year.[6] This *Chronicle* mentions "Mecca, the home of Abraham as they think, which lies between Ur of the Chaldees and the city of Harran (Carras) in the desert."[7] That is not where Mecca is. If Mecca was between Ur and Harran, it would be in present-day Iraq, northeast of where it is actually found

2 Ibid., 26.
3 Crone, *Meccan Trade*, 136.
4 Ibid., 134.
5 Ibid., 137.
6 The Byzantine-Arab Chronicle of 741, 39 (quoted in Hoyland, *Seeing Islam*, 625).
7 Ibid., 34 (quoted in Hoyland, *Seeing Islam*, 622).

in Arabia. So is the Mecca of Muhammad even meant? That cannot be taken for granted.

Mecca is also unlikely ever to have been a thriving trading center; it is far too remote for that. Historian Richard Bulliet notes that "only by the most tortured map reading can it be described as a natural crossroads between a north-south route and an east-west one."[8] Historian Dan Gibson points out that "not one map before 900 AD even mentions Mecca."[9] That's an extraordinary omission if Mecca was anything like what it is described as being in the ninth-century accounts of Muhammad's life.

So where did all this happen, if anywhere?

On What Day was Muhammad Born?

According to a twenty-first-century biographer of Muhammad, the convert to Islam Yahiya Emerick, "on April 20 in the year 570, on a crisp evening under a stunning sky, Aminah gave birth to a beautiful baby boy. Barakah was the first to hold him, and then she reverently handed him to his grateful mother."[10] In Emerick's account, Barakah had good reason to be reverent. This was no ordinary child; accompanying the birth of Muhammad, which took place in Mecca in southwest Arabia, were prophecies about a coming "lord of this nation."[11]

Emerick's relatively straightforward account reflects the consensus of Islamic tradition. But as with virtually every detail regarding the prophet of Islam, the story is not quite as clear and simple as it initially appears. The date of Muhammad's birth, April 20, 570, comes from Ibn Hisham, who states that "the apostle was born on Monday, 12th Rabi'u'l-awwal, in the year of the elephant."[12] *Rabi'u'l-awwal*, or more commonly, *Rabi al-Awwal*, was the third month of the Arabic calendar and became the third month of the Islamic calendar. The date of 12 *Rabi al-Awwal* does indeed correspond to April 20, 570. However, Ibn Sa'd, who wrote his own biography of Muhammad around the time that Ibn Hisham was copying and revising the work of Ibn Ishaq, states: "The Apostle of

---

8 Richard W. Bulliet, *The Camel and the Wheel* (Cambridge, MA: Harvard University Press, 1975), 105 (quoted in Crone, *Meccan Trade*, 6).

9 Dan Gibson, Qur'anic Geography: A Survey and Evaluation of the Geographical References in the Qur'an with Suggested Solutions for Various Problems and Issues (Saskatoon: Independent Scholars Press, 2011), 224.

10 Yahiya Emerick, *The Life and Work of Muhammad* (Indianapolis: Alpha Books, 2002), 29.

11 Ibid.

12 Ibn Ishaq, op. cit., 69.

Allah…was born on Monday, the 10th of the month of *Rabi al-Awwal*; and the invasion of the people of the Elephants (*ashab al-fil*) took place in the middle of Muharram, fifty five days prior to this event."[13]

Ibn Sa'd scrupulously records the variant traditions to which he had access, and he also notes that another early Muslim, Abu Ma'shar Nujayh al-Madani, "used to say that the Apostle of Allah…was born on Monday, 2 *Rabi al-Awwal*."[14]

So was Muhammad born on the 2nd, the 10th, or the 12th? This may seem to be a mere quibble. After all, no one knows the date of Jesus's birth at all. By comparison, three estimates for Muhammad's birth, all within ten days of one another, could be taken as an indication that there is a kernel of historical truth here and that a real Muhammad was indeed born sometime during the first two weeks of the month of Rabi al-Awwal. The exactitude of the traditions, however, and their disagreement with one another does raise questions. These sources are purporting to provide precisely accurate information about the prophet of Islam. Yet at least two of them, and likely all three, are wrong. This epitomizes the Islamic traditions about Muhammad as a whole: we appear to have precise and detailed historical information, but what we actually have is myth, fable, folk tales, sermonizing, factionalism, and guesswork, presented in the guise of historical accounts scrupulously passed on through the generations.

According to tradition, Muhammad was the son of a merchant named Abdullah ibn Abd al-Muttalib and his wife Amina. The early Islamic sources note, as did Emerick, that Muhammad's imminent birth was marked with some fanfare, although even Ibn Hisham relates this account with some reserve. "It is alleged in popular stories (and only God knows the truth)," he says, "that Amina d. Wahb, the mother of God's apostle, used to say when she was pregnant with God's apostle that a voice said to her, 'You are pregnant with the lord of this people and when he is born say, "I put him in the care of the One from the evil of every envier; then call him Muhammad."' As she was pregnant with him she saw a light come forth from her by which she could see the castles of Busra in Syria."[15]

13 Ibn Sa'd, op. cit., I, 109.
14 Ibid., I, 109–10.
15 Ibn Ishaq, op. cit., 69.

Ibn Sa'd records a variant in which Amina elaborates: "I felt no discomfort till I delivered him. But when he was separated from me there emitted with him a light which made everything between the East and the West bright. Then he fell on the earth resting on his hands and took a handful of earth and raised his head to the heaven; and some say that he was reclining on his knees, raising his head to the heaven, and there emitted with him a light which illuminated the palaces of Syria and its markets, till I saw the necks of camels at Busra."[16]

Another variant appears to be an abbreviation or summary of that tradition: "When I delivered him, there emitted a light from my womb which illuminated the palaces of Syria, so I delivered him clean as the lamb without impurities, and he fell on the earth with his hands resting on it."[17] Still another makes the light an even greater portent: "I noticed as if a meteor came out of me with which the earth was lighted."[18]

Yet despite this marvelous portent, apparently no one thought to note, or no one precisely remembered, the exact date of the birth of this favored child. A further marvel, meanwhile, was that according to Ibn Sa'd, "The Prophet was born circumcised and with navel chord cut; this caused Abd al-Muttalib wonder and he was pleased; he remarked: This child of mine will achieve greatness, which he did."[19]

In What Year was Muhammad Born?

There is also some question as to the year of Muhammad's birth. Ibn Hisham says that Muhammad was born in the year of the elephant, which appears to be the year of the events recounted elliptically in the Qur'an: "Haven't you seen how your Lord dealt with the owners of the elephant? Didn't he bring their stratagem to nothing, and send against them swarms of birds, which pelted them with stones of baked clay, and made them like green crops devoured?" (105:1–5).

Ibn Hisham explains that this referred to an expedition into Mecca of the Christian King Abraha of Aksum in what is now Yemen. Abraha, according to Ibn Hisham, had built a great cathedral and sent one of his client emirs, a man named Muhammad ibn Khuza'i, to call people to

16 Ibn Sa'd, op. cit., I, 111.
17 Ibid.
18 Ibid.
19 Ibid., 112.

make pilgrimages to it; however, Muhammad ibn Khuza'i was murdered in Arabia. Abraha, enraged, invaded Mecca with a large army led by an elephant. This expedition came to naught, however, when the elephant proved recalcitrant and the army was afflicted by various plagues, the details of which all correspond exactly to what is recorded in the Qur'an. Later, says Ibn Hisham, Muhammad reminded his tribesmen, the Meccan Arabs of the Quraysh tribe, of this instance of Allah's favor with the words of the Qur'an.[20]

It is generally agreed that this momentous event took place in 570, and so that is the generally accepted date for Muhammad's birth, as per Ibn Hisham. However, a twelfth-century account states: "The Prophet is supposed to have been born that very year, fifty days or two months after the departure of the Elephant, or even ten, fifteen, or even twenty years later."[21] Those who accept the traditional accounts of Muhammad's birth as historically accurate may dismiss this as a late and unreliable tradition. But once again, it must be asked how and why such a tradition could arise in the first place.

If it was generally known and accepted in the ninth century that Muhammad had been born on April 20, 570, and this date was in turn based on oral traditions going back to the sixth century (or at very least to the seventh), why did anyone begin to say that Muhammad could have been born ten to twenty years later than this? Nor is this a singular statement; the twentieth-century Islamic scholar Henri Lammens notes that the twelfth-century Yemeni scholar al-Fayyumi "also mentions an opinion that admits of a ten-year interval between the two events."[22]

Lammens points out that a great deal of the chronology of Muhammad's life appears far more formulaic than real life usually is: "Khadija is said to have given him four sons and as many daughters. At the death of Muhammad, Aisha's eighteen years are divided in this way: nine years before and nine years after her marriage. According to certain biographers, the twenty years of the Prophet's career were divided in two equal sections: ten years at Mecca, ten years at Medina. Others, while they accept twenty-three years for this period, distinguish ten years at Mecca

---

20 Ibn Ishaq, op. cit., 27.

21 Henri Lammens, "The Age of Muhammad and the Chronology of the Sira," *Journal Asiatique* (March-April 1911), 208–50; now in Ibn Warraq, ed., *The Quest for the Historical Muhammad* (Amherst, New York: Prometheus Books, 2000), 189.

22 Ibid.

and ten years at Medina. During those twenty years, he remained under the influence of Gabriel; during the three preceding years, Asrafil is said to have played this role."[23]

Ibn Sa'd likewise recounts a tradition stating that "for ten years he remained at Makkah and for the next ten years he lived at al-Madinah."[24] Like the traditions to which Lammens was referring, this leaves three years unaccounted for. Maybe Muhammad's life did fit into these extremely neat subsections. Or maybe this symmetry is the result of the whole thing having been constructed.

So in the final analysis, while Muhammad *may* have been born on April 20, 570, the divergent traditions indicate that it took some time for the nascent Muslim community to come to an agreement as to his birthdate, and even after it did, some of the earlier variant birthdates continued to circulate. For a man who was supposed to have been born in seventh-century Arabia, when it was not always easy to determine the date, this is not so surprising, but it does recall the same uncertainty we saw regarding the date of his death: Muhammad was supposed to have died in 632, but the *Doctrina Jacobi* has him leading armies into Palestine in 635.

What was the Name of the Prophet of Islam?

According to Ibn Hisham, as we have seen, Muhammad's mother, Amina, said that when her child was not yet born, she heard a voice telling her to name him Muhammad. However, Lammens points out that some Islamic traditions assert that "at his birth Muhammad had received the name Qutham, but since the Book of Allah had given him the name Ahmad and Muhammad, the Tradition, with a slightly apologetic ulterior motive, wants to hear of no other."[25]

Lammens was referring to the late ninth-century Islamic historian Ahmad ibn Yahya ibn Jabir al-Baladhuri, who wrote that Muhammad's grandfather, Abd al-Muttalib, had named him for his son who had died as a child: "As for Qutam b. Abd al-Muttalib: his mother was Safiyyah bt. Jundub, the mother of al-Harit b. Abd al-Muttalib, and he died as a

23 Ibid., 189–90.
24 Ibn Sa'd, op. cit., I, 220.
25 Henri Lammens, "The Koran and Tradition," quoted in Ibn Warraq, ed., *The Quest for the Historical Muhammad,* (Amherst, NY: Prometheus, 2000), 172.

young boy. [Someone] other than al-Kalbi said: "He died three years before the birth of the Prophet, when he was a boy of nine years, whereupon Abd al-Muttalib experienced great anguish, [for] he had been dear to him [and] brought him joy. Then, when the Messenger of God was born, Abd al-Muttalib named him 'Qutam', whereupon his mother Aminah informed him that she had been shown in a dream [that she was] to name him 'Muhammad'—thus, he named him 'Muhammad' [instead]."[26]

Lammens points out that other Islamic scholars said the same thing, including Ibn al-Jawzi, a twelfth-century historian, another historian who flourished a century after that, Sibt ibn al-Jawzi, and the fifteenth-century scholar Ahmad ibn Ali al-Maqrizi.[27] Regarding the name change, he comments: "One needs only to be wakeful in one's pursuit and to research patiently into the remote corners of the Hadith to discover the real significance of what orthodoxy did not or would not understand."[28] However, nothing about Muhammad originally being named Qutham ("The Generous One") actually contradicts Islamic orthodoxy. Al-Baladhuri's tradition is carefully harmonized with the claim that Amina was told by a heavenly voice to name her son Muhammad, and so there is no problem.

The tradition and others like it, however, is important for other reasons. It indirectly highlights the fact that Muhammad, that is, "The Praised One," is more of a title than a proper name, and may indeed have been a title that became affixed in particular to the prophet of Islam, but which had previously been applied to others. In another tradition, one of the Jews, who are frequently cast as skeptics and opponents of Muhammad in Islamic tradition, asks Muhammad: "Why are you named Muhammad and Ahmad and Bashir ['bearer of good news'] and Nadhir ['warner']?" He answered: "As for Muhammad, I am praised on the earth; as for Ahmad, I am more praised in heaven. As for Bashir, I

---

26 Ahmad b. Yahya al-Baladuri (ed. Suhayl Zakkar & Riyad Zirikli), *Kitab Jumal min Ansab al-Asraf*, Vol. 4 (Beirut, Lebanon: Dar al-Fikr, 1997), p. 411, https://islamicorigins.com/was-muhammad-originally-named-qutham/.

27 Ibn al-Jawzi, *Wafa*, p. 32a; idem, *Talqih* (ms. Asir effendi, Constantinople), II, p. 3a; Anonymous, *Sira* (Berlin, no. 9602), p. 155a; al-Barizi (Berlin, no. 2569), p. 81b; Maqrizi, *Imta*, III; Sibt ibn al-Jawzi, *Mirat at az-zaman*, II (ms. Kuprulu, Constantinople), p. 149b (quoted in Ibn Warraq, ed., *The Quest for the Historical Muhammad*, 184).

28 Ibid., 172.

give the good news of heaven to those who obey God. As for Nadhir, I warn those who disobey God of hellfire."[29]

In a similar vein, Bukhari records a hadith in which Muhammad says: "I have five names: I am Muhammad and Ahmad; I am Al-Mahi through whom Allah will eliminate infidelity; I am Al-Hashir who will be the first to be resurrected, the people being resurrected thereafter; and I am also Al-Aqib (i.e. There will be no prophet after me)."[30] Muslim reports a similar statement: "I am Muhammad and I am Ahmad, and I am al-Mahi (the obliterator) by whom unbelief would be obliterated, and I am Hashir (the gatherer) at whose feet mankind will be gathered, and I am Aqib (the last to come) after whom there will be no Prophet."[31] Ibn Sa'd likewise has Muhammad saying: "I am Muhammad (praised), Ahmad (praised), al-Hashir (collector), al-Mahi (one who obliterates), al-Khatim (the Last) and al-Aqib (the last)," and several variants of this.[32]

All of these besides Muhammad are clearly titles, and "Muhammad" itself may be a title as well. If so, this could explain why the mentions of Muhammad in the seventh century don't correspond to the traditional Islamic picture of the prophet: they were referring to someone else altogether.

Also, the use of a title as a proper name in itself suggests that the person so named is more myth than fact. Calling a man "The Praised One" is akin to calling someone "Superman"; even the name itself removes the person from the realm of ordinary human beings. Islamic tradition, of course, insists that Muhammad was anything but ordinary; in fact, he is the "excellent example" (Qur'an 33:21) for Muslims, to be emulated in all things. Yet at the same time, that tradition holds that there was nothing superhuman about Muhammad at all; he was a man like all other men, albeit chosen by Allah for a mission more exalted than that which was given to any other human being before or since. In any case, the very name "Muhammad" is consistent with the idea that he is not a historical figure, but a legend constructed in order to serve various purposes.

The "Qutham" traditions likewise suggest another possibility. Although they don't pose any problems for Islamic orthodoxy, they

29 Qummi, 2:346, quoted in Gabriel Said Reynolds, ed., *The Qur'an and Its Biblical Subtext* (New York: Routledge, 2010), 189.
30 Sahih Bukhari 4.61.3532.
31 Sahih Muslim, book 43, no. 2354a.
32 Ibn Sa'd, op. cit., I, 114.

do raise the question of why they would have been invented in the first place. The primary possibility, of course, is that Muhammad was a historical figure, born in 570 and really named Qutham, only to be renamed Muhammad in light of the voice that his mother heard. This, however, is unlikely in light of the scant mentions of Muhammad in the seventh century and the very late appearance of biographical material about him.

The second possibility, therefore, is that there was a figure named Qutham who was most likely a warrior or a prophet or both, and about whom various traditions circulated that were ultimately incorporated into the new Muhammad myth. As the Qutham stories may still have been circulating in their earlier, pre-Muhammad form, in order to explain the existence of the same stories in the Muhammad legend, the claim was invented that Qutham was Muhammad's original name. Thus the still-circulating Qutham stories were neatly explained away: they were about Muhammad all along.

In his fourteenth-century sira, the renowned Islamic scholar Ibn Kathir has no doubts about the future prophet's name. He asserts that according to Ibn Ishaq, "someone" came to Muhammad's mother Amina as she was about to give birth and told her: "And the sign of that will be that his birth will be accompanied by a light which will fill the palaces of Busra, in the land of Ash-Sham. So when he is born, name him Muhammad, for his name is in the Torah: Ahmad—he is praised by the occupants of the heaven and the occupants of the Earth and his name is in the Gospel: Ahmad—he is praised by the occupants of the heaven and the occupants of the Earth; and his name is in the Qur'an: Muhammad."[33]

A Great Future

Islamic tradition holds that Muhammad's father, Abdullah, died before he was born and that his mother died when he was six. His grandfather Abd al-Muttalib then took him in. When Muhammad would approach Abd al-Muttalib, whose bed was "in the shade of the Ka'ba," his uncles would shoo the small boy away. Abd al-Muttalib, however, would stop them, saying: "Let my son alone, for by Allah he has a great

---

33 Ibn Kathir, The Valley Came Alive: The Life of the Last Messenger, taken from Al-Bidayah wa'l Nihayah, trans. anon. (Riyadh: Darussalam, 2014), 12.

future."[34] Abd al-Muttalib, however, did not live to see that future; he died when Muhammad was eight, whereupon the boy went to live with his uncle, Abu Talib.

At one point, a seer came to Mecca and saw something in young Muhammad. "Bring me that boy," he called out to Abu Talib, but according to Ibn Hisham, when Muhammad's uncle saw the "eagerness" of the seer, he hid Muhammad, whereupon the seer fumed: "Woe to you, bring me that boy I saw just now, for by Allah he has a great future."[35] The fact that Abd al-Muttalib and the seer use the same phrase to refer to the boy suggests yet again that these are stylized fables, not historical accounts. Ibn Hisham concludes his story by writing: "But Abu Talib went away."[36] Abu Talib may have protected Muhammad from the seer in light of the statement in the Qur'an, which was ostensibly revealed after this incident took place but more likely dates from before this story was constructed: "O you who believe, strong drink and games of chance and idols and divining arrows are only an abomination of Satan's handiwork. Leave it aside so that you may succeed" (5:90).

Abd al-Muttalib and the seer were not the only ones who saw that Muhammad had a "great future." When Abu Talib took Muhammad along on a caravan to Syria, a monk named Bahira caught sight of young Muhammad and invited the men of the Quraysh to dine with him so that he could get a closer look at the remarkable boy. One of the Quraysh recalled that Muhammad had been left behind with the caravan's baggage and invoked the Quraysh's goddesses as he exclaimed: "By al-Lat and al-Uzza, we are to blame for leaving behind the son of Abdullah b. Abdu'l-Muttalib."[37] When Muhammad arrived, Bahira "stared at him closely, looking at his body and finding traces of his description (in the Christian books)."[38]

This reflected the Islamic belief that Muhammad's coming was prophesied in the Christian scriptures but that the Christians perfidiously dared to alter the very words of Allah in order to obscure the prophecies that told of the Arabian prophet. Bahira also questioned Muhammad: "Boy, I ask you by al-Lat and al-Uzza to answer my

---

34 Ibn Ishaq, op. cit., 73.
35 Ibid., 79.
36 Ibid.
37 Ibid., 80.
38 Ibid.

question."[39] Ibn Hisham explained that the Christian monk "said this only because he had heard his people swearing by these gods."[40] But he found Muhammad to be a convinced monotheist even at his tender age, as he responded: "Do not ask me by al-Lat and al-Uzza, for by Allah nothing is more hateful to me than these two."[41]

Bahira then tried again with the proper deity: "Then by Allah, tell me what I ask."[42] Muhammad said: "Ask me what you like."[43] Bahira then quizzed the boy about "what happened in his sleep, and his habits, and his affairs generally," and here again, the prophecies were fulfilled: "what the apostle of God told him coincided with what Bahira knew of his description."[44] Bahira then examined Muhammad's back "and saw the seal of prophethood between his shoulders in the very place described in his book."[45] This referred to a distinctive mole that was supposed to be described in the Christian scriptures as a sign of prophethood; no Christian books have ever been found that actually contain this description.

Bahira ultimately told Abu Talib: "Take your nephew back to his country and guard him carefully against the Jews, for by Allah! If they see him and know about him what I know, they will do him evil; a great future lies before this nephew of yours, so take him home quickly."[46] Bahira's warning reflects the antisemitism that runs through the hadith literature as a whole: the Jews are constantly depicted as scheming against Allah and his people and trying to thwart their endeavors. This passage establishes how Jews and Christians are depicted throughout the entirety of the hadith and sira literature: they are enemies of Allah and the Muslims who know that Islam is true and that Muhammad is a genuine prophet but who deliberately conceal this knowledge out of jealousy and hatred of the prophet of Islam.

Khadija

Young Muhammad continued to impress those around him. When he was twenty-five years old, "a merchant woman of dignity and wealth"

39 Ibid.
40 Ibid.
41 Ibid.
42 Ibid.
43 Ibid.
44 Ibid.
45 Ibid.
46 Ibid., 81.

named Khadija, who was herself forty years old, noticed Muhammad's "truthfulness, trustworthiness, and honorable character," and hired him to sell her goods in Syria.[47] Once there, Muhammad sat down under a tree near the dwelling of a monk; when the monk saw him, he declared: "None but a prophet ever sat beneath this tree."[48] As he rode back to Mecca in the intense desert heat, two angels shielded him from the sun's heat.

According to Ibn Hisham, Khadija was a "determined, noble, and intelligent woman possessing the properties with which God willed to honor her."[49] She was "the best born woman in Quraysh, of the greatest dignity and, too, the richest."[50] Ibn Sa'd adds that she was "of the noblest descent, highest in dignity and the wealthiest of the Quraysh," and that "every member of her tribe desired to take her into marriage. They had made proposals and spent money for this purpose."[51] But Khadija had no interest in them; instead, she approached her young employee and asked: "O Muhammad! What prevents you from marriage?"[52] He responded ingenuously that he couldn't afford to get married. She then coquettishly asked: "If you get enough means, and you get a proposal from (a lady of) beauty, wealth, dignity and equal status, will you accept?"[53] Still apparently not perceiving what she was trying to convey to him, Muhammad asked: "Who is she?"[54] Khadija replied: "Khadija."[55]

Despite the fact that Khadija was fifteen years older than Muhammad and that wealthier, more prominent men of the Quraysh had sought her hand, she and Muhammad, who was her first cousin, were duly married. Ibn Sa'd notes the couple's unusual age difference as he records the marriage: "The Apostle of Allah, may Allah bless him, married her when he was twenty-five years old, and Khadijah was forty years old, as she was born fifteen years before the year of Elephant."[56] Tabari, meanwhile, notes that the marriage only came about by way of a subterfuge. Khadija

---

47 Ibid., 82.
48 Ibid.
49 Ibid.
50 Ibid.
51 Ibn Sa'd, op. cit., I, 148.
52 Ibid.
53 Ibid.
54 Ibid.
55 Ibid.
56 Ibid.

"called her father to her house, plied him with wine until he was drunk, slaughtered a cow, anointed him with perfume and clothed him in a striped robe; then she sent for the Messenger of God and his uncles and, when they came in, her father married him to her."[57]

When Khadija's father came to his senses, he had no recollection of what had happened and asked his daughter: "What is this meat, this perfume, and this garment?"[58] She replied: "You have married me to Muhammad b. Abdallah."[59] Appalled, the old man declared: "I have not done so. Would I do this, when the greatest men of Mecca have asked for you and I have not agreed?"[60] Ibn Sa'd recounts much the same story. But other early Islamic authorities maintain that Khadija's father had died before the marriage and thus was never in any position to dispute it.[61]

In any case, the marriage held, and the subtext of Tabari's story was clear: Khadija had unusual powers of discernment, such that she alone could tell that Muhammad was far greater than all of the "greatest men of Mecca." These powers would prove to be of the utmost importance when Muhammad received his first revelation from Allah.

Besides Khadija, others could see what Muhammad would become as well, including non-humans. Ibn Hisham wrote that before Gabriel appeared to Muhammad, the natural world offered intimations of his destiny, as "the glens of Mecca and the beds of its valleys where no house was in sight; and not a stone or tree that he passed by but would say, 'Peace unto you, O apostle of Allah.' And the apostle would turn to his right and left and look behind him and he would see nothing but trees and stones."[62] A hadith ascribes this fantasy to Muhammad himself, having him say: "Indeed in Mecca there is a rock that used to give me Salam during the night of my advent, and I know it even now."[63]

---

57 Abu Ja'far Muhammad bin Jarir al-Tabari, *The History of al-Tabari*, vol. 6, *Muhammad at Mecca*, W. Montgomery Watt and M. V. McDonald, trans. (Albany: State University of New York Press, 1988), 49.
58 Ibid.
59 Ibid.
60 Ibid.
61 Ibn Sa'd, op. cit., I, 149.
62 Ibn Ishaq, op. cit., 105.
63 Jami at-Tirmidhi, vol. 1, book 49, no. 3624.

When was the First Revelation?

Islamic tradition records that Muhammad received his first revelation while he was praying in a cave on Mount Hira, near Mecca. Ibn Sa'd notes that "the angel descended on the Apostle of Allah, may peace be on him, at Hira on Monday, seventeenth of Ramadan, and the Apostle of Allah was then forty years old. It was Gabriel who came down with a revelation to him."[64] Tabari, however, makes clear yet again that the precise date of that tradition was just the illusion of historical precision, not actual scrupulous reporting of the facts; he says that "the Qur'an was revealed to the Messenger of God on the eighteenth of Ramadan. Others say it was revealed on the twenty-fourth of Ramadan.... Others say it was revealed on the seventeenth of Ramadan."[65] He adds that "they quote as evidence for this the words of God: 'And that which we revealed to Our slave on the day of the *furqan*, on the day when the two armies met.' [Qur'an 8:41] This refers to the meeting [in battle] of the Messenger of God with the polytheists at Badr," which Islamic tradition places four years after this, in the year 624, "which took place on the morning of the seventeenth of Ramadan."[66]

What does that verse of the Qur'an have to do with the date of Muhammad's first revelation? *Furqan* is generally translated as "criterion" and refers to the Qur'an itself, as the same book testifies: "Blessed is he who has revealed the *furqan* to his slave, so that he may be a warner for the worlds" (Qur'an 25:1). So if the Battle of Badr took place on the "day of the *furqan*," that is, the anniversary of the day that the Qur'an began to be revealed, and that battle took place on the seventeenth of Ramadan, then Muhammad also received his first revelation on the seventeenth of Ramadan. But then why did other sources say he received his first revelation on the eighteenth or twenty-fourth of that month? Was the seventeenth of Ramadan tradition constructed to validate, make sense of, and flesh out the Qur'anic verse?

---

64 Ibn Ishaq, op. cit., 223–4.
65 Tabari, op. cit., 6, 62–3.
66 Ibid., 63.

How Old was Muhammad When He Received His First Revelation?

"When Muhammad the apostle of God reached the age of forty," says Ibn Hisham, "God sent him in compassion to mankind, 'as an evangelist to all men.'"[67] Tabari attributes to Anas b. Malik, who heard it from Rabiah b. Abi Abd al-Rahman, who heard it from Yahya b. Muhammad b. Qays, who heard it from Amr b. Ali and Ibn al-Muthanna, that "the Messenger of God commenced his mission at the end of his fortieth year."[68] Yet he also attributes a variant tradition to Anas b. Malik and Rabiah b. Abi Abd al-Rahman, but this time via al-Awzai, the unnamed father of al-Abbas b. al-Walid, and finally to al-Abbas b. al-Walid himself: "The Messenger of God commenced his mission at the beginning of his fortieth year."[69] Tabari also notes that "others say that he became a prophet when he was aged forty-three."[70]

The variation in traditions about how old Muhammad was when he became a prophet may have come about from attempts at more of the chronological symmetry that Lammens had noted. According to Tabari, Muhammad once told his daughter Fatima: "Whenever a prophet has been sent, his mission has lasted for a period of half his predecessor's lifetime. Jesus was sent for a period of forty years, and I was sent for twenty."[71] Islamic tradition has generally held throughout the centuries that Muhammad's prophetic career lasted twenty-three years. But making him slightly older and thus his time as a prophet shorter allowed for this congruence with the supposed age of Jesus. The variant traditions—Muhammad was forty, Muhammad was forty-three—also once again remind readers that we are not dealing with scrupulously accurate historical accounts, although their attention to detail may give that impression. Rather, the stories of Muhammad are legends constructed to serve certain purposes.

Yet those three years that throw off the symmetry of Muhammad's prophetic career, which otherwise would be extremely neat and orderly with its ten years in Mecca and ten years in Medina, commencing when he was forty and ending when he was sixty, are so multiply attested

---

67 Ibn Ishaq, op. cit., 104.
68 Tabari, op. cit., 60.
69 Ibid.
70 Ibid., 61.
71 Ibid.

and variously explained that it is possible that they do have their actual origin in the historical career of a real person, whether or not this individual bore the name of Muhammad and claimed prophethood. Ibn Sa'd offers another explanation of these three years: after Muhammad became a prophet, he says, he preached the message of the oneness of Allah "secretly" for three years "till he was commanded to preach openly."[72] Ibn Sa'd also records traditions in which the stray three years come into play regarding the exact identity of the spiritual being who first approached Muhammad.

Who Brought Muhammad His First Revelation?

Whenever it happened, and however old Muhammad was, it was reported to be a visitation from an angel. But which angel? "When it was the night on which God honored him with his mission and showed mercy on His servants thereby," says Ibn Hisham, "Gabriel brought him the command of God."[73] Tabari states that "before Gabriel appeared to him to confer on him his mission as Messenger of God, it is said that he used to see signs and evidences indicated that God wished to ennoble him and to single him out for his favor."[74] Yet even this core element of the Islamic story, that it was the archangel Gabriel who delivered Allah's revelations to Muhammad, is not without its variant traditions. Ibn Sa'd recounts that "verily the Apostle of Allah, may Allah bless him, was commissioned to prophethood when he was forty years old. Saraphel was with him for three years, then he was replaced by Gabriel who remained with him, at Makkah for ten years, and at the city of his migration, al-Madinah, for ten years. The Apostle of Allah, may Allah bless him, breathed his last when he was sixty-three years of age."[75] This recalls the tradition to which Lammens referred, in which Asrafil was the first angel who dealt with Muhammad.

Asrafil and Saraphel have completely disappeared from Islamic tradition, which has held with virtual unanimity since the time of Ibn Sa'd that the angel who appeared to Muhammad was Gabriel, and only Gabriel. Indeed, immediately after recounting this tradition mentioning

---

72 Ibn Sa'd, op. cit., I, 230.
73 Ibn Ishaq, op. cit., 106.
74 Tabari, op. cit., 63.
75 Ibn Sa'd, op. cit., I, 220.

Saraphel, Ibn Sa'd added: "I related this tradition to Muhammad Ibn Umar; he said: The learned men of our city do not know that Saraphel had been with the Prophet, may Allah bless him. Verily the learned and those versed in Sirah literature say: From the time the revelations commenced till he (Prophet) may Allah bless him, breathed his last none except Gabriel was with him."[76]

Who was Saraphel? As may have been the case with Muhammad's original name, Qutham, Saraphel's presence in Islamic tradition could be due to its incorporation of earlier accounts from other traditions. It could be that those who fabricated hadiths had access to a tradition or traditions regarding an angel named Saraphel appearing to a particular prophet and recast these stories as accounts of Muhammad. The circulation of the claim that Saraphel had given Muhammad revelations for three years and then was supplanted by Gabriel was designed to account for the continued spread of the earlier versions that mentioned Saraphel.

Bukhari's account of Muhammad's first revelation doesn't mention the name of the being who appeared to him at all. "The commencement of the Divine Inspiration to Allah's Messenger," according to Muhammad's child bride Aisha in a hadith that Bukhari records, "was in the form of good dreams which came true like bright daylight, and then the love of seclusion was bestowed upon him. He used to go in seclusion in the cave of Hira where he used to worship (Allah alone) continuously for many days before his desire to see his family. He used to take with him the journey food for the stay and then come back to (his wife) Khadija to take his food likewise again till suddenly the Truth descended upon him while he was in the cave of Hira."[77]

The truth took the form of an unnamed angel: "The angel came to him and asked him to read. The Prophet replied, 'I do not know how to read.' The Prophet added, 'The angel caught me (forcefully) and pressed me so hard that I could not bear it any more. He then released me and again asked me to read and I replied, "I do not know how to read." Thereupon he caught me again and pressed me a second time till I could not bear it any more. He then released me and again asked me to read but again I replied, "I do not know how to read (or what shall I read)?" Thereupon he caught me for the third time and pressed me, and then

---

76 Ibid.
77 Sahih Bukhari, vol 1, book 1, no. 3.

released me and said, "Read in the name of your Lord, who has created (all that exists), created man from a clot. Read! And your Lord is the Most Generous.""[78]

That is the beginning of what we find today as sura 96 of the Qur'an: "Recite, in the name of your Lord who creates, creates man from a clot. Recite, and your Lord is the most generous" (96:1–3). This is generally accepted in Islamic tradition as the first revelation of the Qur'an to Muhammad.

What Did the First Revelation Say?

Even the contents of this first message to Muhammad, however, are not undisputed. In his magisterial work *Asbab al-Nuzul* (*Circumstances of Revelation*), the eleventh-century scholar Ali ibn Ahmad al-Wahidi relates a tradition that states that "the first of the Qur'an to be revealed is 'In the Name of Allah, the Beneficent, the Merciful.' This is therefore the first of the Qur'an to be revealed in Mecca while the first Surah revealed is [the Surah which begins with] 'Read: In the name of thy Lord.'"[79] The first sura to begin with "in the name of Allah, the beneficent, the merciful" is the Opening (*Fatiha*), the first sura of the Qur'an.

Al-Wahidi also relates another tradition in which an early Muslim, Abu Salamah ibn Abd al-Rahman, is asked which part of the Qur'an was revealed first and answers: "O you enveloped in your cloak," which is the beginning of sura 74. Another early believer, Jabir ibn Abd Allah al-Ansari, explained: "I will relate to you what Allah's Messenger related to us. Allah's Messenger said: I stayed at Hira for a month. When my stay came to an end, I came down but when I reached the bottom of the valley I was called. I looked in front, behind, on my right and on my left, and then I looked skyward and there he was—i.e. Gabriel—in mid-air sitting on a throne. Trembling seized me. I went to Khadijah; I ordered them to cover me and then throw water on me. Allah, exalted is He, then revealed to me: 'O you enveloped in your cloak, arise and warn!'" (74:1–2).[80]

---

78 Ibid.

79 Ali ibn Ahmad al-Wahidi, *Asbab al-Nuzul*, Mokrane Guezzou, trans. (Amman: Royal Aal al-Bayt Institute for Islamic Thought, 2019), 3.

80 Ibid.

Al-Wahidi adds: "This however does not contradict what we have said initially, for Jabir heard this last report from the Prophet, but did not hear the first report. For this reason he imagined that Surah al-Muddaththir was the first of the Qur'an to be revealed when, in fact, this is not the case. Rather it was the first revealed after Surah Iqra," that is, the "Read!" or "Recite!" portion of sura 96.[81]

Ibn Kathir, however, agrees, stating that the passage beginning "O you enveloped in your cloak, arise and warn" was the first passage to be delivered to Muhammad after there had been a pause in divine revelations to the new prophet. This passage, says Ibn Kathir, "was the first of the Qur'an sent down after the intermission in revelation, though not the very first of all, which was the verse, 'Read: in the name of your Lord who created.'"[82] Somewhat ambiguously, Ibn Kathir then continues: "It is established on the authority of Jabir that the first verse to be revealed was 'O you who are wrapped up.'"[83]

Here again, it may simply be that Jabir did indeed not have access to all the relevant information and so passed on inaccurate data without meaning to do so. Yet it still must be asked why a report about an alleged error and its correction survived into the eleventh century, long enough for al-Wahidi to record it. It could be that at that time, there were still versions of the Qur'an or accounts of its composition that specified that sura 74, not sura 96, was the first revelation. The explanation that this resulted from someone hearing one piece of information from Muhammad but not another would then account for this variant understanding.

How Did Muhammad React to Receiving Revelations?

Aisha is depicted as describing Muhammad's revelations as "good righteous (true) dreams in his sleep." She added: "He never had a dream but that it came true like bright day light."[84] Other accounts, however, make the experience appear more like a nightmare than a good dream. Ibn Sa'd gives an isnad chain going back to an early follower of Muhammad who recalled: "Verily, when revelation dawned upon the Prophet, may Allah bless him, he suffered much pain and his face turned

---

81 Ibid.
82 Ibn Kathir, *The Life of Prophet Muhammad*, Trevor Le Gassick, trans. (Sharjah, United Arab Emirates: Dar ul Thaqafah, 2019), 1, 299.
83 Ibid.
84 Sahih Bukhari, vol. 9, book 91, no. 6982.

dust-colored."[85] Another stated: "The Apostle of Allah, may Allah bless him, experienced great pain when the revelation dawned upon him, so much so that he stirred his lips."[86] According to Ibn Sa'd, Allah accordingly revealed a portion of the Qur'an: "Do not try to hasten it with your tongue. Indeed, upon us the putting together of it and the reading of it. And when we read it, follow the reading, then indeed, upon us is its explanation" (75:16–19).

Still another early source, however, remembered differently, saying that "when the revelation dawned upon the Apostle of Allah, may Allah bless him, he looked fatigued as if overcome by sleep."[87] To his child bride Aisha is attributed this observation: "I witnessed the revelation dawning upon him on an extremely cold day; when it ceased, I noticed that his forehead was perspiring."[88] No one said that after Muhammad received revelations, he looked radiant or enlightened or refreshed.

Others who supposedly witnessed Muhammad receiving revelations likewise recalled it as a terrifying experience even for Muhammad's mount: "I witnessed the revelation coming to the Prophet, may Allah bless him, while he was riding his beast, it screamed and contracted its forelegs, and I thought they would break. Sometimes it sat and sometimes it stood up straightening its forelegs till the burden of the revelation was gone and the Prophet got down from it like a string of pearl."[89]

Muhammad himself is depicted as recounting: "The revelation dawns upon me in two ways—Gabriel brings it and conveys to me as a man conveys to another man and that makes me restless. And it dawns upon me like the sound of a bell till it enters my heart and this does not make me restless."[90] Yet another source has Muhammad being asked: "O Apostle of Allah! How does revelation dawn upon you?"[91] He answers in a manner that contradicts the other report: "Sometimes it dawns upon me in the form of the ringing of a bell, and that is very hard on me; (ultimately) it ceases and I remember what is said. Sometimes the angel appears to me and speaks and I recollect what he says."[92] So the

85 Ibn Sa'd, op. cit., I, 227.
86 Ibid., 229.
87 Ibid., 227–8.
88 Ibid., 228.
89 Ibid.
90 Ibid.
91 Ibid.
92 Ibid.

revelations apparently sometimes came in the manner of a bell ringing, which either did not make him restless or was very hard on him.

How Did Muhammad React to Receiving His First Revelation?

After Muhammad received his first revelation, the being left. Muhammad, according to Ibn Hisham, fell into a deep sleep. When he woke up, according to Tabari, he was considerably agitated. He didn't think of himself as a new prophet, but as someone who was insane or demon-possessed. In Tabari's account, Muhammad, at some unspecified later point, recalled the details of his encounter: "Now none of God's creatures was more hateful to me than an (ecstatic) poet or a man possessed: I could not even look at them," and yet that is what he assumed he now was.[93]

Drastic action was necessary: "I thought, Woe is me poet or possessed—Never shall Quraysh say this of me! I will go to the top of the mountain and throw myself down that I may kill myself and gain rest."[94] But he was saved just in the nick of time by the being who had appeared to him and demanded he recite. According to Ibn Hisham, he continued: "So I went forth to do so and then) when I was midway on the mountain, I heard a voice from heaven saying, 'O Muhammad! You are the apostle of God and I am Gabriel.' I raised my head towards heaven to see (who was speaking), and lo, Gabriel in the form of a man with feet astride the horizon, saying, 'O Muhammad! You are the apostle of God and I am Gabriel.' I stood gazing at him."[95] According to Ibn Sa'd, Muhammad saw Gabriel not standing astride the horizon, but "seated in a chair between the earth and the sky."[96]

Tabari, at this point, has Muhammad adding that the appearance of Gabriel "turned me from my purpose," that is, prevented him from suicide.[97] Gabriel was insistent: in Ibn Hisham's account, Muhammad says that the angel was "moving neither forward nor backward; then I began to turn my face away from him, but towards whatever region of the sky I looked, I saw him as before. And I continued standing there, neither advancing nor turning back, until Khadija sent her messengers in search

---

93 Ibn Ishaq, op. cit., 106.
94 Ibid.
95 Ibid.
96 Ibn Sa'd, op. cit., I, 227.
97 Ibn Ishaq, op. cit., 106.

of me and they gained the high ground above Mecca and returned to her while I was standing in the same place; then he parted from me and I from him, returning to my family."[98]

Whether Muhammad saw Gabriel standing or sitting, this vision should have settled the matter: if Muhammad had any doubts about what he experienced on Mount Hira before this, now the same heavenly being who had appeared to him there had confirmed both his identity—he was the angel Gabriel—and Muhammad's own: he was the new messenger of Allah. Yet Muhammad appeared to be anything but convinced.

He went home to Khadija, but instead of announcing to her that he had conversed with Gabriel and was now a prophet, he repeated his earlier lament: "Woe is me, poet or possessed."[99] Khadija, however, would have none of that: "I take refuge in God from that, O Abu'l-Qasim," calling Muhammad "Father of Qasim," the name of their son, who had died several years earlier at the age of three.[100] She continued: "God would not treat you thus since he knows your truthfulness, your great trustworthiness, your fine character, and your kindness. This cannot be, my dear. Perhaps you did see something."[101] Muhammad then told her of his experience on Mount Hira, to which she responded: "Rejoice, O son of my uncle, and be of good heart. Verily, by Him in whose hand is Khadija's soul, I have hope that you will be the prophet of this people."[102]

For additional confirmation, she went to another one of her cousins, Waraqa bin Naufal. According to Ibn Hisham, Waraqa "had become a Christian and read the scriptures and learned from those that follow the Torah and the Gospel."[103] Bukhari records one tradition that identifies him as "a Christian convert" and adds that he "used to read the Gospels in Arabic."[104] Bukhari also preserves another tradition, however, which states that Waraqa "during the pre-Islamic Period became a Christian and used to write the writing with Hebrew letters. He would write from the Gospel in Hebrew as much as Allah wished him to write."[105]

---

98 Ibid.
99 Ibid.
100 Ibid.
101 Ibid.
102 Ibid., 107.
103 Ibid.
104 Sahih Bukhari, vol. 4, book 60, no. 3392.
105 Sahih Bukhari, vol. 1, book 1, no. 3.

Maybe Waraqa read the Gospel in Arabic and wrote it down in Hebrew, or more likely, these are divergent and contradictory traditions, both clearly meant to establish Waraqa's reliability as a witness to Muhammad's new prophetic status.

Khadija told Waraqa about Muhammad's experience, whereupon Waraqa cried out: "Holy! Holy! Truly by him in whose hand is Waraqa's soul, if you have spoken to me the truth, O Khadija, there has come to him the greatest Namus who came to Moses in former times, and lo, he is the prophet of this people. Bid him be of good heart."[106] Tabari helpfully explains that by "Namus," Waraqa meant Gabriel.[107] Another possibility is that "Namus" is derived from the Greek *nomos* (νομος), that is, "law," which would make sense of Waraqa's reference to Moses. According to Ibn Hisham, Waraqa soon afterward met Muhammad and reiterated what he had told Khadija: "Surely, by him in whose hand is Waraqa's soul, you are the prophet of this people. There has come to you the greatest Namus, who came to Moses."[108] Muhammad's new prophetic mission would not be easy: "You will be called a liar, and they will treat you spitefully and cast you out and fight against you. Truly, if I live to see that day, I will help God in such ways as he knows."[109] According to Tabari, "Waraqa's words added to his confidence and lightened his anxiety."[110]

Every Detail Controverted

Thus, in the earliest available Islamic accounts of Muhammad's birth, early life, and call to become a prophet, virtually every detail is controverted. The ninth-century accounts, which are supposed to have been scrupulously preserved in the memories of the early Muslims and then diligently recorded in the hadith and sira literature with a careful examination of the chains of transmitters of each tradition so as to establish its degree of authenticity, do indeed agree on the main outlines of the story. There was a man born in Mecca, although exactly when is unclear. His name was or became Muhammad, and he received messages from a heavenly being who was Gabriel or became Gabriel at a certain point. These were the contents of the Qur'an, although which

---

106 Ibn Ishaq, op. cit., 107.
107 Ibid.
108 Ibid.
109 Ibid.
110 Ibid.

portion of the Qur'an was revealed when this being first appeared to this new prophet is not undisputed. After receiving this revelation, whatever it was, Muhammad was quite troubled, and even another appearance of Gabriel did not calm his anxiety. Only his wife's cousin, who was a Christian and spoke either Arabic or Hebrew or both, lessened his fears by confirming his prophetic status. Muhammad would continue to find the reception of these revelations to be a trying experience.

The large number of disagreements on small and large aspects of the story cut against the common assumption that this is historical material that was passed on faithfully with a high degree of accuracy. The divergences may stem from differing traditions being invented in different areas. Different sources that agree on some matters but differ on others may be evidence of some material emanating from a common source but diverging as it was developed by others who were not working in the same area. This is not to say that generally reliable accounts will contain no disagreements with one another; the nature of human memory is such that even when someone carefully endeavors to recall all the details of an event with scrupulous accuracy, he may fail to recall some particulars accurately, or his recollections may be colored by subsequent or similar events. It is still possible, however, to provide a generally reliable account of an event.

Can the early traditions about Muhammad be classified as generally reliable accounts of that kind? In light of the two-century gap between the events and the accounts of them and the fact that even his name and the name of the other principal character in the drama, the angel Gabriel, are not universally attested, this cannot be affirmed with any confidence. Yet the commonality of the general outlines of the narrative may indeed hark back to a kernel of historical accuracy. It cannot be stated with any certainty that these accounts even originally referred to Muhammad, the prophet of Islam, or to some other individual who was claiming prophetic status, the stories of whom were subsumed into the Muhammad myth. Nevertheless, there may have been a person about whom at least some of these stories were originally told, and these stories may even have their roots in what this person actually said and did. By the time they become the words and deeds of Muhammad, however, it is impossible to determine which parts of these tales are historically accurate and which are not.

CHAPTER FOUR

A Difficult Beginning

Allah Consoles His Prophet

Even after receiving reassurance from Gabriel himself as well as from
Waraqa bin Naufal, Muhammad did not initially find being a prophet
to be rewarding or fulfilling. Ibn Hisham says that as he began to preach
the message that there was only one God, he encountered "contradiction and charges of falsehood, which saddened him."[1]

Khadija, however, believed in him, which brought him comfort, and
he received considerable comfort from an even more compelling source:
Allah himself. At one point, when Muhammad was upset because he
had not heard from Gabriel for a while, he received a revelation that
was expressly designed to allay the anxieties of the new prophet: "By
the morning hours and by the night when it is most still, your Lord has
not forsaken you, nor does he hate you, and indeed the latter portion
will be better for you than the former, and indeed your Lord will give
to you so that you will be content. Didn't he find you an orphan and
protect? Didn't he find you wandering and direct? Didn't he find you
destitute and enrich? Therefore do not oppress the orphan, therefore do
not drive away the beggar, therefore proclaim the bounty of your Lord"
(Qur'an 93:1–11).

Here again, it is not clear which came first: the revelation or the
explanation of the circumstances of the revelation. The Qur'an most
likely predates the hadith and sira literature, and so it is possible that
the accounts of Muhammad's lack of success as a preacher and his con-
sequent discouragement were constructed in order to provide a context
for this elliptical Qur'anic passage, which is clearly meant to comfort

---

1 Ibn Ishaq, op. cit., 111.

someone, although it is not clear who is being comforted or why he is downcast.

Whatever may be the actual referent for those verses, Allah would show similar solicitude for his prophet throughout Muhammad's prophetic career. This is one reason why it so often seems that contemporary Muslims are far more concerned for the honor of Muhammad than they are for that of Allah himself: in this, they are simply imitating the divinity himself, who was deeply anxious to secure Muhammad's happiness and well-being.

Muhammad, according to Ibn Sa'd, "was commanded to preach in full what was revealed to him by Allah and that he should call people towards Allah, which he did secretly for three years, till he was commanded to preach openly."[2] All that had been revealed to him at this point was essentially that Allah was the one and only God and, hence, that the gods of the Quraysh were false and unworthy of worship. Why he preached secretly for three years is unexplained and may simply be another attempt to harmonize traditions that asserted that Muhammad was forty years old when he began claiming to be a prophet and sixty-three when he died, and yet as a prophet, spent ten years in Mecca and ten in Medina. The three years of secret preaching would make for thirteen years in Mecca and square the chronological discrepancies.

Still, the idea of Allah sending an angel to commission a prophet to recite and then having him do so only in secret to a small, select group of people was difficult to justify. All the earlier prophets had preached openly; why should Muhammad be any different? And so Ibn Sa'd also records a contrary tradition that states that Muhammad "preached Islam secretly and openly" and asserts that he met with success: "those from among the youth and the weak, people embraced Islam whom Allah willed, till their number grew and the unbelievers among the Quraysh did not deny what he said."[3]

Ali ibn Abi Talib Becomes Muhammad's Companion

Muhammad began to attract a small band of followers. Khadija had been the first to believe, and the first male to accept his prophetic claim was a young boy named Ali ibn Abi Talib. Ibn Hisham states: "Ali was

---

2 Ibn Sa'd, op. cit., I, 230.
3 Ibid.

the first male to believe in the apostle of God, to pray with him and to believe in his divine message, when he was a boy of ten."[4] Ma'mar ibn Rashid, however, says that Ali was "fifteen or sixteen years old at the time."[5] Ma'mar also cites a variant tradition: "I asked al-Zuhri and he said: 'We do not know of anyone who became Muslim before Zayd ibn Harithah,'" who was to become Muhammad's adopted son and play a part in one of the most notorious incidents of the entire career of the prophet of Islam.[6]

Abu Talib, Ali's father, was also Muhammad's uncle, so the prophet and his youthful new follower, or companion (*sahaba*), as the followers of Muhammad were known, were cousins. Ali would go on to become one of the pivotal figures of the early Islamic tradition. He would marry Muhammad's daughter Fatima and ultimately become the fourth *caliph*, or successor of Muhammad as the spiritual, military, and political leader of the Muslim community. But his efforts to become the leader of the Muslims met with furious opposition from the beginning. Ali was passed over for the position of caliph three times before he finally attained it, and when he did, he faced furious opposition that became a destructive civil war.

His followers, who were known as the party of Ali (*shiat Ali*), eventually rejected the leadership of the foes of Ali altogether, and a schism arose in the early Islamic community that remains to this day: the split between the Sunnis and the Shi'ites, those who revere Ali. The Sunnis today comprise around 85 to 90 percent of all Muslims worldwide, with the Shi'ites making up most of the remainder. There is an overwhelming Shi'ite majority in Iran, as well as Shi'ite majorities in Iraq and Bahrain, and significant Shi'ite minorities in Saudi Arabia and elsewhere.

When Ali accepted Muhammad's prophetic claim, all that was far off in the future, although when the records of this period were finally written down, the split in the Muslim community had become formal and permanent. Accordingly, all the material about Ali—and there is a great deal in the Sunni hadith and sira literature—may have been formulated in order to explain the split within the community. While this literature may conceivably provide the real reasons for the split and the

---

4 Ibn Ishaq, op. cit., 114.
5 Ma'mar ibn Rashid, *The Expeditions: An Early Biography of Muhammad*, Sean Anthony, trans. (New York: NYU Press, 2015), 1. 5, 71.
6 Ibid., 1.7, 71.

circumstances of it, it is also possible that it is legendary material that was designed to provide an explanation for the split at a time when the true origins of it had been lost in the mists of time and the vagaries of oral tradition.

A Plain Warner

According to Islamic tradition, Muhammad did not initially attract many other followers. This may have been because his message was less than inviting. Warning people of hellfire if they did not submit to Allah was his primary responsibility. Allah also told him: "You are just a warner to him who fears it" (Qur'an 79:45). This was the job that the other prophets did in the past. The Qur'an has Noah telling the people of his day: "O my people, indeed, I am a plain warner to you. Serve Allah and keep your duty to him and obey me, so that he may forgive you some of your sins and give you a respite for an appointed term" (71:2–4). Likewise, the new prophet is directed to tell his people: "The knowledge is with Allah alone, and I am just a plain warner" (Qur'an 67:26). The unbelievers were in no mood to accept this warning: "And they are amazed that a warner from among themselves has come to them, and the unbelievers say, This is a wizard, a charlatan" (Qur'an 38:4). They were enamored of the polytheism that the messenger of Allah was urging them to forsake: "Does he make the gods into one Allah? Indeed, that is an astounding thing" (Qur'an 38:5). It was not so much the preaching about Allah but the denigration of other gods that annoyed his hearers. Ibn Hisham explains: "When the apostle openly displayed Islam as God ordered him his people did not withdraw or turn against him, so far as I have heard, until he spoke disparagingly of their gods."[7]

Some of the Quraysh found all this intolerable and went to Abu Talib to try to get him to rein in his fiery and intransigent nephew: "O Abu Talib, your nephew has cursed our gods, insulted our religion, mocked our way of life and accused our forefathers of error; either you must stop him or you must let us get at him, for you yourself are in the same position as we are in opposition to him and we will rid you of him."[8] Abu

---

7 Ibid., 118.
8 Ibid., 119.

Talib, according to Ibn Hisham, "gave them a conciliatory reply and a soft answer and they went away."[9]

Yet this soft answer did not entirely turn away their wrath; the tensions between Muhammad and the Quraysh began to increase. A conflict appeared inevitable, and it was. Muhammad gained a few more followers, including Abu Bakr and Uthman, who later became the first and third caliphs. Ibn Sa'd says that the second caliph, Umar, was also preaching Islam at this point, but Ibn Hisham says that he only became a Muslim later.[10] These and others, at a time when the number of Muhammad's companions was twenty-two, joined the self-proclaimed prophet in preaching the message of submission or hellfire. "The Quraysh," according to Ibn Sa'd, "became furious. Their jealousy and enmity became open. Some of them openly turned hostile and the others secretly harbored a grudge in their bosoms, but pretended to be non-inimical to him."[11]

Abd al-Uzza

This resistance was strong even among Muhammad's friends and relatives. At one point, Allah told him to "warn your tribe of near relatives" (Qur'an 26:214). Ibn Sa'd recounts that when Muhammad received this revelation, he climbed up the mountain of al-Safa overlooking Mecca and called out to the people in the city below. This call to all the people of the city was made when someone had tremendously important news, and so the Quraysh duly gathered to hear what Muhammad had to say. "O Muhammad!" some called out. "What is the matter?"[12] Muhammad replied: "Suppose I inform you that there is an army behind this mountain; will you believe me?"[13]

They responded, according to this ninth-century Islamic tradition, by praising Muhammad's good character: "Yes, since you have never been blamed, and we have never found you telling a lie."[14] Muhammad then continued: "So I warn you of a severe torment, be ready"—and he named the three tribes of the Quraysh, adding: "Lo! Allah has

---

9 Ibid.
10 Ibn Sa'd, op. cit., I, 231; Ibn Ishaq, 155.
11 Ibn Sa'd, op. cit., I, 232.
12 Ibn Sa'd, op. cit., I, 231.
13 Ibid.
14 Ibid.

commanded me to warn my tribe of near kindred and lo! I do not possess any worldly gains, nor a share in hereafter except that you say: There is no god but Allah."[15] Bukhari states Muhammad's message much more succinctly: "I am a plain warner to you of a coming severe punishment."[16]

So Muhammad's emergency turned out to be a preacher's stunt. As theatrical as it was, this did not impress those who had assembled to hear why Muhammad had called them together. Ibn Sa'd notes that Muhammad's uncle Abd al-Uzza ibn Abd al-Muttalib was particularly annoyed and shouted at Muhammad: "May you perish! Did you assemble us for this?"[17] The name Abd al-Uzza means "Slave of al-Uzza," who was one of the goddesses of the Quraysh. This particular uncle of Muhammad, however, is known throughout history by another name: Abu Lahab, "Father of the Flame," an indication of his having been condemned to hellfire for his opposition to Muhammad.

It is noteworthy that the Nabataeans, who lived in what is today northern Arabia and southern Jordan in and around the city of Petra, worshiped al-Uzza.[18] In many early mosques, the *qibla* doesn't face Mecca but rather Petra.[19] What's more, the linguist Mark Durie points out that "the 'clear Arabic' (*'arabī*; Q26:195) in which the Qur'an was first recited was not the native dialect of Mecca."[20] Instead, "the Qur'an was composed and first recited in a dialect very close or identical to the variety in which the spelling of the *rasm* [the Qur'an's consonantal text] became fixed. This was most likely Nabataean Arabic dialect."[21]

Muhammad's war against al-Uzza and her worshipers may, therefore, be yet another indication that Islam arose not in west-central Arabia, where Mecca and Medina are located, but farther north, in southern Jordan around Petra, the city of the Nabataeans. In any case, the fact that the conflict between Muhammad and the polytheists is so central to the ninth-century biographical material about the prophet of Islam

---

15 Ibid.
16 Sahih Bukhari, vol. 6, book 65, no. 4971.
17 Ibn Sa'd, op. cit., I, 231.
18 "Pre Islamic Goddesses al-Lat, al-Uzza, Manat," BooksFact, January 1, 2016, https://www.booksfact.com/religions/pre-islamic-goddesses-al-lat-al-uzza-manat.html; Nabataean Pantheon, Nabataea.net, n.d., https://nabataea.net/explore/culture_and_religion/gods/.
19 Dan Gibson, Early Islamic Qiblas: A Survey of Mosques Built between 1AH/622 C.E. and 263 AH/876 C.E. (Vancouver: Independent Scholars Press, 2017).
20 Mark Durie, The Qur'an and Its Biblical Reflexes: Investigations into the Genesis of a Religion (New York: Lexington Books, 2018), 91.
21 Ibid., 90.

suggests that Abd al-Uzza may not have been this poor man's name any more than his name was Abu Lahab. Both "Abd al-Uzza" and "Abu Lahab" seem to be names that were deliberately constructed in order to emphasize this man's opposition to Muhammad as a goddess-worshipping polytheist and then to show the outcome of such worship: eternal damnation in hell.

While it is possible that a man in Petra, or possibly Mecca, before the advent of Islam may have had the name "Abd al-Uzza," it's also too convenient: this fellow is remembered in history solely for his conflict with Muhammad over polytheism and the worship of Allah alone, and his name just happens to denote his devotion to one of the goddesses Muhammad was demanding that his people forsake. This is yet another small indication that these accounts are not historical but were constructed in the ninth century in order to make and support various theological points.

Bukhari, meanwhile, makes Abd al-Uzza's statement fit more closely with the Qur'anic verse that Muhammad was shortly to receive, and that apparently refers to this incident: "May your hands perish all this day. Is it for this purpose you have gathered us?"[22] Ibn Hisham has Abd al-Uzza explaining his opposition to Muhammad with a peculiar reference to his hands: "Muhammad promises me things which I do not see. He alleges that they will happen after my death; what has he put in my hands after that?' Then he blew on his hands and said, 'May you perish. I can see nothing in you of the things which Muhammad says.'"[23]

Muhammad, or rather Allah, responded with even greater fury. On the spot, Muhammad received a divine revelation condemning his uncle to hellfire. He even referred to him not by his name, but as Abu Lahab, and picked up on his uncle's reference to his hands: "Perish the hands of Abu Lahab, and may he perish. His wealth and gains will not exempt him. He will be plunged into flaming fire, and his wife, the wood-carrier, will have upon her neck a rope of palm-fiber" (Qur'an 111:1–5).

Ibn Hisham's explanation of this incident is clearly better suited to account for the details of this Qur'anic passage than that of Ibn Sa'd. Ibn Sa'd, however, adds a statement of Muhammad portraying Abd al-Uzza/Abu Lahab as even more irrationally hostile to the new prophet.

---

22 Sahih Bukhari, vol. 6, book 65, no. 4770.
23 Ibn Ishaq, op. cit., 159.

Muhammad is depicted as saying: "I was between two bad neighbors, Abu Lahab and Uqbah Ibn Abi Mu'ayt. They brought excrements and threw it before my door and they brought offensive material and threw [it] before my door."[24] Then Muhammad added: "Is it the (courtesy) of a neighbor?"[25] And he calmly threw away the garbage that Abu Lahab and Uqbah had piled at his door.

This patience in the face of unreasoning hatred, as popular as it is with twenty-first-century Islamic apologists in the West, would prove to be the exception, not the rule. The ferocious rage of the Qur'an's 111th sura, damning Abu Lahab and his wife to eternal torture in hell, is more in keeping with Islam's primary stance toward unbelievers; they are, as Allah informs his prophet in another revelation, "the most vile of created beings" (98:6).

Killing Muhammad, or Being Killed by Him

The episode with Abd al-Uzza was one of the first examples of Muhammad's beginning to preach publicly. This only aroused further antagonism from the Quraysh, for Muhammad could not resist denigrating the objects of their worship, as Ibn Hisham explains: "When the apostle openly displayed Islam as God ordered him his people did not withdraw or turn against him, so far as I have heard, until he spoke disparagingly of their gods."[26] A delegation of the Quraysh approached Abu Talib to complain to him about his troublesome nephew: "O Abu Talib, your nephew has cursed our gods, insulted our religion, mocked our way of life and accused our forefathers of error; either you must stop him or you must let us get at him, for you yourself are in the same position as we are in opposition to him and we will rid you of him."[27]

According to Ibn Hisham, they offered him a "youth of the Quraysh who is handsome, of noble descent, and a poet" in a trade for Muhammad: "We want to hand him over to you so that you may enjoy his support and inheritance and we request you to hand over your brother's son to us so that we may slay him."[28] Abu Talib, however, was dismissive of this idea: "By Allah, you have not done justice to us; you want to hand

---

24 Ibn Sa'd, op. cit., I, 232.
25 Ibid.
26 Ibn Ishaq, op. cit., 118.
27 Ibid., 119.
28 Ibn Sa'd, op. cit., I, 233.

over your son to me to be fed by me for you and hand over my brother's son to you to be killed. Is this justice to a humble and poor person?"[29] They called for Muhammad and appealed to him to "Leave us and our deities, and we will leave you and your Lord."[30]

In response, Muhammad made his own offer: "Will you like to pledge your word to me, if I give this to you? By that word you will overpower Arabia and the part of Persia that adjoins it."[31] One of his adversaries among the Quraysh, Abu Jahl, was excited: "Verily, that word must be advantageous. By your father! We will repeat it and ten others like it."[32] Then Muhammad told them this powerful word: "Say: There is no god but Allah," whereupon "they grew angry and displeased."[33] The Quraysh left Abu Talib and Muhammad and came to an agreement: "We will not approach him again and it is better if Muhammad is slain deceitfully."[34] According to Ibn Hisham, they approached Abu Talib one more time and said to him: "By God, we cannot endure that our fathers should be reviled, our customs mocked and our gods insulted. Until you rid us of him we will fight the pair of you until one side perishes."[35]

Tensions continued to grow. One of the early Muslims heard the Quraysh complaining among themselves about Muhammad and recounted: "I was with them one day when the notables had gathered in the Hijr and the apostle was mentioned. They said that they had never known anything like the trouble they had endured from this fellow; he had declared their mode of life foolish, insulted their forefathers, reviled their religion, divided the community, and cursed their gods. What they had borne was past all bearing, or words to that effect."[36]

Up to this point, the conflict between Muhammad and the Quraysh had been a battle of words, although the Quraysh are depicted as openly speaking of killing Muhammad when they offered their deal to Abu Talib. Now, that threat would be reciprocated. As they were discussing all this, Muhammad himself happened by. "As he passed," the early Muslim continued, "they said some injurious things about him. This I could

---

29 Ibid. Language slightly modernized for clarity.
30 Ibid.
31 Ibid., 234.
32 Ibid.
33 Ibid.
34 Ibid.
35 Ibn Ishaq, op. cit., 119.
36 Ibid., 130–1.

see from his expression. He went on and as he passed them the second time they attacked him similarly. This I could see from his expression. Then he passed the third time, and they did the same. He stopped and said, 'Will you listen to me O Quraysh? By him who holds my life in his hand, I bring you slaughter.'"[37]

The Quraysh were stunned and stood "silent and still."[38] One of them struck a conciliatory tone, saying to Muhammad: "Depart, O Abu'l-Qasim, for by God you are not violent."[39] The next day, however, they surrounded him and accused him: "Are you the one who said so-and-so against our gods and our religion?"[40] Muhammad admitted that he was, whereupon, says the early Muslim, "I saw one of them seize his robe." Then, one of Muhammad's foremost companions, Abu Bakr, placed himself between the Quraysh and Muhammad and demanded: "Would you kill a man for saying Allah is my Lord?"[41] At that, the Quraysh departed. "That is," said the witness, "the worst that I ever saw Quraysh do to him."[42] It was not, however, the worst that Muhammad would do to the Quraysh.

Self-Imposed Exile

Neither side, however, was in a conciliatory mood. Finally, according to Ibn Hisham, Muhammad decided that it would be safer if at least some of the Muslims got away from the Quraysh altogether. He told his companions: "If you were to go to Abyssinia (it would be better for you), for the king will not tolerate injustice and it is a friendly country, until such time as Allah shall relieve you from your distress."[43] In Ibn Sa'd's version, Muhammad says to his companions: "Be scattered in the earth."[44] They then ask him, "Where (are we) to go, O Apostle of Allah?," and he responds: "That way, and pointed towards Abyssinia, and it was the dearest of lands to migrate to."[45]

---

37 Ibid., 131.
38 Ibid.
39 Ibid.
40 Ibid.
41 Ibid.
42 Ibid.
43 Ibid., 146.
44 Ibn Sa'd, op. cit., I, 235.
45 Ibid.

This is indeed the kind of variation that is to be expected from material that is passed on orally for considerable periods, but the fact that there is no verbal congruence at all between what Muhammad says in one version and what he says in the other is still striking. All that the two sources have in common is that some of the Muslims, in view of the difficulties with the Quraysh, emigrated to Abyssinia with Muhammad's approval. What is said in both versions differs widely. This suggests anything but a careful word-by-word preservation of historical accounts reverently passed on from the time the events actually occurred.

Regarding the flight to Abyssinia, Ibn Hisham adds: "This was the first hijra in Islam."[46] Hijra, or emigration, would become a supremely important concept in Islam. Muslims would flee from one land, usually where they were being persecuted or facing other difficulties, and would settle in a new area, where they would strive to plant their religion as well. In placing this practice in the earliest days of Islam, even before Muhammad embarked upon his own and much more famous hijra, Ibn Hisham is emphasizing its importance, an importance that continues to this day with mass Muslim migration into Europe.

The Satanic Verses

The Muslims who had departed Mecca and settled in Abyssinia were safe and free to practice their religion. But Muhammad was not happy; his people's rejection of his message and prophetic status weighed heavily upon him. "I wish," he lamented, that "Allah had not revealed to me anything distasteful to them," that is, the Quraysh, who were, after all, his relatives and friends.[47] Ibn Sa'd's account of what happened as a result of this grief is spare and arresting:

> Then the Apostle of Allah, may Allah bless him, approached them (Quraysh) and got close to them, and they also came near to him. One day he was sitting in their assembly near the Ka'bah, and he recited: "By the Star when it sets," (*Qur'an, 53:1*) till he reached, "Have you thought upon Al-Uzza and Manat, the third, the other." (*Qur'an, 53:19–20*) Satan made him repeat these two phrases: These idols are high and their intercession is expected. The Apostle of Allah, may Allah bless him, repeated them, and he went on reciting

46 Ibn Ishaq, op. cit.
47 Ibn Sa'd, op. cit., I, 237.

the whole surah and then fell in prostration, and the people also fell in prostration with him.[48]

This is a condensed version, perhaps due to the embarrassing nature of the events recounted. This account depicts Muhammad reciting the fifty-third chapter (sura) of the Qur'an up through 53:19–20 ("Have you thought upon Al-Lat and Al-Uzza, and Manat, the third, the other?"), then proclaiming: "These idols are high and their intercession is expected." Then he finished reciting the sura. So did he intend the statement "These idols are high and their intercession is expected" to be understood as part of Allah's revelation? Ibn Sa'd fastidiously refrains from going that far, but that is the clear implication of the account, especially since "the people," which presumably include the Quraysh as well as the Muslims, "fell in prostration with him" after he recited this. Muhammad, after fighting against and insulting the gods of the Quraysh, had now validated them.

Tabari provides a longer and even more embarrassing version:

Now the apostle was anxious for the welfare of his people, wishing to attract them as far as he could. It has been mentioned that he longed for a way to attract them, and the method he adopted is what Ibn Hamid told me that Salama said M. b. Ishaq told him from Yazid b. Ziyad of Medina from M. b. Ka'b al-Qurazi: When the apostle saw that his people turned their backs on him and he was pained by their estrangement from what he brought them from God he longed that there should come to him from God a message that would reconcile his people to him. Because of his love for his people and his anxiety over them it would delight him if the obstacle that made his task so difficult could be removed; so that he meditated on the project and longed for it and it was dear to him. Then God sent down 'By the star when it sets your comrade errs not and is not deceived, he speaks not from his own desire,' and when he reached His words 'Have you thought of al-Lat and al-Uzza and Manat the third, the other', Satan, when he was meditating upon it, and desiring to bring it (sc. reconciliation) to his people, put upon his tongue 'these are the exalted Gharaniq whose intercession is approved.'"[49]

---

48 Ibid.
49 Ibn Ishaq, op. cit., 165–6.

"By the star when it sets..." is the beginning of sura 53. So in this version, Muhammad is again reciting this chapter of the Qur'an and adds in praise for the three goddesses of the Quraysh, al-Lat, al-Uzza, and Manat, after they are mentioned in 53:19–20. *Gharaniq* are cranes that were known to fly very high, near the throne of Allah in paradise.

In this account, the Quraysh immediately grasp the import of what Muhammad has said:

> When Quraysh heard that, they were delighted and greatly pleased at the way in which he spoke of their gods and they listened to him; while the believers were holding that what their prophet brought them from their Lord was true, not suspecting a mistake or a vain desire or a slip, and when he reached the prostration and the end of the Sura in which he prostrated himself the Muslims prostrated themselves when their prophet prostrated, confirming what he brought and obeying his command, and the polytheists of Quraysh and others who were in the mosque prostrated when they heard the mention of their gods, so that everyone in the mosque believer and unbeliever prostrated, except al-Walid b. al-Mughira, who was an old man who could not do so, so he took a handful of dirt from the valley and bent over it. Then the people dispersed and Quraysh went out, delighted at what had been said about their gods, saying, 'Muhammad has spoken of our gods in splendid fashion. He alleged in what he read that they are the exalted Gharaniq whose intercession is approved.'[50]

Peace had finally dawned between the Quraysh and Muhammad, but it had come at an exorbitant price. Ever since he had begun proclaiming that he was a prophet, Muhammad had taught uncompromisingly that there was only one God. He had earned the furious enmity of the Quraysh by mocking their gods and making fun of his tribesmen for believing in them and praying to them. Yet now he was acknowledging al-Lat, al-Uzza, and Manat as heavenly beings who could intercede for the believers before the throne of Allah. So was his earlier monotheistic teaching false? Or was his new teaching, that Allah had three daughters, false?

---

50 Ibid., 166.

The advantages of going with the new teachings were immediate and enormous. Some of the exiles thought it safe to return: "The news reached the prophet's companions who were in Abyssinia," says Tabari, "it being reported that Quraysh had accepted Islam, so some men started to return while others remained behind."[51] Ultimately, however, a higher power made the decision for Muhammad:

> Then Gabriel came to the apostle and said, 'What have you done, Muhammad? You have read to these people something I did not bring you from God and you have said what He did not say to you.' The apostle was bitterly grieved and was greatly in fear of God. So God sent down (a revelation), for He was merciful to him, comforting him and making light of the affair and telling him that every prophet and apostle before him desired as he desired and wanted what he wanted and Satan interjected something into his desires as he had on his tongue. So God annulled what Satan had suggested and God established His verses i.e. you are just like the prophets and apostles. Then God sent down: 'We have not sent a prophet or apostle before you but when he longed Satan cast suggestions into his longing. But God will annul what Satan has suggested. Then God will establish his verses, God being knowing and wise.'[52]

This is Qur'an 22:52, which is more clearly rendered as "We never sent a messenger or a prophet before you who, except that when he recited, Satan would throw into it. But Allah abrogates what Satan proposes. Then Allah establishes his signs. Allah is the knower, the wise one."

Another passage from Tabari, however, has Muhammad not simply being Satan's passive victim, but making the extraordinary admission that he had composed the offending passage under the influence of Satan:

> That evening Gabriel came to him and reviewed the surah with him, and when he reached the two phrases which Satan had cast upon his tongue he said, "I did not bring you these two." Then the Messenger of God said, "I have fabricated things against God and have imputed to Him words which he has not spoken."[53]

51 Ibid.
52 Ibid.
53 Abu Ja'far Muhammad bin Jarir al-Tabari, *The History of al-Tabari*, Volume VI, *Muhammad at Mecca*, W. Montgomery Watt and M. V. McDonald, trans. (Albany: State University of New York Press, 1988), 111.

Tabari adds that this was the occasion for the revelation of this Qur'anic passage: "And they indeed tried hard to seduce you away from what we have inspired you with, so that you would invent against us something other than it, and then they would have accepted you as a friend. And if we had not made you wholly firm, you might almost have inclined to them a little. Then we would have made you taste double of living and double of dying, then you would have found no helper against us" (17:73–5).

Despite this stark warning, in Tabari's account, Allah is primarily concerned with how this incident has affected the state of mind of his beloved prophet, and the deity moves swiftly to make sure that Muhammad was not unduly affected:

> Thus God relieved his prophet's grief, and made him feel safe from
> his fears and annulled what Satan had suggested in the words used
> above about their gods by his revelation 'Are yours the males and His
> the females? That were indeed an unfair division' (i.e. most unjust);
> 'they are nothing but names which your fathers gave them' as far as
> the words 'to whom he pleases and accepts', i.e. how can the interces-
> sion of their gods avail with Him?[54]

This is now what follows in the Qur'an after the mention of al-Lat, al-Uzza, and Manat: "Are yours the males and his the females? That indeed is an unfair division. They are just names that you have named, you and your fathers, for which Allah has revealed no justification. They follow only speculation and what they themselves desire. And now the guidance from their Lord has come to them. Or shall man have what he covets? But to Allah belongs the after and the former. And how many angels are in the heavens whose intercession does not help in any way except after Allah gives permission to those whom he chooses and accepts" (53:21–26). Instead of praising the three goddesses for their ability to intercede for the believers before the throne of Allah, the Quraysh are derided for believing that Allah has daughters when sons are preferable and superior.

The tensions between the Muslims and the Quraysh returned, with relations embittered even further because of this incident. And Muhammad's explanation, that Satan had inspired the offending verses that

---

54 Ibn Ishaq, op. cit., 166.

Allah had subsequently canceled, was hardly convincing. The Quraysh were not hesitant about drawing out its implications. Tabari continues:

> When the annulment of what Satan had put upon the prophet's tongue came from God, Quraysh said: 'Muhammad has repented of what he said about the position of your gods with Allah, altered it and brought something else.' Now those two words which Satan had put upon the apostle's tongue were in the mouth of every polytheist and they became more violently hostile to the Muslims and the apostle's followers. Meanwhile those of his companions who had left Abyssinia when they heard that the people of Mecca had accepted Islam when they prostrated themselves with the apostle, heard when they approached Mecca that the report was false and none came into the town without the promise of protection or secretly.[55]

Late in the tenth century, the Islamic theologian Abu al-Layth al-Samarqandi includes this in his own commentary on the Qur'an:

> When the Prophet recited Surat al-Najm (sura 53), and reached, "Have you seen al-Lat, al-Uzza and Manat, the third, the other…?," there ran upon his tongue: "Those high gharaniq! Indeed, their intercession is to be hoped for." When he reached the prostration, he made the sajdah and the polytheists made the prostration with him. Then Gabriel came and said: "I did not bring you this." So, there came down: "And they strove to tempt you …," until His words, "… in which case they would surely have taken you as a friend." The Prophet remained distressed until there came down, "We have not sent before you a Messenger or a Prophet but that when he desired, Satan cast something into his desire."[56]

There are numerous other early accounts demonstrating that numerous early Islamic authorities took for granted that this incident was as historically accurate as the other material they had about Muhammad. The pioneering contemporary historian of the Satanic verses, Shahab Ahmed, concludes that "in the first two hundred years of Islam, from about 600 to 800, acceptance of the historicity of the Satanic verses incident was the near-universal position. Over the period from about 800

55 Ibid., 166–7.
56 Ahmed, op. cit., 95, slightly edited for clarity.

to 1100, rejection of the incident presents itself more regularly in the literature: in this period it seems that the number of scholars who accept and reject the incident is roughly equal."[57] Only after 1100 did rejection of the incident among Islamic authorities become near-universal. Yet even as late as the fifteenth century, Islamic scholar Jalal al-Din al-Suyuti takes the authenticity of this account for granted and includes it in his commentary on Qur'an 17:73, which says: "And they indeed tried hard to seduce you away from what we have inspired you with, so that you would invent against us something other than it, and then they would have accepted you as a friend."

Al-Suyuti writes:

> God sent down, "By the star when its sets," and the Messenger of God recited this verse to them: "Have you seen al-Lat and al-Uzza...?" And Satan cast two phrases upon him: "Those high gharaniq! Indeed, their intercession is to be hoped for." The Prophet then recited the rest of the surah and made the prostration. And God sent down the verse: "And they strove to tempt you away from that with which We have inspired you...." He remained distressed and anxious until God sent down: "And we have not sent before you a Messenger or a Prophet ..." to His words, "... and God is All-Knowing, All-Wise."[58]

The Apologists' Problem with the Satanic Verses

That rejection, however, was clearly motivated more by apologetic intent than a desire for historical accuracy. After all, the incident raised numerous problems. Not only had Muhammad reversed himself and thus increased hostilities with the Quraysh just at the point when they were calming down, but he had also undermined his entire claim to be a prophet.

For if Satan could fool him once into thinking that he was receiving words from Allah, how could Muhammad or any of his followers be sure that Satan wasn't deceiving them about the whole thing and that the revelations that Muhammad thought he was receiving from Allah were all actually from Satan? Skeptics could likewise conclude that Muhammad

---

57 Ibid., 6.
58 Ibid., 97, slightly edited for clarity.

was obviously a con man who was faking a prophetic gift and fashioning prophecies in a self-serving manner when it suited him until, finally, he was caught in a contradiction that was too large to ignore.

And so the story had to go. One contemporary historian explains that "it was deemed inauthentic and incongruent with the theological project of the Hadith movement, which required the Prophet to be infallible, beyond reproach in the realm of religious matters."[59] Indeed, the story does not appear in the canonical hadith collections, but it is, as we have seen, in the sira literature and passes from there to commentaries on the Qur'an. Ultimately, however, its embarrassing and contradictory aspects won out, and it largely disappeared from view until Rushdie published his notorious novel, *The Satanic Verses*, which is loosely based on this incident, and received a death fatwa for it from the Islamic Republic of Iran.

Because of the prominence this gave to the story, modern-day hagiographers of Muhammad, anxious to present an appealing portrait of the prophet of Islam to Western readers, particularly in light of the jihad terror attacks on September 11, 2001, and the subsequent rise of jihad activity in the West, do not all ignore it entirely. But they do their best to gloss over it. In his book about Muhammad, Islamic apologist Omid Safi briefly discusses Rushdie's novel and its reception but gives no hint that Rushdie is working from anything within the Islamic tradition to fashion his portrait of the prophet of Islam.[60]

In his own biography of Muhammad, Tariq Ramadan, who before he was charged with multiple counts of rape was the foremost Islamic scholar in the Western world, shows no indication of the existence of this incident. Another one of Muhammad's foremost admirers, Karen Armstrong, flatly denies the authenticity of the story: "We have to be clear here that many Muslims believe this story to be apocryphal. They point that there is no clear reference to it in the Qur'an, that it is not mentioned by Ibn Ishaq in the earliest and most reliable account of Muhammad's life..."[61]

---

59 Ahab Bdaiwi, "Word and Deeds," History Today, vol. 72, no. 10, October 2022, https://www. historytoday.com/archive/history-matters/words-and-deeds.

60 Omid Safi, *Memories of Muhammad: Why the Prophet Matters* (New York: HarperOne, 2009), 14.

61 Karen Armstrong, *Muhammad: A Biography of the Prophet* (San Francisco: Harper San Francisco, 1992), 111.

Armstrong is being more than a little disingenuous in claiming that Ibn Ishaq doesn't mention it, as it appears in the lengthy portion of Ibn Ishaq's sira that Tabari preserves. Tabari may have edited or augmented it, but there is no reason to doubt his attribution of it to Ibn Ishaq altogether. What's more, Armstrong's explanation does not offer any reason for why it appears in Tabari's writings or those of other early authorities who likewise appear to have accepted it as authentic.

The Historian's Problem with the Satanic Verses

Yet while Islamic apologists feel free to dismiss or ignore the incident because it doesn't fit the picture of Muhammad they wish to present to the world, no responsible historian can deny that the early Islamic tradition accepts this incident as authentic. That fact, however, leads to a host of new problems.

If Muhammad was not a historical figure and the various accounts of his words and deeds all date from well over a century after he is supposed to have lived, how did this story come to be invented? What believing Muslim would have concocted a tale of the revered prophet being fooled by the devil himself? Surely, the shadow this cast over Muhammad's prophetic claim in its entirety must have occurred to at least some of those who are supposed to have transmitted it, or some who actually did so. Yet it appears in the biography of Muhammad compiled by a pious Muslim, Tabari, and attributed to another, Ibn Ishaq, as well as to the people who are listed in the *isnad* chain as having passed it on.

If the biographical material about Muhammad that appears in the latter half of the eighth and the first half of the ninth century contains any material that is historically accurate, the Satanic verses account must be counted among that material. Yet stories that appear to modern readers to portray Muhammad in a negative light were not always understood by those who composed and disseminated them as doing anything of the kind. There is generally a discernable reason why the eighth- and ninth-century fabricators and compilers of this material included such stories.

In regard to the Satanic verses, the reason for the entire account may be encapsulated in the Qur'anic verse that Tabari says was sent down from Allah in the aftermath of this incident: "We never sent a messenger or a prophet before you who, except that when he recited, Satan would throw into it. But Allah abrogates what Satan proposes. Then Allah establishes his signs" (22:52). "Signs" is *ayat*, the word that is also used for the verses of the Qur'an. Thus the believer can be sure that his Qur'an is the pure word of Allah, protected from Satan, even as the devil tries to contaminate it.

The Qur'anic passage continues: "Allah is the knower, the wise one, so that he may make what Satan proposes a temptation for those in whose hearts is a disease, and those whose hearts are hardened" (22:53). Thus Satan tempts the believers, endeavoring to lead them astray. The evil one even tempted Muhammad and fooled him for a brief period. But Allah hastened to protect him, abrogating the passages that Satan had made Muhammad think were divine revelation and sending him genuine divine revelation. Thus, the believer can be sure that Muhammad's heart is not diseased or hardened, for Allah confounds the designs of Satan and protects his prophet. While the wicked are tempted by Satan and go astray, Allah makes sure that Satan can have no power over Muhammad. Thus, the believer who hews closely to the words and example of Muhammad can be confident of the protection and favor of Allah.

The import of the Satanic verses passage, then, is that the Muslim can place full confidence in both the Qur'an and Muhammad. This was an important message for those who were fashioning the Muhammad myth to convey, for they were faced with the task of constructing a new religion and a biography of their prophet out of an enormous mass of material, which consisted not just of stories that were composed in order to show that Muhammad favored a certain faction's belief or practice, but also of stories from earlier religious traditions, accounts of previous heroes and prophets, and the like. It was inevitable that in the process of constructing their new prophet's life, the creators of Islam would entangle themselves in some contradictions. These would arise from the sheer bulk of the material they were working with, the differing views of various factions, and the differing perspectives and emphases of various sources upon whom they were relying.

They needed an explanation for contradictions that would allow them to make the revisions they needed to adapt their new religion to changing circumstances. How could Allah's chosen prophet say one thing according to one source and the opposite thing according to another? How could revisions in the various versions of the Qur'an be explained? Satan was a ready stand-by: he could always be invoked as trying yet again to confuse the Muslims and lead them astray. But the true believers need not worry: just as Allah had corrected Muhammad when he had said that al-Lat, al-Uzza, and Manat were worthy of veneration, so now he would protect Muhammad's community as well.

The Death of Khadija

Amid all this tension with the Quraysh, Muhammad suffered the loss of two of his foremost champions. Ibn Hisham states: "Khadija and Abu Talib died in the same year, and with Khadija's death troubles followed fast on each other's heels, for she had been a faithful support to him in Islam, and he used to tell her of his troubles. With the death of Abu Talib he lost a strength and stay in his personal life and a defense and protection against his tribe. Abu Talib died some three years before he migrated to Medina, and it was then that Quraysh began to treat him in an offensive way which they would not have dared to follow in his uncle's lifetime. A young lout actually threw dust on his head."[62]

So if Abu Talib and Khadija both died about three years before the hijrah to Medina, this must have been about ten years after Muhammad began proclaiming himself to be a prophet. That is Ibn Sa'd's assessment, as he says that "Abu Talib died passed away about the middle of Shawwal in the tenth year (reckoned) from the time the Apostle of Allah, may Allah bless him, was raised to prophethood, and he (Abd-Talib) was more than eighty years old. One month and five days after his death, Khadijah, who was sixty-five years old, died. Thus two afflictions befell the Apostle of Allah, may Allah, bless him, (the event of) death of Khadijah Bint Khuwaylid and (the event of) the death of his uncle Abu Talib."[63] This accords with the established standard chronology, in which Muhammad was forty years old and Khadija fifty-five when he became a prophet.

Although the Islamic traditions say that Khadija was forty years old when she married Muhammad, they also say that she bore him six children. Ibn Hisham states that Khadija was "the mother of all the apostle's children except Ibrahim," who was born late in Muhammad's life to his concubine Mary the Copt and died at the age of two.[64] Muhammad and Khadija are noted in the traditions to have had two sons, al-Qasim and Abdullah, and four daughters, Zaynab, Ruqayya, Umm Kulthum, and Fatima. The canonical tradition notes that Abdullah, although he only lived to the age of four, came in his brief life to be known as al-Tahir ("the pure") and al-Tayyib ("the good").[65]

Ibn Hisham, however, appears to believe that these are two different sons of Muhammad, giving him eight children in all. He says that "al-Qasim, al-Tayyib, and al-Tahir died in paganism," that is, before Muhammad became a prophet, and shows no awareness of the idea that al-Tayyib and al-Tahir were the same boy.[66] He adds, meanwhile, that all of Muhammad's daughters "lived into Islam, embraced it, and migrated with him to Medina."[67] The fact that his sons did not, however, had an enduring impact upon the development of Islam or was invented in order to explain that development. As Muhammad had no son who lived to adulthood, he had no heir or successor, either as a prophet or as a ruler. Others would have to vie for these positions.

The contemporary Muslim academic Hassan Abbas sings the praises of Muhammad's daughter Fatima, who eventually married Ali ibn Abi Talib. Abbas notes that Fatima (like her brother or brothers al-Tayyib and al-Tahir) has her own titles of honor; she is known as "*al-Zahra* (The Splendid) and *al-Batul* (The Chaste/The Pure), and later famously to be known as *Sayyidatu Nisa al-Alamin*—Leader of The Women of The Worlds."[68] This is a common Shi'ite view, as the Shi'ites revere Fatima for her marriage to Ali and denigrate Aisha, Muhammad's child bride, for opposing Ali.

After noting Fatima's honorifics, however, Abbas unwittingly bears witness to the fluidity of these traditions. He adds that "there is quite a bit of disagreement regarding her birth year and her status as the only child of Muhammad. It is believed that she was born in 605 according to Sunni historians or around 612 as per the Shia record (Shaykh

---

64 Ibn Ishaq, op. cit., 83.
65 Mahdi Rizqullah Ahmed, A Biography of the Prophet of Islam: In the Light of the Original Sources, an Analytical Study, Syed Iqbal Zaheer, trans. (Riyadh: Darussalam, 2005), I, 133.
66 Ibid.
67 Ibid.
68 Hassan Abbas, *The Prophet's Heir: The Life of Ali ibn Abi Talib* (New Haven: Yale University Press, 2021), Kindle edition, loc. 786.

al-Mufid) and, according to most Shia Muslims, she is Muhammad's only biological daughter. While Sunni Muslims believe Zaynab, Ruqayyah, and Umm Kulthum to be the other daughters of Muhammad, Shia believe that they were actually the daughters of Hala, Khadijah's sister, who were adopted by Muhammad and Khadijah following her death. Khadijah and the Prophet also had two sons, Qasim and Abdullah, both of whom died in infancy."[69] It would make more sense for Muhammad and Khadija to have had two children rather than six in light of the fact that the traditions state that she was already forty at the time of their marriage to Muhammad. But the traditions Abbas is relating could simply be a Shi'ite attempt to highlight the centrality of Fatima and, by extension, of Ali. On the other hand, the Sunni accounts of Muhammad having six children could just as easily be efforts to obscure the singularity of Fatima.

However the traditions about Muhammad's children developed, the Khadija accounts stand in contradiction to the common claim of contemporary Islamic apologists that the advent of Islam significantly improved the status of women over what it had been in the pre-Islamic time of *jahiliyya*, that is, the age of ignorance. The apologetics website WhyIslam.org, for example, boasts that "Islam has empowered women with the most progressive rights since the 7th century. In Islam, women are not inferior or unequal to men."[70] Yet one would be hard-pressed to find an accomplished independent woman like Khadija in Sharia states such as Saudi Arabia or Iran, where the strict enforcement of Islamic law reduces female independence, mobility, and opportunity in innumerable ways.

The accounts of Muhammad's other marriages after the death of Khadija also cut against the claim that Islam empowered women in various ways. According to the Islamic sources, Muhammad was fifty years old and newly widowed when he began to amass the many wives for which he has become renowned and notorious. The stories of his various marriages all appear to be designed to make certain points about his character, the nature of his mission, or related issues. His marriage to Khadija, for instance, appears designed to illustrate that he was such a

---

69 Ibid., loc. 786–94.
70 "Women In Islam," WhyIslam.org, September 24, 2014, https://www.whyislam.org/statusof-women/.

remarkable and notable young man that he was able to attract the attention of a highly desirable, sought-after, and successful older woman. Many of these stories, however, are jarring, particularly to modern-day sensibilities, and throughout the history of Islam, they have made Muslims vulnerable to charges that Muhammad was a man who could not control his lusts, which many non-Muslims have contended cut against his prophetic claim.

CHAPTER FIVE

Getting Married
and Going to Paradise

The Heavyset Woman

Muhammad's first marriage after the death of Khadija at least initially exposed him to no such charges. Ibn Hisham records laconically that one of Muhammad's companions, Sakran bin Amr bin Abdu Shams, "died in Mecca before the apostle emigrated," and Muhammad married his widow, Sawdah bint Zamah.[1] There is relatively little about this marriage in the early Islamic sources; Muhammad apparently entered into it out of pity for Sawdah after the death of Sakran. Thus was illustrated the compassion and magnanimity of the prophet of Islam.

However, Aisha, a woman whom Muhammad would also soon marry, recounted that Sawdah was a "heavyset woman."[2] Whether for that or some other reason, Muhammad appears to have grown less than enchanted with her charms and married Aisha while pursuing other women as well. In his commentary on the Qur'an, Ibn Kathir attributes to Muhammad's cousin Ibn Abbas the assertion that "Sawdah feared that the Messenger of Allah might divorce her and she said, 'O Messenger of Allah! Do not divorce me; give my day to Aishah.'"[3]

Sawdah was referring to Muhammad's practice of spending a day and night with each of his wives in turn. Muhammad had no interest, however, in spending a night with the heavyset Sawdah, who nevertheless pleaded with him not to be divorced, as divorce would have meant separation from her friends and loved ones and no means of financial

---

1 Ibn Ishaq, op. cit., 168–9.
2 Sunan an-Nasa'i, vol. 3, book 24, no. 3049. Sunnah.com, https://sunnah.com/nasai:3049.
3 Ibn Kathir, *Tafsir Ibn Kathir* (abridged) (Riyadh: Darussalam, 2000), II, 600.

support. She accordingly offered Muhammad a deal: he wouldn't have to sleep with her and could get extra time with his favorite wife, Aisha, if only he would keep her on as a wife.

Sawdah's plea became the occasion for Allah to give a revelation to Muhammad: "If a woman fears ill treatment from her husband, or desertion, it is no sin for either of them if they make terms of peace between themselves. Peace is better. But greed has been made present in people's minds. If you do good and avoid evil, indeed, Allah is always informed of what you do. You will not be able to deal equally between wives, however much you want to. But do not turn away altogether and leave her in suspense. If you do good and avoid evil, indeed, Allah is always forgiving, merciful" (Qur'an 4:128–9).

As the Qur'an likely predates the *asbab al-nuzul* (occasion of revelation) literature, this story of Sawdah importuning Muhammad may have been invented to explain this Qur'anic passage, rather than the Qur'anic passage being fashioned in order to deal with a specific event in Muhammad's life. It may also have been meant, once again, to illustrate Muhammad's magnanimity in agreeing to keep Sawdah on as a wife despite the fact that she was not desirable to him.

The Child

Muhammad's next marriage was to Aisha bint Abu Bakr, the wife to whom is attributed the judgment that Sawdah was "heavyset." Aisha was the daughter of Abu Bakr, one of Muhammad's most fervent companions and the man who was destined to succeed him as the leader of the Muslim community. The marriage to Aisha is thus routinely explained as a dynastic union, sealing Muhammad's relationship with Abu Bakr and securing his loyalty. Abu Bakr was firmly convinced that the deity was speaking to Muhammad, however, so it is unclear why Muhammad would need to marry Abu Bakr's young daughter in order to ensure the strength of his relationship with him. Aisha is the most famous of Muhammad's wives, and for good reason: numerous Islamic traditions record that she was six when Muhammad contracted the marriage with her and nine when he consummated the marriage.

Since nine years old is hardly an age at which people are generally considered capable of making informed decisions, this is tantamount to saying that Muhammad raped a child and is one of the points on which Islam is most frequently attacked in the Western world today. This is especially true in light of the fact that child marriage is rampant in fervently Islamic Afghanistan.[4] Justifying these marriages is easy, and opposing them is difficult, because of Muhammad's example.

That example is quite clear. Bukhari records several versions of a tradition in which Aisha herself succinctly states the facts of the case: "Narrated Aisha: that the Prophet married her when she was six years old and he consummated his marriage when she was nine years old. Hisham said: I have been informed that Aisha remained with the Prophet for nine years (i.e. till his death)."[5] Bukhari records the same facts attributed to other authorities as well: "Narrated Urwa: The Prophet wrote the (marriage contract) with Aisha while she was six years old and consummated his marriage with her while she was nine years old and she remained with him for nine years (i.e. till his death)."[6] And: "Narrated Hisham's father: Khadija died three years before the Prophet departed to Medina. He stayed there for two years or so and then he married Aisha when she was a girl of six years of age, and he consummated that marriage when she was nine years old."[7]

The same details—that Aisha was six when she was betrothed to Muhammad and nine when he consummated the marriage—also appear in three other hadith collections that, with Bukhari and Muslim, are five of the six such collections that are known as Al-Sahih al-Sittah, "the reliable six": Sunan Abi Dawud, Sunan al-Nasa'i, and Sunan Ibn Majah.[8] Sunan Abi Dawud contains an account in which Aisha misremembers her age at the time of her engagement to Muhammad and is corrected: "Narrated Aishah: The Messenger of Allah married me when I was seven years old. The narrator Sulaiman said: or Six years. He had intercourse with me when I was nine years old."[9]

---

4 "Girls increasingly at risk of child marriage in Afghanistan: Statement by UNICEF Executive Director Henrietta Fore," UNICEF, November 12, 2021, https://www.unicef.org/press-releases/girls-increasingly-risk-child-marriage-afghanistan.

5 Sahih Bukhari, vol. 7, book 67, no. 5134. See also Sahih Bukhari, vol. 7, book 67, no. 5133.

6 Sahih Bukhari, vol. 7, book 67, no. 5158.

7 Sahih Bukhari, vol. 5, book 63, no. 3896.

8 Sunan al-Nasa'i, vol. 4, book 26, no. 3255; vol. 4, book 26, no. 3378; vol. 4, book 26, no. 3379; Sunan Abi Dawud vol. 11, book 12, no. 2121; vol. 42, book 43, no. 4933; Sunan Ibn Majah vol. 3, book, 9, no. 1876.

9 Sunan Abi Dawud, vol. 11, book 12, no. 2121.

Aisha's extreme youth is emphasized in accounts of her still playing with dolls when Muhammad married her. She is depicted as recounting: "I used to play with dolls when I was with the Messenger of Allah, and he used to bring my friends to me to play with me."[10] In another version, she says: "The Messenger of Allah married me when I was six, and consummated the marriage with me when I was nine, and I used to play with dolls."[11] In yet another, sometimes Muhammad would interrupt Aisha while she was playing with dolls with her friends: "I used to play with dolls. Sometimes the Messenger of Allah entered upon me when the girls were with me. When he came in, they went out, and when he went out, they came in."[12] An additional variant of this story depicts Muhammad as more magnanimous toward Aisha and her young friends: "I used to play with the dolls in the presence of the Prophet, and my girl friends also used to play with me. When Allah's Messenger used to enter (my dwelling place) they used to hide themselves, but the Prophet would call them to join and play with me. (The playing with the dolls and similar images is forbidden, but it was allowed for Aisha at that time, as she was a little girl, not yet reached the age of puberty.)"[13]

In another hadith Bukhari collected and published, Aisha provides a number of piquant details:

> The Prophet engaged me when I was a girl of six (years). We went to Medina and stayed at the home of Bani-al-Harith bin Khazraj. Then I got ill and my hair fell down. Later on my hair grew (again) and my mother, Umm Ruman, came to me while I was playing in a swing with some of my girl friends. She called me, and I went to her, not knowing what she wanted to do to me. She caught me by the hand and made me stand at the door of the house. I was breathless then, and when my breathing became all right, she took some water and rubbed my face and head with it. Then she took me into the house. There in the house I saw some Ansari women who said, "Best wishes and Allah's Blessing and a good luck." Then she entrusted me to them and they prepared me (for the marriage). Unexpectedly

---

10 Sunan Ibn Majah, vol. 3, book 9, no. 1982.
11 Sunan al-Nasa'i, vol. 4, book 26, no. 3378.
12 Sunan Abi Dawud, vol. 42, no. 43, no. 4931.
13 Sahih Bukhari, vol. 8, book 78, no. 6130.

Allah's Apostle came to me in the forenoon and my mother handed me over to him, and at that time I was a girl of nine years of age.[14]

The other hadith collection that is respected among Muslims as most reliable, Sahih Muslim, records the same details. Aisha is again depicted as saying: "Allah's Apostle married me when I was six years old, and I was admitted to his house when I was nine years old."[15] It records the same chronology: "Aisha reported that Allah's Apostle married her when she was six years old, and he (the Holy Prophet) took her to his house when she was nine, and when he (the Holy Prophet) died she was eighteen years old."[16] Aisha also tells a similar story of her anxiety at the prospect of marrying the prophet of Islam:

> Allah's Messenger married me when I was six years old, and I was admitted to his house at the age of nine. She further said: We went to Medina and I had an attack of fever for a month, and my hair had come down to the earlobes. Umm Ruman (my mother) came to me and I was at that time on a swing along with my playmates. She called me loudly and I went to her and I did not know what she had wanted of me. She took hold of my hand and took me to the door, and I was saying: Ha, ha (as if I was gasping), until the agitation of my heart was over. She took me to a house, where had gathered the women of the Ansar. They all blessed me and wished me good luck and said: May you have share in good. She (my mother) entrusted me to them. They washed my head and embellished me and nothing frightened me. Allah's Messenger came there in the morning, and I was entrusted to him.[17]

Sunan Ibn Majah includes another variant of Aisha's story of her distress:

> The Messenger of Allah married me when I was six years old. Then we came to Al-Madinah and settled among Banu Harith bin Khaz-raj. I became ill and my hair fell out, then it grew back and became abundant. My mother Umm Ruman came to me while I was on an Urjuhah with some of my friends, and called for me. I went to her,

---

14 Sahih Bukhari, vol. 5, book 63, no. 3894.
15 Sahih Muslim, vol. 8, book 16, no. 1422b.
16 Sahih Muslim, vol. 8, book 16, no. 1422d.
17 Sahih Muslim, vol. 8, book 16, no. 1422a.

and I did not know what she wanted. She took me by the hand and made me stand at the door of the house, and I was panting. When I got my breath back, she took some water and wiped my face and head, and led me into the house. There were some woman of the Ansar inside the house, and they said: "With blessings and good fortune (from Allah)." (My mother) handed me over to them and they tidied me up. And suddenly I saw the Messenger of Allah in the morning. And she handed me over to him and I was at that time, nine years old.[18]

The similarities of these accounts suggest a common source, albeit an oral rather than a written one. The repetition of the accounts, meanwhile, is an indication that numerous sources were telling these stories. The hadith collectors include the repetitions if the isnad chain was different, as the multiple attestation of an account was considered evidence of its authenticity. The numerous sources of the Aisha story and the relative lack of variation in its details stand in contrast to some of the other accounts of various incidents in Muhammad's life, in which the variations are much larger and the sources sparser, as with the date of his birth, his own name at birth, the name of the angel who appeared to him, and so on.

This places contemporary academics of Islam and Islamic apologists in the West (if there is any significant distinction between those two groups at this point) in an excruciatingly difficult position. If they wish to maintain that the hadith and sira literature about Muhammad is generally reliable and provides a picture of the prophet of Islam that is, in the main, historically accurate, then they have to acknowledge (if they are consistent) that the Aisha accounts are among the best indications that this material contains a historical core.

Trying to Explain Aisha Away

For the agreement among the various sources that Aisha was six when Muhammad became engaged to her and nine when he consummated the marriage, as well as the general agreement in the details of Aisha's account of her illness and nervousness and her playing with dolls, could be the result of this material being historically accurate accounts of

---

18 Sunan Ibn Majah vol. 3, book, 9, no. 1876.

incidents that actually happened. There may have been a real child who married a warlord or prophet who was decades older than she was, with the traditions regarding this union being incorporated into the Muhammad myth. Or conceivably, the multiple attestation as to the details is simply because the historical Muhammad married the historical Aisha when she was a child.

That is the traditional Islamic position; it has been influential throughout history and remains so today. Islamic leaders frequently point to Muhammad to justify marrying children. Mufti Fazlul Haque Amini, who is based in Bangladesh, stated in 2011 that banning child marriage would impugn the reputation of Muhammad himself: "Banning child marriage will cause challenging the marriage of the holy prophet of Islam…[putting] the moral character of the prophet into controversy and challenge."[19] Islamonline.com, an influential Salafi website, justified the practice by referring to both Muhammad and the Qur'an:

> The Noble Qur'an has also mentioned the waiting period [i.e. for a divorced wife to remarry] for the wife who has not yet menstruated, saying: "And those who no longer expect menstruation among your women—if you doubt, then their period is three months, and [also for] those who have not menstruated" [Qur'an 65:4]. Since this is not negated later, we can take from this verse that it is permissible to have sexual intercourse with a prepubescent girl. The Qur'an is not like the books of jurisprudence which mention what the implications of things are, even if they are prohibited. It is true that the prophet entered into a marriage contract with Aisha when she was six years old, however he did not have sex with her until she was nine years old, according to al-Bukhari.[20]

Iran's Ayatollah Khomeini said that marriage to a girl before she reached puberty was "a divine blessing" and told fathers: "Do your best to ensure that your daughters do not see their first blood in your house."[21]

---

19 "Islamist leader threatens of waging Jihad," Weekly Blitz, April 20, 2011.

20 "Fatwa: 'It Is Permissible to Have Sexual Intercourse with a Prepubescent Girl,'" Translating Jihad, January 14, 2011. Translated from https://webcitation.org/query?url=http%3A%2F%2Fwww.islamonline.net%2Far%2FIOLCounsel_C%2F1278406761316%2F1278406720653%2F%D9%87%D9%84-%D9%8A%D8%AC%D9%88%D8%B2-%D8%AA%D8%AD%D8%AF%D9%8A%D8%AF-%D8%B3%D9%86-%D8%B2%D9%88%D8%A7%D8%AC-%D9%84%D9%84%D9%81%D8%AA%D9%8A%D8%A7%D8%AA%D8%9F-&date=2011-02-03

21 Amir Taheri, The Spirit of Allah: Khomeini and the Islamic Revolution (Adler and Adler, 1986), 35.

As a result, Islamic apologists in the West, as well as some academics, are extremely anxious to discredit the Aisha accounts, as they put the prophet of Islam in such a bad light and open him to charges of pedophilia. Some even insist that the entirety of the hadith and sira literature is historically unreliable, as it is so late, contradictory, and rife with forgeries, yet at the same time, also maintain that the Aisha accounts are even less reliable than the others due to various inconsistencies or weaknesses they purport to find in the isnad chains, despite the fact that these same "scholars" readily avow that the isnad chains are as susceptible to fabrication as the stories themselves.

Lauded academic studies explain how the isnad chains were forged wholesale, and thus cannot be trusted, and then painstakingly comb through the isnad chains of the various Aisha hadiths, purporting to demonstrate that they are too full of flaws to be considered authentic! The self-contradiction here is naked and obvious and exposes these "scholars" as nothing more than Islamic apologists attempting to give their exoneration of the prophet of Islam an academic patina.

A less ridiculous and consequently more frequently used approach is to claim that the genuinely authentic Islamic sources actually show that Aisha was older than nine when the marriage was consummated. This a difficult argument to make in light of Sahih Bukhari's manifest authority within the Islamic scholarly tradition. Some who try to make it anyway generally handle the problem of Bukhari simply by ignoring him, apparently hoping that non-Muslims will not know the meaning of the word *sahih* ("reliable") or be aware of the respect that is accorded to Bukhari's hadith collection. Others note that the bulk of what Bukhari reports about Aisha's age is attributed to Aisha herself and wave all this material away with the declaration that Aisha couldn't possibly have known for certain how old she was.

Shaykh Dr Ridhwan ibn Muhammad Saleem, chairman of an Islamic proselytizing and apologetics organization known as the Ha Meem Foundation and a senior lecturer at the London College of Islamic Studies, argued in an influential paper in 2010 that Aisha was substantially older than nine when she was married to Muhammad. He bases this claim on several disparate traditions to those recorded in the *Sahih Sittah*. Saleem writes that "Ibn Hajar al-Asqallani states in *al-Isabah*, citing al-Waqidi, on the authority of al-Abbas," that Muhammad's daughter Fatima "was born while the Ka'ba was being built...and the Prophet was thirty-five years of age...and she [Fatima] was about five years older than Aisha."[22] That would mean that Aisha was born when Muhammad was forty. If she lived with him for nine years until his death at age sixty-three, she must have been fourteen when they were married (Saleem says fifteen).

That's not much of an improvement over nine. Saleem also quotes Tabari saying: "In the Age of Ignorance [pre-Islamic period], Abu Bakr married Qutaila daughter of Abd al-Uzza...and she bore for him Abdullah and Asmaa...he also married, in the Age of Ignorance, Umm Ruman daughter of Amir...she bore for him Abd al-Rahman and Aisha. All four of these children were born in the pre-Islamic period."[23] If Aisha was born during the pre-Islamic period, even just before it ended, then she was twenty-three when Muhammad died and, presumably, fourteen when she married him.

Saleem then notes a weakness in his own argument: "However, we know that al-Tabari is aware of the 'six-nine' hadith as he quotes it in the same book."[24] In an attempt to resolve the contradiction thus created, Saleem argues that Tabari painstakingly compiled various traditions and then gave his own opinion as to which was authentic, and asserts that Tabari meant to endorse the tradition suggesting that Aisha was fourteen as authentic.

Then Saleem offers several other indications from Islamic tradition that Aisha was older than nine at the time of the marriage, including this: "Al-Nawawi mentions in *Tahdheeb al-Asmaa wal-Lughaat*, quoting Ibn Abi Zinad, that Asma was ten years older than Aisha, and...was born twenty-seven years before the hijrah of the messenger of Allah..."[25] That would make Aisha seventeen at the time of the hijrah and around that age at the time of the marriage.

These attempts to exonerate Muhammad, however, only make matters worse.

---

22 Ridhwan ibn Muhammad Saleem, "Age of al-Sayyida Aisha When She Married the Prophet Muhammad," West London School of Islamic Studies, Nov. 2010, 5, https://hameem.org/wp-content/uploads/2021/01/Age-of-Aisha.nov2010.pdf.

23 Ibid., 6.

24 Ibid.

25 Ibid., 7.

Why Create Muhammad's Child Bride?

The massive weakness of Saleem's argument and others like it is that Tabari, al-Waqidi, and the other authorities he invokes have no greater claim to authenticity or reliability than does Bukhari. In traditional Islamic theology and law, Bukhari takes precedence over all other hadith collections and is second in authority only to the Qur'an itself and the Hadith Qudsi, the hadiths in which Muhammad quotes Allah saying something that is not in the Qur'an. After Bukhari come the other hadith collections that say Aisha was nine. Thus, from an Islamic standpoint, Saleem's argument holds no water, but of course, he is not writing to Muslims, but to non-Muslims.

What's more, the variant testimony about the age of Aisha also offers further evidence that we are not dealing with historical accounts at any level when it comes to the Islamic material about Muhammad's life. There are differing testimonies about Aisha's age, just as there are about the date of Muhammad's birth, his name at birth, the name of the angel who appeared to him, and so on. There is no resolving the contradictions in the various accounts of Aisha's age; they are simply divergent traditions, among which what Saleem referred to as "the 'six-nine' hadith" clearly won out, as evidenced by its repeated appearance in Bukhari's collection and the other "reliable" ones.

That fact leads to the next question: Why did anyone begin to fabricate traditions asserting that Aisha was nine? And amid the welter of competing traditions asserting that she was older, how did these traditions of Muhammad consummating his marriage with a child find their way into the hadith collections that Muslims consider most reliable? A related question is: Why would those who were constructing the new religion of Islam willingly expose their prophet to pedophilia allegations based on an apparently unbridled and uncontrollable lust that extended even to this child as she innocently played with her dolls?

In order to understand this, it first must be understood that in the time of Muhammad, marriages to very young girls were not altogether uncommon and certainly not as stigmatized as they are today. Islamic apologists are fond of pointing this out today, but it doesn't actually absolve the canonical figure of Muhammad from responsibility for the prevalence of child marriage in some parts of the Islamic world today.

It may, however, point to the prevalence of child marriage during the time that these stories were fabricated. The early Muslims did not have modern Western sensibilities and did not realize the physical and psychological harm this practice did to young girls; it is also unlikely, given the prevailing attitudes toward women, that they would have cared if they had realized the extent of this harm. Once that is understood, the most obvious reason why these stories may have been invented is that these accounts were invented to justify the practice of child marriage among those who were practicing the new religion.

Saleem, on the other hand, suggests that the child marriage accounts were not repudiated throughout the long centuries of Islamic history because they weren't taken seriously as historically accurate in the first place: "It is possible that they," that is, Islamic scholars of earlier centuries, "simply took for granted that particular figures in such reports were not necessarily regarded as chronological data, and did not feel the need to comment further as this was self-evident for people of that time."[26]

Another possibility is that the Aisha accounts were designed to make a different point and were an exercise in theological one-upmanship in the Sunni-Shi'ite quarrel. We have seen that Ibn Hisham states that Ali ibn Abi Talib became Muhammad's first male follower when he was a mere boy of ten years old. The early Islamic literature is full of accounts of the bitter antagonism between Aisha and Ali, which ultimately became the basis for the bitter division between the Sunnis and the Shi'ites. Aisha is even said to have gone to war against Ali when he became caliph. It is thus possible that Aisha was made to be nine when Muhammad consummated his marriage with her so as to give the anti-Ali party an even younger follower of Muhammad than Ali was when he became a Muslim. The point would then not be to justify pedophilia, but simply to take the wind out of the sails of Ali's claim to have been Muhammad's youngest believer and give the Sunnis a claim to have been the first to recognize the new prophet.

Saleem invokes "American professor Denise Spellberg" in support of this view, stating that she "theorises that political factors, in particular the Shi'a-Sunni split, may have been important in the prevalent notion of Aisha's young age at marriage. Her young age, and therefore that she

_____
26 Ibid., 15.

was not known to any man before the Prophet, was an important point for supporters of the Sunni Abbasid caliphate as it proved her status as a divinely-appointed wife, and thus a reliable source regarding the 'thorny' question of his succession. It may have been that Sunni scholars favoured the reports which placed Aisha at nine years of age as it helped raise her status as the only virgin bride of the Prophet."[27]

Saleem is certainly correct about one aspect of this issue: those who fabricated and disseminated the traditions stating that Aisha was nine were certainly motivated by considerations other than historical accuracy.

When Did Aisha Go to Live with Muhammad?

Several of the Aisha hadiths quoted say that she went to live with Muhammad when she was nine, when he consummated the marriage, and lived with him for nine years until his death when she was eighteen. This would suggest that she entered Muhammad's household not in Mecca, but after the hijrah to Medina, where Muhammad is supposed to have lived for the last ten years of his life. One hadith that Muslim records has Aisha essentially saying as much: "Allah's Messenger married me when I was six years old, and I was admitted to his house at the age of nine. She further said: We went to Medina..."[28]

This could, however, suggest that Aisha entered the household of Muhammad just before the move to Medina, as she is depicted as sleeping next to Muhammad during what has become one of the most celebrated events of Islamic tradition: the *miraj*, or Muhammad's nocturnal journey to Jerusalem and visit to Paradise from the Temple Mount. Ibn Hisham states that at the time when tensions between the Muslims and the Quraysh were worse than ever after the Satanic verses incident, "the apostle was carried by night from the mosque at Mecca to the Masjid al-Aqsa, which is the temple of Aelia, when Islam had spread in Mecca among the Quraysh and all the tribes."[29]

Aelia was Aelia Capitolina, the name the Romans gave to Jerusalem when they officially expelled all the Jews from the city in 135 AD. This journey that Muhammad took is generally considered to be the one to

---

27 Ibid.
28 Sahih Muslim, vol. 8, book 16, no. 1422a.
29 Ibn Ishaq, op. cit., 181.

which the Qur'an refers briefly: "May he be glorified who carried his servant by night from the sacred mosque to the farthest mosque, around which we have blessed, so that we might show him some of our signs. Indeed, he, only he, is the hearer, the seer" (17:1).

Yet the Qur'an doesn't mention Jerusalem here or anywhere else. Ibn Hisham, writing early in the ninth century, assumes that the holy city of the Jews was Muhammad's destination. But he may not have been aware that the al-Aqsa Mosque, built late in the seventh century on the Temple Mount, did not exist during Muhammad's lifetime. Thus, if there was a historical Muhammad and he did indeed travel to "the farthest mosque," which is the meaning of *masjid al-aqsa*, that mosque must not have been the one in Jerusalem that came to bear that name.

Also, despite the fact that this account is the sole support for the claim that Jerusalem is a city that is holy to Islam, even the ninth-century accounts don't seem to have a literal journey in mind, although that point is in some dispute. Ibn Hisham depicts Aisha sleeping next to Muhammad in Mecca on the fateful night and says: "One of Abu Bakr's family told me," that is, likely Ibn Ishaq, "that Aisha the prophet's wife used to say: 'The apostle's body remained where it was but God removed his spirit by night.'"[30] This would mean that Aisha lived with Muhammad for longer than the nine years that some hadiths claim; otherwise, she would not have been in his bed in Mecca and able to see that he hadn't gone anywhere.

Yet other accounts suggest that Muhammad claimed that he actually traveled to Jerusalem from Mecca and returned in the space of one night, a miraculous journey, as it would have been physically impossible by the natural means available at the time. For in a Bukhari hadith, Muhammad is made to say: "When the people of Quraish did not believe me (i.e. the story of my Night Journey), I stood up in Al-Hijr and Allah displayed Jerusalem in front of me, and I began describing it to them while I was looking at it."[31] He could only have been able to describe it accurately and thereby silence his detractors if he had actually been there.

Ibn Hisham hedges his bets by saying that the journey "was certainly an act of God by which He took him by night in what way He pleased."[32]

30 Ibid., 183.
31 Sahih Bukhari, vol. 5, book 63, no. 3886.
32 Ibn Ishaq, op. cit., 181–2.

The Night Journey

Whether it was a literal journey or presented as just a dream, in the primary accounts of what happened, Allah sent Muhammad a miraculous animal to enable him to make the extraordinary trip. Ibn Hisham notes that "according to what I have heard Abdullah b. Mas'ud used to say: Buraq, the animal whose every stride carried it as far as its eye could reach on which the prophets before him used to ride was brought to the apostle and he was mounted on it. His companion (Gabriel) went with him to see the wonders between heaven and earth, until he came to Jerusalem's temple," which, of course, had been destroyed over five hundred years before this was supposed to have happened.[33]

Once there, Muhammad "found Abraham the friend of God, Moses, and Jesus assembled with a company of the prophets, and he prayed with them."[34] Bukhari fills in the details. Muhammad is depicted as saying that "while I was lying in Al-Hatim or Al-Hijr," that is, the area inside the low wall surrounding the Ka'ba, "suddenly someone came to me and cut my body open from here to here."[35] Malik bin Sasaa, the companion of Muhammad to whom this story is attributed, recounts: "I asked Al-Jarud who was by my side, 'What does he mean?' He said, 'It means from his throat to his pubic area,' or said, 'From the top of the chest.'" Muhammad continued: "He then took out my heart. Then a gold tray of Belief was brought to me and my heart was washed and was filled (with Belief) and then returned to its original place. Then a white animal which was smaller than a mule and bigger than a donkey was brought to me."[36] This was the Buraq.

In another hadith, Muhammad is depicted as describing the Buraq as "a white animal, smaller than a mule and bigger than a donkey."[37] Ibn Hisham has Muhammad recount that Gabriel "brought me out to the door of the mosque and there was a white animal, half mule, half donkey, with wings on its sides with which it propelled its feet, putting down each forefoot at the limit of its sight and he mounted me on it. Then he went out with me keeping close to me."[38] Ibn Sa'd specifies that

33 Ibid., 182.
34 Ibid.
35 Sahih Bukhari, vol. 5, book 63, no. 3887.
36 Ibid.
37 Sahih Bukhari, vol. 4, book 59, no. 3207.
38 Ibn Ishaq, op. cit.

Muhammad was taken to Jerusalem and has him say: "I was mounted on a beast whose size was between a donkey and a mule, with two wings in its thighs, which came up to its hoofs and were set in them."[39]

Yet an unrelated hadith attributed to Aisha casts doubt on the entire narrative of the night journey as either a miraculous trip or a dream, as it depicts Muhammad as unaware of the idea of a winged equine, and vastly amused at the prospect, years after he was supposed to have ridden Buraq to paradise and met Allah. Aisha recounts: "When the Messenger of Allah arrived after the expedition to Tabuk or Khaybar (the narrator is doubtful), the draught raised an end of a curtain which was hung in front of her store-room, revealing some dolls which belonged to her. He asked: What is this? She replied: My dolls. Among them he saw a horse with wings made of rags, and asked: What is this I see among them? She replied: A horse. He asked: What is this that it has on it? She replied: Two wings. He asked: A horse with two wings? She replied: Have you not heard that Solomon had horses with wings? She said: Thereupon the Messenger of Allah laughed so heartily that I could see his molar teeth."[40]

In Bukhari's principal night journey hadith, however, Muhammad, mounted on the Buraq he evidently forgot all about later, travels with Gabriel to "the nearest heaven"; the hadith does not mention Jerusalem. Muhammad recounts: "I went over the first heaven, I saw Adam there. Gabriel said (to me). 'This is your father, Adam; pay him your greetings.' So I greeted him and he returned the greeting to me and said, 'You are welcomed, O pious son and pious Prophet.'"[41] In the second heaven, Muhammad meets John the Baptist and Jesus, who greet him in the exact words that Adam used. In the third heaven, Muhammad meets Joseph; in the fourth, Idris; in the fifth, Aaron; and in the sixth, Moses. They all greet him in the same way. When Muhammad left Moses, Moses wept: "I weep because after me there has been sent (as Prophet) a young man whose followers will enter Paradise in greater numbers than my followers."[42] In the seventh heaven, Muhammad meets Abraham, who also gives him the same greeting.

---

39 Ibn Sa'd, op. cit., I, 247.
40 Sunan Abi Dawud, vol. 42, book 43, no. 4932.
41 Sahih Bukhari, vol. 5, book 63, no. 3887.
42 Ibid.

Amid this demonstration that Muhammad was a prophet in the illustrious company of his peers, Ibn Hisham states that he is given a test: "Then he was brought three vessels containing milk, wine, and water respectively. The apostle said: 'I heard a voice saying when these were offered to me: "If he takes the water he will be drowned and his people also; if he takes the wine he will go astray and his people also; and if he takes the milk he will be rightly guided and his people also." So I took the vessel containing milk and drank it. Gabriel said to me, "You have been rightly guided and so will your people be, Muhammad.""'[43] Bukhari's account has this take place after the meeting with Abraham, as Muhammad is made to recount: "Then Al-Bait-ul-Ma'mur (i.e. the Sacred House) was shown to me and a container full of wine and another full of milk and a third full of honey were brought to me. I took the milk. Gabriel remarked, 'This is the Islamic religion which you and your followers are following.'"[44]

One of the foundations of the Islamic religion comes from this account. Muhammad says: "Then the prayers were enjoined on me: They were fifty prayers a day."[45] This was the command of Allah himself, but as Muhammad returns, Moses asks him, "What have you been ordered to do?"[46] When he hears about the order to pray fifty times a day, he tells Muhammad: "Your followers cannot bear fifty prayers a day, and by Allah, I have tested people before you, and I have tried my level best with Bani Israel (in vain). Go back to your Lord and ask for reduction to lessen your followers' burden."[47] Muhammad adds:

So I went back, and Allah reduced ten prayers for me. Then again I came to Moses, but he repeated the same as he had said before. Then again I went back to Allah and He reduced ten more prayers. When I came back to Moses he said the same, I went back to Allah and He ordered me to observe ten prayers a day. When I came back to Moses, he repeated the same advice, so I went back to Allah and was ordered to observe five prayers a day. When I came back to Moses, he said, "What have you been ordered?" I replied, "I have been

---

43 Ibn Ishaq, op. cit., 182.
44 Sahih Bukhari, vol. 5, book 63, no. 3887.
45 Ibid.
46 Ibid.
47 Ibid.

ordered to observe five prayers a day." He said, "Your followers cannot bear five prayers a day, and no doubt, I have got an experience of
the people before you, and I have tried my level best with Bani Israel,
so go back to your Lord and ask for reduction to lessen your follower's burden." I said, "I have requested so much of my Lord that I feel
ashamed, but I am satisfied now and surrender to Allah's Order."
When I left, I heard a voice saying, "I have passed My Order and
have lessened the burden of My Worshipers."[48]

This story is reminiscent of the biblical account of Abraham bargaining with God over how many righteous men he must find in Sodom
to prevent him from destroying the city altogether (Genesis 18:22–33).
Muhammad is thus established as a prophet who is a peer of Abraham
and as close to Allah as the earlier prophet was, so close that he can dare
to negotiate with the deity over one of his commands.

Another hadith concludes the story: "So, the two of them remained
upon the back of Al-Buraq until they saw Paradise and the Fire, and all
of what has been prepared for the Hereafter, then they returned back
to where they began."[49] This was, presumably, back in bed in Mecca,
where Aisha testified that he had remained the entire night. Yet when
the Quraysh confronted him about his miraculous journey, he was able
to provide them with details about the geography of Jerusalem.

Ibn Sa'd comes down firmly on the side of those who believed that
the night journey was an actual occurrence. He says that Muhammad
"had disappeared that night, so the members of family of Abd
al-Muttalib went out to search him. Al-Abbas went to Dhu Tuwa and
began to shout: O Muhammad! O Muhammad!"[50] When Muhammad
presents himself, al-Abbas says: "O my mother's son! You have worried
the people since the (beginning of the) night, where had you been?"[51]
Muhammad answers: "I am coming from Bayt al-Muqaddas," that is,
Jerusalem.[52] Surprised, al-Abbas asks: "In one night?" Muhammad
says yes, and then his cousin, Umm Hani, backs up his story, saying:
"He was taken on this journey from our house. He slept that night

---

48 Ibid.
49 Jami at-Tirmidhi, vol. 5, book 47, no. 3147.
50 Ibn Sa'd, op. cit.
51 Ibid.
52 Ibid.

with us; he offered al-Isha prayers, and then he slept."[53] She doesn't mention Aisha.

Umm Hani is convinced that Muhammad really did travel to Jerusalem and back during the night, but she has only his word for it: "When it was pre-dawn we awoke him (to offer) morning (prayers). He got up and when he offered morning prayers he said: 'O Umm Hani! I offered al-Ishaa prayers with you as you witnessed," that is, the last prayers of the night, "then I reached Bayt al-Muqaddas and offered prayers there; then I offered morning prayers before you.'"[54]

Although she evidently believes it, Umm Hani seems aware that this is an implausible tale and warns Muhammad accordingly: "After this he got up to go out; I said to him: 'Do not relate this to the people because they will belie you and harm you.'"[55] Muhammad dismissed this possibility, but Umm Hani was proven right. The Quraysh said: "We have never heard a thing like this," apparently in a disapproving manner, as Muhammad then calls out to his angelic protector: "O Gabriel! My people will not confirm it."[56] Gabriel tells Muhammad: "Abu Bakr will testify to it; and he is al-Siddiq," that is, the truthful or righteous.[57]

How Abu Bakr would know whether or not Muhammad flew to Jerusalem on a winged animal and met the prophets and Allah is not explained, and the people remain skeptical; even some of the Muslims have second thoughts about their religion, as Ibn Sa'd adds: "Many people who had embraced Islam and offered prayers went astray."[58]

This is odd, however, as in the same account, Muhammad says that he was able to answer the skeptics' questions about Jerusalem: "I stood at al-Hijr, visualised Bayt al-Muqaddas and described its signs. Some of them said: 'How many doors are there in that mosque?' I had not counted them so I began to look at it and counted them one by one and gave them information concerning them. I also gave information about their caravan which was on the way and its signs. They found them as I had related." Yet if he had really been able to answer the questions correctly, there was no reason for any of his companions to leave. Ibn

---

53 Ibid., 248.
54 Ibid.
55 Ibid.
56 Ibid.
57 Ibid.
58 Ibid.

Sa'd sums it up as a test from Allah, saying that the Qur'anic verse "we appointed the sight which we showed you as an ordeal for mankind" (17:60) referred to "the vision of the eye which he saw with the eye."[59]

Ibn Hisham also includes an account in which Muhammad tells Umm Hani in the morning about how he had traveled to Jerusalem the previous night and one in which the skeptics go to Abu Bakr, who vouches for Muhammad's veracity. He likewise includes a statement from Mu'awiya, the future caliph, saying that the night journey was "a true vision from God."[60] Ibn Hisham labors to harmonize this with the traditions that it was an actual physical journey that Muhammad took: "What these two latter said does not contradict what Al-Hasan said," al-Hasan being one of those who maintained that Muhammad really went to Jerusalem. Ibn Hisham's evidence for this is Qur'an 17:60; he adds also that Mu'awiya's statement "does it contradict what God said in the story of Abraham when he said to his son, 'O my son, verily I saw in a dream that I must sacrifice thee,' and he acted accordingly. Thus, as I see it revelation from God comes to the prophets waking or sleeping."[61]

Ibn Hisham doesn't include the material that Bukhari has about the prophets welcoming Muhammad as one of their number and Muhammad bargaining Allah down to five prayers a day for his followers. Instead, he depicts Muhammad describing the physical appearance of Abraham, Moses, and Jesus and recounting adventures in the heavenly realms that were substantially different from those that Bukhari recounted. Muhammad is depicted as saying that "after the completion of my business in Jerusalem," which was not specified, "a ladder was brought to me finer than any I have ever seen. It was that to which the dying man looks when death approaches. My companion mounted it with me until we came to one of the gates of heaven called the Gate of the Watchers. An angel called Ismail was in charge of it, and under his command were twelve thousand angels each of them having twelve thousand angels under his command.' As he told this story the apostle used to say, 'and none knows the armies of God but He. When Gabriel brought me in, Ismail asked who I was, and when he was told that I

---

59 Ibid.
60 Ibn Ishaq, op. cit., 183.
61 Ibid.

was Muhammad he asked if I had been given a mission, and on being assured of this he wished me well."[62]

After this reinforcement of his importance and prophetic status, Muhammad is shown a Dantescan vision of hell, with lurid descriptions of the tortures of the damned. These included:

> Then I saw men with lips like camels; in their hands were pieces of fire like stones which they used to thrust into their mouths and they would come out of their posteriors. I was told that these were those who sinfully devoured the wealth of orphans.
>
> Then I saw men in the way of the family of Pharaoh, with such bellies as I have never seen; there were passing over them as it were camels maddened by thirst when they were cast into hell, treading them down, they being unable to move out of the way. These were the usurers.
>
> Then I saw men with good fat meat before them side by side with lean stinking meat, eating of the latter and leaving the former. These are those who forsake the women which God has permitted and go after those he has forbidden.
>
> Then I saw women hanging by their breasts. These were those who had fathered bastards on their husbands.[63]

After this, Muhammad meets John the Baptist, Jesus, Joseph, Idris, Aaron, and Moses. Nothing is said about any conversation they had, if they had any. In the seventh heaven, "there was a man sitting on a throne at the gate of the immortal mansion. Every day seventy thousand angels went in not to come back until the resurrection day. Never have I seen a man more like myself. This was my father Abraham."[64] Once again, the primary point seems to be to demonstrate Muhammad's exalted status. The account continues with an elliptical account that foreshadows the notorious incident involving Muhammad, his adopted son Zayd bin Haritha, and Zayd's wife Zaynab bint Jahsh: "Then he took me into Paradise and there I saw a damsel with dark red lips and I asked her to whom she belonged, for she pleased me much when I saw her, and she told me 'Zayd b. Haritha'. The apostle gave Zayd the good news about her."[65] Ibn

---

62 Ibid., 184–5.
63 Ibid., 185–6.
64 Ibid., 186.
65 Ibid.

Hisham then takes up another account in which Allah tells Muhammad to order the Muslims to pray fifty times a day, and Moses persuades Muhammad to bargain Allah down to five.

With all its fanciful details, clearly, this legend was designed to situate Muhammad among the prophets, enthralling and entertaining audiences while impressing upon them the cardinal importance of obedience to the prophet of Islam. Yet while it is firmly embedded in Islamic tradition and has never been questioned the way the Satanic verses incident has been, apparently those who devised the story of Muhammad late in life discovering Aisha's old dolls were unaware of it, and in their efforts to emphasize Aisha's youth (perhaps once again in an act of one-upmanship over Ali ibn Abi Talib), they provide details that undercut the entire night journey narrative.

All this only serves to highlight that these various traditions lack any clear historical basis and cannot even be reconciled with one another. The proliferation of this mass of contradictory material is what led the early Islamic communities to devise the "science" of hadith and begin the efforts to winnow out the true from the false and fabricated by examining the isnad chains. These offered, however, no reliable pathway out of the morass of legend, fable, and party fabrication, as there was no more of a way to guarantee their authenticity than there was to ensure the reliability of the stories themselves.

The accounts of the night journey also seem intended to show that tensions with the Quraysh were continuing to increase and that matters would have to come to a head sooner or later. This led directly to the narrative of the hijrah, the great emigration to Medina.

CHAPTER SIX

The Hijrah

Outfoxing the Jews

With tensions between the Muslims and the Quraysh at a breaking point, Muhammad began looking for a new home for the believers. According to Ibn Hisham, he began to frequent gatherings of Arabian merchants, where members of different tribes would gather: "The apostle offered himself to the tribes of Arabs at the fairs whenever opportunity came, summoning them to God and telling them that he was a prophet who had been sent. He used to ask them to believe in him and protect him until God should make clear to them the message with which he had charged his prophet."[1]

It was at one of these fairs that Muhammad encountered some men of the Khazraj tribe, who lived in the city of Yathrib. According to Bukhari, Muhammad was supernaturally alerted to the significance of this city: "I was ordered to migrate to a town which will swallow (conquer) other towns and is called Yathrib and that is Medina, and it turns out (bad) persons as a furnace removes the impurities of iron."[2] In Medina, according to Ibn Hisham, there lived Jews who had been taunting the Khazraj with news of a coming prophet who would go to war against the Arab tribe: "A prophet will be sent soon. His day is at hand. We shall follow him and kill you by his aid as Ad and Iram perished."[3]

When the Khazraj heard Muhammad preach, they said to one another, "This is the very prophet of whom the Jews warned us. Don't let them get to him before us!"[4] They said to Muhammad: "We have left

---

1 Ibn Ishaq, op. cit., 194.
2 Sahih Bukhari vol. 3, book 29, no. 1871.
3 Ibn Ishaq, op. cit., 198.
4 Ibid.

123

our people, for no tribe is so divided by hatred and rancor as they. Perhaps God will unite them through you. So let us go to them and invite them to this religion of yours; and if God unites them in it, then no 'man will be mightier than you.'"[5] They accepted Islam and returned to Yathrib as Muslims.

In Ibn Sa'd's account, Muhammad "went out during the season (of pilgrimage) and met six members of al-Ansar," that is, "the helpers," those Medinans who became Muslim, as opposed to *al-muhajiroun*, "the emigrants," the original Muslims who emigrated with Muhammad from Mecca to Medina.[6] In this account, Muhammad stood near these Medinans and asked them: "Are you the allies of the Jews?"[7] They replied simply: "Yes," without telling him any stories about how the Jews had been terrorizing them with stories about a coming prophet who would kill them.[8] "Then he called them to Allah and preached Islam to them and recited the Qur'an before them. They joined the fold of Islam."[9]

Ibn Hisham continues: "When they came to Medina they told their people about the apostle and invited them to accept Islam until it became so well known among them that there was no home belonging to the Helpers but Islam and the apostle had been mentioned therein."[10]

The Two Pledges of Al-Aqaba

The following year, with Muhammad still living in Mecca, a group of twelve Medinans met together at al-Aqaba, a mountain pass near Mecca, to pledge fealty to Muhammad. Because of the location of their meeting and because another oath of fealty followed after it, this pledge has come to be known as the Pledge of al-Aqaba, or the first Aqaba. Ibn Sa'd says that they took an oath "prescribed for women": "We will not associate partners with Allah, we will not steal, will not live in adultery, will not kill our children, will not calumniate knowingly and will not disobey commands."[11]

---

5 Ibid.
6 Ibn Sa'd, op. cit., I, 253.
7 Ibid.
8 Ibid.
9 Ibid.
10 Ibn Ishaq, op. cit.
11 Ibn Sa'd, op. cit., I, 254.

That this is a pledge for women is based on a passage in the Qur'an: "O prophet, if believing women come to you, taking an oath of allegiance to you that they will ascribe no thing as partner to Allah, and will neither steal nor commit adultery nor kill their children, nor produce any lie that they have devised between their hands and feet, nor disobey you in what is right, then accept their allegiance and ask Allah to forgive them. Indeed, Allah is forgiving, merciful" (60:12). Ibn Hisham likewise says that "twelve Helpers" from among the men of Medina "gave the apostle the 'pledge of women.'" Men from the Najjar, a sub-tribe of the Khazraj of Medina, as well as the Amr bin Auf and other tribes, are listed as taking this pledge.[12]

There was nothing necessarily particular to women in any of this. It may be the "pledge of women" simply because it involved words only; no bloodshed was involved. Ibn Hisham goes on to note that "this was before the duty of making war was laid upon them."[13] One of those who took the pledge is depicted as recounting: "I was present at the first Aqaba. There were twelve of us and we pledged ourselves to the prophet after the manner of women and that was before war was enjoined, the undertaking being that we should associate nothing with God; we should not steal; we should not commit fornication; nor kill our offspring; we should not slander our neighbors; we should not disobey him in what was right; if we fulfilled this paradise would be ours; if we committed any of those sins it was for God to punish or forgive as He pleased."[14]

There was also nothing in this pledge that departed from the moral codes of the two monotheistic religions, Judaism and Christianity, that would play such a large role in the history of early Islam. The divergences would come later. This raises the question of the significance of these pledges and how they set apart those who were making them from Muhammad's other companions. Surely all the followers of the new prophet were bound to refrain from idolatry, theft, fornication, lying, and the like. So why was this pledge undertaken?

A clue may lie in another resonance with the Jewish and Christian traditions. Twelve of Muhammad's new followers from among the inhabitants of Medina took this pledge to follow him. Moses sent twelve

---

12 Ibn Ishaq, op. cit.
13 Ibid.
14 Ibid., 199.

men to explore the land of Canaan (Numbers 13:1–15). Jesus had twelve disciples (Matthew 10:1). Ibn Sa'd has Muhammad speaking explicitly about these resonances: "Verily, Moses chose twelve *naqibs* [Ibn Hisham explains this word as "leaders"] from the Israelites, (so twelve will be chosen from amongst you); none of you should grudge him who is chosen, because Gabriel chooses for me. When he had chosen them, he said to them: You are the custodians of others like the *Hawaris* of Jesus, son of Mary, and I am the custodian of my people."[15]

The *hawaris* were the twelve apostles of Jesus. Likewise, Ibn Hisham has the prophet of Islam tell his new group of twelve: "You are the sureties for your people just as the disciples of Jesus, Son of Mary, were responsible to him, while I am responsible for my people, i.e. the Muslims."[16] Thus Muhammad appears to be saying that these twelve men have authority over the new Muslims of Medina, the ansar, while he himself is in charge of the original Muslims from Mecca, the muhajiroun. Obviously, however, the prophet of Islam would actually be in charge of both groups.

After this, at a time when, according to Ibn Sa'd, "Islam had become fully known in al-Madinah," another group came forward to pledge fealty to Muhammad: "Then a party of seventy or a man or two more emerged with a party of al-Aws and al-Khazraj numbering five hundred persons. They came to the Apostle of Allah, may Allah bless him, at Makkah and greeted the Apostle of Allah."[17] Ibn Hisham quotes one of those who were depicted as being present as saying: "There were seventy-three men with two of our women."[18] Muhammad met them, says Ibn Sa'd, "in the mountain pass to the right, which is below Aqabah, when coming down from Mina, and where a mosque has been erected, and is at this time in existence."[19] Ibn Hisham says that they "met the apostle at al-Aqaba in the middle of the days of Tashriq," that is, the eleventh, twelfth, and thirteenth days of the month of Dhul-Hijjah; the pilgrimage to Mecca takes place during the first ten days of the same month.[20] They met Muhammad "when God intended to honor them and to help

---

15 Ibn Sa'd, op. cit., I, 258.
16 Ibn Hisham, op. cit., 204.
17 Ibn Sa'd, op. cit., I, 256.
18 Ibn Ishaq, op. cit., I, 203.
19 Ibn Sa'd, op. cit.
20 Ibn Ishaq, op. cit. 201–2.

His apostle and to strengthen Islam and to humiliate heathenism and its devotees."[21]

Here, says Ibn Sa'd, the seventy "put their hands in his hands and pledged help."[22] Ibn Hisham fills in more details: Muhammad "recited the Quran and invited men to God and commended Islam and then said: 'I invite your allegiance on the basis that you protect me as you would your women and children.'"[23] One of the Medinans asks him: "O apostle, we have ties with other men (he meant the Jews) and if we sever them perhaps when we have done that and God will have given you victory, you will return to your people and leave us?"[24] At this, "the apostle smiled and said: 'Nay, blood is blood and blood not to be paid for is blood not to be paid for. I am of you and you are of me. I will war against them that war against you and be at peace with those at peace with you.'"[25]

Muhammad then said: "Bring out to me twelve leaders that they may take charge of their people's affairs."[26] This was a curious command for him to issue if the first Aqaba pledge had just recently taken place. Had he rejected the original twelve already? Another possibility is that the men who took the first pledge of Aqaba are from various tribes and sub-tribes of the Khazraj, while those who took this second pledge are generally identified as simply from the Khazraj and Aws tribes. Apparently, Muhammad had two sets of twelve men of Medina in charge of Medina's new believers, or the two sets of twelve were a duplication of what was originally the same tradition. The duplication may also be an attempt to harmonize divergent traditions.

Ibn Hisham notes that one of the Muslims then gave the new believers a warning:

O men of Khazraj, do you realize to what you are committing yourselves in pledging your support to this man? It is to war against all and sundry. If you think that if you lose your property and your nobles are killed you will give him up, then do so now, for it would bring you shame in this world and the next (if you did so later); but if you think that you will be loyal to your undertaking if you lose

---

21 Ibid., 202.
22 Ibn Sa'd, op. cit.
23 Ibn Ishaq, op. cit.
24 Ibid.
25 Ibid., 203–4.
26 Ibid., 204.

your property and your nobles are killed, then take him, for by God it will profit you in this world and the next.[27]

In response, the new Muslims "said that they would accept the apostle on these conditions. But they asked what they would get in return for their loyalty, and the apostle promised them paradise."[28] Ibn Hisham notes this as a fundamental difference between the first and second Aqaba pledges: "When God gave permission to his apostle to fight, the second Aqaba contained conditions involving war which were not in the first act of fealty. Now they bound themselves to war against all and sundry for God and his apostle, while he promised them for faithful service thus the reward of paradise."[29]

The number of the men who apparently took this pledge, seventy (although both Ibn Hisham and Ibn Sa'd say there were a few more), was also resonant. Moses chose seventy men to stand before the tabernacle with him (Numbers 11:16), and Jesus had a group of seventy whom he sent to the towns that he himself was about to visit (Luke 10:1).

While it is not inconceivable that two groups of men in these paradigmatic numbers decided to set themselves apart for special allegiance or service to Muhammad, it is much more likely that the stories of these pledges were constructed in order to provide still more support for the claim that Muhammad was a prophet in the established Jewish prophetic line, a line that in this view included Jesus as a prophet. So if Moses and Jesus each had two groups of followers, one numbering twelve and the other seventy, so must Muhammad also. In any case, the intent of the stories was clearly apologetic, with any possible historical content thoroughly obscured by the theological points being made.

Permission to Fight

The Quraysh heard about the conversion of the Medinans, and this made tensions between the Meccans and the Muslims even worse. "When the party of seventy persons returned," says Ibn Sa'd, "the Apostle of Allah, may Allah bless him, was much pleased that Allah had provided him with supporters and had helped him through men of martial spirit and valor. In the meantime the unbelievers had intensified their tyranny on

27 Ibid.
28 Ibid.
29 Ibid., 208.

Muslims since they had learnt of their migration," which, at this point, apparently meant only their plans to migrate from Mecca to Medina, as the move itself had not yet taken place.[30] "Consequently they had rendered their life miserable. They committed cruelties and showered abuses which they had not yet used. The Companions of the Apostle of Allah, may Allah bless him, complained to him and asked him to permit them to migrate."[31] Muhammad gives his permission.

In Ibn Hisham's version, at least some of the Muslims were exiled: "The Quraysh had persecuted his followers, seducing some from their religion, and exiling others from their country. They had to choose whether to give up their religion, be maltreated at home, or to flee the country, some to Abyssinia, others to Medina."[32]

The sources generally agree that this was the occasion of the revelation of the Qur'an's first permission to engage in warfare: "Permission is given to those who fight because they have been wronged, and Allah is indeed able to give them victory, those who have been driven from their homes unjustly only because they said, Our Lord is Allah, for if it had not been for Allah's repelling some men by means of others, monasteries and churches and oratories and mosques, in which the name of Allah is frequently mentioned, would surely have been destroyed. Indeed Allah helps someone who helps him. Indeed, Allah is strong, almighty" (22:39–40). Upon hearing this, Abu Bakr is depicted as remarking sagely: "Then I knew that there would be fighting."[33]

Ibn Hisham notes: "The apostle had not been given permission to fight or allowed to shed blood before the second Aqaba. He had simply been ordered to call men to God and to endure insult and forgive the ignorant."[34] However, "when Quraysh became insolent towards God and rejected His gracious purpose, accused His prophet of lying, and ill-treated and exiled those who served Him and proclaimed His unity, believed in His prophet, and held fast to His religion, He gave permission to His apostle to fight and to protect himself against those who wronged them and treated them badly."[35]

---

30 Ibn Sa'd, op. cit., I, 261.
31 Ibid.
32 Ibn Ishaq, op. cit., 212.
33 Jami al-Tirmidhi, vol. 5, book 47, no. 3171.
34 Ibn Ishaq, op. cit.
35 Ibid.

The fighting would begin in earnest when Muhammad himself relocated to Medina.

Was Muhammad Exiled?

According to a hadith, the Quraysh didn't content themselves with exiling some of the Muslims. They even went so far as to exile Muhammad himself: "When the Prophet was expelled from Makkah, Abu Bakr said: 'They have driven out their Prophet to their own doom.'"[36]

Ibn Hisham, however, doesn't seem to be aware that Muhammad was expelled outright from Medina and depicts him staying on after the exile of some of his companions, waiting for the right moment to leave and apparently not even considering himself to be in any imminent danger: "After his companions had left, the apostle stayed in Mecca waiting for permission to migrate. Except for Abu Bakr and Ali, none of his supporters were left but those under restraint and those who had been forced to apostatize. The former kept asking the apostle for permission to emigrate and he would answer, 'Don't be in a hurry; it may be that God will give you a companion.' Abu Bakr hoped that it would be Muhammad himself."[37]

The Quraysh, meanwhile, were apprehensive "since they knew that he had decided to fight them."[38] The Quraysh leaders met together to discuss what to do with Muhammad, and the possibility of exile, among other plans, was broached, considered, and rejected:

> Another man suggested that they should drive him out of the country. They did not care where he went or what happened to him once he was out of sight and they were rid of him. They could then restore their social life to its former state. Again the shaykh objected that it was not a good plan. His fine speech and beautiful diction and the compelling force of his message were such that if he settled with some Bedouin tribe he would win them over so that they would follow him and come and attack them in their land and rob them of their position and authority and then he could do what he liked with them. They must think of a better plan.[39]

---

36 Jami al-Tirmidhi, vol. 5, book 47, no. 3171.
37 Ibn Ishaq, op. cit., 221.
38 Ibid.
39 Ibid.

Ultimately, the Quraysh decide to kill Muhammad. They devise a plot to do so, and when they are gathered outside Muhammad's door, one of the Islamic prophet's foremost adversaries, Abu Jahl, says: "Muhammad alleges that if you follow him you will be kings of the Arabs and the Persians. Then after death you will be raised to gardens like those of the Jordan. But if you do not follow him you will be slaughtered, and when you are raised from the dead you will be burned in the fire of hell."[40] Muhammad himself then appears and sprinkles dust on the Quraysh chieftains as Allah miraculously prevents them from recognizing or even seeing him. As he does so, he confirms Abu Jahl's succinct summation of the message of Islam: "I do say that. You are one of them."[41]

Muhammad is also depicted as reciting part of the Qur'an: "Ya Sin. By the wise Qur'an, indeed, you are among those sent on a straight path, a revelation of the mighty, the merciful, so that you may warn a people whose fathers were not warned, so they are heedless. Already the judgment has proved true of most of them, for they do not believe. Indeed, we have put shackles on their necks reaching to their chins, so that they are made stiff-necked. And we have set a bar in front of them and a bar behind them, and have covered them so that they do not see" (36:1–9).

The Quraysh end up looking foolish, for they lay in wait for the prophet of Islam until morning, only to see Ali ibn Abi Talib emerging from Muhammad's bedchamber; getting word of the plot from Gabriel, Muhammad had earlier arranged for Ali to sleep in his bed that night. This coincided with another Qur'anic passage: "And when those who disbelieve plot against you, to wound you fatally, or to kill you or to drive you out, they scheme, but Allah schemes, and Allah is the best of schemers" (8:30). Ibn Sa'd tells essentially the same story.

It was only after this foiled plot, according to Ibn Hisham, that Allah "gave permission to his prophet to migrate."[42] By all accounts, Muhammad was by this time clearly unwelcome in Mecca, but there is no trace of any explicit or formal expulsion. Muhammad, by this account, leaves Mecca of his own volition once Allah tells him that it is time to do so. Only in the hadith that Tirmidhi records is there the idea that he was actually exiled.

---

40 Ibid., 222.
41 Ibid.
42 Ibid., 223.

How Long was Muhammad in Mecca?

On Muhammad's departure from Mecca, Ibn Sa'd once again notes some uncertainty about exactly how long the prophet of Islam had been there. He attributes to Aisha and Ibn Abbas the statement that Muhammad "remained in Makkah for ten years, during which period the Qur'an was revealed to him, and he stayed at al-Madinah (also) for ten years."[43] Nothing is said of the other three years that other accounts say filled out Muhammad's prophetic career.

However, Ibn Sa'd also includes another tradition, about which "Yahya Ibn Abbad and Affan Ibn Muslim informed us; they said: Hammad Ibn Salamah informed us; Ammar Ibn Abi Ammar the mawla of Banu Hashim informed us on the authority of Ibn Abbas: The Apostle of Allah remained in Makkah for fifteen years (out of which) for seven years he perceived effulgence and (divine) light and heard sounds; and for eight years he received revelations. Affan added in his narration that he stayed at al-Madinah for ten years."[44] So apparently, the same Ibn Abbas said that Muhammad stayed in Mecca for ten years after Gabriel first appeared to him and also that he stayed there for fifteen years.

The claim that Muhammad heard sounds and perceived the divine light for seven years before he received his first revelation and that his prophetic career in Mecca lasted only eight years flatly contradicts other accounts, with no possibility of harmonization. Yet Ibn Kathir repeats this tradition, among other contradictory ones, four centuries later, and it can be reconciled with another that Ibn Sa'd records, in which Muhammad's prophetic career lasted for eighteen years, rather than the more common twenty-three: "I heard al-Hasan, and he recited: 'And it is a Qur'an that We have divided, that thou mayst recite it unto mankind at intervals, and We have revealed it by successive revelations.' (Qur'an, 17:106) He (Ibn Abbas) said: Allah revealed the Qur'an in parts in succession, one part before the other, since He knew it will last forever among the people. It has reached us that between its first and last parts there was a difference of eighteen years. It was being revealed at Makkah for eight years before migration to al-Madinah, and for ten years there."[45]

---

43 Ibn Sa'd, op. cit., I, 259–60.
44 Ibid., I, 260.
45 Ibid.; Ibn Kathir, *The Life of Prophet Muhammad*, op. cit., 4, 370.

Four hundred years later, Ibn Kathir demonstrates that Muslims are still uncertain of the chronology. He quotes a tradition in which one of the Muslims recounts: "I asked Ibn Abbas how old the Messenger of God was the day he died. He replied, 'I did not know there was anyone in your tribe unaware of this.' I replied, 'I have asked people but received different replies. I wanted to know what you would say about it.' He asked, 'Can you count?' 'Yes,' I replied, 'Then take forty years at which point he received his mission. Then add fifteen he stayed on in Mecca feeling both secure and afraid, and ten more for his life in exile in Medina.'"[46]

Ibn Sa'd, meanwhile, also records several versions of the tradition that Muhammad stayed thirteen years in Mecca before the hijrah, which has become a staple of the canonical Islamic account of the life of the prophet of Islam. But these variants suggest yet again that this man's biography was being formulated by committee, or different committees in different areas, and while there was broad agreement about the overall story, there was no convergence on the details. There is no reason to give any more credence to the standard story that Muhammad spent thirteen years in Mecca and then ten in Medina than to any of these variants. They all come from the same sources, which are of roughly equivalent historical value.

The Covenant with the Jews

When Muhammad arrived in Medina, says Ibn Sa'd, the Muslims numbered "ninety persons, forty-five Muhajirs and forty-five Ansars."[47] But he isn't sure of this and adds: "It is also said: There were one hundred and fifty Muhajirs and fifty Ansars."[48]

As one of the first orders of business in the Muslims' new home, Muhammad ordered a mosque to be built. He also entered into what Ibn Hisham calls a "friendly agreement with the Jews," in which he "established them in their religion and their property, and stated the reciprocal obligations" of both the Jews and the Muslims.[49]

---

46 Ibn Kathir, *The Life of Prophet Muhammad*, op. cit., 4, 370.
47 Ibn Sa'd, op. cit., I, 279.
48 Ibid.
49 Ibid., 231.

Among the directions Muhammad gave to the Muslims was an uncompromising affirmation that a Muslim's first loyalty was to his fellow Muslims: "A believer shall not slay a believer for the sake of an unbeliever, nor shall he aid an unbeliever against a believer.... Believers are friends one to the other to the exclusion of outsiders."[50] This did not mean that alliances with outsiders could not be made: "To the Jew who follows us belong help and equality. He shall not be wronged nor shall his enemies be aided."[51] This was predicated on the alliance being maintained: "The Jews shall contribute to the cost of war so long as they are fighting alongside the believers.... The Jews must bear their expenses and the Muslims their expenses. Each must help the other against anyone who attacks the people of this document. They must seek mutual advice and consultation, and loyalty is a protection against treachery."[52] Meanwhile, "Quraysh and their helpers shall not be given protection."[53]

Changing the Qibla

All was apparently not harmonious, however, between the Muslims and their new Jewish allies. Ibn Sa'd notes that when Muhammad emigrated to Medina, the Muslims were in the habit of facing Jerusalem for prayers and continued to do so for sixteen months in their new home. Ibn Sa'd quotes one source as saying that Muhammad offered prayers facing Jerusalem "for sixteen months after his arrival at al-Madinah; then it was changed in the direction of the Ka'bah two months before (the Battle of) Badr."[54] Mentioning the Battle of Badr, the first full-scale conflict between the Muslims and the Quraysh of Mecca, suggested that the change in the qibla had something to do with Muhammad's ultimate plan to conquer and Islamize Mecca. When the change came, however, the Ka'ba contained, according to Islamic tradition, 360 idols of the pagan Arabs. Thus, it was a curious choice as a place for the Muslims to face in prayer.

Nevertheless, Ibn Sa'd also quotes sources saying that Muhammad maintained prayer in the direction of Jerusalem for seventeen months after the hijrah, and finally, one that says it was for "sixteen or seventeen

50 Ibid., 232.
51 Ibid.
52 Ibid., 232–3.
53 Ibid., 233.
54 Ibn Sa'd, op. cit., I, 284.

months."[55] Ibn Hisham says that the change came "at the beginning of
the seventeenth month after the apostle's arrival in Medina."[56] He also
notes that "it is said that the Qibla was changed in Sha'ban," the eighth
month of the Arabic and Islamic calendar, "at the beginning of the eighteenth month after the apostle's arrival in Medina," suggesting that the
change was not instantaneously accepted, as other accounts suggest.[57]

The change came, according to Ibn Sa'd, because Muhammad was
unhappy with this arrangement. He "wished that the direction be
changed to the Ka'bah."[58] So he asked Gabriel to help him persuade
Allah to make the change: "O Gabriel! I wish that Allah may change my
facing towards the *qiblah* [direction for prayer] of the Jews."[59] Why he
no longer wanted the Muslims to face the same direction that the Jews
faced for prayers is not explained.

Gabriel replies: "I am only a servant, pray to your Lord and request
Him (for the change)."[60] Muhammad duly prays, and Allah quickly
answers his prayer with a revelation of a Qur'anic passage that emphasizes how important Muhammad's happiness is to Allah: "We have seen
the turning of your face to heaven. And now indeed we will make you
turn toward a qibla that is dear to you. So turn your face toward the
sacred mosque, and you, wherever you may be, turn your faces toward
it. Indeed, those who have received the book know this is the truth from
their Lord. And Allah is not unaware of what they do" (2:144).

According to Ibn Sa'd, the new direction for prayer caused friction
with the Muslims' new allies in Medina: "The Jews and the people of
the scripture (ahli-Kitab) liked him when he offered prayers with his
face towards Bayt al-Muqaddas [that is, Jerusalem]. When he turned his
face towards the Ka'bah, they began to dislike it."[61] Ibn Hisham says that
some of the Jewish leaders of Medina "came to the apostle asking why
he had turned his back on the qibla he used to face when he alleged that
he followed the religion of Abraham. If he would return to the qibla in
Jerusalem they would follow him and declare him to be true. Their sole

---

55 Ibid.
56 Ibn Ishaq, op. cit., 258.
57 Ibid., 289.
58 Ibn Sa'd, op. cit., I, 283.
59 Ibid.
60 Ibid.
61 Ibn Sa'd, op. cit., I, 286–7.

intention was to seduce him from his religion."[62] Much later, Ibn Kathir recounts that "the foolish people—the Jews—asked 'What could it be that turned them from the prayer direction they had previously?'"[63]

Allah accordingly scolded the miscreants in a new Qur'anic revelation: "The foolish among the people will say, What has turned them from the qibla which they formerly observed? Say, To Allah belong the East and the West. He guides whom he wills to a straight path" (2:142). He also consoles his prophet: "And even if you brought all kinds of signs to those who have been given the book, they would not follow your qibla. Nor can you be a follower of their qibla. Nor are some of them followers of the qibla of others. And if you followed their desires after the knowledge which has come to you, then surely you were among the evildoers. Those to whom we gave the book recognize this as they recognize their sons. But indeed, a party of them knowingly conceals the truth" (2:145–6).

As the Qur'an depicts the change of the qibla as a command of Allah, it is not surprising that a hadith would depict the Muslims (as opposed to the Jews) accepting the change immediately and with total alacrity. Anas ibn Malik, one of Muhammad's companions, is depicted as recalling that Muhammad prayed toward Jerusalem until Qur'an 2:144 was revealed. Then, one of the Muslims happened upon a group of his coreligionists praying the dawn prayer. "He said in a loud voice: 'Listen! The Qibla has been changed,' and they turned towards (the new) Qibla (Ka'ba) in that very state."[64]

Ibn Sa'd agrees that the change was accepted instantaneously and without question: "Then he turned his face towards the mizab [a waterspout at the top of the building] of the Ka'bah. It is said that the Apostle of Allah offered two rakahs of al-Zuhr (afternoon) prayers in his mosque with the Muslims; then he was commanded (through a revelation) to turn his face towards the inviolable place of worship (Ka'bah), so he turned towards it and the Muslims also turned their faces with him."[65] (Rakahs were and are the prescribed prayers and accompanying movements involved in Islamic prayer; each of the five daily prayers consists of a number of rakahs.) Ibn Sa'd also includes several other stories of

62 Ibn Ishaq, op. cit., 259.
63 Ibn Kathir, *The Life of Prophet Muhammad*, op. cit., 2, 248.
64 Sahih Muslim, book 5, no. 527.
65 Ibn Sa'd, op. cit., I, 284.

Muslims hearing about the change in the qibla and accepting it readily, without the slightest hint of hesitation or complaint.

Muhammad is also depicted as going to the Quba mosque in Medina and personally changing the qibla by making "alterations in the wall of the mosque in its present position."[66] He explained: "Gabriel points out the direction of the Ka'bah to me."[67] According to Ibn Sa'd, it was said that when Allah spoke in the Qur'an about a building that was founded upon "duty to Allah and his good pleasure" (9:109), he was referring to this mosque in Medina.

Two Qiblas?

Yet other hadiths suggest that some of the Muslims continued to pray toward Jerusalem, or at least not toward Mecca. Muhammad was aware of this and apparently tolerated it. Ibn Hisham records a strange tradition in which Muhammad corrects a Muslim who is praying facing the Ka'ba instead of toward Jerusalem. To be sure, this was before Allah made the change in the qibla from Jerusalem to Mecca, but Muhammad gives no indication that praying facing Mecca would be dear to him, as Allah says when announcing the change in Qur'an 2:144.

The story is told about a Muslim named al-Bara b. Marur, who says to several other Muslims during the time before the hijrah, when the Muslims prayed facing Jerusalem: "I have come to a conclusion and I don't know whether you will agree with me or not. I think that I will not turn my back on this building" (meaning the Ka'ba), "and that I shall pray towards it."[68] The Muslims who were with him "replied that so far as we knew our prophet prayed towards Syria and we did not wish to act differently."[69] Al-Bara b. Mariir was unmoved and reiterated his stance: "I am going to pray towards the Ka'ba."[70] The others again refused to join him in this, adding: "We blamed him for what he was doing, but he refused to change."[71]

When this party arrived in Mecca, al-Bara b. Mariir revealed that he was having misgivings: "Let us go to the apostle and ask him about

---

66 Ibid., 287.
67 Ibid.
68 Ibn Ishaq, op. cit., 202.
69 Ibid.
70 Ibid.
71 Ibid.

what I did on our journey. For I feel some misgivings since I have seen your opposition."[72] Finding Muhammad at the Ka'ba, al-Bara said to him: "O prophet of God, I came on this journey God having guided me to Islam and I felt that I could not turn my back on this building, so I prayed towards it; but when my companions opposed me I felt some misgivings. What is your opinion, O apostle of God?"[73] Muhammad was not happy with al-Bara's qibla and said: "You would have had a qibla if you had kept to it."[74] Al-Bara then, according to the story, "returned to the apostle's qibla and prayed with us towards Syria."[75] Then, however, comes a contrary witness: "But his people assert that he prayed towards the Ka'ba until the day of his death; but this was not so. We know more about that than they."[76]

This is an odd story, for if Muhammad himself proclaimed that Allah had changed the qibla to the Ka'ba soon after this, why would al-Bara have continued to pray toward Syria when he himself had been praying facing the Ka'ba even before the change came that validated his direction for prayer? Wasn't al-Bara and his community aware that the change had been made? Why did he persist in praying presumably toward Jerusalem when the rest of the Muslims had abandoned the practice? Is it possible that this tradition reflects a situation before the Qur'anic command to pray toward Mecca had been issued at all and demonstrates that such a command could not actually have been issued at the time when traditionally it has been understood to have been made? Is it possible that the early believers had more than one qibla at the same time and that the al-Bara tradition reflects that situation, while the Qur'anic command is a later attempt to standardize the practice of the believers?

Other traditions appear to assert that Muhammad at least temporarily allowed both qiblas. One hadith states: "The Messenger of Allah has forbidden us to face the two qiblahs at the time of urination or excretion."[77] The two qiblas are presumably Jerusalem and Mecca, but this is left unstated. The idea that there would be two qiblas after Allah himself specifically commanded that Muslims pray facing one direction and not the other is extremely strange, but that is left unexplained as well.

---

72 Ibid.
73 Ibid.
74 Ibid.
75 Ibid.
76 Ibid.
77 Sunan Abi Dawud, book 1, no. 10.

Yet Muhammad is also depicted saying: "Two *qiblas* in one land are not right, and no *jizya* is to be levied on a Muslim."[78] This would not need to be said unless there were some ninth-century people, two hundred years after the qibla is supposed to have been changed from Jerusalem to Mecca, who believed that there were two qiblas, and that both that were equally valid. These people were compounding their infractions against the word of the Qur'an by also collecting jizya from Muslims, when the Qur'an specifies (9:29) that it is to be levied upon the subject people of the book, that is, Jews, Christians, and Zoroastrians. Anas ibn Malik was apparently one of the holdouts: "None remains of those who prayed facing both Qiblas (that is, Jerusalem and Mecca) except myself."[79] The parenthetical "Jerusalem and Mecca" was added by the English translator; the Arabic original does not state what the two qiblas specifically were.

Ibn Sa'd records a tradition that apparently tries to explain away the existence of two qiblas by asserting that this was simply a reference to the change from Jerusalem to Mecca: "The Apostle of Allah, may Allah bless him, visited Umm Bishr Ibn al-Bara Ibn Ma'rur in (the quarter of) Banu Salamah." This was apparently the wife of al-Bara, who prayed facing Mecca before the other Muslims were commanded to do so. "She prepared food for him, and the time of al-Zuhr (prayers) approached. So the Apostle of Allah, may Allah bless him, led the Companions, in prayers and performed two rakahs. Then he was commanded to turn his face towards the Ka'bah. So he turned to the Ka'bah with his face towards the spout. (For this reason) the mosque was known as the mosque of the two qiblahs."[80]

Yet this wouldn't have meant that the mosque continued to mark two directions for prayer or that some of the believers continued to pray in the original direction. These ninth-century traditions suggest that the direction for prayer was still a live controversy at the time that the hadiths were compiled and the inauthentic ones supposedly winnowed out. Yet if the Qur'an had been well known and widely memorized among Muslims by this time, it is hard to see how there could possibly have been any argument or confusion over the plain words of Allah in his

---

78 Mishkat al-Masabih, book 19, no. 4037; see also Jami at-Tirmidhi, vol. 2, book 7, no. 633; Sunan Abi Dawud, book 19, no. 3032.
79 Sahih Bukhari, vol. 6, book 65, no. 4489.
80 Ibn Sa'd, op. cit.

perfect book. The apparent fact that these controversies did take place suggests that the Qur'anic text may not have been solidified by the time these hadiths were fabricated; 2:144 may have been an attempt to resolve an ongoing controversy.

Supporting this idea is another odd fact: while the Qur'an presents the change of the qibla as an utterance of Allah specifically made in order to please Muhammad, a hadith depicts Muhammad himself not observing it. One has a companion of Muhammad, Jabir bin Abdullah, saying: "The Prophet used to offer the Nawafil," a special, non-obligatory prayer, "while riding, facing a direction other than that of the Qibla."[81] Thus, it became Islamic Δ172

law that one need not face the qibla to pray non-obligatory prayers while traveling.[82] Here is a clear example of a hadith being invented in order to settle a disputed question that arose from the day-to-day practice of the new faith; some of the Muslims were apparently wondering if they had to face Mecca for all prayers without exception, no matter the circumstances, and this hadith was invented to settle the matter.

Hadiths that were meant to settle disputed questions, however, did not always accomplish what they were intended to do. Another hadith has Muhammad disregarding laws he himself is supposed to have made. The law is supposed to have been transmitted from one of the Ansar, Muhammad's early followers in Medina: "Yahya related to me from Malik from one of the Ansar that the Messenger of Allah forbade defecating or urinating while facing the qibla."[83] Yet the same Jabir bin Abdullah to whom is attributed the hadith in which Muhammad is not facing the qibla while praying supererogatory prayers is depicted as also saying this: "The Prophet of Allah forbade us to face the qiblah at the time of making water. Then I saw him facing it (qiblah) urinating or easing himself one year before his death."[84] One of the other early Muslims, Abdullah ibn Umar, the son of the future caliph Umar and brother of Muhammad's wife Hafsa, recalls: "I went up to the roof of the house of

81 Sahih Bukhari, vol. 2, book 18, no. 1094.
82 "Situations in which the obligation to face the qiblah is waived," Islam Question & Answer, December 25, 2004, https://islamqa.info/en/answers/65853/situations-in-which-the-obliga-tion-to-face-the-qiblah-is-waived.
83 Muwatta Malik, book 14, hadith 459.
84 Sunan Abi Dawud, book 1, hadith 13.

my sister Hafsa and saw the Messenger of Allah relieving himself facing Syria, with his back to the Qibla."[85]

Still another hadith has Muhammad acting directly against the command he himself is supposed to have issued. Aisha is depicted as recounting that "mention was made in the presence of the Messenger of Allah of some people who did not like to face towards the Qiblah with their private parts. He said: 'I think that they do that. Turn my seat (in the toilet) to face the Qiblah.'"[86] Apparently, one group of Muslims found the command about neither facing toward or away from the qibla while urinating or defecating to be onerous and did their best to mitigate it by showing Muhammad himself contravening it.

Antagonism with the Jews

The change of the direction in which Muslims prayed was not the only cause of growing antagonism between the Muslims and their putative allies, the Jews of Medina. Several hadiths indicate that from the beginning of the Muslims' residency in Medina, Muhammad asserted that they were more fully or properly Jews than the Jews themselves. One says that Muhammad "came to Medina and saw the Jews fasting on the day of Ashura. He asked them about that. They replied, 'This is a good day, the day on which Allah rescued Bani Israel from their enemy. So, Moses fasted this day.' The Prophet said, 'We have more claim over Moses than you.' So, the Prophet fasted on that day and ordered (the Muslims) to fast (on that day)."[87] The idea that the Muslims had more claim to Moses than the Jews was bound to cause tensions to rise.

Another hadith has Muhammad disparaging the religious understanding of both the Jews and the Christians. This episode began when the prophet of Islam "mentioned a matter," and then mused: "That will be at the time when knowledge departs."[88] One of the Muslims, Ziyad bin Labid, then asked him: "How can knowledge depart when we recite the Qur'an and teach it to our children and they will teach it to their children up till the day of resurrection?"[89] To this, Muhammad responded: "I am astonished at you, Ziyad. I thought you were the most learned

85 Sahih Muslim, vol. 2, book 2, no. 266b.
86 Sunan Ibn Majah, vol. 1, book 1, no. 324.
87 Sahih Bukhari, vol. 3, book 30, no. 2004.
88 Mishkat al-Masabih, 277, 278.
89 Ibid.

man in Medina. Do not these Jews and Christians read the Torah and the Injil [Gospel] without knowing a thing about their contents?"[90]

Despite this rhetoric, however, or ignorant of it, Ibn Hisham ascribes the growing rift between the Jews and the Muslims entirely to the Jews' chauvinism: "About this time the Jewish rabbis showed hostility to the apostle in envy, hatred, and malice, because God had chosen His apostle from the Arabs."[91] Some of the Medinan Muslims joined them in their hostility, which Ibn Hisham explains as stemming from their desire to maintain their polytheism. Since the Jews were not polytheists, this was an odd alliance, apparently based on the principle of "the enemy of my enemy is my friend."

Ibn Hisham explains that the Jews "were joined by men from al-Aws and al-Khazraj who had obstinately clung to their heathen religion. They were hypocrites, clinging to the polytheism of their fathers and denying the resurrection; yet when Islam appeared and their people flocked to it they were compelled to pretend to accept it to save their lives. But in secret they were hypocrites whose inclination was towards the Jews because they considered the apostle a liar and strove against Islam."[92]

Muhammad, meanwhile, "invited the Jews to Islam and made it attractive to them and warned them of God's jealousy and His retribution."[93] In response, however, the Jews "repulsed him and denied what he brought them."[94] They would try to trip up the prophet of Islam with sly questions, but Allah himself would often intervene to answer: "It was the Jewish rabbis who used to annoy the apostle with questions and introduce confusion, so as to confound the truth with falsity. The Quran used to come down in reference to these questions of theirs, though some of the questions about what was allowed and forbidden came from the Muslims themselves."[95]

One of the rabbis is depicted as reminding his colleagues that they know Muhammad is a true prophet and are just being obstinate: "Fear God, for you know right well that he is the apostle of God and you used to speak of him to us before his mission and describe him to us."[96]

---

90 Ibid.
91 Ibn Ishaq, op. cit., 239.
92 Ibid.
93 Ibid., 266.
94 Ibid.
95 Ibid., 239.
96 Ibid., 266.

One of the others, however, denied this: "We never said that to you, and God has sent down no book since Moses nor sent an evangelist or warner after him."[97] This prompted Allah to deliver a new revelation in response: "O people of the book, now our messenger has come to you to make things clear to you after an interval between the messengers, so that you would not say, No messenger of good news or any warner came to us. Now a messenger of good news and a warner has come to you. Allah is able to do all things" (Qur'an 5:19).

Amid all this stubborn refusal to recognize Muhammad as a prophet, however, Ibn Hisham notes that one of the rabbis was far more positive toward Muhammad. Abdullah bin Salam recounted: "When I heard about the apostle I knew by his description, name, and the time at which he appeared that he was the one we were waiting for, and I rejoiced greatly thereat, though I kept silent about it until the apostle came to Medina."[98] He told his aunt that Muhammad was "the brother of Moses and follows his religion, being sent with the same mission."[99]

Abdullah quickly became a Muslim but kept his conversion a secret from the other Jews. Then he went to Muhammad and told him: "The Jews are a nation of liars and I wish you would take me into one of your houses and hide me from them, Then ask them about me so that they may tell you the position I hold among them before they know that I have become a Muslim. For if they know it beforehand they will utter slanderous lies against me."[100] The Jews fell right into this trap, telling Muhammad, "He is our chief, and the son of our chief; our rabbi, and our learned man" before they learned that Abdullah had become Muslim, and reviling him as a liar after Abdullah confronted them with his conversion.[101] Abdullah continued: "Then I reminded the apostle that I had said that they would do this, for they were a treacherous, lying, and evil people."[102]

Bukhari records a hadith that asserts that before Abdullah bin Salam converted to Islam, he gave Muhammad a test: "I will ask you about three things which nobody knows unless he be a prophet. Firstly, what

---

97 Ibid.
98 Ibid., 240.
99 Ibid.
100 Ibid., 241.
101 Ibid.
102 Ibid.

is the first portent of the Hour? What is the first meal of the people of Paradise? And what makes a baby look like its father or mother?"[103] This account was ridiculous on its face, for Abdullah could not have known that Muhammad's answers were correct unless he himself was also a prophet. But the story is apparently unaware of this absurdity and intended to establish that Muhammad was indeed a prophet and that this was known to the Jews who broke with the majority of their leaders by being honest enough to admit it.

Muhammad responds: "Just now Gabriel has informed me about that," a claim that elicits yet another antisemitic statement from Abdullah: Gabriel, he says, "among the angels is the enemy of the Jews."[104] This becomes the occasion for Muhammad to receive another revelation: "Say, Who is an enemy to Gabriel? For it is he who has revealed this to your heart by Allah's permission, confirming what was before it, and a guidance and good news to believers" (Qur'an 2:97). Muhammad then gives Abdullah the correct answers to his questions: "As for the first portent of the Hour, it will be a fire that will collect the people from the East to West. And as for the first meal of the people of Paradise, it will be the caudite (i.e. extra) lobe of the fish liver. And if a man's discharge proceeded that of the woman, then the child resembles the father, and if the woman's discharge proceeded that of the man, then the child resembles the mother."[105]

Most of the Jewish leaders remained unconvinced, and soon, Muhammad decided to turn the tables and put them to his own test.

---

103 Sahih Bukhari, vol. 6, book 65, no. 4480.
104 Ibid.
105 Ibid.

CHAPTER SEVEN

Jews, Christians, Hypocrites, Polytheists

Women and Men Taken in Adultery

Muhammad's opportunity to challenge the Jews came soon after the Muslims' arrival in Medina, and according to Ibn Hisham, came when the rabbis tried to subject him to another test. "A married man had committed adultery with a married woman," and rather than judge the case themselves, the rabbis said: "Send them to Muhammad and ask him what the law about them is and leave the penalty to him. If he prescribes *tajbih* (which is scourging with a rope of palm fiber smeared with pitch, the blackening of their faces, mounting on two donkeys with their faces to the animal's tail) then follow him, for he is a king and believe in him. If he prescribes stoning for them, he is a prophet so beware lest he deprive you of what you hold."[1] It is noteworthy that the rabbis instructed their followers to reject Muhammad if he proved to be a prophet; this was designed to illustrate that the Jews were inveterate enemies of Allah, determined to rebel against him.

The rabbis took the guilty couple to Muhammad and explained the situation to them. They designated one of their own, Abdullah ibn Suriya, "the most learned man living in the Torah," to deal with Muhammad on this issue.[2] Muhammad got right to the point, asking Abdullah b. Suriya if the Torah did not call for adulterers to be stoned to death. Abdullah conceded that it did, whereupon Muhammad peremptorily commanded that the pair be stoned to death. Ibn Hisham records,

---

1 Ibn Ishaq, op. cit., 266.
2 Ibid.

without comment or emotion, a tragic scene: "When the Jew felt the first stone he crouched over the woman to protect her from the stones until both of them were killed. This is what God did for the apostle in exacting the penalty for adultery from the pair."[3]

Despite the fact that the rabbis had said among themselves that a sentence of stoning would indicate that Muhammad was indeed a prophet, ibn Suriya then "disbelieved and denied that the apostle was a prophet."[4] This brought yet another revelation from Allah, consoling Muhammad: "O messenger, do not let those who compete with one another in the race to disbelief grieve you, of those who say with their mouths, We believe, but their hearts do not believe, and of the Jews, listeners for the sake of falsehood, listeners on behalf of other people who do not come to you, changing words from their context and saying: If this is given to you, receive it, but if this is not given to you, then beware. He whom Allah dooms to sin, you will not help him at all against Allah. Those are the ones for whom the will of Allah is that he does not cleanse their hearts. Theirs will be disgrace in this world, and in the hereafter an awful doom" (Qur'an 5:41).

Ibn Hisham then offers a different version of this story, in which Muhammad, in giving his judgment about what should be done with the adulterous couple, "asked for a Torah."[5] There was a copy right at hand, for "a rabbi sat there reading it having put his hand over the verse of stoning." Then, the rabbi who had converted to Islam and accused the Jews of being liars, Abdullah bin Salam, "struck the rabbi's hand, saying, 'This, O prophet of God, is the verse of stoning which he refuses to read to you.'"[6] Muhammad then called out: "Woe to you Jews! What has induced you to abandon the judgment of God which you hold in your hands?"[7] They answered that it was all about giving special favors to men of privilege and power: "The sentence used to be carried out until a man of royal birth and noble origin committed adultery and the king refused to allow him to be stoned. Later another man committed adultery and the king wanted him to be stoned but they said No, not until you stone

---

3 Ibid., 267.
4 Ibid.
5 Ibid.
6 Ibid.
7 Ibid.

so-and-so. And when they said that to him they agreed to arrange the matter by tajbih and they did away with all mention of stoning."[8]

Muhammad swept away what seemed to him to be hypocrisy and impiety and proclaimed: "I am the first to revive the order of God and His book and to practice it."[9] In this version also, the couple was stoned to death, and one of the Muslims boasted: "I was among those that stoned them."[10]

In one tradition, Muhammad stones a man to death by his own request. This man, Ma'iz ibn Malik, "came to the Prophet and testified four times against himself that he had had illicit intercourse with a woman," but Muhammad did not appear to be willing to hear about this: "all the time the Prophet was turning away from him."[11] When, however, the guilt-ridden man "confessed a fifth time," Muhammad turned toward him and asked: "Did you have intercourse with her?"[12] When the man replied that he had, Muhammad asked him additional questions to make sure that he realized exactly what he was confessing. The man replied yes to each. Then Muhammad asked him: "What do you want from what you have said?"[13] The man responded: "I want you to purify me."[14] At this, Muhammad "gave orders regarding him and he was stoned to death."[15]

One of Muhammad's companions was incredulous at this, saying: "Look at this man whose fault was concealed by Allah but who would not leave the matter alone, so that he was stoned like a dog."[16] To this, Muhammad "said nothing to them but walked on for a time till he came to the corpse of an ass with its legs in the air." Then he asked his companion who had marveled at the man who wanted to be stoned to death: "Go down and eat some of this ass's corpse."[17] Astonished, the companion said: "Messenger of Allah! Who can eat any of this?"[18] To that,

---

8 Ibid.
9 Ibid.
10 Ibid.
11 Sunan Abi Dawud, book 40, no. 4428. See also Sunan Abi Dawud, book 40, nos. 4422, 4425, 4431.
12 Sunan Abi Dawud, book 40, no. 4428.
13 Ibid.
14 Ibid.
15 Ibid.
16 Ibid.
17 Ibid.
18 Ibid.

Muhammad replied: "The dishonor you have just shown to your brother is more serious than eating some of it. By Him in Whose hand my soul is, he is now among the rivers of Paradise and plunging into them."[19] The sinful Ma'iz ibn Malik had won a place in paradise by submitting to the judgment of Allah. In another version of this tradition, however, Muhammad is less charitable toward the dead man: "People began to speak ill of him but he (the Prophet) forbade them. Then they began to ask forgiveness from him, but he forbade them by saying. He is a man who had committed a sin. Allah will call him to account himself."[20]

This tradition is similar to one in which a woman, rather than a man, comes to Muhammad insisting on confessing her sin and being stoned to death for it. Sunan Abi Dawud records two versions of this; in one, she is "a woman belonging to the tribe of Juhaynah (according to the version of Aban)," and in the other, she is "a woman of Ghamid."[21] This story closely follows the trajectory of the account of Ma'iz ibn Malik: she goes to Muhammad and says, "I have committed fornication."[22] He tells her: "Go back," but she returns the next day and even says to Muhammad: "Perhaps you want to send me back as you did to Ma'iz b. Malik."[23] The other version of this story makes no reference to Ma'iz, however, and the woman's mention of him here may be an attempt to explain the existence of two accounts that are so similar as to make it likely that they are two versions of the same original story.

In the female version of the story, the woman tells Muhammad: "I swear by Allah, I am pregnant."[24] Muhammad tells her: "Go back until you give birth to a child."[25] When she gives birth, she brings the child to Muhammad, who tells her: "Go back, and suckle him until you wean him."[26] Once the boy could eat solid food, she returned to Muhammad. Then: "The boy was then given to a certain man of the Muslims and he (the Prophet) commanded regarding her. So a pit was dug for her, and he gave orders about her and she was stoned to death."[27] When a drop

---

19 Ibid.
20 Sunan Abi Dawud, book 40, no. 4432.
21 Sunan Abi Dawud, book 40, no. 4440; Sunan Abi Dawud, book 40, no. 4442.
22 Sunan Abi Dawud, book 40, no. 4442.
23 Ibid.
24 Ibid.
25 Ibid.
26 Ibid.
27 Ibid.

of her blood splashed onto the cheek of one of the men, stoning her, "he abused her."[28] Muhammad admonished him as he had those who abused Ma'iz after his death: "Gently, Khalid. By Him in whose hand my soul is, she has reported to such an extent that if one who wrongfully takes extra tax were to repent to a like extent, he would be forgiven. Then giving command regarding her, prayed over her and she was buried."[29]

Sahih Muslim includes a tradition that includes both the story of Ma'iz bin Malik and the account of this "woman from Ghamid," who refers to Ma'iz as she is dealing with Muhammad and trying to persuade him to stone her to death.[30] This could be an attempt to harmonize the two stories, but it could also be an earlier version of the story from which the separate accounts developed.

Although several traditions feature men being stoned to death, another hadith has Muhammad stipulating that stoning is only for women, while male adulterers are only to be lashed. A man named Unais approached the prophet of Islam with a request: "Judge us according to Allah's Law and kindly allow me (to speak)."[31] When Muhammad agreed, Unais continued:

My son was a laborer working for this man and he committed an illegal sexual intercourse with his wife, and I gave one-hundred sheep and a slave as a ransom for my son's sin. Then I asked a learned man about this case and he informed me that my son should receive one hundred lashes and be exiled for one year, and the man's wife should be stoned to death.[32]

"Illegal sexual intercourse with his wife" could refer to fornication before they were married or to anal sex. Muhammad responded: "By Him in Whose Hand my soul is, I will judge you according to the Laws of Allah. Your one-hundred sheep and the slave are to be returned to you, and your son has to receive one-hundred lashes and be exiled for one year. O Unais! Go to the wife of this man, and if she confesses, then

28 Ibid.
29 Ibid.
30 Sahih Muslim, book 29, no. 1695b.
31 Sahih Bukhari, vol. 8, book 85, no. 6827, 6828.
32 Ibid.

stone her to death."[33] The hadith continues: "Unais went to her and she confessed. He then stoned her to death."[34]

Yet despite the fact that the hadith literature asserts that several passages of the Qur'an were revealed in the context of the controversy with the Jews over stoning adulterers and that in this controversy itself, Muhammad and the Muslims are depicted as being faithful to the command of Allah to stone adulterers that Jews wish to conceal and ignore, there is no such command in the Qur'an. The Qur'an stipulates lashing only: "The adulterer and the adulteress, lash each one of them a hundred times. And do not let pity for the two prevent you from obedience to Allah, if you believe in Allah and the last day. And let a group of believers witness their punishment" (24:2).

A hadith attributed to the caliph Umar, however, insists that there once was such a passage in the Islamic holy book and that even though it is no longer present there, the command still stands. Umar is depicted as saying: "I am afraid that after a long time has passed, people may say, 'We do not find the Verses of the Rajam (stoning to death) in the Holy Book,' and consequently they may go astray by leaving an obligation that Allah has revealed. Lo! I confirm that the penalty of Rajam be inflicted on him who commits illegal sexual intercourse, if he is already married and the crime is proved by witnesses or pregnancy or confession."[35] He added, "Surely Allah's Messenger carried out the penalty of Rajam, and so did we after him."[36]

Such a hadith is clearly intended to account for the alteration of the Qur'an, although no explanation is offered for why the command for stoning was once in the book and is no longer. This hadith establishes the Muslims in a situation that is the exact opposite of the Jews as depicted in the hadiths about this controversy: the command for stoning is in the Jews' scriptures, but they attempt to conceal it. That same command is not in the Muslims' scriptures, but they behave as if it were and consider stoning to be divinely mandated anyway.

In the Qur'an and hadiths, then, there is a tradition mandating the lashing of both male and female adulterers, as well as traditions calling for the stoning of women but not of men and traditions saying that both

---

33 Ibid.
34 Ibid.
35 Sahih Bukhari, vol. 8, book 86, no. 6829.
36 Ibid.

men and women should be stoned to death. These likely represent the position of various factions among the early Muslims; in Islamic law, the perspective that stoning is the proper penalty and that women, in particular, should be stoned has generally won out.

Challenging Muhammad

Ibn Hisham, meanwhile, depicts the Jews as continuing to devise stratagems to trip up the prophet of Islam. At one point, some of them agree on a plan: "Let us go to Muhammad to see if we can seduce him from his religion, for he is only a mortal."[37] They approached Muhammad with an offer: "You know, Muhammad, that we are the rabbis, nobles, and leaders of the Jews; and if we follow you, the rest of the Jews will follow you and not oppose us. Now we have a quarrel outstanding with some of our people and if we believe in you and say that you are truthful will you, if we appoint you arbitrator between us, give judgment in our favor?"[38] Muhammad refused, and Allah validated his refusal by revealing: "So judge between them by what Allah has revealed, and do not follow their desires, but beware of them, so that they do not seduce you from some part of what Allah has revealed to you. And if they turn away, then know that Allah's will is to afflict them for some sin of theirs. Indeed, many of mankind are transgressors. Is it a judgment from the time of ignorance that they are seeking? Who is better than Allah for judgment to a people that has certainty?" (Qur'an 5:49–50).

The Jewish leaders are also depicted as continuing to challenge Muhammad's claims. Some of them asked him: "Do you not allege that you follow the religion of Abraham and believe in the Torah which we have and testify that it is the truth from God?"[39] Muhammad answered by issuing his own challenge to them: "Certainly, but you have sinned and broken the covenant contained therein and concealed what you were ordered to make plain to men, and I dissociate myself from your sin."[40] When they deny this and insist that they "live according to the guidance and the truth," Allah supplies a new revelation: "Say, O people of the book, you have nothing until you observe the Torah and the Gospel and

---

37 Ibn Ishaq, op. cit., 268.
38 Ibid.
39 Ibid.
40 Ibid.

what was revealed to you from your Lord. What is revealed to you from your Lord is certain to increase the insolence and disbelief of many of them. But do not grieve for the disbelieving people" (Qur'an 5:68).[41]

Ibn Hisham even improbably depicts the Jews as polytheists. Some of the Jewish leaders ask Muhammad: "Do you not know that there is another god with God?"[42] Allah answers this with yet another revelation: "Say, What carries the most weight in testimony? Say, Allah is the witness between me and you. And this Qur'an has been inspired in me so that with it I may warn you and whomever it may reach. Do you actually bear witness that there are gods besides Allah? Say, I bear no such witness. Say, He is only one God. Indeed, I am innocent of what you associate" (Qur'an 6:19).

Continuing with this odd and baseless charge of polytheism among the Jews, other Jewish leaders are depicted as asking Muhammad: "How can we follow you when you have abandoned our Qibla and you do not allege that Uzayr [Ezra] is the son of God?"[43] Once again, Allah supplies an apposite revelation: "And the Jews say, Ezra is the son of Allah, and the Christians say, The Messiah is the son of Allah. That is their saying with their mouths. They imitate the statements of those who disbelieved before. May Allah curse them. How perverse they are" (Qur'an 9:30).

A hadith likewise has Muhammad saying that on the Day of Resurrection, the Jews "will be called upon and it will be said to them, 'Who do you use to worship?' They will say, 'We used to worship Ezra, the son of Allah.' It will be said to them, 'You are liars, for Allah has never taken anyone as a wife or a son. What do you want now?' They will say, 'O our Lord! We are thirsty, so give us something to drink.' They will be directed and addressed thus, 'Will you drink,' whereupon they will be gathered unto Hell (Fire) which will look like a mirage whose different sides will be destroying each other. Then they will fall into the Fire."[44]

Ibn Hisham adds another false claim to the one about Ezra, asserting that the message of Islam could be found in the Torah. The Jewish leaders ask Muhammad: "Is it true, Muhammad, that what you have brought is the truth from God? For our part we cannot see that it is

---

41 Ibid.
42 Ibid., 268–9.
43 Ibid., 269.
44 Sahih Bukhari, vol. 6, book 65, no. 4581.

arranged as the Torah is."[45] Muhammad responds: "You know quite well that it is from God; you will find it written in the Torah which you have. If men and jinn came together to produce its like they could not."[46] He adds: "You know well that it is from God and that I am the apostle of God. You will find it written in the Torah you have."[47] This corresponds to the Qur'anic injunction that the people of the book "have nothing until you observe the Torah and the Gospel" (5:68), but in fact, neither the Torah nor the Gospel contains teachings identical to those of the Qur'an. This gave rise to the common Islamic claim that the Jews and Christians dared to tamper with the texts of the revelations they received from Allah in order to remove correspondences with Islam and mentions of Muhammad, the great prophet who was to come.

Such claims, however, were unknown at the time of the composition of both the Qur'an and the traditions contained in Ibn Hisham's biography of Muhammad. Both take for granted that if the Jews and Christians follow honestly what is written in their scriptures, they will recognize Muhammad as a prophet and embrace Islam. This is the basis for the Qur'an's declaration that "the unbelievers among the people of the book and the idolaters will remain in the fire of Gehenna. They are the most vile of created beings" (98:6). The believers among the people of the book become Muslim. The unbelievers among the people of the book, hardened in their obstinacy, remain Jews and Christians.

A Christian Delegation from Najran

Around this time, another group of unbelievers among the people of the book, this time a delegation of Christians, journeyed from Najran in southern Arabia to meet with Muhammad. Ibn Sa'd places this meeting in the context of a series of meetings Muhammad had with the leaders of the various Arabian tribes after he called them to embrace Islam, but Ibn Hisham doesn't seem to be aware of any such meetings at this time.

Ibn Sa'd says these Christians from Najran were "a deputation consisting of fourteen members of their Christian nobles," but Ibn Hisham

---

45 Ibn Ishaq, op. cit., 269.
46 Ibid.
47 Ibid., 269–70.

states that there were "sixty riders, fourteen of them from their nobles."[48] Ibn Hisham adds that while the Christians were on their way to Medina, their bishop, Abu Haritha bin Alqama, acknowledged that Muhammad was a genuine prophet. One of the Christians cursed Muhammad, and Abu Haritha rebuked him. Asked why he had issued the rebuke, Abu Haritha said: "Because, by God, he is the prophet we have been waiting for."[49]

Abu Haritha was likely familiar with what Muhammad had been preaching. According to a hadith, the Christians of Najran had heard Muhammad's message and had already identified some problematic aspects of it. One of the Muslims, Mughira bin Shu'ba, had gone to Najran with the message of Islam; the Christians there asked him about Qur'an 19:28, in which Mary, the Mother of Jesus, is addressed by her own relatives as "sister of Aaron." Miriam was the sister of Aaron and Moses, and in Arabic, *Miriam* and *Mary* are both *Maryam*; the Qur'an thus appears to conflate the two and envisions Jesus as Moses's nephew. The Christians of Najran point out this error to Mughira, explaining that "Moses was born much before Jesus."[50]

Mughira goes back to Medina and asks Muhammad about this, and the prophet of Islam responds: "The (people of the old age) used to give names (to their persons) after the names of Apostles and pious persons who had gone before them."[51] Thus, "sister of Aaron" is supposed to be just an honorific, not a literal statement of their being blood relatives. The fact that this needed to be explained suggests that Muslims of the ninth century were encountering Christians who were pointing out mistakes in the Qur'an that needed to be answered. The explanation attributed to Muhammad, however, founders on the fact that the Qur'an also refers to Mary's mother as "Imran's wife" (3:35); Imran (Amram) was the father of Moses and Aaron. The Qur'an elsewhere refers to Mary as the "daughter of Imran" (66:12). The idea that these were all titles of honor strains credulity.

The Christian whom Abu Haritha tells that Muhammad is a true prophet responds: "Then if you know that, what stops you from

48 Ibid.; Ibn Sa'd, op. cit., I, 418.
49 Ibn Ishaq, op. cit., 271.
50 Sahih Muslim, book 38, no. 2135.
51 Ibid.

accepting him?"[52] Abu Haritha explained that he could not accept Muhammad because of "the way these people have treated us. They have given us titles, paid us subsidies, and honored us. But they are absolutely opposed to him, and if I were to accept him they would take from us all that you see."[53] Abu Haritha was apparently referring to money his community received from the Roman Empire in Constantinople. The other Christian was so scandalized by the idea that the delegation must reject Muhammad solely due to worldly considerations that he later converted to Islam and, according to Ibn Hisham, "used to tell this story, so I have heard."[54]

Ibn Sa'd does not appear to have heard that story, but he does relate that the Christians appeared in Muhammad's mosque dressed in their most elegant finery: "their garments were of hibrah cloth and their sheets had the patches of silk."[55] Ibn Hisham says that they "came into the apostle's mosque as he prayed the afternoon prayer clad in Yamani garments, cloaks, and mantles, with the elegance of men of B. al-Harith b. Ka'b," a southern Arabian tribe.[56] The Muslims were impressed: "The prophet's companions who saw them that day said that they never saw their like in any deputation that came afterwards."[57] Muhammad himself, however, was not pleased, perhaps sensing that the Christians were displaying in their dress the compensation they were receiving for rejecting him. Ibn Sa'd says that Muhammad allowed them to pray in the mosque, but when they approached him after the prayers, "he turned his face and did not talk to them."[58] Uthman then explained to the puzzled visitors that Muhammad had snubbed them because of the way they were dressed. They accordingly returned the next morning dressed as monks, whereupon Muhammad "invited them to embrace Islam. They declined so there ensued a long discourse and argumentations."[59]

According to Ibn Hisham, in the course of this argumentation, the Christians explained that "they were Christians according to the Byzantine rite, though they differed among themselves in some points, saying

52 Ibn Ishaq, op. cit.
53 Ibid.
54 Ibid.
55 Ibn Sa'd, op. cit., I, 419.
56 Ibn Ishaq, op. cit., 271.
57 Ibid.
58 Ibn Sa'd, op. cit., I, 419.
59 Ibid.

He is God; and He is the son of God; and He is the third person of the Trinity, which is the doctrine of Christianity."[60] This was not an accurate summation either of Christian doctrine or of the standard Islamic understanding of it. Orthodox Christianity does indeed teach that Jesus is the Son of God, who is fully divine, but holds that he is the second, not the third, person of the Trinity. Ibn Hisham, however, came closer to accuracy than the Qur'an, which depicts Allah asking: "O Jesus, son of Mary, did you say to mankind, Take me and my mother as two gods besides Allah?" (5:116) Jesus denies ever having done so, but it remains common to this day for Muslims to assume that the Trinity consists of Allah, Jesus, and Mary because the Qur'an says so.

Muhammad calls upon the Christians to submit to Allah, but they insist that they already have. Muhammad responds acidly: "'You lie. Your assertion that God has a son, your worship of the cross, and your eating pork hold you back from submission."[61] According to Ibn Sa'd, he is even more confrontational, saying: "If you contradict what I say then come on, we will curse each other."[62] The next morning, however, the Christians strike a conciliatory tone, saying to Muhammad: "We think it proper not to curse each other. You may order us as you like and we shall obey you and shall make peace with you."[63] The two concluded an agreement stipulating that the Christians of Najran would pay tribute to the Muslims in return for a declaration from Muhammad that they would receive his protection.

This was much like the Islamic legal system for the *dhimmis*, or protected people, that was beginning to be formulated around the time these traditions were composed. According to the Qur'an, the people of the book who have accepted the hegemony of the Muslims are to "pay the jizya with willing submission and feel themselves subdued" (9:29). In exchange for this payment, the subject people would receive a guarantee from the Muslims to protect their lives and property and allow them to practice their religions, within limits.

According to Ibn Hisham, the Christians of Najran concluded an agreement with the Muslims that is much like this. They agree to give Muhammad two thousand garments and to supply arms in case of a

---

60 Ibn Ishaq, op. cit.
61 Ibid.
62 Ibn Sa'd, op. cit.
63 Ibid.

conflict with other tribes in Yemen. In return, "for the Najran and their neighbors there is the protection of Allah and the guarantee of Muhammad, the Prophet, the Apostle of Allah, over their souls, creed, land, property, those of them who are not present and those who are present and their churches. No bishop will be changed from his bishopric, no monk from his monastery and no testator (waqif) from the property of his endowment."[64] The Christians then returned home, although two of them quickly returned to Medina and embraced Islam.

Ibn Hisham, however, knows of no such agreement, but he does know of the possibility of the Christians and Muslims parting under mutual curses. He has the Christians' leader tell the others: "O Christians, you know right well that Muhammad is a prophet sent (by God) and he has brought a decisive declaration about the nature of your master. You know, too, that a people has never invoked a curse on a prophet and seen its elders live and its youth grow up. If you do this you will be exterminated. But if you decide to adhere to your religion and to maintain your doctrine about your master, then take your leave of the man and go home."[65] They came to Muhammad and "told him that they had decided not to resort to cursing and to leave him in his religion and return home. But they would like him to send a man he could trust to decide between them in certain financial matters in dispute among them."[66] Muhammad accordingly sends a man to "judge between them faithfully in matters they dispute about," but there is no hint of the tribute payments Ibn Sa'd details.[67]

Abraham's Religion and Muhammad's

Along with the Jews and Christians, Ibn Hisham notes that Muhammad in Medina also had to deal with the hypocrites, people who converted to Islam outwardly but remained unbelievers inwardly and did their best to undermine the prophet of Islam. One of these was Abdullah bin Ubayy, who had expected to become the ruler of Medina until Muhammad came along. Abdullah's "people had made a sort of jeweled diadem to crown him and make him their king when God sent His apostle to

---

64 Ibid.
65 Ibn Ishaq, op. cit., 277.
66 Ibid.
67 Ibid.

them; so when his people forsook him in favor of Islam he was filled with enmity realizing that the apostle had deprived him of his kingship. However, when he saw that his people were determined to go over to Islam he went too, but unwillingly, retaining his enmity and dissimulating."[68]

Then, there was Abu Amir, whose objection to Muhammad was based on his religious message rather than his political power. Ibn Hisham says that Abu Amir "had been an ascetic in pagan days and had worn a coarse hair garment and was called 'the monk.'"[69] He was, however, not a Christian, but simply a monotheist who believed the Israelite patriarch Abraham to be the founding figure of his religion. Abu Amir, according to Ibn Hisham, "stubbornly refused to believe and abandoned his people when they went over to Islam and went off to Mecca with about ten followers to get away from Islam and the apostle."[70] Muhammad regarded him with contempt, saying: "Don't call him the monk but the evil-doer."[71]

In connection with Abu Amir, Ibn Hisham also records a significant and revealing tradition about the development of Islam itself. A Muslim about whom we are told that his "memory went back to apostolic days and who was a narrator of tradition" recounts "before he left for Mecca, Abu Amir came to the apostle in Medina to ask him about the religion he had brought."[72] Muhammad answers: "The Hanifiya, the religion of Abraham."[73] Abu Amir, however, objects to this, saying: "That is what I follow."[74] Muhammad replies curtly: "You do not."[75] Abu Amir, however, is insistent: "But I do! You, Muhammad, have introduced into the Hanifiya things which do not belong to it."[76] Muhammad denies the charge: "I have not. I have brought it pure and white."[77]

Ibn Hisham goes on to note that Abu Amir then declared, "May God let the liar die a lonely, homeless, fugitive!"[78] Ibn Hisham adds that Abu

68 Ibid., 278.
69 Ibid.
70 Ibid.
71 Ibid.
72 Ibid.
73 Ibid.
74 Ibid.
75 Ibid.
76 Ibid.
77 Ibid.
78 Ibid.

Amir was referring to Muhammad, "as if he had falsified his religion."[79] Muhammad, however, agrees, saying, "Well and good. May God so reward him!," and sure enough, when Muhammad conquered Arabia, Abu Amir "went to Syria and died there a lonely, homeless, fugitive."[80]

The Qur'an states that "Abraham was not a Jew, nor was he a Christian, but he was a Muslim hanif, and he was not one of the idolaters" (3:67). In Islamic theology, a hanif is a monotheist before the time of Muhammad. Muhammad himself, however, according to the Qur'an as well as the hadith and sira literature, insists that his religion is nothing more than the pure monotheism of Abraham, as the prophet of Islam in this story insists to Abu Amir. Abu Amir, however, maintains that Muhammad has "introduced into the Hanifiya things which do not belong to it."[81]

This tradition reflects an anxiety to assure people that Muhammad's religion is indeed simply pure Abrahamic monotheism and to silence charges to the contrary. At a time when the figure of Muhammad and the teachings of the religion of Islam were being developed and built upon this Abrahamic monotheism, such traditions would be necessary in order to silence the inevitable objections of those whose "memory went back to apostolic days."[82] This was the time when numerous innovations were being introduced among these monotheists, such as the late eighth-century recollection of an old man who said that "reading from the *mushaf*"—a copy of the Qur'an—"at the Mosque was not done by people in the past. It was Hajjaj b. Yusuf who first instituted it."[83] People with such long memories had to be reassured that while it may appear that all manner of new beliefs and practices were being introduced, in fact, that was not the case, and those who made such claims were actually, like Abu Amir, the ones who were in the wrong.

Raiding the Quraysh

Rather than set up his followers in their new community as farmers or merchants, Muhammad, according to Ibn Hisham, began a series of raids on the Quraysh of Mecca. The Muslims would live off what they

---

79 Ibid.
80 Ibid.
81 Ibid.
82 Ibid.
83 Ali al-Samhudi, Wafa al-Wafa bi-akhbar dar al-Mustafa, op. cit.

were able to seize from the polytheists of Mecca, who had dared to reject the prophetic claim of their kinsman. Ibn Hisham's account of the raids was apparently designed to emphasize that the Muslims should expect, and require whenever possible, the unbelievers to pay for their upkeep, in accord with the Qur'an's stipulation that the subjugated "people of the book" must submit to the Muslims and pay the jizya.

At one point, Muhammad sent one of the Muslims, Abdullah bin Jahsh, along with eight of those who had migrated from Mecca and Medina and thus would know the Quraysh personally, on one of these raids. Muhammad wrote Abdullah a letter and "ordered him not to look at it until he had journeyed for two days, and to do what he was ordered to do, but not to put pressure on any of his companions."[84] Abdullah obeyed, opening the letter only after he and his companions had journeyed two days away from Medina. The letter said: "When you have read this letter of mine proceed until you reach Nakhla between Mecca and Al-Ta'if. Lie in wait there for Quraysh and find out for us what they are doing."[85] Abdullah murmured: "To hear is to obey," and told his comrades about the mission in a manner that made it clear that he understood the mission to involve much more than mere reconnaissance. The Muslims were going to attack the Quraysh, and some of the believers might be killed: "The apostle has commanded me to go to Nakhla to lie in wait there for Quraysh so as to bring him news of them. He has forbidden me to put pressure on any of you, so if anyone wishes for martyrdom let him go forward, and he who does not, let him go back; as for me I am going on as the prophet has ordered."[86] No one dropped out.

At Nakhla, "a caravan of Quraysh carrying dry raisins and leather and other merchandise of Quraysh passed by them."[87] This caravan was ripe for raiding, but as it happened, the Muslims had spotted this caravan on the last day of the month of Rajab, which was one of the four months of the Arabic calendar that were designated as sacred: fighting was forbidden during them. The Muslims realized that if they refrained from attacking, the Quraysh caravan would make it safely back to Mecca before the end of the sacred month, but if they attacked, they would

---

84 Ibn Ishaq, op. cit., 286–7.
85 Ibid., 287.
86 Ibid.
87 Ibid.

violate the sacred month's prohibition on fighting. After some discussion, "they encouraged each other, and decided to kill as many as they could of them and take what they had."[88]

The Muslims killed one of the Quraysh; two others surrendered, and a third escaped. Abdullah and his companions brought the entire caravan and the two prisoners back to Medina, where Abdullah instructed the others that "a fifth of what we have taken belongs to the apostle."[89] Ibn Hisham states that "this was before God had appointed a fifth of the booty to him."[90] Soon, this rule would pass into the Qur'an, where, unlike the mandate to stone adulterers, it remains to this day: "And know that whatever you take as spoils of war, indeed, a fifth of it is for Allah, and for the messenger and for the relatives and orphans and the needy and the traveler" (8:41).

Muhammad, however, was not pleased with either the gift or the raid itself. "I did not order you to fight in the sacred month," he said icily to Abdullah, and he "held the caravan and the two prisoners in suspense and refused to take anything from them."[91] Abdullah and his fellow raiders "were in despair and thought that they were doomed."[92] For their part, the Quraysh made the most of the situation, charging that "Muhammad and his companions have violated the sacred month, shed blood therein, taken booty, and captured men."[93] The Jews "turned this raid into an omen against the apostle."[94]

As so often happens in these accounts, it was Allah who had the last word, siding with Abdullah and his companions in a new revelation: "They ask you about warfare in the sacred month. Say, Warfare during it is an awesome sin, but to turn people away from the way of Allah, and to disbelieve in him and expelling his people from the sacred mosque, is more serious with Allah, for persecution is worse than slaughter" (Qur'an 2:217). The Quraysh had turned people away from following Muhammad and expelled the Muslims from the mosque in Mecca (which, at this time, was full of the idols of the various Arab tribes). In

---

88 Ibid.
89 Ibid.
90 Ibid.
91 Ibid.
92 Ibid.
93 Ibid., 288.
94 Ibid.

doing this, they had forfeited the protection of the sacred month. The Muslims could lawfully ignore such laws for the greater good of Islam, in order to strike back at the enemies of religion.

Ibn Hisham notes that this revelation peacefully resolved the tensions among the Muslims: "And when the Quran came down about that and God relieved the Muslims of their anxiety in the matter, the apostle took the caravan and the prisoners."[95]

Whitewashing Muhammad

In a striking indication of the dishonesty that pervades the contemporary academic and popular discourse about Islam, the popular Islamic apologist Karen Armstrong uses this passage of the Islamic holy book to refer to the Qur'an's "condemnation of all warfare as an 'awesome evil.'"[96] The Qur'an, however, never issues such a blanket condemnation of all warfare, either at 2:217 or anywhere else. What it characterizes as an "awesome evil" or "awesome sin" is fighting during the sacred month, but it only says this in the context of setting aside this very prohibition to fight in the case of a severe persecution of the Muslims. This establishes an overarching principle that is essentially the diametric opposite of a blanket prohibition on warfare during certain periods: Muslims are allowed to set aside any law or custom if they consider themselves to be suffering persecution.

This encourages a rhetoric of grievance and victimhood that has been present in Islam from the beginning and has intensified in our age of the celebration and lionization of victims. It also establishes a relativism in which nothing whatsoever can be said to be absolutely wrong in Islam. This relativism entirely eluded the glib analysts of the West in the aftermath of the jihad attacks in the United States on September 11, 2001, when both Muslim and non-Muslim commentators rushed to assure the public that the attacks violated numerous tenets of Islam and that the Islamic rhetoric of the attackers and their allies represented a "hijacking" of the religion itself.

In light of the fact that the public mastermind of the attacks, Osama bin Laden, asserted that the US had persecuted Muslims in Palestine,

---

95 Ibid.
96 Karen Armstrong, "Balancing the Prophet," *Financial Times*, April 27, 2007, https://www.ft.com/content/4a05a4a4-f134-11db-838b-000b5df10621.

Somalia, Iraq, and elsewhere, it was clear that he and many other Muslims believed that the attacks were justified no matter what prohibitions on attacking civilians or innocent people (both more elastic terms than is usually noted in any case) would not be in play, for as the Qur'an states at 2:217, "persecution is worse than slaughter."[97] This key Islamic concept, however, was never discussed amid the extensive post-9/11 examinations of "why they hate us." American foreign policy from the moment of those attacks was based on fantasy, wishful thinking, and propaganda about Islam, not the facts about what the Islamic texts actually teach.

This fantasy, wishful thinking, and propaganda took firm hold even in the face of numerous accounts of Muhammad waging offensive war against unbelievers simply because of the fact that they were unbelievers.

---

97 Osama bin Laden, "Full text: bin Laden's 'letter to America,'" *Observer*, November 24, 2002, https://web.archive.org/web/20040615081002/http://observer.guardian.co.uk/worldview/story/0,11581,845725,00.html.

CHAPTER EIGHT

Muhammad Deals with His Enemies

Going to War

Emboldened by the success of the Nakhla raid and the seal of approval that Allah had given to it, Muhammad determined to escalate his campaign against the Quraysh. He ordered a raid on another Quraysh caravan traveling back to Mecca from Syria: "This is the Quraysh caravan containing their property. Go out to attack it, perhaps God will give it as a prey."[1] Ibn Hisham adds that despite Muhammad's previous bellicosity, this surprised some of the Muslims: "The people answered his summons, some eagerly, others reluctantly because they had not thought that the apostle would go to war."[2]

In his *Kitab al-Tarikh wa al-Maghazi* ("Book of History and Campaigns"), another biographer of Muhammad, Abu Abd Allah ibn Waqidi (747–823), agrees, saying that "many of the Prophet's companions held him back. They hated his going out raiding and there were many words of dispute about it. Those who stayed behind were not censured because a battle had not been intended."[3]

Yet according to several hadiths, those who stayed behind were indeed censured after the successful conclusion of the battle, whether it had been intended or not. Muhammad's cousin Ibn Abbas, who was only around five years old at the time of the Battle of Badr, is depicted as later declaring: "Not equal are those believers who sat (at home) and

---

1 Ibn Ishaq, op. cit., 289.
2 Ibid.
3 Muhammad ibn Umar al-Waqidi, *The Life of Muhammad: Al-Waqidi's Kitab al-Maghazi*, Rizwi Faizer, Amal Ismail and AbdulKader Tayob, trans., Rizwi Faizer, ed. (London: Routledge, 2011), 12.

did not join the Badr battle and those who joined the Badr battle."[4] This judgment was based on words attributed to Muhammad himself: to Rifaa, one of the Muslims who fought at Badr, is ascribed the tradition that "Gabriel came to the Prophet and said, 'How do you look upon the warriors of Badr among yourselves?'"[5] Muhammad answered: "As the best of the Muslims,' or said a similar statement."[6]

Another tradition adds that on the day of the battle itself, Allah sent a revelation making it absolutely clear that those who held back and didn't fight at Badr had made a catastrophic and possibly eternal mistake: "O you who believe, when you meet those who disbelieve in battle, do not turn your backs on them. Whoever turns his back on them on that day, unless he is maneuvering for battle or intent on joining a company, he indeed has incurred wrath from Allah, and his dwelling place will be Gehenna, an evil destination" (Qur'an 8:15–16). A hadith states that according to Abu Sa'id, one of Muhammad's companions to whom are attributed numerous hadiths, said: "The verse 'If any do turn his back to them on such a day' was revealed on the day of the Battle of Badr."[7]

A Booth at Badr, Three Booths on Mount Tabor

Ibn Hisham relates that as it became clear that the Muslims were going to go to war with the Quraysh, Muhammad and his men traveled about eighty miles from Medina to the town of Badr. It was there that one of Muhammad's companions, Sa'd ibn Mu'adh, said to him:

> O prophet of God, let us make a booth [Tabari adds "of palm-branches" here] for you to occupy and have your riding camels standing by; then we will meet the enemy and if God gives us the victory that is what we desire; if the worst occurs you can mount your camels and join our people who are left behind, for they are just as deeply attached to you as we are. Had they thought that you would be fighting they would not have stayed behind. God will protect you by them; they will give you good counsel and fight with you.[8]

4 Sahih Bukhari, vol. 6, book 65, no. 4595.
5 Sahih Bukhari, vol. 5, book 64, no. 3992.
6 Ibid.
7 Sunan Abi Dawud, book 15, no. 2648.
8 Ibn Ishaq, op. cit., 297.

Muhammad, Ibn Hisham continues, "thanked him and blessed him. Then a booth was constructed for the apostle and he remained there."[9]

While there is abundant evidence of the influence of both Jewish and Christian tradition upon the Qur'an and Islamic tradition in general, with numerous biblical and extrabiblical stories recast and retold in an Islamic context, there is little to no textual dependence. It doesn't appear as if those who composed the Qur'an and the vast body of biographical material about Muhammad were familiar with the exact words of either the Hebrew or Christian scriptures or of other Jewish and Christian literature, although there are a few notable exceptions. One of the most striking can be found in Qur'an 5:32, which states: "For that reason, we decreed for the children of Israel that whoever kills a human being for anything other than manslaughter or corruption on the earth, it will be as if he had killed all mankind, and whoever saves the life of one person, it will be as if he had saved the life of all mankind." This directly recalls a passage from the *Mishnah Sanhedrin*: "he that kills an Israelite is, by the plural here used, counted as if he had killed the world at large; and he who saves a single Israelite is counted as if he had saved the whole world."[10]

The account of Sa'd ibn Mu'adh offering to build a booth for Muhammad to await the arrival of the Quraysh at Badr does not involve any textual dependence upon the New Testament account of the Transfiguration. But there is a clear correspondence between the two stories: they both feature a key follower of the central holy figure offering to build a temporary structure for that revered figure at a site of supreme importance. The English translator of Ibn Hisham's sira invokes that correspondence by using the word "booth," which is used in many translations of the gospels for the accounts of the Transfiguration. Matthew's version, according to the Revised Standard Version of the Bible in English, goes this way:

> And after six days Jesus took with him Peter and James and John his brother, and led them up a high mountain apart. And he was transfigured before them, and his face shone like the sun, and his garments became white as light. And behold, there appeared to them Moses and Elijah, talking with him. And Peter said to Jesus,

---

9 Ibid.

10 William St. Clair Tisdall, "The Sources of Islam," in Ibn Warraq, ed., *The Origins of the Koran: Classic Essays on Islam's Holy Book* (Amherst, NY: Prometheus Books, 1998), 239.

"Lord, it is well that we are here; if you wish, I will make three booths here, one for you and one for Moses and one for Elijah." He was still speaking, when lo, a bright cloud overshadowed them, and a voice from the cloud said, "This is my beloved Son, with whom I am well pleased; listen to him." When the disciples heard this, they fell on their faces, and were filled with awe. But Jesus came and touched them, saying, "Rise, and have no fear." And when they lifted up their eyes, they saw no one but Jesus only (Matthew 17:1–8).

The "high mountain" is traditionally identified with Mount Tabor. In the Christian tradition, this is a supremely important incident, for it reveals Jesus to be the Son of God, confirms this by the presence of Moses (who stands for the Jewish law) and Elijah (who stands for the Jewish prophets), and brings the three disciples who were closest to Jesus into the presence of God the Father as he speaks from heaven to identify his Son. In light of all this, Peter's offer to build three booths for Jesus, Moses, and Elijah appears to be an attempt to prolong this supernatural experience and remain as long as possible at this intersection of the human and the divine. Sa'd ibn Mu'adh, by contrast, offers to build a booth for Muhammad at the place of a battle.

Victory Is from Allah

The Battle of Badr, however, would not prove to be an ordinary battle. It looms extremely large in the Qur'an and other Islamic traditions as a clear sign of Allah's favor upon the Muslims. Allah himself reminds the believers of this: "Allah had already given you the victory at Badr, when you were contemptible" (Qur'an 3:123), that is, a tiny force that had no chance, according to worldly calculations, of overcoming the Quraysh, who according to Islamic traditions numbered about a thousand, three times more than the Muslims.

As the Quraysh advanced, according to Ibn Hisham, Muhammad made it clear that this was a great struggle between the forces of good and evil: "O God, here come the Quraysh in their vanity and pride, contending with you and calling your apostle a liar. O God, grant the help which you promised me. Destroy them this morning!"[11] Allah complied. Despite its superiority, the Quraysh force was decimated.

---

11 Ibn Ishaq, op. cit., 297.

The Qur'an states that it was angels who achieved the victory at Badr in view of the obedience of the Muslims to Allah: "So observe your duty to Allah so that you may be thankful. When you said to the believers, Is it not sufficient for you that your Lord should support you with three thousand angels sent down? No, but if you persevere and avoid evil, and they attack you suddenly, your Lord will help you with five thousand angels sweeping in. Allah ordained this only as a message of good cheer for you, and that thereby your hearts might be at rest. Victory comes only from Allah, the mighty, the wise" (3:123–126).

This encapsulates a supremely important principle: Success in earthly battles is achieved not by means of military might, which the Muslims did not possess, but by means of persevering and avoiding evil. Allah rewards piety with earthly victory.

These points, which are so central to the message of Badr in the Qur'an and the biographical material about Muhammad, open the possibility that Sa'd ibn Mu'adh's offer to build a booth for Muhammad is very much akin to Peter's offer to build booths for Jesus and the two prophets. For the Battle of Badr is, in an Islamic context, as much of an encounter of the human with the divine as the New Testament account of the Transfiguration. In Islam, however, Allah is interacting with human beings not on a peaceful mountaintop, but on the field of battle. The Muslims' warfare against unbelievers is an opportunity for them to gain the fruits of their piety and devotion to Allah by winning the victories he promised to the righteous.

Warfare in Islam is thus not primarily a grim necessity for the defense of the community, or even a harsh but indispensable means for the expansion of that community; it is a great deal more than that. It is an occasion for him to give his blessings and rewards to those who have served him faithfully. It is an encounter with Allah himself, akin to Peter, James, and John hearing the voice of God the Father and seeing Moses and Elijah with Jesus on Mount Tabor.

How Many Muslims Fought at Badr?

The precision and detail of the ninth-century Islamic biographical material about Muhammad give the illusion of scrupulous historical accuracy. Yet here again, there are telling indications that the available accounts are not historical records, but exhortatory texts designed to convince people of the truths of Islam and inspire them to follow in the footsteps of the heroes of the great battle. The details do not demonstrate historical exactness so much as the appearance thereof, such as one might find in a well-crafted novel, so as to heighten the overall impact of the story. The small detail of exactly how many Muslims fought at Badr demonstrates that the compilers of these traditions were less precise and accurate than they attempted to appear to be; although they generally agree that there were around three hundred Muslims fighting at Badr, numerous traditions offer different exact numbers.

Modern-day hagiographers of Muhammad likewise offer the illusion of passing on careful, detailed, and precise historical accounts but disagree with one another. The number 313 has captured the contemporary jihadi imagination, such that the Taliban have a "special force" called the Badri 313 unit.[12] Al-Islam.org states confidently that at Badr, "the pagan army consisted of 950 fighters" and the "Islamic defense" of 314 men, "including the Messenger."[13] Omid Safi attributes his certainty to Ibn Ishaq, Muhammad's eighth-century biography whose work has been largely preserved, with an unknowable amount of editing and revision, in the work of Ibn Hisham: "Muhammad's biography by Ibn Ishaq covers the details of each battle in full glory, down to the lists of the 314 Muslims who fought in the Battle of Badr and the 50 Meccan pagans who were killed."[14] Yahiya Emerick says that there were "305 men who were so poorly equipped that every three soldiers had to take turns riding a camel."[15] Tariq Ramadan is less sure, saying that "Muhammad set off at the head of 309 (or 313, according to some accounts) of his Companions."[16]

The ninth-century accounts aren't sure, either. Ibn Sa'd says that Muhammad "set out with three hundred and five men."[17] He also quotes another source saying that there were "three hundred thirteen to three hundred nineteen" men.[18] Tabari offers a variety of traditions, stating

12 "Explainer: What is Badri 313 unit? Taliban's so-called 'special force,'" WION, August 31, 2021, https://www.wionews.com/south-asia/explainer-what-is-badri-313-unit-talibans-so-called-special-force-409665.

13 "The Battle of Badr," al-Islam.org, n.d., https://www.al-islam.org/articles/battle-badr.

14 Safi, op. cit., 128.

15 Emerick, op. cit., 161.

16 Ramadan, op. cit., 101.

17 Ibn Sa'd, Kitab al-Tabaqat al-Kabir, S. Moinul Haq, trans. (New Delhi: Kitab Bhavan, n.d.), II, 10.

18 Ibid., 19.

that the number of Muslim warriors was 307, 313, 314, 318, and simply "over three hundred and ten."[19]

These are minor differences over a small detail. A defender of the historical accuracy of these accounts might emphasize the fact that they all agree that the number of Muhammad's men was slightly over three hundred. Still, they give the impression of scrupulous historical exactitude, as Safi clearly intends to convey when he notes that Ibn Ishaq/Ibn Hisham gives a list of all the warriors who fought at Badr. Yet the disagreements as to the exact number among the various accounts demonstrate that the appearance of careful historical accuracy is illusory.

Another group of Islamic traditions, moreover, suggests that all of these numbers were given in order to convey once again that Muhammad is a prophet in the line of the biblical accounts. These traditions assert that the number of Muslim warriors at Badr corresponded to the number of warriors in a biblical story of King Saul. If there were indeed as many Muslims at Badr as Israelites fighting alongside this ancient king, this could either be a sign from Allah, a remarkable coincidence, or an indication that the stories of the Battle of Badr were constructed in order to make various theological points, not to provide a sober and accurate historical account.

Talut, who is identified with Saul, appears in the Qur'an in precisely the role of a commander whose forces are vastly outnumbered. The Qur'an mixes up the story of Saul with that of Gideon, who is depicted in the Hebrew scriptures as being ordered by God to reduce the number of his forces and doing so by means of a test involving water:

> And the LORD said to Gideon, "The people are still too many; take them down to the water and I will test them for you there; and he of whom I say to you, 'This man shall go with you,' shall go with you; and any of whom I say to you, 'This man shall not go with you,' shall not go." So he brought the people down to the water; and the LORD said to Gideon, "Every one that laps the water with his tongue, as a dog laps, you shall set by himself; likewise every one that kneels down to drink." And the number of those that lapped, putting their

19 Abu Ja'far Muhammad bin Jarir al-Tabari, *The History of al-Tabari*, vol. 7, *The Foundation of the Community*, M. V. McDonald and W. Montgomery Watt, trans. (Albany: State University of New York Press, 1987), 49.

hands to their mouths, was three hundred men; but all the rest of the people knelt down to drink water. And the LORD said to Gideon, "With the three hundred men that lapped I will deliver you, and give the Midianites into your hand; and let all the others go every man to his home" (Judges 7:4–7).

The Qur'an recasts this as an incident involving Saul and makes the water test into a loyalty test:

And when Saul set out with the army, he said, Indeed, Allah will test you by a river. Whoever therefore drinks from it is not with me, and whoever does not taste it is with me, except the one who takes it in the hollow of his hand. But they drank from it, all except a few of them. And after he had crossed, he and those who believed with him, they said, We have no power this day against Goliath and his hosts. But those who knew that they would meet Allah exclaimed, How many little companies have defeated mighty hosts by Allah's permission. Allah is with the persevering (2:249).

How little was Saul's company exactly? The Qur'an doesn't say, but several hadiths do, proclaiming proudly that the number of Muslim warriors at Badr was the same as the number of warriors that the biblical figure of Saul commanded. One has al-Bara stating that "the companions of (the Prophet) Muhammad who took part in Badr told me that their number was that of Saul's (i.e. Talut's) companions who crossed the river (of Jordan) with him and they were over three-hundred-and-ten men."[20] Another has al-Bara offering a slightly different number of warriors but noting the same correspondence between the number of Muhammad's men and that of Saul's men: "We used to say that the participants of Badr on the Day of Badr were like the number of companions of Talut, three hundred and thirteen men."[21]

Variants aside, the number of Muslims fighting at Badr is explicitly related to the three hundred men God raised up under the command of Gideon (although Islamic tradition confuses him with Saul) to defeat the Midianites. Just as that was a miraculous victory, so also was Badr.

---

20 Sahih Bukhari, vol. 5, book 64, no. 3957.
21 Jami at-Tirmidhi, vol. 3, book 21, no. 1598.

Miracles Abounding

In keeping with the presence of the angels securing the Muslims' victory at Badr, there were a number of other miracles there as well. Ibn Sa'd notes that "verily Ukkashah Ibn Milan broke his sword on the day of Badr. The Apostle of Allah, may Allah bless him, gave him a stick which changed in his hand into a sharp sword of pure iron and of strong blade."[22]

In Ibn Kathir's much later version, which he attributes to al-Waqidi, the man who broke his sword is different, as is the material the miracle-working prophet uses to make a new one:

> Al-Waqidi stated, "Usama b. Zayd related to me, from Daud b. al-Husayn, from some men of the Banu al-Ashhal, several of whom said, 'The sword of Salama b. Huraysh broke during the battle of Badr. Without a sword, he was unable to fight, so the Messenger of God gave him a staff he carried made of a green palm tree frond. He told him, "fight with this!" And it turned into a fine sword. He kept it with him until he was killed at the battle of Jisr Abu Ubayda.'"[23]

Ibn Kathir, again ascribing the tradition to earlier authorities, also depicts Muhammad as having miraculous healing powers. One of the Muslims' "eye was wounded at Badr and that its pupil came down on to his cheekbone. They were about to slice it off, but asked the Messenger of God, who said that they should not do this. He then said a prayer for him, covering his cheek with his palm. And later you could not tell which of his eyes had been struck!"[24] Ibn Kathir adds: "According to one account, this became his better eye."[25]

Muhammad is also depicted as having Allah's ear to the extent that the people he called upon to be killed before the Battle of Badr were all indeed killed there. A hadith states that while Muhammad was prostrating himself in prayer, a group of men of the Quraysh surrounded him, intent on humiliating him:

> Uqba bin Abi Muait came and brought the intestines of a camel and threw them on the back of the Prophet. The Prophet did not raise

22 Ibn Sa'd, op. cit., I, 216.
23 Ibn Kathir, *The Life of Prophet Muhammad*, op. cit., 2, 298.
24 Ibid.
25 Ibid.

his head from prostration till Fatima (i.e. his daughter) came and removed those intestines from his back, and invoked evil on whoever had done (the evil deed). The Prophet said, "O Allah! Destroy the chiefs of Quraish, O Allah! Destroy Abu Jahl bin Hisham, Utba bin Rabia, Shaiba bin Rabia, Uqba bin Abi Muait, Umaiya bin Khalaf (or Ubai bin Kalaf)." Later on I saw all of them killed during the battle of Badr and their bodies were thrown into a well except the body of Umaiya or Ubai, because he was a fat person, and when he was pulled, the parts of his body got separated before he was thrown into the well.[26]

Accounts of this kind directly contradicted the Qur'an's frequent avowal that the messenger of Allah could not actually perform miracles: "They say, Why has no sign been sent down upon him from his Lord? Say, Indeed, Allah is able to send down a sign. But most of them do not know" (6:37). Yet surely if Muhammad had been able to ask Allah that certain people be killed and then they were indeed killed, that would constitute a sign from the deity. The Qur'an, however, never envisions Muhammad doing anything of the kind and even dismisses the requests for miracles with the claim that even if Muhammad were given a miracle to perform, the unbelievers would persist in their rejection of Islam: "Indeed, if you came to them with a miracle, those who disbelieve would indeed exclaim, You are just tricksters" (30:58). "And they say, If only he would bring us a miracle from his Lord. Hasn't there come to them the proof of what is in the former scriptures?" (20:133)

In contrast to that excuse-making, Muhammad is so powerful in the hadith literature that he is even able to exert control over the heavenly bodies. In one tradition, he delays the coming of the new moon, which some of the believers were looking for in order to know when to begin the Ramadan fast. They meet up with Ibn Abbas and tell him that they had seen the new moon but couldn't agree when exactly it had first appeared. Ibn Abbas explained: "God's messenger deferred it till the time it is seen, so it is to be reckoned as being on the night you saw it."[27] The same story depicts Muhammad himself as being more modest, giving Allah the credit for the miracle: "God most high has deferred

---

26 Sahih Bukhari, vol. 4, book 58, no. 3185.
27 Mishkat al-Masabih, book 7, no. 1981.

it till it is seen."[28] The hadith collection Mishkat al-Masabih says of this tradition that "Muslim transmitted it," but Sahih Muslim's version doesn't contain Ibn Abbas saying that Muhammad was the one who had deferred the new moon.[29] Instead, Muhammad attributes the miracle to Allah alone: "Verily Allah deferred it till the time it is seen, so it is to be reckoned from the night you saw it."[30]

The difference between those two versions may indicate how the miracle stories of Muhammad grew in number and impressiveness as his stature and importance in Islam increased. The presence of the miracle stories in the hadith and sira material but not in the Qur'an has been taken as an indication that the Qur'an was assembled closer to the time of Muhammad, if not written directly by him, before all these miracle stories were fabricated or attached to his legend.

It is arresting, however, that the hadith and sira literature never offers a clear or adequate explanation for why Muhammad is no longer making excuses for his lack of ability to perform miracles, as he does in the Qur'an, but is instead a prolific miracle worker whose powers are apparently limitless. There are traces, to be sure, of the older Qur'anic tradition; one hadith has Muhammad saying: "Every Prophet was given miracles because of which people believed, but what I have been given, is Divine Inspiration which Allah has revealed to me. So I hope that my followers will outnumber the followers of the other Prophets on the Day of Resurrection."[31] Yet the same collection (Sahih Bukhari) that has Muhammad opposing his divine revelation to the miracles other prophets received also depicts him performing miracles.

Contemporary Islamic apologists tend to gloss over this anomaly by claiming that the Qur'an is actually full of miracles of Muhammad. The book is often presented as a miracle: sublime words of Allah that could not have been written by an "unlettered prophet" (7:157). In the Qur'an, we are told that "the hour drew near and the moon was split in two. And if they see a sign, they turn away and say, Prolonged illusion. They denied and followed their own lusts" (54:1–3). Although there is no mention of Muhammad or any other prophet or messenger in connection with this passage, a hadith makes it a miracle of Muhammad:

---

28 Ibid.
29 Ibid.
30 Sahih Muslim, book 13, no. 1088a.
31 Sahih Bukhari, vol. 6, book 66, no. 4981.

"The people of Mecca asked the Prophet to show them a sign (miracle). So he showed them (the miracle) of the cleaving of the moon."[32]

The Qur'an itself, however, never makes any such claim. And if Muhammad had done something as spectacular as split the moon, why does the Qur'an depict his detractors as asking: "Why has no sign been sent down upon him from his Lord?" (6:37) Yet while there is a super-abundance of hadiths that quote the Qur'an and whole sections of the various hadith collections that offer stories explaining in what circumstances various portions of the Qur'an came to be sent down, there is no acknowledgment of any problem with Muhammad's miracle working in light of the Qur'anic passages saying he can't do miracles.

Clearly, the authors and compilers of these stories of Muhammad's life had read the Qur'an. It is possible, however, that the Qur'an they read was not identical to the version that most Muslim believers read today. One possible reason why they don't explain why Muhammad can't perform miracles in the Qur'an but can in later traditions is because the difference didn't exist at the time those later traditions were being written and compiled: either the Qur'an had him able to perform miracles and that material was removed, or the passages about him being unable to perform miracles were not yet in the book.

Why, however, if numerous stories existed of Muhammad performing miracles, would anyone fabricate traditions where he cannot do so and tries to explain away this uncomfortable fact? This may have been an effort to buttress the authority of the Qur'an itself as Muhammad's lone miracle and, indeed, a miracle greater than splitting the sun or delaying the appearance of the new moon or anything else. The Qur'an, as the perfect and eternal words of Allah, was clearly not the work of Muhammad, who was so much an ordinary man that he didn't even have the miraculous powers that other prophets had possessed. Could the Qur'an's authors have made a conscious decision to reject miracle accounts and present the prophet of Islam as unable to perform them so as to enhance his reception of the Qur'an itself as a singular supernatural achievement? Does the Qur'an's avowals of the messenger's inability to perform miracles thus represent the views of a party that was (in this and possibly on other issues as well) opposed to the faction or factions that were responsible for the manufacture of the bulk of the hadiths?

---

32 Sahih Bukhari, vol. 6, book 65, no. 4867.

Another Wife for Muhammad

After the great victory at Badr, says Ibn Hisham, Muhammad "divided the booty which God had granted to the Muslims equally."[33] The Muslims were in an ebullient mood; as they congratulated one another on defeating the Quraysh, they delighted in belittling the force that had appeared so very formidable not long ago. Muhammad's nephew Salama ibn Salama responded: "What are you congratulating us about? By God, we only met some bald old women like the sacrificial camels who are hobbled, and we slaughtered them!"[34] At this, Muhammad grinned and said: "But, nephew, those were the chiefs."[35]

There was also a special reward for the prophet of Islam. Hafsa bint Umar, daughter of Muhammad's companion and eventual successor Umar bin al-Khattab, was widowed at Badr. Umar offered her hand to two other future caliphs, first Uthman and then Abu Bakr. Uthman refused, and Abu Bakr did not respond at all, which made Umar angry. "Some days later," Umar is depicted as recounting, "Allah's Messenger demanded her hand in marriage and I married her to him."[36] After this, Abu Bakr said to Umar: "Perhaps you were angry with me when you offered me Hafsa for marriage and I gave no reply to you?"[37] Umar admitted that to be the case, whereupon Abu Bakr explained: "Nothing prevented me from accepting your offer except that I learnt that Allah's Messenger had referred to the issue of Hafsa and I did not want to disclose the secret of Allah's Messenger, but had he (i.e. the Prophet) given her up I would surely have accepted her."[38] Muhammad's wishes always came first; Hafsa became his fourth wife.

Muhammad also took a fifth wife, another Badr widow, Zaynab bint Khuzaymah. Zaynab was known as Umm al-Masakin, "mother of the poor," for her charitable work, but survived only a few months after her marriage to the prophet of Islam.[39]

---

33 Ibn Ishaq, op. cit.
34 Ibid.
35 Ibid.
36 Sahih Bukhari, vol. 5, book 64, no. 4005.
37 Ibid.
38 Ibid.
39 Mishkat al-Masabih, book 6, no. 1875; Tabari, op. cit., 150.

Confronting the Jews

Emboldened by his success against the Quraysh, Muhammad determined to compel the Jews of Medina to accede to his wishes as well. According to Ibn Hisham, after Badr, Muhammad called together the Jews of the Qaynuqa tribe and demanded their conversion to Islam: "O Jews, beware lest God bring upon you the vengeance that He brought upon Quraysh and become Muslims. You know that I am a prophet who has been sent—you will find that in your scriptures and God's covenant with you."[40]

The threat did not impress them: "Don't deceive yourself, Muhammad. You have killed a number of inexperienced Quraysh who did not know how to fight. But if you fight us you will learn that we are men and that you have met your equal."[41] Allah then responded to them in a new revelation: "There was a sign for you in two armies that met, one army fighting in the way of Allah, and another disbelieving, whom they saw as twice their number, clearly, with their own eyes" (Qur'an 3:13). "Twice their number" is noteworthy, as the various reckonings of the numbers at the Battle of Badr generally agree that the Quraysh were about three times the number of the Muslims.

The Qur'an continues: "In this way Allah strengthens those whom he wills with his help. Indeed, in this there is truly a lesson for those who have eyes" (3:13). For Ibn Hisham, this is a warning to the Jews that even if they think they are stronger than Muhammad and can defeat him, Allah bestows his favor upon those whom he pleases, and other passages make it clear that it is obedience to Allah that wins his favor and thus earthly success.

After relating Muhammad issuing this threat, Ibn Hisham records a tradition stating that the members of the Qaynuqa tribe "were the first of the Jews to break their agreement with the apostle and to go to war, between Badr and Uhud, and the apostle besieged them until they surrendered unconditionally."[42] Yet in light of the threat Muhammad had given them, the Qaynuqa Jews had little choice; the prophet of Islam had made it quite clear that he intended to attack them as he had attacked the Quraysh. Other early Islamic sources appear to be aware of how this

---

40 Ibn Ishaq, op. cit., 363.
41 Ibid.
42 Ibid.

makes the hero of their story appear, and so they emphasize that the Jews began scheming against Muhammad before he issued his threat. Ibn Sa'd says that the Qaynuqa were "the bravest of the Jews, and were goldsmiths. They had entered into a pact with the Prophet," but adds that "when the Battle of Badr took place, they transgressed and showed jealousy, and violated the pact and the covenant."[43] The awe-inspiring specificity of the hadith and sira literature in general eludes him at this point, and he offers no details about how exactly the Banu (that is, tribe) Qaynuqa "transgressed and showed jealousy."

Ibn Sa'd adds that this was the occasion of the revelation of another passage of the Qur'an: "And if you fear treachery from any people, then throw it back to them fairly. Indeed, Allah does not love the treacherous" (8:58). Yet that passage envisions a scenario in which the Muslims break a treaty because they "fear treachery" from the other party in the agreement, not because any actual treachery has been committed. Tabari says that as soon as Gabriel had delivered this revelation to Muhammad, the prophet of Islam responded, "I fear the Banu Qaynuqa."[44]

About what triggered the breakdown in relations between the Muslims and the Qaynuqa Jews, Tabari is as vague as Ibn Sa'd, saying that "after the Messenger of God killed many polytheists of Quraysh at Badr," the Jews "were envious and behaved badly toward him."[45] He says that "they also infringed the contract in various ways."[46] This has remained the Islamic understanding of what triggered the conflict between the Muslims and the Qaynuqa Jews to this day. Tariq Ramadan asserts, likewise without offering any supporting evidence, that "alarming news of treason and a possible plot came to the Prophet" from within the ranks of the Banu Qaynuqa.[47]

The only evidence of any such treason or plot that Ramadan offers comes from a story that al-Waqidi tells. Al-Waqidi begins by stating the case in vague terms similar to those of Ibn Sa'd and Tabari, saying that "when the Prophet overcame the companions of Badr and arrived in Medina, the Jews acted wrongfully and destroyed the agreement that

---

43 Ibn Sa'd, op. cit., II, 32.
44 Tabari, op. cit., 86.
45 Ibid., 85.
46 Ibid.
47 Ramadan, op. cit., 108.

was between them and the Messenger of God."[48] He prefaces this to his version of Muhammad's threat and the Jews' response, which are both similar to the versions Ibn Hisham presents but take on an entirely different character coming after the statement that the Jews had "acted wrongfully and destroyed the agreement" they had with Muhammad. Al-Waqidi then attempts to buttress his case against the Jews by telling the story of a Muslim woman who "came to the market of the Banu Qaynuqa" and "sat down at a goldsmith's with a trinket of hers."[49] Then she fell victim to a nasty prank: "A Jew of the Banu Qaynuqa came and sat behind her, and without her knowledge fixed her outer garment to her back with a pin. When the woman stood up her pudenda showed and they laughed at her."[50]

Enraged at this, one of the Muslims killed the prankster; then the Banu Qaynuqa "gathered and surrounded and killed the Muslim."[51] It was at this point that the Jews "abandoned the agreement with the Prophet and opposed him, fortifying themselves in their fortress."[52]

Muhammad determined to exile the Banu Qaynuqa from Medina. Al-Waqidi says that Muhammad "besieged them in their fortress for fifteen nights most vigorously until God put fear in their hearts. The Jews said, 'May we surrender and leave?' The Prophet said, 'No, except upon my judgment.' The Jews surrendered unconditionally to the Prophet and he ordered that they be tied up."[53]

Ibn Hisham says that one of the Muslims, Abdullah ibn Ubayy, was friendly with the Banu Qaynuqa and asked Muhammad to "deal kindly" with them, but "the apostle put him off."[54] Abdullah was insistent, to the point that Muhammad became "so angry that his face became almost black."[55] Abdullah still stood by his friends and even prevailed upon Muhammad not to kill them: al-Waqidi says that in the face of Abdullah's insistent importuning, Muhammad finally exclaimed: "Set them free, and may God curse them and curse him with them!"[56] Al-Waqidi

---

48 Al-Waqidi, op. cit., 87.
49 Ibid., 88.
50 Ibid.
51 Ibid.
52 Ibid.
53 Al-Waqidi, op. cit., 88.
54 Ibn Ishaq, op. cit., 363.
55 Ibid.
56 Al-Waqidi, op. cit.

adds: "When Ibn Ubayy spoke for them the Prophet refrained from killing them, and commanded that they be exiled from Medina."[57]

However, another Muslim who had been friendly with the Banu Qaynuqa, Ubada ibn al-Samit, saw the error of his ways at this point and told Muhammad: "O apostle of God, I take God and His apostle and the believers as my friends, and I renounce my agreement and friendship with these unbelievers."[58] At that point, says Ibn Hisham, Allah revealed this passage regarding Abdullah ibn Ubayy and the error of his ways: "O you who believe, do not take the Jews and the Christians for friends. They are friends of one another. He among you who takes them for friends is of them. Indeed, Allah does not guide wrongdoing people" (5:51).

The word translated here as "friends," *awliya*, does not necessarily refer to personal friendships between individuals; *awliya* means friend and protector, that is, a political ally or a patron, someone entrusted with another's safety. Thus it repudiates not just the friendship Abdullah and Ubada had with the Banu Qaynuqa, but more generally, it rejects the kind of alliance that Muhammad is depicted as having made with the Jews of Medina.

Confronting the Poet

After the hijrah, says al-Waqidi, "the polytheists and Jews among the people of Medina hurt the Prophet and his companions grievously but God most high commanded His prophet and the Muslims to be patient and forgiving."[59] One was a poet named Ka'b ibn al-Ashraf, whom a hadith identifies solely as "a Jew," and who, says al-Waqidi, "refused to abstain from insulting the Prophet and the Muslims."[60] Ka'b was deeply grieved at the defeat of the Quraysh at Badr and composed verses lamenting the event; according to Ibn Hisham, in one such poem, K'ab sang acidly of the prophet of Islam:

> Drive off that fool of yours that you may be safe
> From talk that has no sense!
> Do you taunt me because I shed tears

---

57 Ibid.
58 Ibn Ishaq, op. cit.
59 Al-Waqidi, op. cit., 91.
60 Ibid., 92; Sahih Bukhari, vol. 4, book 56, no. 3032.

For people who loved me sincerely?
As long as I live I shall weep and, remember
The merits of people whose glory is in Mecca's houses.[61]

Ibn Hisham adds that Ka'b also "composed amatory verses of an insulting nature about the Muslim women."[62] Al-Waqidi claims that Ka'b went even farther, hoping to rouse the Quraysh to take on Muhammad again: "I will go out to the Quraysh and incite them."[63] Ibn Sa'd agrees, saying that Ka'b "used to satirize the Prophet, may Allah bless him, and his Companions, and used to instigate (polytheists) against them, and offended them."[64] Ka'b even "went to Makkah and made the Quraysh lament for the dead at Badr and exhorted them in verses (to take revenge)."[65] Ibn Hisham, however, doesn't mention Ka'b inciting the Quraysh against Muhammad, aside from the call to "drive off that fool of yours"; nor does Bukhari, who offers no justification for what happens to Ka'b other than that he "hurt Allah and His Apostle."[66]

For these hurt feelings, Bukhari has Muhammad asking his companions, "Who is willing to kill Ka'b bin Al-Ashraf?"[67] Ibn Hisham, Tabari, al-Waqidi, and Ibn Sa'd all mitigate this. Ibn Hisham and Tabari have Muhammad asking, "Who will rid me of Ibnu'l-Ashraf?"[68] Al-Waqidi has, "Who will bring me Ibn al-Ashraf, for he has harmed me?"[69] Ibn Sa'd makes Muhammad out to be even more of the innocent aggrieved party, having him say: "Who is for me against Ka'b Ibn al-Ashraf, as he has offended me?"[70]

All the accounts agree, however, that whether it was his own suggestion or that of one of his companions, Muhammad ibn Maslama, the prophet of Islam gives permission for Ka'b to be murdered. Muhammad ibn Maslama even asks for, and receives, permission from his prophet to lie to Ka'b in order to gain his confidence and get him to put his guard down so that he can be murdered more easily. Oddly, even as he

61 Ibn Ishaq, op. cit., 366.
62 Ibid., 367.
63 Al-Waqidi, op. cit., 92.
64 Ibn Sa'd, op. cit., II, 35.
65 Ibid., 35–6.
66 Sahih Bukhari, vol. 3, book 48, no. 2510; vol. 4, book 56, no. 3031.
67 Ibid.
68 Ibn Ishaq, op. cit.; Tabari, op. cit., 95.
69 Al-Waqidi, op. cit., 93.
70 Ibn Sa'd, op. cit., II, 36.

portrays one of Maslama's confederates, Abu Naila, deceiving Ka'b and luring him into the trap that enabled his murder, Ibn Hisham portrays Muhammad's enemy as noble and courageous:

> Now it was a moonlight night and they journeyed on until they came to his castle, and Abu Naila called out to [Ka 'b]. He had only recently married, and he jumped up in the bed sheet, and his wife took hold of the end of it and said, "You are at war, and those who are at war do not go out at this hour." He replied, "It is Abu Naila. Had he found me sleeping he would not have woken me." She answered, "By God, I can feel evil in his voice." Ka'b answered, "Even if the call were for a stab a brave man must answer it."[71]

That was exactly what the call was for. Once those who had deceived Ka'b and gained his confidence had duly murdered him. According to al-Waqidi, the killers beheaded Ka'b and then ran, carrying their victim's head, "until they found the Messenger of God standing at the door of the mosque."[72] Never depicted as magnanimous or gracious in victory, Muhammad was delighted at Ka'b's death and said to the attackers: "May your faces prosper!"[73] The killers "threw Ibn al-Ashraf's head before him, and he praised God for his death."[74] In the scuffle as Ka'b was killed, one of the killers, al-Harith, was lightly wounded; now, however, the miracle-working prophet "spat in his wound and it no longer hurt him."[75]

Attacking the Jews

Besides demonstrating that Muhammad, and hence Allah, would reward killing blasphemers, the Ka'b ibn al-Ashraf accounts seem designed to justify aggression against the Jews. Ka'b was identified as Jewish, and in Ibn Hisham's version, Maslama declares after the killing that "our attack upon God's enemy cast terror among the Jews, and there was no Jew in Medina who did not fear for his life."[76] After the murder of Ka'b, Muhammad gives a blanket command: "Kill any Jew that fails into

---

71 Ibn Ishaq, op. cit., 368.
72 Al-Waqidi, op. cit., 95.
73 Ibid.
74 Ibid.
75 Ibid.
76 Ibn Ishaq, op. cit.

your power."[77] Ibn Sa'd records Muhammad's statement this way: "Kill every Jew whom you come across."[78] Al-Waqidi has: "Who ever from among you can get the better of men from among the Jews, kill him."[79] Al-Waqidi adds: "The Jews became fearful. Not one of their leaders ventured out. They did not speak for they feared they would be sought out in their homes just as Ibn al-Ashraf was."[80]

According to Ibn Hisham, one of Muhammad's companions, Muhayyisa ibn Masud, took this command to heart and made no effort to distinguish between warriors and civilians, or even enemies of Muhammad, as opposed to those who had not expressed any opposition to him. Muhayyisa "leapt upon Ibn Sunayna, a Jewish merchant with whom they had social and business relations, and killed him."[81] Muhayyisa's elder brother, Huwayyisa, who was not a Muslim, was appalled; he began beating Muhayyisa while saying: "You enemy of God, did you kill him when much of the fat on your belly comes from his wealth?"[82] Muhayyisa replied: "Had the one who ordered me to kill him ordered me to kill you I would have cut your head off."[83] Huwayyisa asks his brother: "By God, if Muhammad had ordered you to kill me would you have killed me?"[84] Muhayyisa's answer is unequivocal: "Yes, by God, had he ordered me to cut off your head I would have done so."[85] Instead of further rebuking his brother for his unthinking fanaticism, Huwayyisa is depicted as being deeply impressed, saying: "By God, a religion which can bring you to this is marvelous!"[86] Huwayyisa became a Muslim, thereby providing a foundation for the reflexive fanaticism that has run through the history of Islam and has continued right up to the present day.

Al-Waqidi states that the Jews tried to reason with Muhammad, going to him and arguing that Ka'b ibn al-Ashraf had been murdered without any justification. They don't seem to be aware of the claim

---

77 Ibid., 369.
78 Ibn Sa'd, op. cit., II, 37.
79 Al-Waqidi, op. cit.
80 Ibid.
81 Ibn Ishaq, op. cit.
82 Ibid.
83 Ibid.
84 Ibid.
85 Ibid.
86 Ibid.

that he had engaged in any incitement against the Muslims. They are depicted as saying to Muhammad: "Our companion, who was one of our lords, was knocked up at night and murdered treacherously with no crime or incident by him that we know of."[87]

Muhammad's justification for the killing made no reference to any incitement, either, but only to Ka'b's verses that had insulted him: "If he had remained as others of similar opinion remained he would not have been killed treacherously. But he hurt us and insulted us with poetry, and one does not do this among you, but he shall be put to the sword."[88] Al-Waqidi adds that Muhammad and the Jews then signed a joint document but says nothing about what was in it. Whatever it said, however, was of no comfort to the Jews, for they "became cautious and were fearful and humbled from the day Ibn al-Ashraf was murdered."[89]

Their worst fears would be borne out.

87 Al-Waqidi, op. cit., 96.
88 Ibid.
89 Ibid.

CHAPTER NINE

Defeat, Revenge, and Exile

The Battle of Uhud

After the victory at Badr and the killing of Ka'b ibn al-Ashraf, Muhammad and his men embarked on a series of raids upon the neighboring
Arab tribes. Al-Waqidi relates that after one of these, "included among
the prisoners was al-Furat b. Hayyan. He was brought before the Prophet
and it was said to him, 'Convert—if you convert, we will not kill you.' So
he converted and was not killed."[1] Ibn Sa'd's version is much the same:
Furat "was asked to embrace Islam and then his life would be safe. He
embraced Islam and the Apostle of Allah, may Allah bless him, saved
him from being killed."[2]

A hadith has Muhammad stating this as a general principle: the Muslims must wage war against non-Muslims until they bore witness to the
truth of Islam, which, as the Islamic system developed, came to mean
either conversion to Islam or submission to the Muslims as a conquered
and captive people. The only way that non-Muslims could prevent the
Muslims from killing them and confiscating their property was by bearing witness to Muhammad's status as a prophet. Muhammad is depicted
as saying: "I have been ordered (by Allah) to fight against the people
until they testify that none has the right to be worshipped but Allah and
that Muhammad is Allah's Messenger, and offer the prayers perfectly
and give the obligatory charity, so if they perform that, then they save
their lives and property from me except for Islamic laws and then their
reckoning (accounts) will be done by Allah."[3]

---

1 Al-Waqidi, op. cit., 99.
2 Ibn Sa'd, op. cit., II, 42.
3 Sahih Bukhari, vol. 1, book 2, no. 25.

The Quraysh, however, despite their defeat at Badr, were unwilling either to convert or to submit. Some of the Quraysh warriors raised funds for a new campaign, appealing to their fellow tribesmen on the basis of revenge: "Men of Quraysh, Muhammad has wronged you and killed your best men, so help us with this money to fight him, so that we may hope to get our revenge for those we have lost."[4] According to Ibn Hisham, this was the occasion for Allah to reveal another passage of the Qur'an: "Indeed, those who disbelieve spend their wealth so that they may bar people from the way of Allah. They will spend it, then it will become a source of anguish for them, then they will be conquered. And those who disbelieve will be gathered to Gehenna" (8:36).

This time, however, the Quraysh force was even more formidable than it had been at Badr. Al-Waqidi says that they had three thousand troops, as well as "many weapons," along with "two hundred horses," plus "seven hundred coats of mail and three thousand camels."[5] According to Ibn Hisham, Muhammad "marched out with a thousand of his companions," but by the time he "drew up his troops for battle," he only had "about 700 men."[6] According to Ibn Hisham, some of the Muslims asked him: "O apostle, should we not ask help from our allies, the Jews?"[7] Muhammad answered: "We have no need of them."[8] Yet al-Waqidi has him burdened with dark foreboding: "Indeed I fear defeat."[9] He told the Muslims: "Pay attention to my commands and follow them. Go, by the name of God, and victory will be yours if you are patient."[10] Just before the battle began, he expanded on this: "O people, let me advise you as God has advised me in His book: Do good works in obedience to Him, and abstain from His taboos. Then indeed he who remembers his duty and devotes himself to it with patience and certitude with effort and zeal shall have a place of reward and treasure. Fighting the enemy is hard. Strong is his distress, and few are those who are patient about it unless God decides to bring him to his senses. For surely God is with he who obeys Him, and

4 Ibn Ishaq, op. cit., 370.
5 Al-Waqidi, op. cit., 101.
6 Ibn Ishaq, op. cit., 372, 373.
7 Ibid., 372.
8 Ibid.
9 Al-Waqidi, op. cit., 106.
10 Ibid.

indeed the devil is with he who resists Him."[11] Just as at Badr, victory would come to the pious.

Yet it did not come. As it turned out, the Muslims could have used some help, whether from the Jews or others. The two armies met in a valley north of Mount Uhud, near Medina. This time, the outcome was much different from what it had been at Badr. According to Ibn Hisham, "the Muslims were put to flight and the enemy slew many of them. It was a day of trial and testing in which God honored several with martyrdom."[12] This debacle was, according to a hadith, the handiwork of Satan himself, who snatched victory from the Muslims by deceiving them. Aisha is depicted as recounting that "the pagans were defeated on the day (of the battle) of Uhud."[13] But then, "Satan shouted among the people on the day of Uhud, 'O Allah's worshippers! Beware of what is behind you!' So the front file of the army attacked the back files (mistaking them for the enemy)."[14]

Muhammad Is Injured

Even Muhammad was injured. In Ibn Hisham's version, "the enemy got at the apostle who was hit with a stone so that he fell on his side and one of his teeth was smashed, his face scored, and his lip injured. The man who wounded him was Utba b. Abu Waqqas."[15] Ibn Hisham adds that "the blood began to run down his face and he began to wipe it away, saying the while, 'How can a people prosper who have stained their prophet's face with blood while he summoned them to their Lord?'"[16] Allah then sent down a new revelation: "It is not at all your concern whether he is merciful toward them or punishes them, for they are evildoers" (3:128).

The nature and extent of Muhammad's wounds was disputed. Al-Waqidi has them as much more serious than does Ibn Hisham, quoting a tradition he traces back to Aisha and Abu Bakr to the effect that Muhammad "was shot in his face until the two rings of his helmet

---

11 Ibid., 110.
12 Ibn Ishaq, op. cit., 380.
13 Sahih Bukhari, vol. 9, book 87, no. 6883.
14 Ibid.
15 Ibn Ishaq, op. cit.
16 Ibid.

entered his cheeks."[17] One of Muhammad's companions, Abu Ubayda bin al-Jarrah, pleads: "I ask you, by God, O Abu Bakr, let me remove it from the face of the Prophet."[18] Abu Bakr allows this, and Abu Ubayda removes the ring of the helmet with his teeth, becoming toothless in the process. However, al-Waqidi quotes another source saying that "verily he who removed the rings from the face of the Prophet was Uqba b. Wahb b. Kalada."[19] Al-Waqidi adds: "Others said, Abu'l-Yasar."[20]

Al-Waqidi concludes: "Uqba b. Wahb b. Kalada is confirmed with us."[21] Yet he then immediately repeats another tradition, in which another one of the companions, Malik ibn Sinan, "began to suck the blood with his mouth and then swallow it."[22] Seeing this, Muhammad said: "Whoever desires to see one who mixes his blood with mine, let him look at Malik b. Sinan."[23] Al-Waqidi notes that people would ask Malik about this, and he would respond: "Yes, I drank the blood of the Messenger of God."[24] Muhammad is depicted as saying: "Whoever touches his blood and my blood, the fire of hell will not wound him."[25]

Al-Waqidi also quotes another companion of Muhammad who saw the prophet of Islam after the battle: "I looked at his face, and lo and behold, there was the mark of a dirham in each cheek; a fracture in his forehead at the root of his hair, his lower lip bled, and his central incisor on the right was broken, and on his wound was something black."[26]

In the confusion of the battle, rumors flew that Muhammad was not just wounded, but had been killed. Ibn Sa'd states that "Iblis, may Allah damn him, cried, Muhammad is slain."[27] This only increased the disorder in the ranks of the Muslims: "The Muslims were confused and began to fight against their custom," that is, not in the usual way they had fought up to this point.[28] "In haste and confusion they began to

---

17 Al-Waqidi, op. cit., 121.
18 Ibid.
19 Ibid.
20 Ibid.
21 Ibid.
22 Ibid.
23 Ibid.
24 Ibid.
25 Ibid.
26 Ibid., 122.
27 Ibn Sa'd, op. cit., II, 49.
28 Ibid.

strike each other."[29] Ibn Sa'd notes also that "the angels were present that day, but they did not fight."[30] One of the Quraysh, Ibn Qamiah, claimed that he had killed Muhammad, "and this filled the Muslims with awe and disheartened them."[31]

The confusion was quickly resolved, however; al-Waqidi explains that a search for Muhammad's body proved fruitless, and Ibn Qamiah was exposed as a liar: the prophet of Islam was still alive. Ibn Qamiah himself, however, would not remain alive for long. Al-Waqidi states that Muhammad prayed, "May God humiliate him!" Al-Waqidi then adds: "When Ibn Qamia approached a sheep to milk it, it butted him with its horns while he was holding it, and it killed him. He was found dead among the mountains because of the prayer of the Messenger of God."[32]

Muhammad Gets Revenge

As the battle continued, Muhammad revealed his undying thirst for vengeance. At one point, one of the Quraysh "shot an arrow that struck the hem of Umm Ayman," a Muslim woman "who had come, at that time, to give water to the wounded."[33] As a result, "she tripped and was revealed," and her Quraysh attacker found this a source of great mirth; "his laughter was loud."[34] Muhammad saw all this, and it "grieved the Prophet, so he gave Sa'd b. Abi Waqqas an arrow without an arrowhead and said, 'Shoot!'"[35] The Muslim shot the warrior of the Quraysh who had exposed and humiliated Umm Ayman, and the Qurayshi "fell down, exposing his buttocks."[36] Muhammad was delighted: "Sa'd said, 'I saw the Messenger of God laugh then, until his teeth could be seen.'"[37]

A hadith offers what is clearly a variant of the same story. The motif of Muslims saving a woman's modesty or striking back when it is outraged by unbelievers who are so lost in their lusts as to take delight in such humiliation is often seen not just in the sira literature but throughout Islamic history. It is, however, absent in this version of the story:

---

29 Ibid.
30 Ibid.
31 Ibid.
32 Al-Waqidi, op. cit., 121.
33 Ibid., 119.
34 Ibid.
35 Ibid.
36 Ibid.
37 Ibid.

Amir b. Sa'd reported on the authority of his father that Allah's Apostle gathered for him on the Day of Uhud his parents when a polytheist had set fire to (i.e. attacked fiercely) the Muslims. Thereupon Allah's Apostle said to him: (Sa'd), shoot an arrow, (Sa'd), may my mother and father be taken as ransom for you. I drew an arrow and I shot a featherless arrow at him, aiming at his side; then he fell down and his private parts were exposed. Allah's Messenger laughed that I saw his front teeth.[38]

Yet another hadith tells a very similar story, situating it during a later battle, the Battle of the Trench:

Amir ibn Sa'd said: Sa'd [Ibn Abi Waqqas] said: 'I had seen the Prophet laugh at the Battle of the Trench, so hard that his molar teeth became apparent.' I said: 'How was his laughter?' He said: 'There was a man holding a shield while Sa'd was shooting, and the man was saying such-and-such and such-and-such, with the shield covering his forehead. Sa'd therefore aimed an arrow at him and shot it when he raised his head, so it did not miss this part of him— meaning his forehead—and the man toppled over and kicked up his foot. The Prophet then laughed so much that his molar teeth became apparent.' I asked: 'What made him laugh?' He replied: 'What he did to the man!"[39]

While it is remotely possible that on two different occasions, in two separate battles, Sa'd ibn Abi Waqqas shot an opposing warrior with an arrow in a way that made Muhammad laugh heartily so that his back teeth were visible, it is much more likely that these are two different versions of the same story, fine-tuned to fit into different battles as they were disseminated among different groups of people.

In both versions, however, Muhammad is depicted as laughing heartily at the embarrassment of an opponent, in revenge for the opponent's humiliation of a Muslim woman (al-Waqidi's version) or in revenge for the apparent boasting of the opponent (the hadith version). The Christian idea of "love your enemies, and pray for those who persecute you" (Matthew 5:43), and the Judeo-Christian one of "do not rejoice when

38 Sahih Muslim, book 44, no. 2412c.
39 Ash-Shama'il al-Muhammadiyah 233.

your enemy falls, and let not your heart be glad when he stumbles" (Proverbs 24:17) is completely foreign to this mindset. Yet in a bizarre example of the West's willful blindness regarding Islam, and infatuation with it, the contemporary academic Eric Ormsby refers to these stories, which in all their variants depict Muhammad reveling in the destruction of his enemies, as revealing the Islamic prophet's charm: "And he loved to laugh, we are told, to the extent that when he did laugh—admittedly, not often—he did so 'until his back teeth showed'. These are charming reports; they make a figure remote in time and place startlingly present and credible."[40]

When the battle of Uhud had ended, the Quraysh were sure they had the upper hand. Quraysh commander Abu Sufyan climbed to a high place and called out to his men: "You have done a fine work; victory in war goes by turns. Today in exchange for the day" of the Quraysh defeat at Badr.[41] Then he prayed to one of his gods: "Show your superiority, Hubal."[42] Hearing this in the Muslim camp, Muhammad, according to Ibn Hisham, "told Umar to get up and answer him and say, 'God is most high and most glorious. We are not equal. Our dead are in paradise; your dead in hell.'"[43]

Forestalling Ridicule

In the aftermath of Uhud, Muhammad took one step to ensure that he would not be subject to the ridicule that appeared to be the weapon his enemies knew he feared and hated the most. At Badr, the Muslims had taken prisoner a poet, Abu Azza Amr ibn Abdullah ibn Umayr al-Jumahi. Al-Waqidi says that Muhammad set him free after Abu Azza pleaded: "I have five daughters who have nothing. Grant me life and be charitable to them, O Muhammad."[44] In response to this show of mercy from the prophet of Islam, Abu Azza offered a promise: "I give you my word that I will not fight you nor increase against you ever."[45] Mindful of this promise, Muhammad sent Abu Azza back to Mecca in peace.

---

40 Eric Ormsby, "Making a Prophet," *Literary Review*, November 2013, https://literaryreview.co.uk/making-a-prophet.
41 Ibn Ishaq, op. cit., 386.
42 Ibid.
43 Ibid.
44 Al-Waqidi, op. cit., 56.
45 Ibid.

Abu Azza, however, was not to keep his promise. When his fellow Quraysh exhorted him to join them in fighting the Muslims again at Uhud, Abu Azza was reluctant, saying: "I have given a promise to Muhammad that I will not fight him nor increase against him ever. He was kind to me, and he was not kind to any other but rather killed him or took ransom from him."[46] The Quraysh leader Safwan then lured Abu Azza with his own promise: if Abu Azza survived the battle, "he would give him so much wealth that his debt would not consume it."[47] And if Abu Azza were killed, Safwan "would keep his daughters with his own daughters."[48]

This won over Abu Azza, and he went out with the Quraysh to fight the Muslims again at Uhud. For him, the outcome was the same as it had been at Badr: the Muslims once again took him captive. Abu Azza pleaded with the prophet of Islam, saying: "O Muhammad, surely I went out, hating it. I have daughters and I am their guarantor."[49] Muhammad replied: "Where is what you gave me of promise and trust? No, by God, you will not wipe your two cheeks in Mecca to say, 'I made fun of Muhammad a second time.'"[50] Al-Waqidi offers a variant of the story in which Abu Azza, captured a second time, pleads: "O Muhammad, be kind to me!"[51] Muhammad has no interest in his appeal, saying: "Indeed, a believer will not be bitten from a snake hole twice. And you will never go back to Mecca to boast that you deceived Muhammad twice."[52] Then, he commanded one of the Muslims to behead Abu Azza.

Mutilation

Meanwhile, one of the women of the Quraysh, Hind bint Utba, who was the wife of Abu Sufyan, was looking for vengeance of her own. Her father, son, brother, and uncle had been killed fighting the Muslims at Badr; after the Battle of Uhud, she and "the women with her," according to Ibn Hisham, "stopped to mutilate the apostle's dead companions." Ibn Hisham continues:

---

46 Ibid.
47 Ibid.
48 Ibid.
49 Ibid.
50 Ibid.
51 Ibid., 149.
52 Ibid.

They cut off their ears and noses and Hind made them into anklets and collars and gave her anklets and collars and pendants to Wahshi, the slave of Jubayr b. Mutim. She cut out Hamza's liver and chewed it, but she was not able to swallow it and threw it away. Then she mounted a high rock and shrieked at the top of her voice:

> We have paid you back for Badr
> And a war that follows a war is always violent.
> I could not bear the loss of Utba
> Nor my brother and his uncle and my first-born.
> I have slaked my vengeance and fulfilled my vow.[53]

Hamza was Muhammad's uncle. Abu Sufyan attempted to calm the situation, calling out to the Muslims: "There are some mutilated bodies among your dead. By God, it gives me no satisfaction, and no anger. I neither prohibited nor ordered mutilation."[54] When Muhammad came upon his uncle's mutilated body, however, he was overcome with rage and exclaimed: "If God gives me victory over Quraysh in the future, I will mutilate 30 of their men."[55]

Muhammad's grief and anger inspired the Muslims with him: "When the Muslims saw the apostle's grief and anger against those who had thus treated his uncle, they said, 'By God, if God gives us victory over them in the future we will mutilate them as no Arab has ever mutilated anyone.'"[56] However, Allah then stepped in with a note of proportionality: "If you punish, then punish with the equivalent of what you were afflicted with. But if you endure patiently, indeed it is better for the patient" (Qur'an 16:126). Accordingly, says Ibn Hisham, Muhammad "pardoned them and was patient and forbade mutilation."[57] One of the Muslims recalled: "The apostle never stopped in a place and left it without enjoining on us almsgiving and forbidding mutilation."[58] In another Qur'anic verse, however, Allah instructed Muslims to retaliate against their foes in the same way they had been attacked, and even to "transgress" against existing laws, without any accompanying exhortation to

---

53 Ibn Ishaq, op. cit., 385.
54 Ibid., 386.
55 Ibid., 387.
56 Ibid.
57 Ibid.
58 Ibid., 388.

endure wrongs patiently: "Then whoever transgresses against you, you transgress in the same way against him" (2:194). This opened the door for mutilation and other atrocities to be practiced lawfully if they had been perpetrated against the Muslims.

Explaining Uhud

After Uhud, Allah reinforced with new revelations the proposition that victory and defeat were decided by him alone and on the basis of the piety of the warriors: "And when you left your house at daybreak to assign to the believers their positions for the battle, Allah was the hearer, the knower. When two parties of you almost fell away, and Allah was their protecting friend. In Allah let believers put their trust" (3:121-2). Allah had given the Muslims victory in the previous battle and would do so again in the future if they remained steadfast in the faith:

> Allah had already given you the victory at Badr, when you were contemptible. So observe your duty to Allah so that you may be thankful. When you said to the believers, Is it not sufficient for you that your Lord should support you with three thousand angels sent down? No, but if you persevere and avoid evil, and they attack you suddenly, your Lord will help you with five thousand angels sweeping in. Allah ordained this only as a message of good cheer for you, and that thereby your hearts might be at rest. Victory comes only from Allah, the mighty, the wise (3:123-6).

The defeat at Uhud was apparently due to the Muslims' disobedience, as Allah now exhorts them: "O you who believe, do not devour usury, doubling and quadrupling. Observe your duty to Allah, so that you may be successful" (3:130). But the Muslims must be patient, for the reward of their obedience—victory over their enemies—might not come immediately, but it would come: "Do not grow weary and do not grieve, for you will overcome them if you are believers" (3:139). Uhud was a gigantic test for the believers, as well as for the unbelievers: "And that Allah may purify those who believe, and may destroy the unbelievers. Or did you think that you would enter paradise when Allah did not yet know which of you would really wage jihad, and did not know which are steadfast?" (3:141-2)

Allah promised to punish the Muslims' foes: "We will cast terror into the hearts of those who disbelieve because they ascribe partners to Allah, for which no justification has been revealed. Their dwelling is the fire, and wretched is the dwelling place of the wrongdoers" (3:151). The difference between Badr and Uhud was a matter of the Muslims' devotion to Allah: "Allah indeed made good on his promise to you when you routed them by his permission" at Badr, "until your courage failed you, and you disagreed about the order and you disobeyed, after he had shown you what you long for. Some of you desired this world, and some of you desired the hereafter. Therefore he made you flee from them" at Uhud "that he might test you. Yet now he has forgiven you. Allah is a Lord of kindness to believers" (3:152).

Satan had deceived those who desired the world rather than the here-after: "Indeed, those of you who turned back on the day when the two armies met, it was Satan alone who caused them to backslide, because of some of what they have earned. Now Allah has forgiven them. Indeed, Allah is forgiving, merciful" (3:155).

All this appears to be exactly what it is represented as being in Islamic tradition: a rationalization of a defeat and an exhortation to the defeated force to arise and fight again with renewed courage. Passages such as this clearly refer to an event with which the hearers are assumed to be familiar but which has been lost to succeeding generations: "When you climbed and paid no heed to anyone, while the messenger, in your rear, was calling you. Therefore he rewarded you trouble for trouble, so that you would not be sorry either for what you missed or for what happened to you. Allah is aware of what you do" (3:153).

Muhammad is generally assumed to be the messenger, and this is universally taken as a reference to a detail of the Battle of Uhud. But there is no explicit reference either to Muhammad or to Uhud in the Qur'anic texts that are generally understood to be discussing this battle. Here, as in other instances, it is just as possible that the ninth-century accounts of Uhud were invented or adapted from texts describing an entirely different battle in order to explain the elliptical and obscure Islamic text rather than that they were the actual context in which these "revelations" were received.

Another Wife and a Book That Can (or Cannot) Be Changed

After the Battle of Uhud, Muhammad took another wife, Hind bint Suhayl, better known as Umm Salama, who had been widowed in the battle. Umm Salama is revered in some circles today as an Islamic proto-feminist, for according to Tabari, she once asked Muhammad: "Why are men mentioned in the Qur'an and why are we not?"[59] Umm Salama later recounted:

> I had asked the Prophet why the Qur'an did not speak of us as it did of men. And what was my surprise one afternoon, when I was combing my hair, to hear his voice from the minbar. I hastily did up my hair and ran to one of the apartments from where I could hear better. I pressed my ear to the wall, and here is what the Prophet said: "O people! Allah has said in his book: 'Men who surrender unto Allah, and women who surrender, and men who believe and women who believe,'" etc. And he continued in this vein until he came to the end of the passage where it is said: "Allah hath prepared for them forgiveness and a vast reward."[60]

This was a new Qur'anic revelation (33:35), appearing to grant equality to men and women. Unfortunately, it was not the Qur'an's only word on the subject.

Around the time that Muhammad married Umm Salama, according to Tabari, he commanded one of his companions, Zayd bin Thabit, "to study the Book of the Jews, saying 'I fear that they may change my Book."[61] This is a curious tradition. Apparently, it is designed to account for discrepancies in the Qur'anic text and to explain, at least in part, Islam's similarities to elements of Jewish tradition. Yet it was strange that Muhammad would be depicted as fearing that the Jews would change the Qur'an, as the Qur'an itself says that it cannot be changed: "And recite what has been revealed to you of the book of your Lord. There is no one who can change his words, and you will find no refuge besides him" (18:27). The Qur'anic text may have represented more of

---

59 Tabari, *Tafsir*, vol. 22, 10, in Fatima Mernissi, *The Veil and the Male Elite: A Feminist Interpretation of Women's Rights in Islam*, Mary Jo Lakeland, trans. (Reading, Massachusetts: Addison-Wesley Publishing Company, 1987), 118.

60 Ibid.

61 Tabari, *History*, op. cit., 167.

an aspiration than a reality; as the new religion was developing, changes were inevitably made, and so they had to be explained away. One easy recourse was to blame the recurring villains of the entire hadith and sira literature: the Jews.

Confronting the Jews Again

Meanwhile, trouble was brewing between the Muslims and the Jews of the Banu Nadir, one of the two remaining Jewish tribes of Medina. A hadith depicts the Nadir Jews as plotting with the pagan Quraysh against Muhammad for a considerable period, beginning after the Battle of Badr. According to this story, the Quraysh initiated the plot with a threatening letter to the Nadir Jews: "You are men of weapons and fortresses. You should fight our companion or we shall deal with you in a certain way. And nothing will come between us and the anklets of your women."[62]

The hadith continues by stating that the Banu Nadir then wrote to Muhammad: "Come out to us with thirty men from your companions, and thirty rabbis will come out from us till we meet at a central place where they will hear you. If they testify to you and believe in you, we shall believe in you."[63] However, instead of coming out to discuss theology, "when the next day came, the Messenger of Allah went out in the morning with an army, and surrounded them. He told them: 'I swear by Allah, you will have no peace from me until you conclude a treaty with me. But they refused to conclude a treaty with him. He therefore fought them the same day.'"[64]

According to al-Waqidi, however, matters came to a head after the Battle of Uhud, when one of the Muslims, Amr ibn Umayya al-Damri, killed two members of the Banu Amir, an Arab tribe. When Amr presented Muhammad with the booty he had seized after the murders, Muhammad was not pleased, saying (in al-Waqidi's version): "What you have done is unfortunate. The two of them had a protection and an agreement from us!"[65] Amr pleaded ignorance; as far as he had known, they were just polytheists whom he could lawfully kill and plunder: "I

---

62 Sunan Abi Dawud, book 20, no. 3004.
63 Ibid.
64 Ibid.
65 Al-Waqidi, op. cit., 178.

did not know. I saw them in their polytheism, their people taking what they took from us by deceit."[66] Muhammad, al-Waqidi states, "commanded that their plunder be set aside until he sent it with their blood money," as the leader of the Banu Amir had sent him a message asking for blood money to atone for the deaths of his men.[67]

Muhammad was willing to pay, but he wanted the Banu Nadir to put up the money, as they were allies of the Banu Amir. According to al-Waqidi, the Jews greeted him as a dear friend, saying: "O Abu'l-Qasim," that is, the father of Qasim, one of Muhammad's sons who had died in early childhood, "we will do whatever you desire. It is about time that you visited us, so come to us. Be seated until we bring you food!"[68]

Their conviviality was deceptive, however, as they said among themselves: "O community of Jews, Muhammad has come to you with less than ten of his companions, including Abu Bakr, Umar, Ali, al-Zubayr, Talha, Sa'd b. Muadh, Usayd b. Hudayr, and Sa'd b. Ubada. Throw a stone upon him from above this house, which he is under, and kill him, for you will never find him with less companions than he has with him now."[69] Al-Waqidi depicts one of the Nadir Jews, Sallam ibn Mishkam, as aware of the treachery involved in this and urging his people to be more prudent: "Obey me this once, my people, and you may disagree with me forever after, for by God, if you do this (throw a stone on Muhammad), he will surely be informed that we are acting treacherously against him. Surely this is the violation of the agreement, which is between us and him, so do not do it! By God, if you do what you intend, this religion will surely stay among them until the Day of Judgment. He will destroy the Jews and his religion will triumph."[70]

Even within the logic of the Islamic traditions, this was not a gratuitous attack. After Muhammad had exiled the Banu Qaynuqa, the Banu Nadir had good reason to suspect that he would turn upon them as well, and so were endeavoring to protect themselves. Allah, however, was protecting Muhammad; Ibn Hisham states that "as the apostle was with a number of his companions among whom were Abu Bakr, Umar, and Ali, news came to him from heaven about what these people intended,

66 Ibid.
67 Ibid.
68 Ibid.
69 Ibid.
70 Ibid.

so he got up and he went back to Medina."[71] By all accounts, the Nadir Jews lived in Medina as well, so al-Waqidi must mean by this the area of Medina where the Muslims were living at the time. After a while, the companions left as well, leaving some of the Banu Nadir bewildered at their unexplained departure.

Then, according to al-Waqidi, one of the Jews, Kinana ibn Suwayra, gives another example of a common theme in the Islamic traditions: that at least some of the Jews knew very well that Muhammad was a prophet but were rejecting him out of obstinacy and self-interest. Kinana asked the others: "Did you know why Muhammad got up?"[72] They replied: "No, by God, we do not know, and you do not know!" But Kinana insisted:

> But certainly, by the Torah, I do know! Muhammad was informed about the treachery you planned against him. Do not deceive yourselves. By God, he is surely the Messenger of God, for he would not have stood up except that he was informed about what you planned against him. Surely he is the last of the prophets. You desire him to be from the Banu Harun [the tribe of Aaron], but God has placed him as He pleases. Surely our books and what we studied of the Torah that were not changed and altered, state that his birth is in Mecca and the land of his emigration is Yathrib. His exact description does not disagree by a letter from what is in our book. What he brings you is better than his fighting you. But it appears to me as if I see you departing. Your children scream, for you have left your homes and your possessions that are the basis of your nobility behind. So obey me in two things, for the third has no virtue in it."[73]

They ask him: "What are the two?" Kinana answers: "Convert and enter with Muhammad, and secure your possessions and children. Thus, you will be among the highest of his companions, and your possessions will remain in your hands, for you will not leave from your homes."[74] But the men of Banu Nadir are unwilling to become Muslims and respond: "We will not depart from the Torah and the covenant of Moses."[75]

---

71 Ibn Ishaq, op. cit., 437.
72 Al-Waqidi, op. cit., 179.
73 Ibid.
74 Ibid.
75 Ibid.

Kinana then repeated his warning that Muhammad would exile the Nadir Jews from Medina: "Surely he will send to you to 'Leave from my land.'"[76] He advised them to accept exile so that they would not be killed and their possessions taken as plunder: "Say, 'Yes,' and then surely he will not deem your blood and money lawful, and your possessions will remain. If you wish you may sell it, and if you wish you may keep it."[77] They agree, but Kinana is unhappy with the whole matter, saying: "By God, would it not have disgraced you, I would have converted to Islam, but by God, Sha'tha shall never be reproached for my conversion, so I will share your fate."[78] Al-Waqidi explains: "His daughter was Sha'tha whom Hassan used to flirt with."[79]

In Ibn Sa'd's version, Muhammad states explicitly that Allah informed him about the Jews' plot, telling his companions when they asked him why he had left the Banu Nadir so abruptly: "The Jews had intended to act treacherously; Allah informed me and I left."[80] He told Muhammad ibn Maslama to go back to the Nadir Jews and tell them: "Go out from my land and you shall not live here because of the treachery you had intended to commit. You are given ten days' time (to leave). He who is seen after this time would be beheaded."[81]

Confronted with this demand, the leader of the Nadir Jews was defiant, sending word to Muhammad: "We shall not leave our houses; you may do what you like."[82] Muhammad "said the *takbir* loudly, and the Muslims said the *takbir* in response."[83] That is, Muhammad exclaimed, "Allahu akbar," Allah is greater, a declaration of Allah's superiority over the gods of the infidels that was ever after to be the cry of Muslims when waging war. Al-Waqidi states that Muhammad "proclaimed *takbir* and the Muslims magnified it. He said, 'The Jews have chosen war!'" Ibn Sa'd asserts that "the Jews had waged war," but they had not actually chosen war or waged it; all they had really done was reject Muhammad's ultimatum.[84]

76 Ibid.
77 Ibid.
78 Ibid.
79 Ibid.
80 Ibn Sa'd, op. cit., II, 69.
81 Ibid.
82 Ibid.
83 Ibid.
84 Ibid., al-Waqidi, op. cit., 181.

Cutting Down the Trees

In response to this rejection, Muhammad, according to Ibn Hisham, ordered the Muslims "to prepare for war and to march against them."[85] The Nadir Jews "took refuge in their forts and the apostle ordered that the palm trees should be cut down and burnt, and they called out to him, 'Muhammad, you have prohibited wanton destruction and blamed those guilty of it. Why then are you cutting down and burning our palm-trees?'"[86]

It was a valid question. A hadith depicts Muhammad giving some general instructions for the conduct of warfare: "I advise you ten things: Do not kill women or children or an aged, infirm person. Do not cut down fruit-bearing trees. Do not destroy an inhabited place. Do not slaughter sheep or camels except for food. Do not burn bees and do not scatter them. Do not steal from the booty, and do not be cowardly."[87]

The Qur'an also seems to be aware of a contradiction between two Islamic traditions regarding the cutting of trees, as it goes out of its way to emphasize that Allah explicitly permitted what was done against the Nadir Jews: "Any palm-trees you cut down or left standing on their roots, it was by Allah's permission, so that he might frustrate those who are evil" (59:5). Either the Muslim community reversed itself on this issue or there were two factions, one favoring "wanton destruction" in battle and the other rejecting it. The resulting ambiguity allows contemporary Islamic apologists in the West to maintain that Muhammad laid down humane rules for warfare that even respected the environment; meanwhile, jihadis have the Qur'anic exhortation to emulate Muhammad (33:21) as justification to fight with no such restraints.

Expelling the Jews

The Banu Nadir held out against the Muslims' siege for fifteen days. The Banu Qurayzah, the other Jewish tribe that remained in Medina after Muhammad had exiled the Banu Qaynuqa, did not join the Banu Nadir in fighting against Muhammad. They still had a nominal alliance with the prophet of Islam, and so, according to al-Waqidi, "the Qurayza kept

---

85 Ibn Hisham, op. cit.
86 Ibid.
87 Muwatta Malik book 21, hadith 10.

away from them," that is, the Nadir, "and did not help them with weapons or men, and did not come near them."[88]

Bukhari, however, records a conflicting tradition: "Bani An-Nadir and Bani Quraiza fought (against the Prophet, violating their peace treaty), so the Prophet exiled Bani An-Nadir and allowed Bani Quraiza to remain at their places (in Medina) taking nothing from them till they fought against the Prophet again."[89] This was a reference to the Battle of the Trench, which took place later. But if the Banu Qurayza fought Muhammad "again" at the Battle of the Trench, they must have done so previously, which contradicts al-Waqidi's statement that they refused to join the Banu Nadir against Muhammad.

Whether or not the Qurayzah were with the Nadir, al-Waqidi notes that when the women of the Nadir saw the Muslims cutting down the date palms, they "tore their dresses, struck their cheeks, crying out in affliction."[90] Hearing them, Muhammad asked: "What is wrong with them?"[91] He was informed that "they are saddened by the cutting of the Ajwa," that is, the particular variety of date that was growing on the palms the Muslims were cutting down. Muhammad took the opportunity to explain the beneficial properties of this particular date: "The mellowed Ajwa, and the dry—the male with which the female date palm is pollinated—are the date palms of Paradise. The Ajwa are a cure for poison."[92] A hadith depicts him as being quite specific about this: "Whoever takes seven Ajwa dates in the morning will not be effected by magic or poison on that day."[93]

Meanwhile, one of the Jews tried to console the weeping women, telling them: "If the Ajwa are cut over here, we have Ajwa in Khaybar," an oasis nearly a hundred miles north of Medina, where the Banu Qaynuqa had settled after Muhammad had exiled them. But in a dark portent of things to come, al-Waqidi adds that "an old woman among them said, 'Khaybar will see the same fate!'"[94] The Jewish leader, Abu Rafi, replied:

---

88 Al-Waqidi, op. cit., 181.
89 Sahih Bukhari, vol. 5, book 64, no. 4028.
90 Al-Waqidi, op. cit., 182.
91 Ibid.
92 Ibid.
93 Sahih Bukhari, vol. 7, book 76, no. 5779.
94 Al-Waqidi, op. cit., 182–3.

"May God break your jaw! Surely my confederates at Khaybar are ten thousand warriors."[95]

The warriors of the Nadir would soon be adding to those numbers. The Jews surrendered and asked Muhammad for permission to leave Medina with as much as they could carry on their camels, except for weapons, which he granted. Despite this victory, however, Muhammad was not in a magnanimous mood; he was still enraged over the Banu Nadir plot. "Having expelled them," says al-Waqidi, "the Messenger of God said to Ibn Yamin, 'Did you not see how your cousin Amr b. Jihash plotted to kill me?'" Ibn Yamin declared: "I will protect you from him, O Messenger of God." Ibn Yamin paid a man to kill Amr ibn Jihash; "then Ibn Yamin came to the Prophet and informed him of the killing and the Prophet was pleased."[96]

Ibn Hisham, however, states that a man from the Banu Muharib, one of the Arab tribes, made an offer to the men of his own tribe and to the Ghatafan, a confederation of other Arab tribes: "Shall I kill Muhammad for you?"[97] They "encouraged him to do so and asked him how he proposed to carry out his design."[98] The would-be assassin explained that he would take Muhammad by surprise; he then approached the prophet of Islam, who was "sitting with his sword in his lap, and asked to be allowed to look at it."[99] Muhammad readily handed it over, whereupon the man "drew it and began to brandish it intending to strike him, but God frustrated him."[100] Despite the fact that an unseen force was preventing him from carrying out his plan, the man asked Muhammad: "Aren't you afraid of me when I have a sword in my hand?"[101] Muhammad answered: "No, God will protect me from you."[102]

Thwarted, the man handed Muhammad back his sword, and Allah revealed: "O you who believe, remember Allah's favor to you, how a people intended to stretch out their hands against you but he kept their hands from you, and keep your duty to Allah. In Allah let believers put their trust" (Qur'an 5:11). There were, however, apparently two

---

95 Ibid., 183.
96 Ibid.
97 Ibn Ishaq, op. cit., 445.
98 Ibid.
99 Ibid.
100 Ibid.
101 Ibid.
102 Ibid.

circulating versions of the tradition surrounding the revelation of this passage: Ibn Hisham then notes that another source told him "that this came down in reference to Amr b. Jihash, brother of B. Al-Nadir, and his intention. But God knows the truth of the matter."[103]

Allah once again took credit for the Muslims' victory over the Nadir Jews in a new revelation:

> All that is in the heavens and all that is on the earth glorifies Allah, and he is the mighty, the wise. It is he who has caused those among the people of the book who disbelieved to go forth from their homes to the first exile. You did not think that they would go forth, while they thought that their strongholds would protect them from Allah. But Allah reached them from a place they did not expect, and cast terror in their hearts so that they ruined their houses with their own hands and the hands of the believers. (Qur'an 59:1–2)

Al-Waqidi explains that "while they were besieged, the Jews were destroying their own homes that were on their side, and the Muslims were destroying what was on their side, until peace was settled."[104] Why the Jews would destroy their own houses is left unexplained. Here again, it is impossible to know if the canonical account accurately elucidates the circumstances of the Qur'anic revelation or was constructed in order to make sense of an opaque text.

This idea of the infidels being led by Allah to destroy themselves looms large in the contemporary jihadist consciousness. The Muslim Brotherhood echoed this idea as it detailed its goals for the United States in an internal communication that was never intended to be published but which the FBI seized in 2005 in the course of its investigation of an Islamic charity known as the Holy Land Foundation, which at that time was the largest Islamic charity in the United States.

The document, which was entitled "An Explanatory Memorandum on the General Strategic Goal for the Group in North America," exhorted members of the Muslim Brotherhood inside the US to "understand that their work in America is a kind of grand jihad in eliminating and destroying the Western civilization from within and 'sabotaging' its miserable house by their hands and the hands of the believers, so

---

103 Ibid.
104 Ibid.

that it is eliminated and Allah's religion is made victorious over all other religions."[105] The idea of the non-Muslims in America working for their own destruction, with help from the Muslims, came straight from this Qur'anic passage about the defeat and exile of the Nadir Jews.

Al-Qaeda also quoted this Qur'anic passage about the infidels destroying their own houses in an edition of its glossy, slickly produced magazine, *Ummah Wahidah* ("One Ummah," that is, one global Islamic community) that was published in September 2023 in commemoration of the twenty-second anniversary of the jihad attacks of September 11, 2001. The jihad terror group vowed an attack on the United States that would be even more devastating than those attacks had been.[106] Likewise, Gholamreza Qasemian, director of the library, museum, and archives of the Iranian Majles, said in an August 2023 lecture that "Israel only has three years left to exist. There is even no need for a war. 'They destroy their homes with their own hands.' [Israel] will self-destruct. There are now all kinds of signs of its annihilation."[107]

The Qur'an continues by noting that exile was a merciful punishment for the Banu Nadir:

So learn a lesson, O you who have eyes. And if Allah had not decreed migration for them, he indeed would have punished them in the world, and in the hereafter theirs is the punishment of the fire. That is because they were opposed to Allah and his messenger, and whoever is opposed to Allah, Allah is indeed stern in reprisal. (Qur'an 59:2–4)

When the Nadir Jews left Medina, some children who had been in their company remained behind. A hadith has Muhammad's cousin Abdullah ibn Abbas recounting that, before the hijrah and the conversion

105 Mohamed Akram, "An Explanatory Memorandum on the General Strategic Goal for the Group in North America," May 22, 1991, Government Exhibit 003-0085, U.S. vs. HLF, et al. P. 7 (21).

106 "Al-Qaeda Magazine Released On 9/11 Anniversary Threatens Future Attack on U.S. More Devastating Than 9/11," Middle East Media Research Institute (MEMRI), Top of FormBottom of FormSeptember 11, 2023, https://www.memri.org/jttm/al-qaeda-maga-zine-released-911-anniversary-threatens-future-attack-us-more-devastating-911.

107 "Gholamreza Qasemian, Director of the Iranian Majles's Library, Museum, and Archives: Israel Will Self-Destruct Within Three Years; After That, We Will Fight Saudi Arabia and Conquer Mecca," Middle East Media Research Institute (MEMRI), August 26, 2023, https://www.memri.org/tv/head-of-iranian-majles-archives-qasemian-israel-destroy-final-war-con-quer-mecca-ghasemian.

of the Ansar to Islam, if one of the pagan Arab women of Medina had a child who died, she would make a vow that if she had another child who survived, she would turn that child over to the Jews to raise as a Jew." Accordingly, "when Banu an-Nadir were expelled, there were some children of the Ansar among them."[108]

The hadith continues with the Ansar saying: "We shall not leave our children."[109] That is, the Ansar, who were now Muslims, didn't want the Arab children who were being raised as Jews to accompany the Banu Nadir into exile. But then, "Allah the Exalted revealed: 'Let there be no compulsion in religion. Truth stands out clear from error.'"[110] Thus, the children cannot be forced to become Muslims; they must be allowed to go with the Nadir into exile rather than stay in Medina with the Muslims.

This is Qur'an 2:256, a passage that is frequently quoted in our age in order to demonstrate that Islam is a peaceful and tolerant faith. Ibn Kathir tells this story in his exegesis of this Qur'anic passage, which he says means, "Do not force anyone to become Muslim, for Islam is plain and clear, and its proofs and evidence are plain and clear. Therefore, there is no need to force anyone to embrace Islam. Rather, whoever Allah directs to Islam, opens his heart for it and enlightens his mind, will embrace Islam with certainty. Whoever Allah blinds his heart and seals his hearing and sight, then he will not benefit from being forced to embrace Islam."[111]

These are high-minded sentiments; unfortunately, throughout Islamic history, they have all too often been honored in the breach. And before too long, according to the Islamic traditions, the Banu Nadir would have abundant reason to regret having brought these children along.

---

108 Sunan Abi Dawud book 15, no. 2682.
109 Sunan Abi Dawud book 15, no. 2682.
110 Sunan Abi Dawud book 15, no. 2682.
111 Ibn Kathir, *Tafsir Ibn Kathir*, op. cit., II, 30.

CHAPTER TEN

Problems and Solutions

Aisha Is Accused

After exiling the Banu Nadir, Muhammad embarked upon a series of raids on Arab tribes. It was during one of these that a crisis arose that roiled the Muslim community and led ultimately to a split that continues to this day. Alternatively, a story was composed and situated during one of those raids that attempts to explain several important issues, including the reasons for that deep schism in the community.

The story is told by Aisha, Muhammad's child bride, who was about thirteen or fourteen years old by the time of the events she recounts. In Bukhari's version, she explains that "whenever Allah's Messenger intended to go on a journey, he used to draw lots amongst his wives, and Allah's Messenger used to take with him the one on whom lot fell."[1] Aisha won the drawing and so joined Muhammad and the Muslims on the raid. She explains that this was "after Allah's order of veiling (the women) had been revealed."[2] That order was contained in a new Qur'anic revelation: "O prophet, tell your wives and your daughters and the women of the believers to draw their veils close around them. That will be better, so that they may be recognized and not molested. Allah is always forgiving, merciful" (33:59).

Aisha was, therefore, fully veiled as she was loaded onto a camel's back in a howdah by men who were forbidden to see her or even to speak to her. After the raid, when Muhammad announced that it was time for the Muslims to make their way back to Medina, "I got up and went away from the army camps," Aisha recounts, but once she was back

---

1 Sahih Bukhari, vol. 5, book 64, no. 4141.
2 Ibid.

at her camel, she realized she had lost her necklace.[3] She went back to look for it, and while she was gone, "the people who used to carry me on my camel, came and took my howdah and put it on the back of my camel on which I used to ride, as they considered that I was in it. In those days women were light in weight for they did not get fat, and flesh did not cover their bodies in abundance as they used to eat only a little food."[4] Also, Aisha was still a very young girl.

Once Aisha found her necklace, the Muslims had left. Aisha was alone in the desert, and no one among the Muslims realized that she was not with them. As it happened, a young Muslim warrior, Safwan bin al-Muattal Al-Sulami Al-Dhakwani, was "behind the army. When he reached my place in the morning, he saw the figure of a sleeping person and he recognized me on seeing me as he had seen me before the order of compulsory veiling (was prescribed)."[5] When Aisha saw him, she is depicted as recounting: "I veiled my face with my head cover at once, and by Allah, we did not speak a single word, and I did not hear him saying any word besides his Istirja," a prayer Muslims often recite in times of stress.[6]

Safwan carried Aisha back to the Muslim army. Yet it was after this instance of being saved that her worst troubles began. Rumors immediately started spreading in the Muslim camp that Safwan and Aisha were guilty of adultery. These rumors made even Muhammad distance himself from her. Aisha states: "After we returned to Medina, I became ill for a month. The people were propagating the forged statements of the slanderers while I was unaware of anything of all that, but I felt that in my present ailment, I was not receiving the same kindness from Allah's Messenger as I used to receive when I got sick. (But now) Allah's Messenger would only come, greet me and say, 'How is that (lady)?' and leave."[7]

Aisha Is Exonerated

When Aisha found out that she had been accused of adultery, "I kept on weeping that night till dawn I could neither stop weeping nor sleep

---

3 Ibid.
4 Ibid.
5 Ibid.
6 Ibid.
7 Ibid.

then in the morning again, I kept on weeping."[8] Ibn Hisham, who places the incident later, after the Muslims' raid on an Arab tribe, the Banu Mustaliq, depicts Aisha's mother offering comforting words that included a backhanded critique of polygamy: "My little daughter, don't let the matter weigh on you. Seldom is there a beautiful woman married to a man who loves her but her rival wives gossip about her and men do the same."[9]

She was facing being stoned to death and was by no means the only one who was distraught at the prospect. As even "the Divine Inspiration was delayed," and Muhammad called Ali bin Abi Talib and another of his companions, Usama bin Zayd, "to ask and consult them about divorcing me."[10] Usama bin Zayd said, "O Allah's Messenger! She is your wife and we do not know anything except good about her."[11] Ali, however, was less gallant, answering that Muhammad could easily replace Aisha, as there were plenty of fish in the sea: "O Allah's Messenger! Allah does not put you in difficulty and there are plenty of women other than she, yet ask the maid-servant who will tell you the truth."[12] Ibn Hisham has Ali speak even more bluntly: "Women are plentiful, and you can easily change one for another. Ask the slave girl, for she will tell you the truth."[13]

According to Islamic tradition, at that moment was born the everlasting enmity between Aisha and Ali. When he was vying to be Muhammad's successor upon his death, she argued against his candidacy. She did so again after the deaths of Abu Bakr, Umar, and Uthman. When Ali finally became caliph anyway after the Uthman's death, she convinced a Muslim commander, Muawiya, to rebel against him. She even led armies against him herself, commanding them from the back of a camel, where she was safely ensconced in a howdah as she had been on the fateful occasion when she was left behind and rescued by Safwan. This enmity ultimately became the split between the majority of the Muslims, who revered Aisha, and the *shiat Ali*, the party of Ali, which came to be known as the Shi'ites.

---

8 Ibid.
9 Ibn Ishaq, op. cit., 495.
10 Sahih Bukhari, vol. 5, book 64, no. 4141.
11 Ibid.
12 Ibid.
13 Ibn Ishaq, op. cit., 496.

The initial controversy was resolved after Barira, the maidservant to whom Ali had directed Muhammad, told the prophet of Islam: "By Him Who has sent you with the Truth. I have never seen anything in her (i.e. Aisha) which I would conceal, except that she is a young girl who sleeps leaving the dough of her family exposed so that the domestic goats come and eat it."[14] Ibn Hisham says that when Muhammad called this slave girl over to ask her about Aisha, "Ali got up and gave her a violent beating, saying, 'Tell the apostle the truth.'"[15] Could this wholly undeserved thrashing have influenced Barira to speak well of Aisha since the man who had beat her was so cavalier about the fate of Muhammad's child bride? Islamic tradition does not consider this question.

Muhammad then asked his companions from the pulpit for help against Aisha's accuser: "O you Muslims! Who will relieve me from that man who has hurt me with his evil statement about my family? By Allah, I know nothing except good about my family and they have blamed a man about whom I know nothing except good and he used never to enter my home except with me."[16] One of the companions volunteered to kill the accuser, Abdullah bin Ubayy, if he was from the al-Aws tribe but not if he was from the al-Khazraj tribe. At this, an argument broke out between the members of the two tribes, and nothing was resolved.

Aisha remained disconsolate, weeping for days. According to al-Waqidi, her father, Abu Bakr, advised her to beg Muhammad for forgiveness. Conscious of her own innocence, Aisha indignantly refused: "By God, I will not ask for forgiveness of God for what you mention, ever."[17] She lamented her fate and longed for Allah to send down a new revelation exonerating her: "'Woe unto me, I am, by God, more scorned in my heart and too diminished a thing that He should reveal a Qur'an about me that people would read in their prayers.' And yet I hoped that the Messenger of God would see in his sleep something to indicate that God disbelieves them about me for what He knows of my innocence, or that news would reach him. And as for a Qur'an, no by God, how could I think it!"[18]

---

14 Sahih Bukhari, vol. 5, book 64, no. 4141.
15 Ibn Ishaq, op. cit., 496.
16 Sahih Bukhari, vol. 5, book 64, no. 4141.
17 Al-Waqidi, op. cit., 212.
18 Ibid.

Yet it was indeed Allah who saved Aisha, providing the solution to the problem in a new revelation for which she had dared to hope. Aisha is depicted as witnessing this: "The sweat was dropping from his body like pearls though it was a wintry day and that was because of the weighty statement which was being revealed to him."[19] Once he had received the divine message, Muhammad "got up smiling, and the first word he said was, 'O Aisha! Allah has declared your innocence!'"[20] The new revelation first disparaged Aisha's accusers: "Indeed, those who spread the slander are a gang among you. Do not think it is a bad thing for you, no, it is good for you. To every man among them, what he has earned of the sin, and as for him among them who had the greater share in it, his will be an awful doom" (Qur'an 24:11).

Then Allah established rules of evidence that Aisha's accusers had not met: "Why didn't the believers, men and women, when you heard it, think good of their own people, and say, It is an obvious untruth? Why didn't they produce four witnesses? Since they do not produce witnesses, they indeed are liars in the sight of Allah" (24:12–13). Henceforth, it would be a law: "And those who accuse honorable women but do not bring four witnesses, lash them eighty times and never accept their testimony, they indeed are evildoers" (24:4). Aisha's accusers did not have four witnesses, and so she was exonerated.

Why was This Story Told?

The account of Aisha being accused of adultery and then exonerated with a convenient revelation that cleared Muhammad's favorite wife of wrongdoing is often invoked as evidence of the general reliability of the hadith and sira literature, for it falls into the category of stories that present Muhammad in an unfavorable light, thus raising the question of why such stories would be invented at all. Muhammad is depicted as receiving a revelation from Allah that conveniently gets him out of a difficult situation in which he is facing the loss of someone who is dear to him. Among many of his alleged revelations that have been characterized as self-serving, this one stands out.

Yet it is equally possible that this story was invented in order to illustrate Allah's solicitude for even the smallest details of Muhammad's life

19 Sahih Bukhari, vol. 5, book 64, no. 4141.
20 Ibid.

and thereby to highlight his centrality in the religion and the importance for believers of making him central to their own lives as well.
It also could have been fashioned in order to establish and/or justify
the legal requirement of four witnesses to establish crimes of a sexual
nature, e.g., adultery, fornication, and even rape. It is also possible that it
is a fable that is designed to explain the Sunni/Shi'ite split, with Ali's cavalier attitude toward the prospect of Aisha being stoned to death meant
to illustrate that the Shia do not have the best interests of Muhammad,
or Islam, at heart. None of these possibilities are either conclusive or
mutually exclusive; the story may have been invented for some other
reason altogether.

The least likely possibility, however, is that this is a seventh-century
account of an incident that actually happened in the lives of Muhammad and Aisha. Like the rest of the available biographical material about
Muhammad, this account appears fully developed in the ninth-century
literature, without any clear or certain antecedents that would take it
any closer to the actual lives of its protagonists. Al-Waqidi prefaces his
version of the story with a brief list of those who have passed it down
to his day: "Yaqub b. Yahya b. Abbad related to me from Isa b. Mamar
from Abbad b. Abdullah b. al-Zubayr saying: I said to Aisha 'Tell us
your version of the raid of al-Muraysi,' the raid after which this controversy began."[21]

Muslim attributes his version of the story, which is substantially the
same in all sources, to an entirely different and lengthier group of people,
in an isnad chain going all the way back to the woman who was accused
and exonerated: "Habban bin Musa told us, Abdullah bin Al-Mubarak
told us, Yunus bin Yazid, Al-Ayli told us, and Ishaq bin Ibrahim Al-Han-
athili told us. And Muhammad bin Rafi, and Abd bin Humayd. Ibn Rafi
said he told us and the other two said, Abd al-Razzaq told us, Muammar
told us, and the context is a hadith of Muammar from the narration
of Abd and Ibn Rafi, Yunus and Muammar all said on the authority of
Al-Zuhri: Sa'id bin Al-Musayyab, Urwa bin Al-Zubayr, Alqamah bin
Waqqas told me, and Ubayd Allah ibn Abdullah ibn Utbah ibn Masoud,
on the authority of Aisha, the wife of the Prophet, when the people of
fiqh told her what they said, and God exonerated her."[22]

---

21 Al-Waqidi, op. cit., 208.
22 Sahih Muslim, book 50, no. 2770a.

This is a fairly typical chain of transmitters; the believer is expected to accept that each member of this large group passed on the story faithfully and without alteration. There is no room even for any of them to have gotten some of the details wrong simply due to the vagaries of memory while intending to pass on the tradition in all good faith. In traditional Islamic theology, if all the members of the chain of narration are men of solid reputation, then the tradition is considered authentic. Yet this list itself, and others like it, first appears in ninth-century sources; how can anyone be sure that these were really the people who passed on this tradition? There is no way to do so.

While Islamic tradition readily admits that thousands upon thousands of hadiths were forged, there is no acknowledgment of the fact that the isnad chains could just as easily be forged as well. Even some revisionist scholars who readily avow that the chains of transmissions cannot be trusted any more than the stories themselves then try to use these chains to establish which stories, among this huge mass of material, are more likely to be authentic. Once one realizes that this is all ninth-century material at best and that the chains of narration themselves are all recorded along with the stories in sources that are at least two centuries removed from the facts they purport to record, it becomes clear that trying to determine the relative authenticity of any of this material is a fool's errand.

The commonality of the details among the various accounts points to their being adapted from a single source. But there is no indication that this original source dates from significantly earlier than the various extant versions.

The Beautiful Zaynab

Muhammad had troubles with another woman as well. At one point, he came to the house of his adopted son, Zayd ibn Haritha, who had come to be known to everyone after the adoption as Zayd ibn Muhammad. Zayd was not home, but his wife Zaynab bint Jahsh, who was Muhammad's first cousin, was; according to Tabari, she greeted her father-in-law while "dressed only in a shift."[23] Muhammad piously turned away from her, but Zaynab, oblivious to his discomfort,

---

23 Abu Ja'far Muhammad bin Jarir al-Tabari, *The History of al-Tabari*, Volume VIII, *The Victory of Islam*, Michael Fishbein, trans. (Albany: State University of New York Press, 1997), 2.

welcomed him: "He is not here, Messenger of God. Come in, you who are as dear to me as my father and mother!"[24] Muhammad, however, hurried away, muttering: "Glory be to God the Almighty! Glory be to God, who causes hearts to turn!"[25]

When Zayd, who was unhappy in his marriage, returned home and heard about this, he hastened to Muhammad and made an offer: "Messenger of God, perhaps Zaynab has excited your admiration, and so I will separate myself from her."[26] As the Qur'an records, Muhammad refused, saying: "Keep your wife to yourself and fear Allah" (33:37). A hadith depicts Aisha recounting later: "If Allah's Apostle were to conceal anything (of the Quran), he would have concealed this verse."[27]

This was because although Muhammad told him repeatedly to keep his wife, Zayd ultimately did separate from Zaynab. Then Allah intervened. One day, according to Tabari, Muhammad was in the middle of a conversation with Aisha when "a fainting overcame him."[28] When he came to, "he smiled and said, 'Who will go to Zaynab to tell her the good news, saying that God has married her to me?'"[29]

The new revelation rebuked him for not wanting to take Zaynab as his wife in the first place: "And when you said to him on whom Allah has conferred favor and you have conferred favor, Keep your wife to yourself and fear Allah. And you hid in your mind what Allah was going to bring to light, and you feared mankind, whereas Allah has a better right that you should fear him. So when Zayd had performed that necessary formality from her, we gave her to you in marriage, so that there may be no sin for believers in regard to the wives of their adopted sons, when the latter have performed the necessary formality from them. The commandment of Allah must be fulfilled" (33:37).

The whole incident, according to the Qur'an, was designed to annul adoption. Zayd would henceforth be known once again as Zayd ibn Haritha, not Zayd ibn Muhammad, and thus Muhammad was cleared of the scandal of marrying his daughter-in-law; Zaynab was never actually his daughter-in-law in the first place.

---

24 Ibid.
25 Ibid.
26 Ibid.
27 Sahih Bukhari, vol. 9, book 97, no. 7420.
28 Tabari, op. cit., 3.
29 Ibid.

Zaynab and the Historicity of Muhammad

The story of Zaynab is one of the primary reasons why many non-Muslims continue to believe in the historicity of Muhammad: clearly, here is an incident that depicts Muhammad in such a bad light that it could not possibly have been invented by the fabricators of traditions about the prophet of Islam. Muhammad here is lustful, opportunistic, self-serving, and unscrupulous enough to claim the sanction of the creator of the universe for stealing his adopted son's wife. Then, he adds insult to injury with the transparently flimsy claim that the whole charade was staged so that Allah could outlaw adoption.

Yet even this story could have been invented to serve the purposes of the creators of the nascent religion. Immediately after the passage referring to Zayd's wife marrying the messenger, the Qur'an continues:

> There is no reproach for the prophet in what Allah has prescribed for him. That was Allah's way with those who passed away of old, and the commandment of Allah is certain destiny, who delivered the messages of Allah and feared him, and feared no one except Allah. Allah keeps good account. Muhammad is not the father of any of your men, but he is the messenger of Allah and the seal of the prophets, and Allah is always aware of all things (33:38–40).

"Muhammad is not the father of any of your men" could be another instance of the Qur'an's tendency to careen without warning from one subject to another, or it could be the key to the entire legend of Zaynab. The Qur'an depicts many of the prophets as being of the lineage of Abraham and, thus, relatives of one another:

> And we bestowed upon him Isaac and Jacob, each of them we guided, and Noah we guided previously, and of his descendants, David and Solomon and Job and Joseph and Moses and Aaron. In this way we reward the good. And Zachariah and John and Jesus and Elias. Each one was among the righteous. And Ishmael and Elisha and Jonah and Lot (6:84–86).

"David and Solomon and Job and Joseph and Moses and Aaron" were "of his descendants," that is, they were all descendants of Abraham. In the same vein, the Qur'an says that "Allah preferred Adam and Noah and the family of Abraham and the family of Imran over the worlds"

(3:33). The Qur'an also envisions Jesus as being Moses's nephew, calling Mary "sister of Aaron," the brother of Moses (19:28), and stating that Mary was the daughter of Imran, the wife of Moses (3:36).

If the prophetic gift could be passed on from father to son, Muhammad could not have been the "seal of the prophets" if he had a son, for that son would have been a prophet as well. Thus, Islamic tradition emphasizes that Muhammad is the final prophet by depicting all of Muhammad's natural sons as dying at an early age and his adopted son becoming no longer his adopted son when Allah reveals that Muhammad is to marry Zaynab.[30]

Thus, the Zaynab story may have been fabricated so as to emphasize the central place of Muhammad in Islam; the last prophet would never and could never be supplanted by any later prophet, for his line died with him. Another tradition has Aisha saying: "Had Zayd outlived Muhammad, he would have appointed him as his successor."[31] But Zayd did not outlive Muhammad, and so Muhammad remained the final prophet.

Another Jewish Plot

Exiled from Medina, the Banu Nadir resettled with the Banu Qaynuqa in Khaybar, but according to Islamic tradition, they thirsted for revenge. Al-Waqidi notes that a delegation of ten men from the Nadir Jews "set out for Mecca, and asked the Quraysh and their followers to join them in fighting Muhammad. They said to the Quraysh, 'We will be with you until we destroy Muhammad.'"[32]

The Quraysh commander Abu Sufyan asked them: "Is this what brought you here?"[33] They responded: "Yes. We come as your confederates, in enmity against Muhammad in order to fight him."[34] Abu Sufyan was delighted, saying: "Greetings. The most loved of the people to us are those who help us against the enmity of Muhammad."[35] The pagan Arabs and the Jews went to the Ka'ba, where they swore a solemn agreement not to betray one another. Amid this convivial atmosphere, Abu

---

30 David S. Powers, *Muhammad Is Not the Father of Any of Your Men: The Making of the Last Prophet* (Philadelphia: University of Pennsylvania Press, 2009), 9, 25.

31 Ibid., 91.

32 Al-Waqidi, op. cit., 216.

33 Ibid.

34 Ibid.

35 Ibid.

Sufyan asked: "O community of Jews, you are the people of the first books and knowledge, so inform us of what we have become, for we are in dispute with Muhammad. Is our religion good or is the religion of Muhammad good? We are the keepers of the house, we slaughter the cattle, we quench the thirst of the pilgrims, and we worship images."[36]

To this, the Jews answered: "By God, you are the first in truth about it. Indeed, you magnify this house, you maintain the provision of water, you slaughter the sacrifice, you worship what your forefathers worshiped. You, rather than he, are the first in truth."[37] Ibn Hisham and al-Waqidi both state that it was in response to this exchange that Allah revealed another section of the Qur'an: "Haven't you seen those to whom a portion of the book has been given, how they believe in *jibt* and *taghut*, and how they say of those who disbelieve, These people are more rightly guided than those who believe?" (4:51) *Jibt* is commonly translated as "idols," but this is a consensus interpretation that has been established by conjecture. The twentieth-century Islamic scholar Arthur Jeffery says that "the exegetes knew not what to make of it, and from their works we can gather a score of theories as to its meaning, whether idol, or priest, or sorcerer, or sorcery, or satan, or what not."[38] *Taghut* is an Ethiopic word that has likewise been the subject of interpretation by conjecture and consensus in Islamic tradition. According to one Islamic scholar, it was the name of one of the idols of the Quraysh; some of the Jews also honored it as a demonstration to the Quraysh of their friendship.[39]

That raises the possibility that this understanding of the word was derived from the story of the Nadir Jews traveling to Mecca to conclude an alliance with the Quraysh. In any case, it is left unexplained how this Qur'anic verse rebuking the Jews for praising the idolaters came to be revealed, for within the parameters of the story told in the sira literature, Muhammad was not present and was unaware of the machinations of his enemies. Did Muhammad receive this revelation before he knew of this alliance between the Jews and the Meccan Arabs to kill him, or was it revealed while Allah was giving his prophet miraculous knowledge

---

36 Ibid., 216–7.
37 Ibid.
38 Ibn Warraq, "Introduction," in Ibn Warraq, ed., *What the Koran Really Says* (Amherst, New York: Prometheus, 2002), 42.
39 "Taghut," in Thomas Patrick Hughes, ed., *A Dictionary of Islam* (Ottawa: Laurier Publications, 1996), 625.

of the plot? Alternatively, did Allah reveal it later, when these conflicts were but a dimming memory?

The likeliest explanation is that the account of the Quraysh conspiring with the Jews, and the Jews praising the Quraysh's pagan practices, was invented in order to explain and elucidate this Qur'anic passage, and none of those who invented it paused to consider the difficulty they had created: How could Muhammad have received a revelation about a secret plot against him that was supposed to be proceeding without his knowledge? And if he did receive miraculous knowledge of this plot, why didn't he act immediately against the plotters rather than wait for them to attack him?

Instead, according to al-Waqidi, "when the Quraysh departed from Mecca to Medina, a group of riders from the Khuzaa," another Arab tribe in Mecca, "set out to the Prophet and informed him of the departure of the Quraysh. They went from Mecca to Medina in four days."[40] In al-Waqidi's account, Muhammad seems to be aware of the Quraysh movements, although he seems to think they intend to attack the Khuzaa: "That was when the Prophet called and informed them of the news of their enemy. He consulted them about the affair with seriousness and effort, and he promised them help if they were patient and God fearing. He commanded them to obey God and His prophet."[41]

The Battle of the Trench

It quickly became clear that the Quraysh intended to attack the Muslims, and so Muhammad ordered that a trench be dug around Medina. Not all the Muslims were enthusiastic about this effort; according to Ibn Hisham, "the Muslims worked very hard with him, but the disaffected held back from them and began to hide their real object by working slackly and by stealing away to their families without the apostle's permission or knowledge."[42] This became the occasion for another revelation, impugning the sincerity of the faith of those who shrank back from this work: "They only are the true believers who believe in Allah and his messenger and, when they are with him on some common errand, do not go away until they have asked permission from

---

40 Al-Waqidi, op. cit., 218.
41 Ibid.
42 Ibn Ishaq, op. cit., 450–1.

him. Indeed, those who ask permission from you, those are the ones who believe in Allah and his messenger. So if they ask your permission for some matter of theirs, give permission to those whom you will of them, and ask forgiveness of Allah for them. Indeed, Allah is forgiving, merciful. Do not make the call of the messenger among you like your calling of one another. Allah knows those of you who steal away, hiding themselves. And let those who conspire to evade orders beware, so that grief or painful punishment do not come upon them" (Qur'an 24:62–3).

Al-Waqidi notes that "as they worked, they borrowed many tools of iron, hoes and baskets from the Banu Qurayza," the last remaining Jewish tribe in Medina.[43] "They dug the trench with him, for they were at that time at peace with the Prophet and they hated the bold daring of the Quraysh."[44] Neither Ibn Hisham nor Ibn Sa'd mention the Qurayza Jews helping Muhammad dig the trench. The accounts of the digging of the trench include several that featured Muhammad performing miracles; in one, says Ibn Hisham, "a large rock caused great difficulty," and those who were digging "complained to the apostle."[45] In response, Muhammad "called for some water and spat in it; then he prayed as God willed him to pray; then he sprinkled the water on the rock. Those who were present said, 'By Him who sent him a prophet with the truth it was pulverized as though it were soft sand so that it could not resist axe or shovel.'"[46]

Ibn Hisham also records another tradition featuring Salman the Persian, a companion of Muhammad who has been accused of teaching the prophet of Islam what Muhammad then disseminated as revelations from Allah, a charge that is denied in the Qur'an: "And we know well that they say, Only a man teaches him. The speech of him about whom they falsely hint is foreign, and this is clear Arabic" (16:103). Salman recounts, according to Ibn Hisham: "I was working with a pick in the trench where a rock gave me much trouble. The apostle who was near at hand saw me hacking and saw how difficult the place was. He dropped down into the trench and took the pick from my hand and gave such a blow that lightning showed beneath the pick. This happened a second

43 Al-Waqidi, op. cit., 218.
44 Ibid.
45 Ibn Ishaq, op. cit., 451.
46 Ibid.

and a third time. I said: 'O you, dearer than father or mother, what is the meaning of this light beneath your pick as you strike?'"[47]

Muhammad responds with a vision of Islam spreading throughout the region by the force of arms: "Did you really see that, Salman? The first means that God has opened up to me the Yaman; the second Syria and the west; and the third the east."[48] Ibn Hisham adds that according to a different source, "when these countries were conquered in the time of Umar and Uthman and after, 'Conquer where you will, by God, you have not conquered and to the resurrection day you will not conquer a city whose keys God had not given beforehand to Muhammad.'"[49]

In al-Waqidi's account, Muhammad's miraculous softening of the rock and his imperialistic vision are combined into a single story. Unlike Ibn Hisham, al-Waqidi also knows the identity of the person who was having difficulty with the hard stone: the future caliph Umar.

> Umar b. al-Khattab was digging at that time with a hoe, when he struck at a hard stone that he had not expected to find. The Messenger of God took the hoe from Umar, he was at Mount Ubayd, and struck once, and the first strike brought a spark that went like lightening to Yemen. Then he struck again, and the lightening went towards al-Sham. Then he struck again and the lightening went towards the East, and the stone broke at the third stroke. Umar b. al-Khattab used to say: By Him who sent him with the truth, it became like sand.
>
> Salman said, "O Messenger of God, I observed the hoe whenever you struck with it, and it lit up what was under it." And the Prophet said, "Did you see that?" And he said, "Yes." The Prophet said, "Indeed, I saw with the first, the castles of al-Sham [Syria and the Levant]; with the second, the castles of al-Yemen. And with the third, the white castles of Khusrau [Chosroes, emperor of Persia], of the nobility in Madain." He began to describe it to Salman, who said, "You speak the truth. By Him who sent you with the truth, indeed this is the description. I witness that you are indeed the messenger of God!" The Messenger of God said, "This conquest of God will open for you after me, O Salman, for al-Sham will be open to

---

47 Ibid., 452.
48 Ibid.
49 Ibid.

you. Heraclius [the Roman emperor] will flee to the most distant kingdom, and you will be victorious over al-Sham and no one will contest you. Yemen will be open to you. The East will be conquered and Khusrau killed after it." Salman said, "All this did I see."

Al-Waqidi not only knows the identity of the man whom Muhammad helped with these miraculous blows of the hoe; he also has Muhammad explicating the meaning of his statement about Syria and Yemen and the other lands that the Muslims will conquer, while Ibn Hisham leaves the explanation to Umar.

Meanwhile, despite the clear evidence of the divine favor that this miracle provided, the atmosphere inside the city grew tense as the Quraysh began to lay siege to Medina. Ibn Hisham states: "The situation became serious and fear was everywhere. The enemy came at them from above and below until the believers imagined vain things, and disaffection was rife among the disaffected."[50] One of the angry Muslims complained: "Muhammad used to promise us that we should eat the treasures of Chosroes and Caesar and today not one of us can feel safe in going to the privy!"[51] Allah sent a new revelation to scold this malcontent: "And when the hypocrites, and those in whose hearts is a disease, were saying, Allah and his messenger promised us nothing but delusion" (33:12).[52]

To make matters even worse, the last remaining Jewish tribe of Medina, the Banu Qurayza, had turned against the Muslims, but they were still inside Medina with them. Muhammad heard rumors to this effect and called together three of his most trusted companions. He told them the rumors and directed them to determine whether or not they were true: "Indeed it has reached me that the Banu Qurayza have destroyed the agreement which was between us, and gone to war. Go and observe if what has reached me is true. If it is baseless, proclaim it aloud. If it is true say it in code and I will know. Do not undermine the support of the Muslims."[53] Apparently, Muhammad was calculating that if the news turned out to be false, the public airing of it would lead the Qurayza Jews to redouble their efforts to prove their loyalty to

---

50 Ibid., 453–4.
51 Ibid., 454.
52 Ibid., 243.
53 Al-Waqidi, op. cit., 224.

Muhammad. And if it were true, of course, keeping the Banu Qurayza unaware of the fact that Muhammad knew of their betrayal would be to his advantage.

Here again, even if one takes the Islamic traditions at face value, this is not the perfidious betrayal that it is often represented to be in contemporary Islamic sources. Muhammad had attacked and exiled the Banu Qaynuqa Jews entirely unprovoked. Even if it were true that the Banu Nadir then plotted against him, it is understandable under the circumstances that they would want to avoid the Qaynuqa Jews' fate, and the same can be said at the Battle of the Trench of the Banu Qurayza. Al-Waqidi even depicts the Qurayza Jews explaining their actions in this way, saying of Muhammad: "Surely, the matter of this man is a trial. You saw what he did with the Banu Qaynuqa and the Banu Nadir. He expelled them from their land after taking their wealth."[54]

Muhammad, however, thought of the Banu Qurayza only as having betrayed him and continued to devise stratagems to deceive them. At the darkest moment for the Muslims, one of the Ghatafan, who were fighting alongside the Quraysh against the Muslims, came to Muhammad to tell him, according to Ibn Hisham, "that he had become a Muslim though his own people did not know of it, and let him give him what orders he would."[55] Muhammad replied: "You are only one man among us, so go and awake distrust among the enemy to draw them off us if you can, for war is deceit."[56]

Nuaym went to the Banu Qurayza and sowed distrust among them of Muhammad's foes: "Now Quraysh and Ghatafan have come to fight Muhammad and his companions and you have aided them against him, but their land, their property, and their wives are not here, so they are not like you. If they see an opportunity they will make the most of it; but if things go badly they will go back to their own land and leave you to face the man in your country and you will not be able to do so if you are left alone. So do not fight along with these people until you take hostages from their chiefs who will remain in your hands as security that they will fight Muhammad with you until you make an

---

54 Ibid., 235.
55 Ibn Ishaq, op. cit., 458.
56 Ibid.

end of him."[57] The Jews, according to Ibn Hisham, agreed that this was "excellent advice."[58]

Then, however, Nuaym went to the Quraysh and the Ghatafan in turn and told them: "You know my affection for you and that I have left Muhammad. Now I have heard something which I think it my duty to tell you of by way of warning, but regard it as confidential. Mark my words, the Jews have regretted their action in opposing Muhammad and have sent to tell him so, saying: 'Would you like us to get hold of some chiefs of the two tribes Quraysh and Ghatafan and hand them over to you so that you can cut their heads off? Then we can join you in exterminating the rest of them.' He has sent word back to accept their offer; so if the Jews send to you to demand hostages, don't send them a single man."[59] The trap was set: the Banu Qurayza sent word to the Arabs that they would not "fight Muhammad with them until they give us hostages."[60] Ibn Hisham says that "Quraysh and Ghatafan refused to do so, and God sowed distrust between them, and sent a bitter cold wind against them in the winter nights which upset their cooking-pots and overthrew their tents."[61]

The crisis for the Muslims was averted. Ibn Sa'd says that "both of the parties trusted" Nuaym, so he "sowed the seed of discord among the people so the al-Ahzab (armies) retreated crushed, without fighting."[62] According to al-Waqidi, when two of the Ghatafan arrived back at their campsite, their comrades asked them: "What happened to you?"[63] One of them replied: "The affair was not completed," that is, the pagan Arabs were not able to enter Medina and defeat the Muslims.[64] He continued: "We saw a people who have a vision, and who will give themselves for their leader. We and the Quraysh are destroyed. The Quraysh will return and not even speak to Muhammad. The anger of Muhammad will fall on the Banu Qurayza. If we turn back, he will sit on them and besiege them together until they give him what is before them."[65] One of the

---

57 Ibid., 458–9.
58 Ibid., 459.
59 Ibid.
60 Ibid.
61 Ibid.
62 Ibn Sa'd, op. cit., II, 90.
63 Al-Waqidi, op. cit., 235.
64 Ibid.
65 Ibid.

others responded with a foretaste of what was to come: "May they be destroyed. Muhammad is more dear to us than the Jews."[66]

The Final Solution for the Banu Qurayza

Soon after the pagan Arabs' siege of Medina was broken, according to Ibn Hisham, "Gabriel came to the apostle wearing an embroidered turban and riding on a mule with a saddle covered with a piece of brocade. He asked the apostle if he had abandoned fighting, and when he said that he had he said that the angels had not yet laid aside their arms and that he had just come from pursuing the enemy. 'God commands you, Muhammad, to go to B. Qurayza. I am about to go to them to shake their stronghold.'"[67] In Bukhari's version, the angel says, "You have put down your arms! By Allah, I have not put down my arms yet."[68]

Ibn Hisham states that Muhammad "ordered it to be announced that none should perform the afternoon prayer until after he reached B. Qurayza."[69] This was apparently meant to induce the Muslim forces to hurry so that they could perform their prayers on time. Meanwhile, Muhammad sent Ali ahead; Ali "advanced until when he came near the forts he heard insulting language used of the apostle."[70] Then he went back to Muhammad "and told him that it was not necessary for him to come near those rascals."[71] Muhammad, of course, immediately surmised the reason for this: "Why? I think you must have heard them speaking ill of me," and when Ali acknowledged this, Muhammad added: "If they saw me they would not talk in that fashion."[72] He did not approach the forts of the Qurayza in a conciliatory mood, saying: "You brothers of monkeys, has God disgraced you and brought His vengeance upon you?"[73] They then confirmed his prediction that they would speak kindly to him in person after reviling him behind his back, as they responded: "O Abu'l-Qasim, you are not a barbarous person."[74] But Muhammad would not be placated: "The apostle besieged them for

66 Ibid.
67 Ibn Ishaq, op. cit., 461.
68 Sahih Bukhari, vol. 4, book 56, no. 2813.
69 Ibn Ishaq, op. cit.
70 Ibid.
71 Ibid.
72 Ibid.
73 Ibid.
74 Ibid.

twenty-five nights until they were sore pressed and God cast terror into their hearts."[75]

According to al-Waqidi, one of the Muslims called out to the Banu Qurayza: "O enemies of God, we will not leave your fortress until you die of starvation. You in your homes are like foxes in their dens."[76] The Jews pleaded with the Muslims, insisting that they, not the Arabs of Medina, were their allies. But the Muslims would have none of it, as one responded: "There is no agreement between me and you, and no alliance."[77] Muhammad called out to them: "O brothers of monkeys and pigs and worshipers of evil, did you insult me?"[78] This echoed the Qur'anic passages in which Allah turns sabbath-breaking and otherwise disobedient Jews into apes and pigs (2:63–5; 5:59–60; 7:166). Ultimately, Muhammad ordered marksmen to shoot arrows into the Qurayza fortress; one of them recalled: "With me were about fifty men, and we shot at them for a while such that our arrows were like the locust. They hid in their den, and not one of them came out."[79] Al-Waqidi adds that "the Messenger of God did not stop shooting at the enemy until he was certain of their destruction."[80]

Amid this dire situation, according to Ibn Hisham, the chief of the Banu Qurayza, Ka'b bin Asad, addressed his people, offering them three choices. The first was to convert to Islam, "for by God it has become plain to you that he is a prophet who has been sent and that it is he that you find mentioned in your scripture; and then your lives, your property, your women and children will be saved."[81] Ka'b's people, however, were determined to remain true to their own traditions, saying: "We will never abandon the laws of the Torah and never change it for another."[82] Ka'b's second proposal was bluntly barbaric: "Let us kill our wives and children and send men with their swords drawn to Muhammad and his companions leaving no encumbrances behind us, until God decides between us and Muhammad. If we perish, we perish, and we shall not leave children behind us to cause us anxiety. If we conquer

75 Ibid.
76 Al-Waqidi, op. cit., 245.
77 Ibid.
78 Ibid.
79 Ibid.
80 Ibid., 246.
81 Ibn Ishaq, op. cit., 461–2.
82 Ibid., 462.

we can acquire other wives and children."[83] To that, the Qurayza Jews responded: "Should we kill these poor creatures? What would be the good of life when they were dead?"[84] Ka'b had one more idea: "Tonight is the eve of the sabbath and it may well be that Muhammad and his companions will feel secure from us then, so come down, perhaps we can take Muhammad and his companions by surprise."[85] Ibn Hisham has the Jews reply in a manner that suggested that they accepted the truth of the Qur'anic accounts about how Allah had punished them for breaking the sabbath: "Are we to profane our sabbath and do on the sabbath what those before us of whom you well know did and were turned into apes?"[86] Ka'b gave up, saying: "Not a single man among you from the day of your birth has ever passed a night resolved to do what he knows ought to be done."[87]

This story is unusual in the corpus of biographical material about Muhammad in that it is not entirely unfavorable to the Jews, who are relentlessly demonized in numerous accounts. Here, they demonstrate a tender human concern for their wives and children and are even depicted as being obedient to Allah enough to keep the sabbath, even when doing so could mean their defeat and destruction. The Qurayza Jews, however, are still seen here through a decidedly Islamic lens, for they take for granted that Allah had transformed their forbears into apes for their disobedience, specifically their sabbath-breaking (Qur'an 2:65).

Checkmated, the Qurayza appealed to Muhammad himself. Neither Ibn Hisham nor Ibn Sa'd repeat or even seem to be aware of this tradition, but al-Waqidi states that their representative, Nabbash bin Qays, appealed to the prophet of Islam to treat them the way he had treated the other Jews of Medina: "O Muhammad, we will accept what the Banu Nadir accepted. To you will be our property and weapons, and in return our blood will be saved. We will set out from your land with our women and children. We will take what the camels can carry except for the weapons."[88] Muhammad, however, had hardened in his attitude

---

83 Ibid.
84 Ibid.
85 Ibid.
86 Ibid.
87 Ibid.
88 Al-Waqidi, op. cit., 246.

toward the Jews and declined this offer. Nabbash then offered another proposal: they would leave their property behind for the Muslims. "Save our blood and give us our women and children, and we will not load our camels."[89] Muhammad, however, was unyielding: "No. You will submit only to my judgment."[90]

In the event, however, he turned the decision of what would be the fate of the Banu Qurayza over to one of his companions, Sa'd ibn Muadh, who declared: "I give judgment that the men should be killed, the property divided, and the women and children taken as captives."[91] This judgment was executed swiftly: "The Messenger of God breakfasted at the market and gave instructions for a furrow to be dug there between the house of Abu Jahm al-Adawi and the Ahjar al-Zayt in the market. His companions were digging there. The Messenger of God sat with the distinguished among his companions. He called for the men of the Banu Qurayza, and they came out at a leisurely pace, and their heads were cut off."[92] As this grisly operation continued, al-Waqidi depicts Muhammad displaying a peculiar sort of compassion for the victims, as he tells the Muslims: "Be good to your captives. Let them rest; quench their thirst until they are cool. Then, kill those who remain. Do not apply both the heat of the sun and the heat of the weapons."[93] There were many people to be killed, and so the killing went on for many hours: "Aisha used to say that the Banu Qurayza continued to be killed that day until it was night and that they were killed throughout the night with the help of a torch."[94]

Ibn Hisham, however, depicts Muhammad as much more actively involved in executing Sa'd's judgment: "Then the apostle went out to the market of Medina (which is still its market today) and dug trenches in it. Then he sent for them and struck off their heads in those trenches as they were brought out to him in batches. Among them was the enemy of Allah Huyayy b. Akhtab and Ka'b b. Asad their chief. There were 600 or 700 in all, though some put the figure as high as 800 or 900."[95]

---

89 Ibid.
90 Ibid.
91 Ibn Ishaq, op. cit. 464.
92 Al-Waqidi, op. cit., 252.
93 Ibid.
94 Ibid., 254.
95 Ibn Ishaq, op. cit., 464.

A hadith has Aisha also recalling that Muhammad did the killing himself, as she remembers the only woman among the Banu Qurayza to be killed: "No woman of Banu Qurayzah was killed except one. She was with me, talking and laughing on her back and belly (extremely), while the Messenger of Allah was killing her people with the swords."[96] Aisha seems mystified by the woman's laughter, but it seems to have been an emotional reaction to the horror of the scene. Aisha states that when it came to be this woman's time to die, "suddenly a man called her name: Where is so-and-so?"[97] According to Ibn Hisham, Aisha exclaimed: "Good heavens, what is the matter?"[98] The woman replied: "I am to be killed."[99] Aisha then asks: "What for?," and the woman answers: "Because of something I did," without elaborating.[100] Aisha adds: "The man took her and beheaded her."[101] She continues: "I shall never forget my wonder at her good spirits and her loud laughter when all the time she knew that she would be killed."[102]

As is so often the case, al-Waqidi knows a great many details of this story that are not known to the others who passed on these traditions, including the name of this unfortunate woman and the reason why she is being put to death:

When it was the day the Messenger of God commanded that they be killed, Nubata came before Aisha and began to laugh hysterically. She said, "The leaders of the Banu Qurayza are being killed." All of a sudden she heard the voice of a speaker say, "O Nubata!" She said, "I am, by God, she who is being called." Aisha said, "For what?" She said, "My husband killed me." She was a soft-spoken girl. Aisha said, "How did your husband kill you?" She said, "I was in the fortress of al-Zabir b. Bata, and he commanded me to push the millstone on the companions of Muhammad. It crushed the head of a man among them to death, and I killed him. And the Messenger of God commanded that I be killed for Khallad b. Suwayd." Aisha said, "I

---

96 Sunan Abi Dawud, book 15, no. 2671.
97 Ibid.
98 Ibn Ishaq, op. cit., 465.
99 Ibid.
100 Ibid.
101 Sunan Abi Dawud, book 15, no. 2671.
102 Ibn Ishaq, op. cit.

shall never forget the good soul of Nabata and her hysterical laughter when she knew that she would be killed."[103]

Al-Waqidi phrased Sa'd's ruling on the fate of the Banu Qurayza in this way: "Indeed I judge about them, that whoever shaves a beard be killed; their women and children be enslaved; and their property be apportioned."[104] The distinction between those who shaved and those who did not was a matter of life and death. A hadith depicts one of the Qurayza Jews, Atiyyah al-Qurazi, recalling: "I was among the captives of Banu Qurayzah. They (the Companions) examined us, and those who had begun to grow hair (pubes) were killed, and those who had not were not killed. I was among those who had not grown hair."[105] One of the Muslims recalled, according to al-Waqidi: "They were slaughtered until twilight withdrew. Then they were covered with the dust in the trench. Whoever they doubted had reached puberty they looked into his underwear. If he had grown hair he was killed, and if not he was taken prisoner."[106]

---

103 Al-Waqidi, op. cit., 254.
104 Ibid., 251.
105 Sunan Abi Dawud, book 40, no. 4404.
106 Al-Waqidi, op. cit., 254.

CHAPTER ELEVEN

A Time of Peace

Two More Wives for Muhammad

Once the men had all been killed, says Ibn Hisham, Muhammad divided their "property, wives, and children of B. Qurayza among the Muslims, and he made known on that day the shares of horse and men, and took out the fifth."[1] He sent one of his companions to Najd with "some of the captive women of B. Qurayza" and "sold them for horses and weapons."[2] According to al-Waqidi, "the prisoners included a thousand women and children. The Messenger of God took his fifth before selling the plunder. He apportioned the prisoners into five parts, and he took a fifth and he set free from it, and he gifted from it, and he gave favors from it to those who desired. Thus he did with what he obtained of their old clothes that were divided before they were sold; and thus with the dates."[3]

Al-Waqidi depicts an elderly Muslim recounting a scene of immense sorrow, although neither the storyteller nor al-Waqidi himself appears to take any notice of the tragedy involved: "I attended the Messenger of God who was selling the prisoners of the Banu Qurayza. Abu al-Shahm al-Yahudi bought two women, with each one of them three male children, for one hundred and fifty dinars. He kept saying, 'Are you not of the Jewish faith?' The two women replied, 'We will not depart from the religion of our people until we die!' They were crying."[4]

Muhammad kept one of the female captives, Rayhana bint Zayd, for himself, not as another wife, but as a slave. Ibn Hisham recounts that Muhammad "had proposed to marry her and put the veil on her," as the

---

1 Ibn Ishaq, op. cit., 466.
2 Ibid.
3 Al-Waqidi, op. cit., 257.
4 Ibid., 256–7.

veil was for the wives of Muhammad and later for all Muslim women, while slave women remained uncovered. The early Islamic sources depict Muhammad and his men taking the morality of slavery, including the enslavement and rape of captive infidel women, for granted. One Muslim recounts in a hadith: "We used to sell our slave women and the mothers of our children (*Umahat Awaldina*) when the Prophet was still living among us, and we did not see anything wrong with that."[5]

Despite the massive difference between the life of a slave woman and that of a wife of the Islamic prophet, however, Rayhana declined the honor of becoming one of Muhammad's wives: "Nay, Leave me in your power," that is, as a slave, "for that will be easier for me and for you."[6] Muhammad complied. Her reluctance to become his wife, according to Ibn Hisham, was due to the fact that "she had shown repugnance towards Islam when she was captured, and clung to Judaism."[7] This irked Muhammad, so he "put her aside and felt some displeasure."[8] At one point, Allah solved the problem: Muhammad heard footsteps and told his companions: "This is Thalaba b. Sa'ya coming to give me the good news of Rayhana's acceptance of Islam."[9] After Rayhana's belated conversion to Muhammad, she became his latest wife.

Al-Waqidi, however, first tells a similar story but then also relates a significantly different version. He notes that as the possessions of the Banu Qurayza were being divided up among the Muslims, Muhammad saw Rayhana among the captive women and "took her for himself as the leader's share. She was beautiful."[10] He asked her to become a Muslim, but she refused, which "grieved" Muhammad, but ultimately she agrees to become a Muslim and marries Muhammad.[11] However, al-Waqidi goes on to note an alternate version in which Muhammad tells Rayhana: "If you desire that I set you free and marry you, I will do so. If you desire to be my concubine and that I co-habit with you, I will do so."[12] She responds: "O Messenger of God, it is easier for you and me that I be your

---

5 Sunan Ibn Majah, vol. 3, book 19, no. 2517.
6 Ibn Ishaq, op. cit.
7 Ibid.
8 Ibid.
9 Ibid.
10 Al-Waqidi, op. cit., 255.
11 Ibid.
12 Ibid., 256.

property."[13] Al-Waqidi adds: "So she was the property of the Prophet and he co-habited with her until she died as his property."[14]

Al-Waqidi concludes that the version in which Muhammad marries Rayhana "is the more confirmed of the two traditions with us" but offers no explanation of how the alternative tradition could have arisen if there had been a historical Muhammad who married a historical Rayhana.[15] If that had been the case, why would anyone have opted for a less satisfying version of the story in which Rayhana refuses Muhammad's entreaties to convert and remains a slave? If either version has any basis in history, it is more likely to be the version in which Rayhana remains in Judaism as a slave rather than become a Muslim and marry Muhammad, for this version depicts the desires of the prophet of Islam being thwarted. On the other hand, it is possible that this version was formulated and disseminated in order to show once again the perversity of the Jews. In any case, once again, the slippage and variations among various Islamic traditions testify to the non-historical character of what is being related.

After administering his final solution to the Banu Qurayza, Muhammad resumed his raids on pagan Arab tribes, including the Banu Mustaliq. Ibn Hisham puts it succinctly: "There was a fight and God put the B. al-Mustaliq to flight and killed some of them and gave the apostle their wives, children, and property as booty."[16] Many of the Muslims found the captive women of the Banu Mustaliq particularly alluring. One recounted:

> We went out with Allah's Messenger on the expedition to the Bi'l-Mustaliq and took captive some excellent Arab women; and we desired them, for we were suffering from the absence of our wives, (but at the same time) we also desired ransom for them. So we decided to have sexual intercourse with them but by observing *azl* (withdrawing the male sexual organ before emission of semen to avoid conception). But we said: We are doing an act whereas Allah's Messenger is amongst us; why not ask him? So we asked Allah's

---

13 Ibid.
14 Ibid.
15 Ibid.
16 Ibn Ishaq, op. cit., 490.

Messenger, and he said: It does not matter if you do not do it, for every soul that is to be born up to the Day of Resurrection will be born.[17]

The legal problem that preoccupied the Muslims was regarding the permissibility of *coitus interruptus*; both Muhammad and his companions are depicted as taking for granted that the rape of the captive women was perfectly acceptable.

Among the captive women, Muhammad found yet another wife for himself. Ibn Hisham has Aisha recount that when Muhammad distributed the captured Banu Mustaliq prisoners among the Muslims as slaves, he allotted Juwayriya, a "most beautiful woman" who "captivated every man who saw her," to a Muslim named Thabit b. Qays b. al-Shammas, "or to a cousin of his."[18]

Juwayriya was displeased with this outcome and came to appeal to Muhammad. Aisha was not happy: "As soon as I saw her at the door of my room I took a dislike to her, for I knew that he would see her as I saw her."[19] Juwayriya explained to Muhammad that she was the daughter of al-Harith bin Abu Dirar, the leader of the Banu Mustaliq. She lamented: "You can see the state to which I have been brought."[20] Muhammad immediately offered to solve her problem by marrying her, and she accepted. Ibn Hisham adds that this changed the situation of all the captives of the Banu Mustaliq: "The news that the apostle had married Juwayriya was blazed abroad and now that B. Mustaliq were the prophet's relations by marriage the men released those they held. When he married her a hundred families were released. I do not know a woman who was a greater blessing to her people than she."[21]

Tensions Among the Muslims

The outcome for the Banu Mustaliq was happy, but all was not, however, harmonious among the Muslims themselves. A fight broke out between the Muhajiroun, the Muslims who had migrated from Medina to Mecca, and the Ansar, the Medinans who had converted at the time of that migration. Abdullah bin Ubayy, a leader of the Ansar and a man

---

17 Sahih Muslim, book 16, no. 1438a.
18 Ibn Ishaq, op. cit., 493.
19 Ibid.
20 Ibid.
21 Ibid.

who had already been identified as a villain of the sira literature, as he was one of the chief accusers of Aisha, was furious. He declared: "Have they actually done this? They dispute our priority, they outnumber us in our own country, and nothing so fits us and the vagabonds of Quraysh as the ancient saying 'Feed a dog and it will devour you.' By Allah when we return to Medina the stronger will drive out the weaker." He told the Ansar: "This is what you have done to yourselves. You have let them occupy your country, and you have divided your property among them. Had you but kept your property from them they would have gone elsewhere."[22]

A young boy, Zayd bin Arqam, heard Abdullah say all this and reported it to Muhammad. Umar, who was with Muhammad, was enraged and peremptorily ordered one of the Muslims to kill Abdullah. Muhammad, however, countermanded the order, telling Umar: "But what if men should say Muhammad kills his own companions?" Ibn Hisham does not mention a salient Qur'anic verse in this connection: "It is not for a believer to kill a believer except by mistake" (4:92). Since he spends a great deal of time explaining the circumstances of the various Qur'anic revelations, this is a curious omission that may indicate that the Qur'anic text regarding this issue was still in flux at the time that these traditions were initially formulated.

In any case, when Abdullah found out that Muhammad had heard what he said, he hastened to undo the damage. Ibn Hisham says that Abdullah went to the prophet of Islam "and swore that he had not said what he did say."[23] Others among the Ansar also defended him, saying: "It may well be that the boy was mistaken in what he said, and did not remember the man's words."[24] Ibn Hisham states that Allah himself informed Muhammad that what Zayd bin Arqam had said was true: "The sura came down in which God mentioned the disaffected with Ibn Ubayy and those like-minded with him. When it came down the apostle took hold of Zayd b. Arqam's ear, saying, 'This is he who devoted his ear to Allah.'"[25]

Al-Waqidi, who places this story much earlier, before the Battle of the Trench and right before Aisha is accused of adultery, elaborates,

---

22 Ibid., 491.
23 Ibid.
24 Ibid.
25 Ibid., 491–2.

having Zayd bin Arqam recount: "Before long, I saw the Messenger of God have a severe fit. His forehead was sweating, and his hand was heavy on his camel. No sooner was it revealed, than I knew that the Messenger of God had been inspired, and I hoped that it would reveal to him the honesty of my news."[26] And sure enough, "as soon as the Prophet was released from the fit, he took my ear—and I was on my beast and I was lifted from my seat—and directed it to the heavens, saying, 'Your ear is perfect, lad. God confirms your news.'"[27] The entirety of the sixty-third chapter of the Qur'an is said to be about this incident. Abdullah bin Ubayy is not mentioned, but what the traditions claim that he said is: "They say, Surely, if we return to Medina, the honorable ones will soon drive out the dishonorable, when honor belongs to Allah and to his messenger and to the believers, but the hypocrites do not know. O you who believe, do not let your wealth or your children distract you from the remembrance of Allah. Those who do so, they are the losers" (63:8–9).

Muhammad, meanwhile, tried to defuse the tension. According to Ibn Hisham, he "walked with the men all that day till nightfall, and through the night until morning and during the following day until the sun distressed them. Then he halted them, and as soon as they touched the ground they fell asleep. He did this to distract their minds from what Abdullah b. Ubayy had said the day before."[28]

The next day, the Muslims were further distracted by some good news: the death of one of their foremost opponents. Muhammad "continued his journey through the Hijaz as far as water a little above al-Naqi called Baq'a. As he traveled at night a violent wind distressed the men and they dreaded it. He told them not to be afraid because the wind announced the death of one of the greatest of the unbelievers, and when they got to Medina they found that Rifaa b. Zayd b. al-Tabut of B. Qaynuqa, one of the most important Jews and a secret shelterer of the disaffected, had died that day."[29] Respect for one's foes as human beings and children of the single creator was never part of Islam. The ninth-century literature never shies away from depicting Muhammad and his companions receiving news of the deaths of their enemies or misfortune befalling them with unbridled glee.

---

26 Al-Waqidi, op. cit, 205.
27 Ibid.
28 Ibn Ishaq, op. cit., 491.
29 Ibid.

In this case, his patience regarding Abdullah bin Ubayy paid off. Abdullah's son even approached Muhammad, asking for permission to murder his father. Here, there is another reference to the prohibition of a believer killing another believer, but once again, Ibn Hisham makes no mention of the relevant Qur'anic verse. Abdullah's son says to Muhammad: "I have heard that you want to kill Abdullah b. Ubayy for what you have heard about him. If you must do it, then order me to do it and I will bring you his head, for al-Khazraj know that they have no man more dutiful to his father than I, and I am afraid that if you order someone else to kill him my soul will not permit me to see his slayer walking among men and I shall kill him, thus killing a believer for an unbeliever, and so I should go to hell."[30] Muhammad replied: "Nay, but let us deal kindly with him and make much of his companionship while he is with us."[31] Once word got out among the wider population of the Ansar of what Abdullah said, "it was his own people who reproached and upbraided him roughly."[32] This was just what Muhammad had wanted, and he explained what had happened to Umar: "Now what do you think, Umar? If I had killed him on the day you wanted me to kill him, the leading men [of the Ansar] would have trembled with rage. If I ordered them to kill him today, they would kill him."[33] By not acting precipitously against Abdullah, Muhammad had eradicated discontent among the Ansar, who would, by this time, gladly kill their own leader if their warlike prophet told them to do so. Umar was duly impressed and observed: "I know that the apostle's order is more blessed than mine."[34]

The Treaty of Hudaybiyya

Around this time, according to Ibn Hisham, Muhammad decided to make a pilgrimage to Mecca "with no intention of making war."[35] This was not the time of year for the great pilgrimage, the hajj, which Islamic tradition states that he later made into a core requirement of Islam, but the *umra*, a lesser pilgrimage. Al-Waqidi states that Muhammad got this idea in a dream: "The Messenger of God had seen in his sleep that he

---

30 Ibid., 492.
31 Ibid.
32 Ibid.
33 Ibid.
34 Ibid.
35 Ibid., 499.

entered the 'House,' his head shaven, taken the key to the 'House,' and stood at the place of the halting at al-Arafat. So, he called his companions to perform the *Umra*. They hastened their preparations to set out."[36]

As tensions with the Quraysh were still high, "he called together the Arabs and neighboring Bedouin to march with him, fearing that Quraysh would oppose him with arms or prevent him from visiting the temple, as they actually did."[37] The "temple" was, of course, the Ka'ba in Mecca. Muhammad did all he could to telegraph his peaceful intentions: "He took the sacrificial victims with him and donned the pilgrim garb so that all would know that he did not intend war and that his purpose was to visit the temple and to venerate it."[38] The sacrificial victims were seventy camels that Muhammad intended to offer to Allah at the sacred place. Muhammad told his men: "I will not carry weapons. Surely I am setting out as a pilgrim for *Umra*."[39] Quickly, however, Muhammad was informed that "there are Quraysh who have heard of your coming" and were "swearing that you will never enter Mecca in defiance of them."[40]

Muhammad was annoyed and exclaimed: "Alas, Quraysh, war has devoured them! What harm would they have suffered if they had left me and the rest of the Arabs to go our own ways? If they should kill me, that is what they desire, and if God should give me the victory over them they would enter Islam in flocks. If they do not do that, they will fight while they have the strength, so what are Quraysh thinking of? By Allah, I will not cease to fight for the mission with which God has entrusted me until He makes it victorious or I perish."[41] But despite his willingness to fight, he did not want a confrontation with the Quraysh and asked his men: "Who will take us out by a way in which we shall not meet them ?"[42]

Ibn Hisham states that "a man of Aslam" offered to help the Muslims avoid the Quraysh and "took them by a rugged, rocky track between passes which was very hard on the Muslims."[43] Once this was done and the Muslims were once again on "the easy ground," at Hudaybiyya, near

---

36 Al-Waqidi, op. cit., 281.
37 Ibn Ishaq, op. cit.
38 Ibid., 500.
39 Al-Waqidi, op. cit.
40 Ibn Ishaq, op. cit.
41 Ibid.
42 Ibid.
43 Ibid.

the sacred precincts of the Ka'ba, Muhammad said to his men: "Say, We ask God's forgiveness and we repent towards Him."[44] They complied, whereupon Muhammad added: "That is the 'putting away' that was enjoined on the children of Israel; but they did not say the words."[45] The putting away, or *hitta*, referred to the forgiveness of sins, and once again, the obedience of the Muslims and disobedience of the Jews was reinforced.

Toward the Quraysh, however, Muhammad was feeling conciliatory and told his men: "Today whatever condition Quraysh make in which they ask me to show kindness to kindred I shall agree to."[46] Yet the Quraysh remained hostile, saying: "He may have come not wanting war but by Allah he shall never come in here against our will, nor shall the Arabs ever say that we have allowed it."[47] Ibn Hisham says that the Quraysh even "sent forty or fifty men with orders to surround the apostle's camp and get hold of one of his companions for them, but they were caught and brought to the apostle, who forgave them and let them go their way. They had attacked the camp with stones and arrows."[48]

Suspicion ran high on both sides. Ibn Hisham states that one of the Quraysh, Urwa bin Mas'ud, came to meet with the prophet of Islam and asked him: "Muhammad, have you collected a mixed people together and then brought them to your own people to destroy them?"[49] He added a prediction: by the next day, the Muslims would desert Muhammad. This enraged Abu Bakr, who responded crudely: "Suck al-Lat's nipples! Should we desert him?"[50] Al-Waqidi has Urwa bin Mas'ud speak more clearly to Muhammad, presenting him with "one of two possibilities. To destroy your people—the Quraysh—and before you, we have not heard of a man who exterminates his roots; or those who follow you will let you down. Indeed we do not see with you except a confused mix of people, I do not know their faces nor their genealogy."[51] In this version, Abu Bakr responds even more vulgarly, saying: "Suck the clitoris of al-Lat!

---

44 Ibid.
45 Ibid.
46 Ibid.
47 Ibid., 501.
48 Ibid., 503.
49 Ibid., 502.
50 Ibid.
51 Al-Waqidi, op. cit., 292.

Shall we abandon him?"[52] This incenses Urwa, who replies: "By God, if I did not owe you a debt that I have not fulfilled, I would react."[53]

Muhammad didn't want a battle, however, and at length, the two sides agreed to negotiate. Muhammad's companions were dumbfounded when he began making sweeping concessions to the Quraysh. Ibn Hisham states that "after a long discussion peace was made and nothing remained but to write an agreement," whereupon "Umar jumped up and went to Abu Bakr saying, 'Is he not God's apostle, and are we not Muslims, and are they not polytheists?'"[54] Abu Bakr affirmed that this was so, and Umar continued: "Then why should we agree to what is demeaning to our religion?"[55] To that, Abu Bakr said: "Stick to what he says, for I testify that he is God's apostle."[56] Umar reassured Abu Bakr of his loyalty and asked Muhammad about the agreement. Muhammad counseled patience, saying: "I am God's slave and His apostle. I will not go against His commandment and He will not make me the loser."[57]

Umar's patience, however, would be sorely tried. Muhammad called for Ali ibn Abi Talib to have him write down the agreement he had concluded with the Quraysh. Muhammad told him to head the document "In the name of Allah the Compassionate, the Merciful."[58] Suhayl ibn Amr, the Quraysh negotiator, found that unacceptable and said: "I do not recognize this; but write 'In thy name, O Allah.'"[59] Muhammad directed Ali to comply and then said: "Write: 'This is what Muhammad, the apostle of God has agreed with Suhayl b. Amr.'"[60] Suhayl would have none of that, either, and responded: "If I witnessed that you were God's apostle I would not have fought you. Write your own name and the name of your father."[61]

Muhammad acquiesced to that as well, telling Ali:

Write: "This is what Muhammad b. Abdullah has agreed with Suhayl b. Amr: they have agreed to lay aside war for ten years during which

---

52 Ibid.
53 Ibid.
54 Ibn Ishaq, op. cit., 504.
55 Ibid.
56 Ibid.
57 Ibid.
58 Ibid.
59 Ibid.
60 Ibid.
61 Ibid.

men can be safe and refrain from hostilities on condition that if anyone comes to Muhammad without the permission of his guardian
he will return him to them; and if anyone of those with Muhammad
comes to Quraysh they will not return him to him. We will not show
enmity one to another and there shall be no secret reservation or
bad faith. He who wishes to enter into a bond and agreement with
Muhammad may do so and he who wishes to enter into a bond and
agreement with Quraysh may do so."[62]

The fact that someone could flee from the Muslims to the Quraysh
and not be returned, while someone could flee from the Quraysh to the
Muslims and the Muslims were bound to return him, was a significant
concession. The Quraysh even made an additional demand: "You must
retire from us this year and not enter Mecca against our will, and next
year we will make way for you and you can enter it with your companions, and stay there three nights. You may carry a rider's weapons, the
swords in their sheaths. You can bring in nothing more."[63]

Al-Waqidi has Umar recount much later: "I was suspicious that day
in a manner that I had never been since I converted. If on that day, I had
found a group separating from the Muslims because they disliked the
contract I would have joined them. Then God made its outcome good
and guided. Indeed, the Messenger of God was most knowledgeable."[64]
But Allah sent a new revelation promising that all would work out in the
end in the Muslims' favor: "Indeed, we have given you a clear conquest,
so that Allah may forgive you of your sin what is past and what is to
come, and may perfect his favor to you, and may guide you on a right
path...Allah has fulfilled the vision for his messenger in very truth. You
will indeed enter the sacred mosque, if Allah wills, secure, shaven and
with hair cut, not fearing. But he knows what you do not know, and has
given you a near conquest beforehand" (Qur'an 48:1–2, 27).

Ibn Hisham was enthusiastic about the results of this agreement
despite its appearing to be so lopsided in favor of the Quraysh: "No previous victory in Islam was greater than this. There was nothing but battle
when men met; but when there was an armistice and war was abolished
and men met in safety and consulted together none talked about Islam

---

62 Ibid.
63 Ibid.
64 Al-Waqidi, op. cit., 298.

intelligently without entering it. In those two years double as many or more than double as many entered Islam as ever before."[65]

The reason for his enthusiasm, and Muhammad's confidence, would soon become clear. Ibn Hisham relates that a woman, Umm Kulthum bint Uqba, "migrated to the apostle during this period. Her two brothers Umara and al-Walid, sons of Uqba, came and asked the apostle to return her to them in accordance with the agreement between him and the Quraysh at Hudaybiya, but he would not. God forbade it."[66] Al-Waqidi, as usual, has an abundance of piquant detail. In his version, Umm Kulthum pleads with Muhammad to be allowed to stay with the Muslims: "O Messenger of God, indeed I fled with my religion to you, so keep me and do not return me to them, they will prevent me and hurt me. I have no patience with pain. I am a woman and women are weak, as you know. I have seen you return two men to the polytheists until one of them refused. But I am a woman!"[67] Muhammad was happy to comply, saying: "Indeed, God has revoked the agreement concerning women."[68] Al-Waqidi states that Muhammad "returned those who came from the men, but he did not return those who came from the women," and that he "judged about that with wisdom, satisfying all of them."[69]

The Muslims may have been satisfied, but the Quraysh, of course, were not. Al-Waqidi turns Ibn Hisham's summary account into a dialogue in which Muhammad himself declares that Allah has revoked the treaty. When Umm Kulthum's two brothers say, "O Muhammad, return her to us in accordance with our laws and what you contracted with us," Muhammad replies, "God has revoked it."[70]

The treaty of Hudaybiyya established the pattern for all treaty-making in Islamic law, and that may have been the purpose of the formulation of this legend. Treaties with non-Muslims were to be for a period of ten years, but the Muslims could revoke them at any time if the conditions that led to their being concluded no longer prevailed. In the case of the treaty of Hudaybiyya itself, Muhammad initially negotiated it from a position of weakness, but after "double as many or more than

---

65 Ibn Ishaq, op. cit., 507.
66 Ibid., 509.
67 Al-Waqidi, op. cit., 310–1.
68 Ibid., 311.
69 Ibid.
70 Ibid.

double as many entered Islam as ever before," as Ibn Hisham says, the Muslims were in a stronger position, and so had no need of the treaty. The flight of Umm Kulthum from Mecca to Medina to join the Muslims gave Muhammad a pretext to break the treaty, which he did not hesitate to do now that he was in a position of strength.

Yet despite the fact that these principles have been part of Islamic law regarding treaties since the ninth century, Western governments today still pursue treaties with Islamic states and organizations, assuming that they will, like Western entities, consider those treaties sacrosanct and inviolable.

Appealing to the Rulers

Having secured this uneasy peace with the Quraysh, Muhammad wrote a series of letters to the rulers of various nations, inviting them to accept his new religion. Ibn Sa'd says that in May of the year 628, six messengers went out with letters from Muhammad. Two letters went to Najashi, the ruler of Aksum, in present-day Ethiopia and Eritrea; upon receiving them, he immediately accepted Islam. Another letter went to the Roman Emperor Heraclius, who was in Emessa at the time. Heraclius was deeply impressed and addressed the Roman grandees in a church at Emessa, saying: "Follow this Arabian Prophet."[71] At that, however, the notable Romans Heraclius was addressing "ran away like wild asses, snorting and with their crosses raised."[72] Heraclius "was disappointed as to their joining the faith of Islam and became apprehensive of the safety of his person and authority. So he consoled them and said: I said this to test your steadfastness in your religion and now I have seen what I like most. They prostrated before him," an indication of their idolatry, for in Islam, the believers prostrated before Allah alone.[73]

Bukhari has a wealth of additional detail in his version. He has Heraclius summoning Abu Sufyan, the Quraysh chieftain who had fought against the Muslims, to ask him about Muhammad. Abu Sufyan appeared before Heraclius and the Roman court in Jerusalem; several of the Quraysh were accompanying him, and they all knew Muhammad personally. Abu Sufyan recounts: "By Allah! Had I not been afraid of my

---

71 Ibn Sa'd, I, 306.
72 Ibid.
73 Ibid.

companions labeling me a liar, I would not have spoken the truth about the Prophet."[74] In response to Heraclius's questions, Abu Sufyan admits that Muhammad is of a noble family, that no one who had become a Muslim had later become disenchanted and left Islam (a claim that was not exactly true, according to other traditions), that Muhammad was not a liar, and that he kept his promises. Abu Sufyan later recalled telling his men that Muhammad "has become so prominent that even the King of Bani Al-Asfar," that is, the Roman emperor, "is afraid of him."[75]

Abu Sufyan was as impressed as Heraclius, recounting: "Then I started to become sure that he (the Prophet) would be the conqueror in the near future till I embraced Islam (i.e. Allah guided me to it)."[76] Meanwhile, Heraclius "invited all the heads of the Byzantines to assemble in his palace at Homs. When they assembled, he ordered that all the doors of his palace be closed. Then he came out and said, 'O Byzantines! If success is your desire and if you seek right guidance and want your empire to remain then give a pledge of allegiance to this Prophet (i.e. embrace Islam).'"[77] But when they heard this, "the people ran towards the gates of the palace like onagers but found the doors closed. Heraclius realized their hatred towards Islam and when he lost the hope of their embracing Islam, he ordered that they should be brought back in audience. (When they returned) he said, 'What already said was just to test the strength of your conviction and I have seen it.' The people prostrated before him and became pleased with him, and this was the end of Heraclius's story (in connection with his faith)."[78]

There is no record of this letter, or any communication from Muhammad, in the writings of the Roman chroniclers of the day. If Heraclius did receive a communication from an Arabian prophet, no record of this survived, and there is no indication that this letter or Heraclius' affinity for Islam existed at all until they appear in accounts that were composed two centuries later.

Muhammad is depicted as writing to others as well. When the Persian emperor Chosroes received his message, says Ibn Sa'd, "he took it

74 Sahih Bukhari, vol. 1, book 1, no. 7.
75 Ibid.
76 Ibid.
77 Ibid.
78 Ibid.

and tore it (into pieces)."[79] When Muhammad was told about this reaction, he said: "O Allah: Tear (break) his kingdom (into pieces)."[80]

Maria the Copt

Muhammad's letter to al-Muqawqis, ruler of Egypt, had a better result for the prophet of Islam. This is an even more dubious tradition than most of the others about Muhammad, for no one is sure who exactly al-Muqawqis was. He has often been identified with the last Roman prefect of Egypt before the Arab conquest, Cyrus of Alexandria, but this is uncertain, and others suggest he was a Persian who ruled in Alexandria during the Persian occupation of Egypt early in the seventh century.

Whoever al-Muqawqis was, Ibn Hisham says that he received one of Muhammad's letters and responded with a gift: "al-Muqawqis gave to the apostle four slave girls, one of whom was Mary mother of Ibrahim the apostle's son."[81] Mary the Copt, as she was known, became one of Muhammad's favorites among the many women in his life, and according to a hadith, this aroused the jealousy of some of his wives: "It was narrated from Anas, that the Messenger of Allah had a female slave with whom he had intercourse, but Aishah and Hafsah would not leave him alone until he said that she was forbidden for him. Then Allah, the Mighty and Sublime, revealed: 'O Prophet! Why do you forbid (for yourself) that which Allah has allowed to you.' until the end of the Verse."[82]

This refers to what we find today as the beginning of the sixty-sixth chapter of the Qur'an, which begins with Allah scolding his prophet for taking an oath in order to please his wives. The nature of the oath is not specified, but Allah repeats that the prophet is free from it and warns the wives that if they continue to trouble the messenger, he will divorce them and get other wives:

> O prophet, Why do you prohibit what Allah has made lawful for you, trying to please your wives? And Allah is forgiving, merciful. Allah has made lawful for you absolution from your oaths, and Allah is your protector. He is the knower, the wise one. When the prophet confided a fact to one of his wives and when she afterward

79 Ibid.
80 Ibid.
81 Ibn Ishaq, op. cit., 653.
82 Sunan al-Nasai, vol. 4, book 36, no. 3959.

revealed it and Allah told him about this, he made part of it known and passed over a part. And when he told it to her, she said, Who has told you? He said, The knower, the aware has told me. If you two turn in repentance to Allah for what your hearts desired, and if you help one another against him, then indeed, Allah, even he, is his protecting friend, and Gabriel and the righteous among the believers, and furthermore the angels are his helpers. It may happen that his Lord, if he divorces you, will give him in your place wives who are better than you, Muslim, believing, pious, penitent, devout, inclined to fasting, widows and maidens. (66:1–5)

Bukhari records a lengthy hadith explaining this oblique passage as involving Aisha and Hafsa being angry at Muhammad because he had spent a night with Mary the Copt out of turn as he made the rounds among his women.[83] They confront him, whereupon he takes an oath to stay away from Mary. Allah, however, absolves him from this oath in this Qur'anic passage and threatens Aisha and Hafsa with divorce if they don't get back in line.

Some Muslims, however, evidently considered this story to portray the prophet of Islam in far too scandalous a light, and so Bukhari also includes another tradition saying that the Qur'anic passage in question was all about Muhammad's bad breath. Aisha is depicted as recounting that Muhammad would dally for long periods at the home of Zaynab bint Jahsh "and drink honey at her house," affecting his breath.[84] Aisha explained that "Hafsa and I decided that if the Prophet came to any one of us, she should say to him, 'I detect the smell of Maghafir (a nasty smelling gum) in you. Have you eaten Maghafir?'"[85] When they did this, Muhammad promised not to eat any more: "Never mind, I have taken some honey at the house of Zainab bint Jahsh, but I shall never drink of it anymore."[86] At this point, in this version, Allah revealed the beginning of the Qur'an's sixty-sixth chapter, scolding Muhammad for making this oath and rebuking his wives.

---

83 Sahih Bukhari, vol. 3, book 46, no. 2468.
84 Sahih Bukhari, vol. 7, book 68, no. 5267.
85 Ibid.
86 Ibid.

Mary the Copt bore Muhammad his son Ibrahim, who was said to have died before reaching the age of two, thereby maintaining Muhammad's status as the seal of the prophets.

According to a hadith, Muhammad once ordered the murder of a man who was said to have had a sexual liaison with Mary the Copt, but the killing proved to be unnecessary: "Anas reported that a person was charged with fornication with the slave girl of Allah's Messenger. Thereupon Allah's Messenger said to Ali: 'Go and strike his neck.' Ali came to him and he found him in a well making his body cool. Ali said to him: 'Come out,' and as he took hold of his hand and brought him out, he found that his sexual organ had been cut. Hadrat Ali refrained from striking his neck. He came to Allah's Apostle and said: 'Allah's Messenger, he has not even the sexual organ with him.'"[87] This saved his life.

---

87 Sahih Muslim, book 50, no. 2771.

CHAPTER TWELVE

Triumph

The Khaybar Raid

Now that Muhammad was confident that the Muslim forces were stronger than those of the Quraysh, he turned his attention to the other group he regarded as his great rivals: the Jews. The remnants of the three Jewish tribes of Medina, the Banu Qaynuqa, Banu Nadir, and Banu Qurayza, had settled at the oasis of Khaybar, north of Medina, after Muhammad had exiled the first two and massacred the men of the third. But the prophet of Islam was not disposed to let them live there in peace. The only peace that he would accept for the Jews of Medina was the peace of the grave. Accordingly, he now marched with his forces to Khaybar.

Al-Waqidi prefaces his account of the Khaybar raid by providing a lengthy list of those who "have related portions of this tradition about Khaybar to me" in "the year three hundred and seventy-seven AH," that is, the year 938 AD.[1] Thus, here again, the reader is confronted with the incredible claim that several generations of transmitters, over more than three centuries, were able to preserve and pass on, with scrupulous accuracy, a detailed and multifaceted report about Muhammad's activities. Al-Waqidi adds that "some were more reliable than others," but provides no details about how he determined the reliability of the various accounts.[2]

Al-Waqidi begins his account by saying that some of the hypocrites who had refused to join Muhammad on earlier raids were eager for this one, telling him: "We will go out with you to Khaybar. Surely it is the

1 Al-Waqidi, op. cit., 311–2.
2 Ibid., 312.

countryside of the Hijaz with rich food and property."[3] Muhammad immediately rebukes their materialism: "You will not go out with me unless you desire *jihad*. As for plunder, there will be none."[4] Emphasizing the point, Muhammad "sent a herald out to cry, 'Only those desiring *jihad* will go out with us. And as for plunder there will be none!'"[5] The prophet of Islam was apparently intent solely on massacring the Jews because of their earlier machinations against him, which are reported only in the hadith and sira literature.

Muhammad did not, however, launch an attack immediately upon arrival. According to Ibn Hisham, one of the Muslims in Muhammad's force recounted: "When the apostle raided a people he waited until the morning. If he heard a call to prayer he held back; if he did not hear it he attacked."[6] That is, if there were Muslims present, Muhammad would not attack; he was only intent on making war against non-Muslims. The Muslim warrior continued: "We came to Khaybar by night, and the apostle passed the night there; and when morning came he did not hear the call to prayer, so he rode and we rode with him, and I rode behind Abu Taiha with my foot touching the apostle's foot."[7] The Jews of Khaybar were taken completely by surprise: "We met the workers of Khaybar coming out in the morning with their spades and baskets. When they saw the apostle and the army they cried, 'Muhammad with his force,' and turned tail and fled. The apostle said, 'Allah Akbar! Khaybar is destroyed. When we arrive in a people's square it is a bad morning for those who have been warned.'"[8]

Muhammad "seized the property piece by piece and conquered the forts one by one as he came to them." Although he had told the hypocrites before the conquest that there would be no booty, in the event, the spoils were plentiful. A hadith says that the "Khaybar was divided among the people of al-Hudaybiyyah. The Messenger of Allah divided it into eighteen portions. The army contained one thousand and five hundred people. There were three hundred horsemen among them. He gave

---

3 Ibid.
4 Ibid.
5 Ibid.
6 Ibn Ishaq, op. cit., 511.
7 Ibid.
8 Ibid.

double share to the horsemen, and a single to the footmen."[9] Another tradition, however, says that "Khaybar was divided by the Messenger of Allah into three sections: two for Muslims, and one as a contribution for his family. If anything remained after making the contribution of his family, he divided it among the poor Emigrants."[10]

Among the spoils were women of Khaybar whom the Muslims had captured: "The apostle took captives from them among whom was Safiya d. Huyayy b. Akhtab who had been the wife of Kinana b. al-Rabi b. Abu'l-Huqayq, and two cousins of hers. The apostle chose Safiya for himself. Dihya b. Khalifa al-Kaib had asked the apostle for Safiya, and when he chose her for himself he gave him her two cousins. The women of Khaybar were distributed among the Muslims."[11] Ibn Sa'd notes that Safiya "was a handsome girl."[12] One Muslim recalled, according to Ibn Hisham, that Muhammad forbade "carnal intercourse with pregnant women who were captured"; those who were not pregnant, however, were fair game.[13]

Not all of the women of Khaybar were willing to accept their fate. Ibn Hisham recounts that Safiya was brought before Muhammad "along with another woman."[14] They were led "past the Jews who were slain," and "when the woman who was with Safiya saw them she shrieked and slapped her face and poured dust on her head."[15] Muhammad was disgusted, saying: "Take this she-devil away from me."[16] Nevertheless, he demonstrated understanding, asking his companion Bilal, who had led the women to him: "Had you no compassion, Bilal, when you brought two women past their dead husbands?"[17]

In his version, al-Waqidi softens Muhammad's reaction. He scolds Bilal: "Has graciousness left you that you take a young girl past the dead?"[18] Unlike Ibn Hisham, al-Waqidi has Bilal's response: "O Messenger of God, I did not think that you would hate that. I wanted her to

---

9 Sunan Abi Dawud, book 20, no. 3015.
10 Sunan Abi Dawud, book 20, no. 2967.
11 Ibn Ishaq, op. cit.
12 Ibn Sa'd, op. cit., II, 145.
13 Ibn Ishaq, op. cit., 512.
14 Ibid., 514.
15 Ibid., 515.
16 Ibid.
17 Ibid.
18 Al-Waqidi, op. cit., 331.

see the destruction of her people."[19] Instead of demanding that the "she-devil" be taken out of his sight, Muhammad then consoles the upset girl, telling her, "This is only a devil," apparently in reference to the loyal but overzealous Bilal.[20]

Meanwhile, Ibn Hisham notes that Muhammad's reaction to Safiya was quite different from his revulsion before the "she-devil": "He gave orders that Safiya was to be put behind him and threw his mantle over her, so that the Muslims knew that he had chosen her for himself."[21] Safiya, according to Ibn Hisham, had seen this coming, having had a dream before the Muslims invaded Khaybar; in her dream, the moon fell in her lap. Hearing of this dream, Safiya's husband, Kinana ibn al-Rabi, declared: "This simply means that you covet the king of the Hijaz, Muhammad."[22] He then "gave her such a blow in the face that he blacked her eye. When she was brought to the apostle the mark was still there, and when he asked the cause of it she told him this story."[23]

This story may have been designed to reduce sympathy for Kinana ibn al-Rabi, for he "had the custody of the treasure of B. al-Nadir."[24] Kinana was captured and brought before Muhammad, who asked him: "Do you know that if we find you have it, I shall kill you?"[25] Kinana said yes, he was aware of this. Some of this treasure was found, but Kinana refused to tell Muhammad where he could find the rest, so Muhammad issued an order: "Torture him until you extract what he has."[26] The Muslims then "kindled a fire with flint and steel on his chest until he was nearly dead."[27] After that, Kinana was beheaded.

Al-Waqidi's version considerably softens the cruelty and rapacity of Muhammad and his men. Kinana doesn't have custody of the Banu Nadir's treasure, but solely that of his own family, "and the jewelry from their jewelry, and what there was of the skin of the camel. Their nobility was known by it."[28] But Kinana tells Muhammad that it was all gone:

19 Ibid.
20 Ibid.
21 Ibn Ishaq, op. cit.
22 Ibid.
23 Ibid.
24 Ibid.
25 Ibid.
26 Ibid.
27 Ibid.
28 Al-Waqidi, op. cit., 330.

"O Abu'l-Qasim, we spent it during our war and there does not remain anything from it. We saved it for such a day as this. The war and provisions for the warriors left nothing behind."[29] The Jews even take an oath to this effect, whereupon Muhammad warns them: "The protection of God and His prophet will be denied you if it is discovered with you."[30]

Kinana agrees, but Muhammad still takes a further step: he "asked Abu Bakr, Umar, Ali and ten Jews to witness the agreement."[31] One of the Jews gives Kinana a further warning, that Muhammad has prophetic powers: "If you have what Muhammad is seeking from you or you know of it, inform him, for surely you will protect your blood. If not, by God, it will appear to him. He has come to know about other things we did not know."[32] Kinana, however, scoffs at this.

Muhammad does indeed find the treasure, whereupon he commands one of the Muslims to torture Kinana "until he revealed all that he had with him." The Muslim "came to him with a firebrand and pierced him in his chest."[33] Then Muhammad commanded that Kinana be put to death and that Kinana's brother also be tortured and then killed.

In Ibn Hisham's account, Muhammad further commanded that the Jews of Khaybar be exiled: "The apostle besieged the people of Khaybar in their two forts al-Watih and al-Sulalim until when they could hold out no longer they asked him to let them go, and spare their lives, and he did so."[34]

A hadith, however, states that he let the Jews stay in Khaybar as long as they paid him tribute in the form of a share of the fruits of the land. This tradition also differs from the sira accounts in asserting that the Muslims conquered Khaybar without a fight: "When Allah bestowed Khaybar on His Prophet as *fay* (as a result of conquest without fighting), the Messenger of Allah allowed (them) to remain there as they were before, and apportioned it between him and them. He then sent Abdullah ibn Rawahah who assessed (the amount of dates) upon them."[35] *Fay* was the treasure of Muslims that they gained from people they had

---

29 Ibid.
30 Ibid., 330–1.
31 Ibid.
32 Ibid.
33 Ibid.
34 Ibn Ishaq, op. cit., 515.
35 Sunan Abi Dawud, book 23, no. 3414.

conquered. In a related hadith, Muhammad says to the Khaybar Jews, "I confirm you in it," that is, in Khaybar itself, "as long as Allah, the Mighty, the Majestic, establishes you in it, provided that the fruits are divided between us and you."[36]

The continued existence of the Jews in Khaybar, however, was decidedly conditional and temporary. A hadith depicts Umar saying: "The Messenger of Allah had transaction with the Jews of Khaybar on condition that we should expel them when we wish. 'If anyone has property (with them), he should take it back, for I am going to expel the Jews.' So he expelled them."[37]

Once Khaybar was thoroughly subdued, Muhammad commanded one of the captive Jewish women, Zaynab bint al-Harith, to prepare a meal for him. Zaynab (not to be confused with Muhammad's two wives of that name) "prepared for him a roast lamb, having first inquired what joint he preferred. When she learned that it was the shoulder, she put a lot of poison in it and poisoned the whole lamb. Then she brought it in and placed it before him. He took hold of the shoulder and chewed a morsel of it, but he did not swallow it."[38] One of the other Muslims, Bishr ibn al-Bara, swallowed a bit of the poisoned meat, but Muhammad "spat it out, saying, 'This bone tells me that it is poisoned.'"[39]

In al-Waqidi's version, both Muhammad and Bishr swallow bites of the meat, but then Muhammad cries out: "Stop! Surely this forearm informs me that it is poisoned."[40] Although he is not a prophet, Bishr says that he also knew that the meat was poisoned: "By God, I found that from the bite I ate, and what prevented me from spitting it out was that I hated to spoil your pleasure at your food, for when you swallowed what was in your hand I would not favor myself over you. I hoped only that you did not eat what was bad in it."[41] So evidently, the forearm did not inform Muhammad that it was poisoned before he had swallowed at least part of it. Al-Waqidi states that Bishr died, but not immediately: "his pain did not last a year."[42]

---

36 Muwatta Malik, book 33, no. 1.
37 Sunan Abi Dawud, book 20, no. 3007.
38 Ibn Ishaq, op. cit., 516.
39 Ibid.
40 Al-Waqidi, op. cit., 334.
41 Ibid.
42 Ibid.

Ibn Hisham records that Muhammad confronted Zaynab, and she immediately confessed, saying: "You know what you have done to my people. I said to myself, If he is a king I shall ease myself of him and if he is a prophet he will be informed (of what I have done)."[43] Apparently, because she had implied that he was a prophet, Muhammad did not have her killed; Ibn Hisham adds: "So the apostle let her off."[44] Bukhari reports: "A Jewess brought a poisoned (cooked) sheep for the Prophet who ate from it. She was brought to the Prophet and he was asked, 'Shall we kill her?' He said, 'No.' I continued to see the effect of the poison on the palate of the mouth of Allah's Messenger."[45] However, another hadith states: "The Messenger of Allah then ordered regarding her and she was killed."[46] Al-Waqidi offers both versions: "There was disputation among us about her. A sayer said: The Messenger of God commanded about her and she was killed, then crucified. Another said that he had pardoned her."[47]

This incident was to cast a long shadow over the rest of Muhammad's life. Several years later, when Muhammad was in his final illness, he told the sister of the man who had been poisoned: "O Umm Bishr, this is the time in which I feel a deadly pain from what I ate with your brother at Khaybar."[48] "Umm Bishr," however, means "mother of Bishr," and al-Waqidi states that this woman was indeed Bishr's mother, not his sister: "The mother of Bishr b. al-Bara used to say: I visited the Messenger of God during the sickness of which he died. He was feverish and I felt him and said, 'I have not found what makes you sick on any other.' The Messenger of God said, 'Just as rewards are given us, so are trials inflicted on us. People claim that the Messenger of God has pleurisy. God would not inflict it upon me. Rather, it is the touch of Satan caused by eating what I, and your son ate on the day of Khaybar. I will continue to feel pain until the time of death overwhelms me.'"[49]

---

43 Ibn Ishaq, op. cit.
44 Ibid.
45 Sahih Bukhari, vol. 3, book 51, no. 2617.
46 Sunan Abi Dawud, book 41, no. 4511.
47 Al-Waqidi, op. cit.
48 Ibn Ishaq, op. cit.
49 Al-Waqidi, op. cit.

The Muslims thus departed from Khaybar in an atmosphere of suspicion and distrust. An impatient Muhammad married Safiya, says Ibn Hisham, "in Khaybar or on the way" out of the area, even as she was grieving over the murder of her father and husband at the hands of her new husband.[50] Safiya had been duly prepared for her new role as a wife of the prophet: she was "beautified and combed, and got in a fit state for the apostle by Umm Sulaym d. Milhan mother of Anas b. Malik."[51]

And so Muhammad "passed the night with her in a tent of his," right in the midst of the dead bodies of Safiya's countrymen. Suspicious after the poisoning, one Muslim "passed the night girt with his sword, guarding the apostle and going round the tent until in the morning the apostle saw him there and asked him what he meant by his action. He replied, 'I was afraid for you with this woman for you have killed her father, her husband, and her people, and till recently she was in unbelief, so I was afraid for you on her account.'"[52] Touched at his concern, Muhammad replied with a prayer: "O God, preserve Abu Ayyub, as he spent the night preserving me."[53]

Al-Waqidi depicts Safiya as warming to her new role but grieved by the unkindness of her fellow wives: "I suffered his wives who looked down on me saying, 'O daughter of a Jew.' But I used to see the Messenger of God, and he was gracious and generous to me. One day when he visited me I was crying. He said, 'What is the matter with you?' I said, 'Your wives look down on me and say, "O daughter of a Jew."'" Safiya continued: "I saw that the Messenger of God was angry. He said, 'When they speak to you or dismiss you, say, "My father is Aaron and my uncle, Moses."'"[54] After twice exiling the Banu Qaynuqa and Banu Nadir and massacring the Banu Qurayza, his words appeared less generous than they might have otherwise.

Indeed, Khaybar became a watchword, an enduring warning to the Jews that they could be massacred again. In our own day, foes of Israel frequently chant, "Khaybar, Khaybar, O Jews, the army of Muhammad

---

50 Ibn Ishaq, op. cit.
51 Ibid., 517.
52 Ibid.
53 Ibid.
54 Al-Waqidi, op. cit., 332.

will return," threatening modern-day Jews with the punishment that the prophet of Islam meted out to their ancestors.[55]

A Pilgrimage to Mecca

The Islamic traditions state that Muhammad, having destroyed the Jewish tribes of Medina and conquered many of the pagan tribes of Arabia, now turned toward Mecca, the city in which he was said to have been born, and set his sights upon a final victory over the Quraysh, his own people who had rejected his claim to be a prophet of Allah.

Ibn Hisham states that at first, Muhammad contented himself with the raids that provided the plunder that was the livelihood of the community: "When the apostle returned from Khaybar to Medina he stayed there from the first Rabi until Shawwal," that is, for six months, "sending out raiding parties and expeditions."[56] Then, he decided to make another attempt to make the lesser pilgrimage, the *umra*, to Mecca. This time, in a telling reflection of the change in the balance of power, "when the Meccans heard of it, they got out of his way," although the Quraysh did console themselves with the apparent poverty of the Muslim pilgrims: "Muhammad and his companions are in destitution, want, and privation."[57]

---

55 Melissa Koenig, "'Allahu Akhbar!': Pro-Palestinian Protesters Chant as They BURN Israeli Flag in March Through NYC that Left Diners Shocked and Saw 'Blood' Thrown at BlackRock Offices," *Daily Mail*, June 12, 2021, https://www.dailymail.co.uk/news/article-9678709/Pro-Palestinian-group-BURNS-Israeli-flag-protest-businesses-ties-Israel.html; Robert Spencer, "South Africa: Muslim Demonstrators Scream 'Khaybar' Jihad Chant Vowing New Genocide of Jews," Jihad Watch, May 18, 2021, https://www.jihadwatch.org/2021/05/south-africa-muslim-demonstrators-scream-khaybar-jihad-chant-vowing-new-genocide-of-jews; Robert Spencer, "Belgium: Muslims Scream 'Khaybar' Jihad Chant Vowing New Genocide of Jews," Jihad Watch, May 17, 2021, https://www.jihadwatch.org/2021/05/belgium-muslims-scream-khaybar-jihad-chant-vowing-new-genocide-of-jews; "London Rally for Jews Killed in Arab Countries Disrupted by Men Shouting in Arabic about Killing Jews," *Jewish Telegraphic Agency*, November 9, 2018, https://www.jta.org/2018/11/09/global/men-shouting-arabic-killing-jews-end-london-kristallnacht-vigil; Benjamin Weinthal, "Vienna Police Charge 3 Men for Waving Israeli Flag at Rally," *Jerusalem Post*, January 10, 2018, https://www.jpost.com/international/vienna-police-charge-3-men-for-waving-israeli-flag-at-rally-533313; Robert Spencer, "Video: Muslim Protesters in London Scream 'Death to America,' 'Death to Israel,' Genocidal Anti-Jewish Jihad Chant," Jihad Watch, December 11, 2017, https://www.jihadwatch.org/2017/12/video-muslim-protesters-in-london-scream-death-to-america-death-to-israel-genocidal-anti-jewish-jihad-chant; Danielle Avel, "CAIR-Affiliated Protest: 'We Are Hamas!,'" *Breitbart News*, July 23, 2014, https://www.breitbart.com/national-security/2014/07/23/cair-affiliated-protest-we-are-hamas/.

56 Ibn Ishaq, op. cit., 530.

57 Ibid.

Muhammad entered Mecca without incident. When he entered the great mosque, he "threw the end of his cloak over his left shoulder leaving his right upper arm free," saying: "God have mercy on a man who shows them today that he is strong."[58] He performed the duties of the pilgrimage as they stood for the pagan Arabs then and for Muslims to this day, kissing the black stone and walking repeatedly around the Kaʻba. Ibn Abbas confirmed that these pagan practices were being incorporated into the new religion: "People used to think that this practice was not incumbent on them because the apostle only did it for this clan of Quraysh because of what he had heard about them until when he made the farewell pilgrimage he adhered to it and the *sunna* carried it on."[59]

As Muhammad performed these rituals, one of the Muslims began a bellicose chant:

> Get out of his way, you unbelievers, make way.
> Every good thing goes with His apostle.
> O Lord, I believe in his word,
> I know God's truth in accepting it.
> We will fight you about its interpretation
> As we have fought you about its revelation
> With strokes that will remove heads from shoulders
> And make friend unmindful of friend.[60]

While on this pilgrimage, which lasted for three days, Muhammad made the most of the time and seized the opportunity to take yet another wife, Maymuna bint al-Harith. On the third day of his stay in Mecca, some of the Quraysh came to him in a less than hospitable mood, saying: "Your time is up, so get out from us."[61] Muhammad replied in full conciliatory mode: "How would it harm you if you were to let me stay and I gave a wedding feast among you and we prepared food and you came too?"[62] The Quraysh, however, were not interested in conciliation, saying: "We don't need your food, so get out."[63] Muhammad

---

58 Ibid.
59 Ibid., 531.
60 Ibid.
61 Ibid.
62 Ibid.
63 Ibid.

sacrificed some oxen, consummated his marriage with Maymuna, and returned to Medina.

A Dispute Among the Pagans

Shortly thereafter, however, a dispute among the pagan Arabs. One of the stipulations of the Treaty of Hudaybiyya was that any Arab tribe could conclude a treaty with either the Muslims or the Quraysh. Presently, the Quraysh became embroiled in a conflict with a tribe that had an alliance with the Muslims; this led Abu Sufyan, the Quraysh chieftain, to travel to Medina to try to smooth matters over with Muhammad, who was clearly now the stronger party.

In Medina, Abu Sufyan encountered his daughter Ramla bint Abi Sufyan, who was known as Umm Habiba. She had become a Muslim early in Muhammad's career and left for Abyssinia when tensions between the Muslims and the Quraysh began increasing. Once in Abyssinia, her husband left Islam, whereupon Ramla left her husband and married Muhammad from a distance; she did not journey to Medina and begin to live in his household until several years later.

Ramla was there by the time her father arrived, however, and she was not welcoming. According to Ibn Hisham, "having arrived at Medina," Abu Sufyan "went in to his daughter Umm Habiba, and as he went to sit on the apostle's carpet she folded it up so that he could not sit on it."[64] Abu Sufyan exclaimed: "My dear daughter, I hardly know if you think that the carpet is too good for me or that I am too good for the carpet!"[65] Umm Habiba shot back: "It is the apostle's carpet and you are an unclean polytheist. I do not want you to sit on the apostle's carpet."[66]

Abu Sufyan was saddened as only a parent confronted by a wayward child can be. He replied: "By God, since you left me you have gone to the bad."[67] But when he tried to appeal to Muhammad himself, the prophet of Islam would not speak to him. Abu Sufyan then went to Abu Bakr, who refused to help. Abu Sufyan turned to Umar, who responded: "Should I intercede for you with the apostle! If I had only an ant I would fight you with it."[68] Then Abu Sufyan went to Muhammad's daughter

---

64 Ibid., 543.
65 Ibid.
66 Ibid.
67 Ibid.
68 Ibid.

Fatima; seeing Hasan, the young son she had with Ali ibn Abi Talib, Abu Sufyan said: "O daughter of Muhammad, will you let your little son here act as a protector between men so that he may become lord of the Arabs forever?"[69] According to Ibn Hisham, "she replied that her little boy was not old enough to undertake such a task and in any case, none could give protection against God's apostle."[70] Ali told Abu Sufyan: "I do not see anything that can really help you, but you are the chief of B. Kinana, so get up and grant protection between men and then go back home"; however, when Abu Sufyan asked Ali "if he thought that that would do any good, he replied that he did not, but that he could see nothing else."[71] Abu Sufyan proclaimed this protection, which amounted to an assurance that the Quraysh would not behave belligerently toward any other group, in the mosque in Medina. Then he returned to Mecca.

Muhammad then made the momentous decision: he would take an expedition of Muslims to Mecca himself. He prayed: "O God, take eyes and ears from Quraysh so that we may take them by surprise in their land."[72] However, one of the Muslims, Hatib ibn Abu Baitaa, wrote to the Quraysh, warning them that Muhammad was going to invade. According to Ibn Hisham, Hatib gave this letter to a woman whom he paid to take it to the Quraysh, but the identity of this woman was a matter of disagreement: "He gave it to a woman whom Muhammad b. Jafar alleged was from Muzayna while my other informant said she was Sara, a freed woman of one of the B. Abdul-Muttalib."[73] Al-Waqidi, however, is sure that she was "a woman of the Muzayna."[74]

Whoever she was, she hid the letter in her hair. Allah warned Muhammad about this, however, and the Muslims overtook her before she could reach the Quraysh. At length, she took the letter to Muhammad. Muhammad thereupon confronted Hatib, whom Umar wanted to behead summarily. Hatib explained: "O Messenger of God, indeed I am a believer in God and His Messenger. I have not altered nor changed! But I am a man with neither lineage nor kinship among the people, and I have, in their [Quraysh] midst, a family and a son, and I did it to

---

69 Ibid., 544.
70 Ibid.
71 Ibid.
72 Ibid.
73 Ibid., 545.
74 Al-Waqidi, op. cit., 393.

flatter and bribe them."[75] Muhammad responded magnanimously, spar-
ing Hatib's life, but Allah issued a warning: "O you who believe, do not
choose my enemy and your enemy for allies. Do you give them friendship when they disbelieve in that truth which has come to you, driving
out the messenger and you because you believe in Allah, your Lord? If
you have come forth to wage jihad in my way and seeking my good pleasure, do you show friendship to them in secret, when I am best aware of
what you hide and what you proclaim? And whoever does this among
you, he indeed has strayed from the right path" (Qur'an 60:1).

Abu Sufyan Converts

As Muhammad and the Muslim troops approached Mecca, they embarked upon a fast, mindful that Allah had granted victory to the pious
at Badr and always promised worldly success as a reward for obedience
and devotion. Abu Sufyan saw the writing on the wall; he and another
one of the Quraysh approached Muhammad, who initially was reluctant to receive them: "I have no use for them. As for my cousin he has
wounded my pride; and as for my aunt's son and my brother-in-law he
spoke insultingly of me in Mecca."[76] But Abu Sufyan overcame Muhammad's wounded pride with a threat: "By God, he must let me in or I will
take this little boy of mine and we will wander through the land until we
die of hunger and thirst."[77] Muhammad then took pity upon them and let
them in; Abu Sufyan became a Muslim. After his conversion, according
to Ibn Hisham, he recited a poem that included these verses:

> By thy life when I carried a banner
> To give al-Lat's cavalry the victory over Muhammad
> I was like one going astray in the darkness of the night,
> But now I am led on the right track.
> I could not guide myself, and he who with God overcame me
> Was he whom I had driven away with all my might.
> I used to do all I could to keep men from Muhammad
> And I was called a relative of his, though I did not claim
> the relation....[78]

75 Ibid.
76 Ibn Ishaq, op. cit., 546.
77 Ibid.
78 Ibid.

Ibn Hisham adds that "when he recited his words 'He who with God overcame me was he whom I had driven away with all my might,' the apostle punched him in the chest and said, 'You did indeed!'"[79]

Then, Ibn Hisham records a different tradition, in which Muhammad's uncle and companion, al-Abbas, brings Abu Sufyan to see Muhammad. As they converse, Muhammad says to him: "Woe to you, Abu Sufyan, isn't it time that you recognize that I am God's apostle?"[80] Abu Sufyan replies: "As to that I still have some doubt."[81] Fed up, al-Abbas declares to Abu Sufyan: "Submit and testify that there is no God but Allah and that Muhammad is the apostle of God before you lose your head."[82] Abu Sufyan complies.

Immediately after threatening to murder Abu Sufyan if he doesn't convert to Islam, al-Abbas becomes sensitive to his well-being: "I pointed out to the apostle that Abu Sufyan was a man who liked to have some cause for pride and asked him to do something for him."[83] Muhammad was equally interested in salvaging the pride of their former enemy and offered a guarantee of safety to the Meccans: "He who enters Abu Sufyan's house is safe, and he who locks his door is safe, and he who enters the mosque is safe."[84]

In al-Waqidi's account, pride is the farthest thing from Abu Sufyan's mind as he makes a fulsome confession of his weakness before Muhammad: "O Muhammad, I asked help of my God, and you asked help of your God. No, by God, whenever I confront you, you are victorious over me. And if my God were true and your God false, I would be victorious over you."[85] Here, again, is the one-to-one equation between obedience to Allah and earthly prosperity. The idea of the wicked prospering and the righteous having to endure suffering is entirely foreign to this perspective.

Abu Sufyan confesses that Muhammad is a prophet and then observes blandly: "O Muhammad, you come with a mix of people who are known and not known to your close relatives and your roots."[86]

---

79 Ibid.
80 Ibid., 547.
81 Ibid.
82 Ibid.
83 Ibid.
84 Ibid., 547–8.
85 Al-Waqidi, op. cit., 401–2.
86 Ibid., 402.

Muhammad, however, is not pacified by Abu Sufyan's conversion and immediately challenges the new convert: "You are most unjust and corrupt. You broke the agreement of al-Hudaybiyya," an extraordinary charge in light of the fact that Muhammad clearly broke it by refusing to send Umm Kulthum back to the Quraysh.[87]

Muhammad had more criticism of Abu Sufyan, to which the new Muslim finally replied that the prophet of Islam would do better to turn his wrath against the Hawazin, an Arab tribe that was "more distant in relationship and stronger to you in enmity!"[88] Muhammad's reply indicated that he had been longing to take for himself the property of the Hawazin, as well as the most vulnerable among them: "Indeed, I hope that my Lord will gather them to me, all of them through the conquest of Mecca, and strengthen Islam through them and defeat the Hawazin. I wish that God would grant me plunder from their wealth and their children. Indeed, I beg that of God!"[89]

The Kill List

First, however, Mecca had to be conquered. As the Muslim armies approached—"ten thousands," according to al-Waqidi—al-Abbas told Abu Sufyan to "hurry to his people" and warn them of what was coming so that they could accept Islam and head off a bloody battle.[90] Abu Sufyan entered Mecca shouting: "O Quraysh, this is Muhammad who has come to you with a force you cannot resist. He who enters Abu Sufyan's house is safe."[91] One of those who heard him was his wife, Hind bint Utba, who had eaten the liver of one of the Muslims who had been slain in the Battle of Uhud. Aware that her life hung in the balance with the Muslims about to enter Mecca, she approached Abu Sufyan and, "seizing his moustaches, cried, 'Kill this fat greasy bladder of lard! What a rotten protector of the people!'"[92] Abu Sufyan appealed directly to the Meccans: "Woe to you, don't let this woman deceive you, for you cannot resist what has come. He who enters Abu Sufyan's house will be safe."[93]

---

87 Ibid.
88 Ibid.
89 Ibid.
90 Ibid., Ibn Ishaq, op. cit., 548.
91 Ibn Ishaq, op. cit.
92 Ibid.
93 Ibid.

The Meccans were skeptical, saying to Abu Sufyan: "God slay you, what good will your house be to us?"[94] Abu Sufyan then expanded the protection: "And he who shuts his door upon himself will be safe and he who enters the mosque will be safe."[95] The Meccans, according to Ibn Hisham, then "dispersed to their houses and the mosque."[96]

Most of the Meccans had nothing to fear. Ibn Hisham explains that Muhammad "had instructed his commanders when they entered Mecca only to fight those who resisted them, except a small number who were to be killed even if they were found beneath the curtains of the Ka'ba."[97] These were people who had particularly offended Muhammad. One of them was Abdullah ibn Sa'd, about whom Ibn Hisham offers this explanation: "The reason he ordered him to be killed was that he had been a Muslim and used to write down revelation; then he apostatized and returned to Quraysh."[98]

Why would someone leave Islam after occupying the exalted position of being a scribe for Muhammad and writing down the revelations he received from Allah? Al-Waqidi explains that when Abdullah ibn Sa'd "used to write the revelation for the Messenger of God," there were some discrepancies that the scribe found disturbing: "Maybe the Prophet dictated it as '*samiun alimun*' but he wrote '*alimun hakimun*,' and yet the Prophet established it, saying God established it thus."[99]

Samiun alimun is "all-hearing, all-knowing," while *alimun hakimun* is "all-knowing, wise." All are attributes of Allah, but Muhammad was apparently cavalier about exactly which wording Allah had revealed and agreed to wording that came not from the angel Gabriel, but from Abdullah ibn Sa'd, but which Muhammad affirmed as being the word of Allah anyway. So, says al-Waqidi, Abdullah "was tempted away from Islam and he said, 'Muhammad does not know what he says! Indeed, I wrote for him what I wished. This, which I wrote, was revealed to me just as it was revealed to Muhammad."[100] Abdullah accordingly "went out fleeing from Medina to Mecca, an apostate."[101] But it did not appear

94 Ibid.
95 Ibid.
96 Ibid.
97 Ibid., 550.
98 Ibid.
99 Al-Waqidi, op. cit., 421.
100 Ibid.
101 Ibid.

that he could escape: "The Messenger of God permitted the shedding of his blood on the day of the Conquest."[102]

Uthman, however, was Abdullah ibn Sa'd's adoptive brother and pleaded for his life; a reluctant Muhammad remains silent in the face of his entreaties but finally agrees. When Abdullah is gone, however, Muhammad says furiously to his companions: "I kept silent so that one of you might get up and strike off his head!"[103] One of them responds: "Then why didn't you give me a sign, O apostle of God?"[104] Muhammad, says Ibn Hisham, "answered that a prophet does not kill by pointing."[105]

The story of Abdullah ibn Sa'd is often invoked today as evidence that Muhammad was clearly a false prophet: he readily agrees to an alteration, however minor, in the wording of what was supposed to be a revelation to him through an angel of the perfect book that had existed forever in paradise with the one true God. For the same reason, this is one of the traditions that is often seen as supporting the historicity of Muhammad; why would Muslims invent a story in which Muhammad is casual regarding the wording of Allah's revelation and then wants a man dead simply for discovering that the Qur'an isn't really the pure words of the divinity after all? The criterion of embarrassment, the proposition that if the stories of Muhammad were fabricated, the fabricators would not invent stories that portrayed their hero in a bad light, appears to be in play here.

From an Islamic standpoint, however, the story must be understood in light of Allah's solicitude for Muhammad and his constant protection of his prophet. From the perspective of a convinced believer, Abdullah ibn Sa'd was at fault when he first doubted Muhammad. Instead of being scandalized that Muhammad was taking his own words and making them part of the Qur'an, Abdullah should have been grateful that Allah used him, even if just for one moment, as a prophetic instrument.

The fact that Muhammad put him on the list of people to be killed in Mecca is also, in the view of the Islamic orthodoxy that was being solidified around the time these accounts were written, an indication that there was nothing embarrassing about the stories of Abdullah ibn Sa'd as far as the Muslims of the ninth and tenth centuries were concerned. The

102 Ibid.
103 Ibn Hisham, op. cit.
104 Ibid.
105 Ibid.

Qur'an tells Muslims: "Fight them, and Allah will punish them by your hands, and he will lay them low and give you victory over them, and he will heal the hearts of people who are believers. And he will remove the anger of their hearts" (9:14–15). If Allah punishes his enemies by the hands of the believers, how much more is this true of Muhammad, the last and greatest of the prophets? Muhammad's judgment against Abdullah ibn Sa'd is Allah's judgment and a demonstration of Muhammad's role as the prophet of Allah.

The mercy Muhammad ultimately shows to Abdullah, under the pleading of Uthman, doesn't change this. It is clear that everyone in the story takes it for granted that Muhammad has absolute power of life and death over him, and this is how later believers are to regard him: as the ultimate judge and arbiter, essentially identical in this role with Allah himself, albeit a mere mortal who is not to be worshipped as a god. Abdullah, according to al-Waqidi, returned to Islam, and though he fled from Muhammad in fear at first, he eventually was calmed after Muhammad said that what he had done before his return to Islam was of no importance.

Next on the kill list, according to Ibn Hisham, was a man who had been a Muslim but had committed murder, apostatized, and fled to Mecca. "He had two singing girls, Fartana and her friend, who used to sing satirical songs about the apostle, so he ordered that they should be killed with him."[106] Al-Waqidi, as usual, has more detail, knowing both of their names, but even he isn't sure of exactly what happened, saying self-contradictorily that "one of them was killed: Arnab or Fartana. As for Fartana, he granted her protection until she believed."[107]

The messenger of Allah was not to be mocked; next on the list was a man who was to be killed for the same reason. Al-Waqidi notes: "As for Huwayrith b. Nuqaydh, who was the son of Qusayy, indeed he used to insult the Messenger of God. So the Prophet permitted the taking of his blood."[108] Various others whose only crime was insulting Muhammad were on the list as well.

Most of those on the list were duly killed on Muhammad's orders. Al-Waqidi tells the story of a singer and professional mourner named Sara; "insulting poetry was dictated to her about Messenger of God and

106 Ibid., 551.
107 Al-Waqidi, op. cit., 423.
108 Ibid., 421.

she would sing it."[109] She had once appealed to Muhammad in Medina when she was in need; Muhammad asked her: "Did not your singing and lamenting help you?"[110] She answered: "O Muhammad, indeed the Quraysh, since those who were killed among them in Badr, have stopped listening to the singers."[111] Muhammad took pity upon her and packed her off to Mecca on a camel loaded with food. On the day Muhammad entered Mecca, however, the time of mercy was over: "On the day of the Conquest," says al-Waqidi, "the Messenger of God commanded that she be killed, and she was killed at that time."[112]

Muhammad Takes Mecca

The Meccans were overawed at the size and power of the Muslim force and offered no significant resistance. Nevertheless, there was some, for "the Apostle of Allah, may Allah bless him," says Ibn Sa'd (the collector of traditions about Muhammad, not to be confused with Abdullah ibn Sa'd, the erstwhile apostate) "forced his entry" into Mecca. Once he had entered the city, Ibn Sa'd adds, "the people embraced Islam willingly or unwillingly."[113]

The prophet of Islam, meanwhile, immediately made his way to the Ka'ba and circumambulated it on his mount. "There were three hundred and sixty idols around the Ka'bah," according to Ibn Sa'd, and whenever Muhammad would pass one, he would point at it with a staff he was holding and utter a passage from the Qur'an: "And say, Truth has come and falsehood has vanished away" (17:81). Ibn Hisham adds a miraculous touch: when Muhammad pointed at each of the idols, they "collapsed on their backs one after the other."[114] According to a Bukhari hadith, however, Muhammad didn't just point at the idols but stabbed them with the stick he was holding: "The Prophet entered Mecca and (at that time) there were three hundred-and-sixty idols around the Ka'ba. He started stabbing the idols with a stick he had in his hand and reciting: 'Truth (Islam) has come and Falsehood (disbelief) has vanished.'"[115]

---

109 Ibid., 423.
110 Ibid.
111 Ibid.
112 Ibid.
113 Ibn Sa'd, op. cit., II, 168.
114 Ibn Ishaq, op. cit., 552.
115 Sahih Bukhari, vol. 3, book 46, no. 2478.

After prayer, he "ordered that all the idols which were round the Ka'ba should be collected and burned with fire and broken up."[116] In the Ka'ba was a picture, likely an icon, of Jesus and Mary that Muhammad allowed to remain.

Muhammad announced to the Meccans that he did not plan to kill them wholesale; he was even merciful when he encountered Hind bint Utba. He declared that Mecca had now "regained its former holiness. Let those here now tell those that are not here. If anyone should say, The apostle killed men in Mecca, say God permitted His apostle to do so but He does not permit you."[117] He also had a herald cry out: "Whoever is a believer in God will not leave an idol in his house, but will break it or burn it, for its price is forbidden."[118] Al-Waqidi says that even Hind bint Utba fell into line: when she "converted to Islam, she began to break the idol in her house with a hammer, bit by bit, saying, 'We were deceived about you!'"[119]

Reluctance to Confront the Romans

Muhammad, according to al-Waqidi, stayed in his native city for fifteen days. Then, he set out to conquer and Islamize what was left of polytheistic Arabia. Soon, however, he returned to Medina and set his sights on a much more formidable foe: the Roman Empire. Known today as the Byzantine or Eastern Roman Empire, the target in question understood itself, throughout its long life, to be simply the Roman Empire, the political entity that Julius and Augustus Caesar created, and that was now, by this time, based in the New Rome: Constantinople. The Roman Empire was one of the two great powers of the world (Persia was the other) and the primary global exponent of Christianity. In taking it on, Muhammad and the Muslims were challenging the other proselytizing Abrahamic religion and what many regarded as the foremost earthly power of his day.

According to al-Waqidi, the Muslims were well aware of Roman might: "A group arrived which mentioned that the Byzantines had gathered many groups in al-Sham [the Levant], and that Heraclius,"

---

116 Ibn Ishaq, op. cit.
117 Ibid., 555.
118 Al-Waqidi, op. cit., 428.
119 Ibid.

the Roman emperor, "had provisioned his companions for a year."
Al-Waqidi adds, however: "That was not a fact, but rather something
that was said to them that they repeated. There was not an enemy more
fearful to the Muslims than them. That was because of what they saw
of them, when they used to arrive as merchants, of preparedness, and
numbers, and sheep."[120]

Yet in fact, by this time, the Romans existed more on the power
of their reputation than on their actual might. When Islamic tradition states that Muhammad embarked upon his expedition to Tabuk,
where there was a Roman garrison, the Roman Empire was exhausted
and depleted after a series of wars with the Persians. It was that Roman
weakness that enabled the Arab conquests that began in the 630s, after
Muhammad's death, according to Islamic tradition.

According to the ninth-century Islamic accounts, however, when
Muhammad ordered this expedition against the great Christian empire,
Muslims were hardly in a stronger position. Muhammad, says Ibn
Hisham, "ordered his companions to prepare to raid the Byzantines at
a time when men were hard pressed; the heat was oppressive and there
was a drought; fruit was ripe"—here, Tabari adds that "shade was eagerly
sought"—"and the men wanted to stay in the shade with their fruit and
disliked traveling at that season."[121]

Ibn Hisham notes that Muhammad usually was cagey about where
the Muslims would be raiding next and "announced that he was making
for a place other than that which he actually intended."[122] That diminished the possibility of hypocrites and secret apostates informing his
enemies of his plans. This time, however, the prophet of Islam "said
plainly that he was making for the Byzantines because the journey was
long, the season difficult, and the enemy in great strength, so that the
men could make suitable preparations."[123] Tabari adds that the Muslims began making preparations with a certain reluctance: "the men got
ready in spite of their dislike for the journey in itself to say nothing of
their respect for the reputation of the Byzantines."[124]

120 Ibid., 485.
121 Ibn Ishaq, op. cit., 602.
122 Ibid.
123 Ibid.
124 Ibid.

Muhammad had some trouble inspiring enthusiasm for this expedition across the desert sands in the heat of summer. He asked one of the Muslims, Jadd ibn Qays: "Would you like to fight the B. Asfar, Jadd?"[125] The "Banu Asfar" was "the pale tribe," that is, the light-skinned Romans. Jadd, however, had a unique excuse: "Will you allow me to stay behind and not tempt me, for everyone knows that I am strongly addicted to women and I am afraid that if I see the Byzantine women I shall not be able to control myself."[126]

Muhammad excused him, but Allah was ready with a revelation that ruled Jadd out of the Muslim community altogether for his unwillingness to go on this jihad: "Among them is he who says, Give me permission and do not tempt me. Surely it is into temptation that they have fallen. Indeed, Gehenna truly is all around the unbelievers" (Qur'an 9:49). What's more, Jadd's excuse was curious, for he could have seized as many Roman women as he wanted as the spoils of war, as the Muslims had in numerous earlier jihad raids, and not had to bother to control himself. Al-Waqidi tries to correct this oddity in his version by having Muhammad ask Jadd: "When you come out with us for this battle, perhaps you might bring back Byzantine girls with you?"[127] Al-Jadd's answer here, however, is even more unsatisfactory: "You grant me permission but you do not tempt me. Surely my people know there is none with a greater vanity about women than I. But I fear that if I saw a woman of the Byzantines I would not be patient about them."[128] Yet there was nothing in Islamic directives regarding the treatment of captive infidel women that would have required any patience from Jadd at all.

Ibn Hisham explains that Jadd actually had a hidden motive: "It was not that he feared temptation from the Byzantine women: the temptation he had fallen into was greater in that he hung back from the apostle and sought to please himself rather than the apostle."[129] Pleasing Muhammad was, as we have seen, the foremost concern of Allah himself and should also have been uppermost in the minds of the Muslims. Ibn Hisham appends another Qur'anic verse to his account of the

---

125 Ibid.
126 Ibid.
127 Al-Waqidi, op. cit., 486.
128 Ibid.
129 Ibid., 603.

unfortunate Jadd: "Gehenna is before him, and he is made to drink fetid water" (14:16). Accompany Muhammad on his jihad or go to hell.

Al-Waqidi adds that even Jadd's young son was disgusted with his reluctance to fight and asked him why he rejected Muhammad's invitation. Jadd responded: "O my little son, why should I go out in the wind and heat and difficulties to the Byzantines? By God, I am not secure from fear of the Byzantines in my own house in Khurba, so how will I go out to them and raid them? Indeed, my little son, I am knowledgeable about the cycles of life."[130] Al-Waqidi continues: "His son was rude to him. He said, 'No, by God, it is hypocrisy! By God, a Qur'an will be revealed about you to the Messenger of God and they will read it.' He said: And he [the father] raised his sandal and struck his son's face with it. And his son turned from him and did not speak to him."[131]

Even though his unwillingness to accompany Muhammad earned him a place in hell and the disgust of his own son, Jadd wasn't alone in not being happy with this particular jihad. Ibn Hisham says that "the disaffected said one to another, 'Don't go forth in the heat,' disliking strenuous war, doubting the truth, and creating misgivings about the apostle."[132] Allah responded with another Qur'anic revelation: "Those who were left behind rejoiced at sitting still behind the messenger of Allah, and were averse to waging jihad with their wealth and their lives in Allah's way. And they said, Don't go forth in the heat. Say, The fire of Gehenna is more intense heat, if only they understood. Then let them laugh a little, they will weep much, as the reward of what they used to earn" (9:81–2).

Although not a few Muslims begged off, some did agree to accompany Muhammad. Some were even enthusiastic about the prospect of taking on the Romans. Al-Waqidi says that "Uthman bin Affan supplied a third of that army. He spent the most, until that army had sufficient supplies, and it was said that every need was met. He even provided the ropes for their water containers. It was said: Indeed the Messenger of God said at that time, 'After this, nothing will harm Uthman whatever he does!'"[133] This was a curious tradition for al-Waqidi to include, for Islamic tradition records that Uthman later became caliph, only to

130 Al-Waqidi, op. cit.
131 Ibid.
132 Ibid.
133 Ibid.

meet a violent death at the hands of Muslims who rebelled against his rule. Either Muhammad was wrong in proclaiming that nothing would henceforth harm Uthman, or the tradition of this saying was formulated among people who did not know of or rejected the stories of Uthman's downfall as caliph and violent death.

CHAPTER THIRTEEN

The End of the Prophet

Muhammad Appoints a Successor—Or Does He?

When the Muslims finally set out for Tabuk, says Ibn Hisham, Muhammad left Ali in Medina "to look after his family, and ordered him to
stay with them."[1] Some in Medina were unhappy with this arrangement:
"The hypocrites spoke evil of him, saying that he had been left behind
because he was a burden to the apostle and he wanted to get rid of him."[2]
This upset Ali, so he took his weapons and caught up with Muhammad.
Finding the Muslim warriors resting on their way to the Roman garrison, a furious Ali told Muhammad what the hypocrites back home
were saying about him. Muhammad replied: "They lie. I left you behind
because of what I had left behind, so go back and represent me in my
family and yours. Are you not content, Ali, to stand to me as Aaron
stood to Moses, except that there will be no prophet after me?"[3] Mol-
lified, Ali went back to Medina, while Muhammad continued on his
way to Tabuk.

A party of the Muslims, supporters of Ali, took this to mean that
Muhammad was appointing Ali as his successor, particularly in light
of a Qur'anic passage that depicted Moses saying to Aaron: "Take my
place among the people" (7:142). Bukhari, the foremost Sunni hadith
collection, records a version of this incident that makes the idea of succession even more explicit. Sa'd ibn Abi Waqqas, the expert archer of
other hadiths, is depicted as recounting that Ali was unhappy at being
left behind in Medina and says to Muhammad: "Do you want to leave

---

1 Ibn Ishaq, op. cit., 604.
2 Ibid.
3 Ibid.

me with the children and women?"[4] Muhammad replies: "Will you not be pleased that you will be to me like Aaron to Moses? But there will be no prophet after me."[5]

In this additional statement, Muhammad appears to be clarifying the exact nature of the authority he is bestowing upon Ali. His successor will not be another prophet after Muhammad; his role as Aaron to Muhammad's Moses is to take his place among the people, that is, to be the leader of the community after Muhammad's death. In case the Bukhari version was still not clear enough, Muslim makes it even clearer. In a tradition attributed to Amir, the son of Sa'd ibn Abi Waqqas, Muhammad is depicted as saying: "You are in the same position with relation to me as Aaron (Harun) was in relation to Moses but with (this explicit difference) that there is no prophet after me."[6] Those who composed and disseminated this tradition were aware of how controversial it would be, and so the next link on the chain of transmitters, Said bin al-Musayyab, who is supposed to have heard the story from Amir bin Sa'd, is depicted as saying: "I had an earnest desire to hear it directly from Sa'd, so I met him and narrated to him what (his son) Amir had narrated to me, whereupon he said: Yes, I did hear it. I said: Did you hear it yourself? Thereupon he placed his fingers upon his ears and said: Yes, and if not, let both my ears become deaf."[7]

Al-Waqidi, however, for all the wealth of detail he includes that is not in the earlier material, notably omits all mention of this incident. Apparently, by the time he was writing, the split in the Islamic community was becoming deeper and more difficult to heal. And as al-Waqidi was not a member of the party of Ali, he apparently did not choose to continue to spread a story that gave the impression that Muhammad had appointed this widely disliked individual as his successor.

Islamic tradition holds that after Muhammad died, only a year or two after the expedition to Tabuk, Ali thrice attempted to make good on what he and his followers understood as this designation of himself as Muhammad's successor but was thwarted by other Muslims, who passed over him in favor of Abu Bakr, Umar, and Uthman. Behind it all was Aisha, who nurtured a burning hatred of Ali ever since she had

---

4 Sahih Bukhari, vol. 5, book 64, no. 4416.
5 Ibid.
6 Sahih Muslim, book 44, no. 2404a.
7 Ibid.

been accused of adultery and he had so cavalierly told Muhammad that he could just as easily get another wife. All this was the beginning of the Sunni/Shia split in the global Islamic community that persists to this day. But it is more likely, given their long distance from the events recounted, that these traditions regarding Ali and Aisha were invented in order to explain the schism, the actual causes of which were lost in the mists of time.

The Expedition to Tabuk

The journey through the desert in high summer was arduous. But Ibn Hisham depicts the Muslims receiving divine assistance, as Allah remained ever solicitous for the well-being of his prophet: "In the morning when the men had no water they complained to the apostle, so he prayed, and God sent a cloud, and so much rain fell that they were satisfied and carried away all the water they needed."[8] Yet the hypocrites among the Muslims remained obstinate. One Muslim recalled later that when this miraculous rain fell at Muhammad's command, some of the Muslims confronted one of the hypocrites: "We went to him, saying 'Woe to you! Have you anything more to say after this?' He said, 'It is a passing cloud!'"[9]

As usual, al-Waqidi's account has a wealth of additional detail. One of the Muslims recounts: "I saw the Messenger of God face the *qibla* and pray. And by God, I did not see a cloud in the sky. And he did not stop praying until I saw clouds assemble from every direction. He did not leave his place until the heavens came down upon us with fresh water. I heard the Messenger of God proclaim God's praises in the rain. Then Allah cleared the sky. Since that time the land is like pools pouring into each other. People brought water and quenched the thirst of the last of them. I heard the Messenger of God say, 'I witness that I am the messenger of God.' I said to one of the Hypocrites, 'Woe unto you, after this have you any more doubts?' He replied, 'It is only a passing cloud!'"[10]

Muhammad was confident during the trip, according to al-Waqidi, saying to his longtime companion Bilal: "Indeed God has promised me the two treasures of Persia and Byzantium and helps me with the kings

8 Ibn Ishaq, op. cit., 605.
9 Ibid.
10 Al-Waqidi, op. cit., 494.

of the kings of Himyar. They will strive in the path of God and eat the booty of God."[11] By the time this account was committed to writing, the Muslims had conquered Persia and much of the Middle Eastern and North African territories of the Romans; there is no record dating from before these conquests that depicts Muhammad making this prediction.

During the journey, Muhammad's camel went astray, leading another hypocrite, whose name was Zayd ibn al-Lusayt (not to be confused with Muhammad's erstwhile adopted son), to taunt the Muslims: "Does Muhammad allege that he is a prophet and can tell you news from heaven when he doesn't know where his camel is?"[12] Muhammad, however, according to Ibn Hisham, not only knew where the camel was but also knew of the taunt. He said to one of his companions: "A man has said: 'Now Muhammad tells you that he is a prophet and alleges that he tells you of heavenly things and yet doesn't know where his camel is.' By God, I know only what God has told me and God has shown me where it is. It is in this wadi in such-and-such a glen. A tree has caught it by its halter; so go and bring it to me."[13]

Ibn Hisham is unsure how the story concluded: "Some people allege that Zayd subsequently repented; others say that he was suspected of evil until the day of his death."[14] Even al-Waqidi is likewise unsure: "Zayd b. al-Lusayt said, 'It was as if I had not converted until today! I had doubts about Muhammad. I rose in the morning and I was the possessor of insight. I testify that he is the Messenger of God!' People claim that Zayd asked for forgiveness."[15] One of the Muslim women, however, the daughter of another Zayd, was said to have disputed this version: "Kharija b. Zayd b. Thabit used to deny that he asked for forgiveness saying: He continued to be deceitful until his death."[16]

When the Muslims reached Tabuk, several Arab tribes of northern Arabia submitted to Muhammad. Ibn Hisham notes that the "governor of Ayla came and made a treaty with him and paid him the poll tax. The people of Jarba and Adhruh also came and paid the poll tax."[17] The

---

11 Ibid., 495.
12 Ibn Ishaq, op. cit.
13 Ibid., 605–6.
14 Ibid., 606.
15 Al-Waqidi, op. cit., 495.
16 Ibid.
17 Ibn Ishaq, op. cit., 607.

Qur'an refers to this poll tax and stipulates that it is to be collected from the people of the book, that is, Jews and Christians as well as Zoroastrians and some others, presumably in addition to being collected from groups such as the pagan Arabs: "Fight against those do not believe in Allah or the last day, and do not forbid what Allah and his messenger have forbidden, and do not follow the religion of truth, even if they are among the people of the book, until they pay the jizya with willing submission and feel themselves subdued" (9:29).

Muhammad quickly enforced that submission upon his new subjects. He directed the governor of Ayla that he and those with him "all have the protection of God and the protection of Muhammad the prophet."[18] However, "should anyone of them break the treaty by introducing some new factor then his wealth shall not save him; it is the fair prize of him who takes it."[19]

Obtaining the submission of northern Arab tribes was a welcome development, but it was not what the Muslims had come to Tabuk to accomplish. Yet the Romans were nowhere to be seen; the ranks of their military were so depleted that they did not have the personnel to staff all the border outposts on a permanent basis; the Muslims had come at a time when the troops were manning one of the other outposts. Muhammad waited awhile but to no avail. Ibn Hisham states: "The apostle stayed in Tabuk some ten nights, not more. Then he returned to Medina."[20] Al-Waqidi has him staying longer: "The Messenger of God arrived in Tabuk and stayed there for twenty nights. He prayed two bowings. Heraclius was at that time in Hims."[21] Al-Waqidi adds that while he waited in Tabuk, Muhammad preached a sermon that included these assertions: "Poetry is from Satan. Wine is the gathering of sin; Satan uses women for ensnaring. Youth is a branch of madness; evil are the earnings from usury."[22] Financial institutions all over the West have by now adopted interest-free arrangements to accommodate the prophet of Islam's distaste for usury.

Al-Waqidi also says that even though there were no Roman troops on hand to confront the prophet of Islam militarily, the Roman emperor

---

18 Ibid.
19 Ibid.
20 Ibid.
21 Al-Waqidi, op. cit., 497.
22 Ibid., 498.

was keenly interested in Muhammad. "Heraclius had sent a man from the Ghassan to observe the Prophet, his ways, his characteristics, the redness of his eyes, and the seal of prophecy between his shoulders."[23] This was a fist-shaped mole surrounded by warts that the sira literature claims was to be a physical characteristic of the prophet the Jews and Christians were supposedly expecting, and Muhammad, of course, had it. Heraclius asked the man he had sent to gather certain information about Muhammad; when the messenger returned to make his report to the emperor, the monarch was deeply impressed, to the extent that he asked his people to accept Islam: "he invited the people to believe in the Messenger of God, but they refused, until he feared they would go against his authority."[24]

Yet as we have seen, Bukhari and Ibn Sa'd have Heraclius hearing about Muhammad earlier, when the prophet wrote to the emperor inviting him to accept Islam after the Islamic prophet concluded the treaty of Hudaybiyya. In both stories, the outcome is the same: Heraclius is deeply impressed by what he learns about Muhammad and wants the Romans to accept Islam but is deterred by the violently negative reaction of his court. Did this drama play out on two separate occasions? Or is this yet another example of traditions that have come down to us in two widely divergent versions?

Dealing with Rivals and Critics

On his way to Tabuk from Medina, Muhammad stopped in a town called Dhu Awan, where there was what Ibn Hisham calls "the mosque of opposition."[25] There were many mosques that were gathering places for prayer that predated Islam, as the Qur'an itself bears witness when it says: "And do not let your hatred of a people who stopped your going to the sacred mosque seduce you to transgress" (5:2).

Muslim commentators on the Qur'an have generally explained this as referring to the run-up to the treaty of Hudaybiyya, when the polytheists were barring Muhammad from making the pilgrimage to the sacred mosque in Mecca. In the fourteenth century, Ibn Kathir records a tradition that states: "The Messenger of Allah and his Companions

---

23 Ibid., 499.
24 Ibid.
25 Ibn Ishaq, op. cit., 609.

were in the area of Al-Hudaybiyyah when the idolators prevented them from visiting the House, and that was especially hard on them. Later on, some idolators passed by them from the east intending to perform Umrah. So the Companions of the Prophet said, 'Let us prevent those (from Umrah) just as their fellow idolators prevented us.' Thereafter, Allah sent down this Ayah."[26] Thus, the polytheists not only controlled the sacred mosque but were making pilgrimages to it, a practice that Muhammad ended when he removed the idols from the Ka'ba. There were, however, other mosques that had to be brought into line as well.

The proprietors of the mosque in Dhu Awan tried to calm Muhammad's suspicions, telling him: "We have built a mosque for the sick and needy and for nights of bad weather, and we should like you to come to us and pray for us there."[27] Muhammad, according to Ibn Hisham, made excuses: "He said that he was on the point of traveling, and was preoccupied, or words to that effect, and that when he came back if God willed he would come to them and pray for them in it."[28]

Despite this, according to Ibn Hisham, when Muhammad was returning from Tabuk, he visited this town again and did not come to pray at this mosque as he had said he would. When Muhammad "stopped in Dhu Awan, news of the mosque came to him," whereupon he called two of the Muslims "and told them to go to the mosque of those evil men and destroy and burn it."[29] Obediently, "the two of them ran into the mosque where its people were and burned and destroyed it and the people ran away from it."[30] Allah supplied a Qur'anic revelation that accused the conciliatory chiefs of the Dhu Awan mosque of lying: "And as for those who chose a mosque out of opposition and disbelief, and in order to cause dissent among the believers, and as an outpost for those who made war against Allah and his messenger previously, they will surely swear, We intended nothing but good. Allah bears witness that they indeed are liars. Never stand there. A mosque that was founded upon duty from the first day is more worthy that you should stand in it, in which are men who love to purify themselves. Allah loves the purifiers" (9:107–8).

---

26 Ibn Kathir, *The Life of Prophet Muhammad*, op. cit., 3, 81.
27 Ibn Ishaq, op. cit., 609.
28 Ibid.
29 Ibid.
30 Ibid.

Al-Waqidi, as always, has a great deal more detail. One of the Muslims observes, "this mosque was built by Hypocrites, well known for their hypocrisy."[31] Al-Waqidi explains that one of the hypocrites, Abdullah bin Nabtal, "used to come to the Messenger of God and listen to his conversation and then bring it to the Hypocrites. The angel Gabriel said, 'O Muhammad, indeed a man from the Hypocrites comes to you and listens to your conversation and takes it to the Hypocrites.' The Messenger of God said, 'Which of them is it?' Gabriel replied, 'The black man who possesses much hair, and red eyes like two pots of brass; his liver is the liver of a donkey and he watches with the eye of Satan.'"[32] At length, Muhammad gives the order to destroy this mosque: "Go to this mosque whose people are evil, and demolish it and burn it!"[33]

Al-Waqidi's version makes sense of Ibn Hisham's elliptical account by making this doomed mosque a nest of hypocrites. But it is likely that this story was originally composed in order to account both for the continued existence of non-Islamic mosques and to justify their forced Islamization. At a time when Islam was just taking shape as a religious tradition and making a place for itself among the existing religious traditions of southern Iraq and northern Arabia, such stories would give carte blanche to any group of Muslims who desired to claim a local mosque as one of their own.

Muhammad was no more generous with other rivals. A hadith notes the existence of a rival Ka'ba, which is noteworthy in light of the fact that the early mosques do not point toward Mecca and may have originally been oriented toward a Ka'ba in another place. The contemporary archaeologist Barbara Finster has pointed out that the Meccan Ka'ba has "the same orientation, rectangular ground plan," and "possibly apsidal closure in the northwest" that are found in "similar temples in southern Arabia, such as the sanctuary of Sirwah" in Yemen.[34] This may have been the Ka'ba referred to in this hadith: "Jabir reported that there was in pre-Islamic days a temple called Dhu'l-Khalasah and it was called the Yamanite Ka'ba or the northern Ka'ba. Allah's Messenger said unto me: 'Will you rid me of Dhu'l-Khalasah and so I went forth at the head

---

31 Al-Waqidi, op. cit., 513.

32 Ibid.

33 Ibid., 512.

34 Barbara Finster, "Zu Der Neuauflage Von K.A.C. Creswells 'Early Muslim Architecture,'" *Kunst Des Orients* 9, no. 1/2 (1973), 94. Author's translation.

of 350 horsemen of the tribe of Ahmas and we destroyed it and killed whomsoever we found there. Then we came back to him (to the Holy Prophet) and informed him and he blessed us and the tribe of Ahmas."[35]

Ibn Hisham notes that around the time that he dealt with the "mosque of opposition," Muhammad received a letter from another self-proclaimed prophet, a man named Musaylima. He wrote insolently to Muhammad: "From Musaylima the apostle of God to Muhammad the apostle of God. Peace upon you. I have been made partner with you in authority. To us belongs half the land and to Quraysh half, but Quraysh are a hostile people."[36] Musaylima sent two messengers to Muhammad with this letter. One of the Muslims recounted that when the reputedly illiterate prophet "read his letter," he asked Musaylima's messengers: "What do you say about it?"[37] They replied, "that they said the same as Musaylima."[38]

Enraged, Muhammad declared: "By God, were it not that heralds are not to be killed, I would behead the pair of you!"[39] Ibn Hisham continues: "Then he wrote to Musaylima: 'From Muhammad the apostle of God to Musaylima the liar. Peace be upon him who follows the guidance. The earth is God's. He lets whom He will of His creatures inherit it and the result is to the pious."[40] Musaylima was willing to acknowledge Muhammad as a fellow apostle of Allah, but Muhammad was adamantly unwilling to return the favor.

Musaylima, however, was fortunate that Muhammad didn't have him killed. The prophet of Islam had taught his followers to deal extremely harshly with those who opposed and criticized him. Muhammad sent his former adopted son Zayd ibn Haritha on a raid of one Arab tribe, the Banu Fazara, which had participated in the Quraysh's siege of Medina that faltered before Muhammad's trench. Zayd killed some members of this tribe and took several prisoners, including Umm Qirfa, a leading figure of the tribe who was, says Ibn Hisham, "a very old woman."[41] According to Tabari, Zayd "ordered Qays to kill Umm Qirfah, and he

35 Sahih Muslim, book 44, no. 2476a.
36 Ibn Ishaq, op. cit., 649.
37 Ibid.
38 Ibid.
39 Ibid.
40 Ibid.
41 Ibid., 665.

killed her cruelly. He tied each of her legs with a rope and tied the ropes to two camels, and they split her in two."[42] A Muslim warrior, Salama ibn Amr, captures Umm Qirfah's daughter and presents her to Muhammad as a war prize; the prophet of Islam gives her to his uncle Hazn ibn Abi Wahb.

Tabari, however, also offers another version of the story, in which Abu Bakr, not Zayd, is the commander of the expedition, and Umm Qirfa and her cruel murder are not mentioned at all. In this version, "a woman of the Banu Fazarah wearing a worn-out piece of leather" is captured, along with her daughter, who was "among the fairest of the Arabs."[43] Muhammad sees Salama ibn Amr with the young woman and says: "Salamah—how excellent the father who begot you!—give me the woman."[44] Salama, however, is reluctant, saying: "Messenger of God, I like her, by God, and I have not uncovered her garment," that is, he had not yet raped her.[45] Muhammad, however, is insistent, and finally, Salama relents and hands her over. Muhammad then "sent her to Mecca, and with her he ransomed some Muslim captives who were in the hands of the polytheists."[46]

Umm Qirfa was by no means the only victim of the Muslims' cruelty. Abu Afak was an elderly poet who had criticized Muhammad in his verses; Muhammad asked his followers, "Who will deal with this rascal for me?"[47] Ibn Hisham says that upon hearing that, one of Muhammad's companions, Salim ibn Umayr, "went forth and killed him."[48]

When news of this circulated, a woman named Asma bint Marwan "displayed disaffection" and also composed verses critical of Muhammad.[49] Ibn Hisham states that when Muhammad heard her verses, he asked his companions: "Who will rid me of Marwan's daughter?"[50] A Muslim named Umayr ibn Adiy al-Khatmi "heard him, and that very night he went to her house and killed her."[51] When Muhammad heard

---

42 Al-Tabari, *The Victory of Islam*, op. cit., 96.
43 Ibid., 97.
44 Ibid.
45 Ibid.
46 Ibid.
47 Ibn Ishaq, op. cit., 675.
48 Ibid.
49 Ibid.
50 Ibid., 676.
51 Ibid.

what he had done, he was delighted and said: "You have helped God and His apostle, O Umayr!"[52] Umayr was still worried, however, and asked Muhammad "if he would have to bear any evil consequences," but Muhammad was reassuring: "Two goats won't butt their heads about her."[53] Ibn Hisham notes that the murder of Asma bint Marwan became the occasion for the conversion of one of the remaining pagan Arab tribes: "The day after Bint Marwan was killed the men of B. Khatma became Muslims because they saw the power of Islam."[54]

Other traditions make plain that there was to be no penalty for killing those who insulted Muhammad either, as many traditions make plain. Another one, attributed to Ibn Abbas, states: "A blind man had a pregnant slave, who used to abuse the Messenger of Allah and defame him. The blind man forbade her but she did not stop. One night she began to slander the Prophet so he [that is, the blind man] took an axe, placed it on her belly, pressed it and killed her. The Messenger of Allah was told about it, and thereupon he said, 'Oh people! Be witnesses that no Diyah is to be paid for her blood.' Related by Abu Dawud with a trustworthy chain of narrators."[55] Diyah was blood money, compensation paid by a murderer to the family of his victim in lieu of other punishment. In this case, it was forfeited because the victim had insulted Muhammad.

Such stories were designed to teach the power of intimidation, terror, and violence.

A hadith depicts Muhammad enunciating a general principle that reflects his indifference over the murders of those who had mocked him. "Narrated Amr bin Shuaib from his father, from his grandfather that the Messenger of Allah said: 'The Muslim is not killed for disbeliever.' And with this chain, it has been narrated that the Prophet said: 'The blood-money paid for disbeliever is half of the blood-money paid for a believer.'"[56]

The idea that the life of a non-Muslim is worth less than the life of a Muslim would carry over into Islamic law. The Shafi'i Sharia manual *Reliance of the Traveller* stipulates that if someone kills a male Muslim, he may pay a certain amount of blood money in compensation. But if he

---

52 Ibid.
53 Ibid.
54 Ibid.
55 Bulugh al-Maram, book 9, no. 47.
56 Jami at-Tirmidhi, vol. 3, book 16, no. 1413.

kills a Jew or a Christian, he needs to pay only a third of the amount he would pay for killing a male Muslim.[57]

Sheikh Sultanhussein Tabandeh, a twentieth-century Iranian Sufi jurist, says that a male Muslim adulterer should receive "100 lashes, the shaving of his head, and one year of banishment."[58] However, "if the man is not a Muslim and commits adultery with a Muslim woman, his penalty is execution."[59]

The difference arises from the differing values of a Muslim's life and that of a non-Muslim: "Since Islam regards non-Muslims as on a lower level of belief and conviction, if a Muslim kills a non-Muslim...then his punishment must not be the retaliatory death, since the faith and conviction he possesses is loftier than that of the man slain...Again, the penalties of a non-Muslim guilty of fornication with a Muslim woman are augmented because, in addition to the crime against morality, social duty and religion, he has committed sacrilege, in that he has disgraced a Muslim and thereby cast scorn upon the Muslims in general, and so must be executed."[60] The guiding principle was clear: "Islam and its peoples must be above the infidels, and never permit non-Muslims to acquire lordship over them."[61]

To be sure, legal systems are generally designed to protect the people who develop them, and there are other legal systems that penalize the killing of someone who is in the group more severely than the killing of someone outside the group. Islamic law, however, remains distinct in actually calling for the creation of a legal system that institutionalizes the deprivation of basic rights from those who are not in the favored group.

The Final Pilgrimage

Muhammad's victory at this point was total: he had defeated those from his home city who doubted his claim to be a prophet and had conquered Mecca. He had exiled and massacred the Jews, who likewise rejected his prophetic claim. He had also defeated many of the other Arab tribes, and now the rest of them came to pledge their fealty to the prophet of

---

57 Ahmed ibn Naqib al-Misri, *Reliance of the Traveller: A Classic Manual of Islamic Sacred Law*, Nuh Ha Mim Keller, trans. (Beltsville, Maryland: Amana Publications, 1999), xx; o4.9.

58 Sultanhussein Tabandeh, *A Muslim Commentary on the Universal Declaration of Human Rights*, translated by F. J. Goulding, 1970.

59 Ibid.

60 Ibid.

61 Ibid.

Islam. "Deputations from the Arabs," says Ibn Hisham, "came to him from all directions."[62] Allah sent down a celebratory revelation: "When Allah's help and the conquest comes, and you see mankind entering the religion of Allah in crowds, then sing the praises of your Lord, and seek his forgiveness. Indeed, he is always ready to show mercy" (110:1–3).

Muhammad embarked upon one more pilgrimage to Mecca, this time the major pilgrimage, the hajj. He approached Mecca as the master of all he surveyed. In the course of it, according to Ibn Hisham, a controversy arose when one of Ali's companions dressed a Muslim army in clothes that belonged to Ali; when Ali saw them, he ordered the men to return the clothes, which caused resentment in the ranks. Muhammad is depicted as defending Ali in terms that would resonate in emerging Shi'ite piety: "Do not blame Ali, for he is too scrupulous in the things of God, or in the way of God, to be blamed."[63]

While on his pilgrimage, Muhammad "showed the men the rites and taught them the customs of their hajj. He made a speech in which he made things clear."[64] He made a speech about Muslim practices, beginning with: "O men, listen to my words," which made it clear that he was speaking as master of his community and not delivering divine revelation.[65] In the course of his speech, however, according to Ibn Hisham, he said: "Postponement is only an excess of disbelief whereby those who disbelieve are led astray, they allow it in one year and forbid it in another year, so that they may make up the number of the months which Allah has made sacred, so that they allow what Allah has forbidden. The evil of their deeds is made to seem good to them. Allah does not guide the disbelieving people."

This is Qur'an 9:37. Ibn Hisham, however, gives no hint of it being a revelation that Muhammad received, although, throughout his biography of Muhammad, he notes frequently that Allah at various points delivered divine revelations commenting on events in Muhammad's life, answering disputed questions, and the like. Al-Waqidi likewise puts this Qur'anic passage in Muhammad's mouth without identifying it as a divine revelation.[66]

---

62 Ibn Ishaq, op. cit., 627.
63 Ibid., 650.
64 Ibid., 650–1.
65 Ibid., 651.
66 Al-Waqidi, op. cit., 543–4.

This in itself creates problems for the standard understanding that the Qur'an is the perfect word of Allah, existing with him forever in paradise and delivered to Muhammad through the angel Gabriel, not composed by Muhammad. It opens the possibility that this passage was not part of the Qur'anic text at the time that Ibn Hisham and al-Waqidi wrote and was added later. It also creates an enormous problem for the sira literature in general. Qur'an 9:37 is part of a longer passage about leap months. In pre-Islamic times, the pagan Arab calendar, a 354-day lunar calendar, would insert an extra month every three years in order to keep pace with the 365-day solar calendar. The Islamic calendar, however, has no leap months; accordingly, its year is about ten days shorter than the solar year, and as the years go by, Islamic feast days move throughout the solar year. The Qur'an abolishes the leap months in this passage, which begins: "Indeed, the number of the months with Allah is twelve months by Allah's decree on the day that he created the heavens and the earth" (9:36).

The Dutch scholar of Islam Johannes J. G. Jansen points out that "for every event which took place in the life of Muhammad, Ibn Ishaq meticulously recorded in his *Sira* in which month it took place." Thus, the activities of Muhammad can be plotted throughout the year and for the length of his prophetic career. This is one of the details that impresses modern-day historians. Jansen continues: "this meticulous and systematic dating by month which is Ibn Ishaq's wont, is, of course, one of the main reasons why Western historians classified his book as historiography in the normal sense of that word."[67]

If the chronology of the life of Muhammad in the early sira literature is to be believed, Allah abolished the leap month during the revelation of sura 9, which came after the expedition to Tabuk and was one of the last suras of the Qur'an to be revealed. That would mean, however, that Muhammad lived most of his life at a time when there were leap months every few years. "How then," Jansen asks, "is it possible that not a single one of the numerous events Ibn Ishaq describes and attaches a date to, took place during a leap month? If his narrative of the life of Muhammad would be based on historical memories and on real events, however distorted, but remembered by real people, how

---

67 Johannes J. G. Jansen, "The Gospel According to Ibn Ishaq (d. 773)" (Conference paper, Skepticism and Scripture Conference, Center for Inquiry, Davis, California, January 2007)."

can half a solar year (or more) remain unmentioned and have disappeared from the record?"[68]

The biography of Muhammad by Ibn Ishaq/Ibn Hisham, Jansen, therefore, concludes, "can only date from a period in which people had forgotten that leap months had once existed."[69] And it can only be fiction or largely fiction. "These stories by Ibn Ishaq," Jansen states, "do not attempt to describe memories of events that took place in the past, but they want to convince the reader that the protagonist of these stories, Muhammad, is the Messenger of God."[70]

Muhammad Falls III

The conqueror of Arabia and messenger of Allah did not have long to savor his triumph. About a year after he returned from Tabuk, Muhammad fell ill. "It began, so I have been told," says Ibn Hisham, "when he went to Baqiul-Gharqad in the middle of the night and prayed for the dead. Then he returned to his family and in the morning his sufferings began."[71] Ibn Hisham records a tradition in which one of Muhammad's companions recounts that Muhammad had actually opted to die sooner rather than later:

> In the middle of the night the apostle sent for me and told me that he was ordered to pray for the dead in this cemetery and that I was to go with him. I went; and when he stood among them he said, "Peace upon you, O people of the graves! Happy are you that you are so much better off than men here. Dissensions have come like waves of darkness one after the other, the last being worse than the first." Then he turned to me and said, "I have been given the choice between the keys of the treasuries of this world and long life here followed by Paradise, and meeting my Lord and Paradise (at once)." I urged him to choose the former, but he said that he had chosen the latter. Then he prayed for the dead there and went away. Then it was that the illness through which God took him began."[72]

---

68 Ibid.
69 Ibid.
70 Ibid.
71 Ibn Ishaq, op. cit., 678.
72 Ibid.

That illness apparently began immediately. Ibn Hisham depicts Aisha as recounting: "The apostle returned from the cemetery to find me suffering from a severe headache and I was saying, 'O my head!' He said, 'Nay, Aisha, O my head!'"[73] Then Muhammad asked her: "Would it distress you if you were to die before me so that I might wrap you in your shroud and pray over you and bury you?"[74] To this, she responded tartly: "Methinks I see you if you had done that returning to my house and spending a bridal night therein with one of your wives."[75] This made Muhammad smile, but Ibn Hisham adds that Aisha continued: "Then his pain overcame him as he was going the round of his wives, until he was overpowered in the house of Maymuna. He called his wives and asked their permission to be nursed in my house, and they agreed."[76]

As his illness progressed, Muhammad became more and more incapacitated. Ibn Hisham records a tradition in which Aisha says that at one point, Muhammad "went out walking between two men of his family, one of whom was al-Fadl b. al-Abbas. His head was bound in a cloth and his feet were dragging as he came to my house."[77] The other man who was apparently helping Muhammad to walk was, according to another of his companions, Ali ibn Abi Talib; Tabari adds that Aisha did not identify him because she "could not bring herself to speak well of him though she was able to do so."[78]

Muhammad, says Ibn Hisham, "suffered much pain" as his illness worsened. At one point, he was made to sit in a tub while water was poured over him, but this did nothing to improve his condition. He made his way to the mosque one day "with his head bound up, and sat in the pulpit."[79] After asking forgiveness from the men of Uhud, who were now Muslims and praying a lengthy prayer, Muhammad announced: "God has given one of his servants the choice between this world and that which is with God and he has chosen the latter."[80]

Abu Bakr, says Ibn Hisham, "perceived that he meant himself and he wept, saying, 'Nay, we and our children will be your ransom.'"[81] To

---

73 Ibid.
74 Ibid., 678–9.
75 Ibid., 679.
76 Ibid.
77 Ibid.
78 Ibid.
79 Ibid.
80 Ibid.
81 Ibid.

that, Muhammad said: "Gently, Abu Bakr. See to these doors that open on to the mosque and shut them except one from Abu Bakr's house, for I know no one who is a better friend to me than he."[82] He added: "If I were able to choose a friend on earth I would choose Abu Bakr, but comradeship and brotherhood in the faith remain until God unites us in His presence."[83] This provided the justification for the community's choice of Abu Bakr to be Muhammad's first successor, passing over Ali, who, as Muhammad is depicted as saying in a competing tradition, was to be the Aaron to Muhammad's Moses.

His sermon completed, Muhammad "came down and entered his house and his pain increased until he was exhausted."[84] Several of his wives decided to "force him to take medicine."[85] Muhammad disliked this and asked why it was done; his uncle Abbas responded: "We were afraid that you would get pleurisy."[86] Muhammad was dismissive and angry, replying: "That is a disease which God would not afflict me with. Let no one stop in the house until they have been forced to take this medicine, except my uncle."[87] In another tradition, Muhammad says: "That is something which comes from the devil, and God would not let it have power over me."[88] Everyone present (except Abbas) had to take the pleurisy medicine "as a punishment for what they had done to him."[89]

Poison

As his pain increased, Muhammad related it to the pain he experienced when he was poisoned at Khaybar by one of the captive women whom he had ordered to prepare a meal for him. He exclaimed: "O Aisha! I still feel the pain caused by the food I ate at Khaybar, and at this time, I feel as if my aorta is being cut from that poison."[90] It was a significant admission, for this was supposed to be the same prophet to whom Allah had revealed the Qur'an. Allah had said of the Qur'an, in the Qur'an itself, that "it is a revelation from the Lord of the worlds. And if he had

---

82 Ibid.
83 Ibid.
84 Ibid., 680.
85 Ibid.
86 Ibid.
87 Ibid.
88 Ibid.
89 Ibid.
90 Sahih Bukhari, vol. 5, book 64, no. 4428.

invented false sayings about us, we surely would have taken him by the right hand and then severed his aorta" (69:43–6).

A Shi'ite tradition also relates his distress to the poisoning at Khaybar: "It is mentioned in reliable traditions that the Messenger of Allah departed from the world with the status of a martyr as Saffar has narrated through authentic chains of narrators from Imam Ja'far Sadiq that on the day of the Battle of Khaybar, the Prophet was administered poison in a shoulder of a lamb. When the Prophet took a morsel from it, that meat spoke up and said: 'O Messenger of Allah, I have been laced with poison."[91] Once again, why the meat didn't warn Muhammad before he ingested the poison is left unexplained. The tradition continues: "That is why the Messenger of Allah used to say during his terminal illness that 'the morsel that I took in Khyber has broken by back. And no prophet or successor of the prophet has departed from the world without martyrdom.'"[92]

The Shi'ite source goes on to echo another Sunni tradition of Khaybar, saying: "In another authentic traditional report he said that a Jewess had fed the Prophet with poisoned mutton. When the Prophet ate a piece of it, it said: I have been laced with poison. The Prophet threw it away and that poison continued to affect him till he passed away under its effect."[93] Then, however, it adds a startling alternative view: "And Ayyashi has narrated through authentic chains of narrators from Imam Ja'far Sadiq that Aisha and Hafasa had poisoned the Prophet with that poison, so it is possible that both poisons caused his death."[94]

Would two of Muhammad's wives, including his favorite Aisha, actually have murdered him? We have seen that they were angry with him over his unscheduled dalliance with Mary the Copt and received a rebuke from Allah in the Qur'an (66:1–5), threatening them with divorce over this. The idea that they would have gone as far as acting to kill him is rooted in the Shi'ite animus against Aisha for being the foremost opponent of Ali ibn Abi Talib. The antagonism between the two is explained as arising from his cavalier attitude toward her when she was accused of adultery and in danger of being executed. The claim

---

91 Allamah Baqir al-Majlisi, *Hayat al-Qulub*, Sayyid Athar Husayn S. H. Rizvi, trans. (Qum: Ansariyah Publications, 2010), vol. 2, Kindle edition, loc. 20756.
92 Ibid.
93 Ibid.
94 Ibid.

that this tradition was "narrated through authentic chains of narrators," however, is no more or less true in this instance than it is in the case of the Sunni traditions. This story was fabricated in order to put a heroine of the Sunnis in a bad light; Sunnis fabricated their own traditions in a similar way for their own purposes.

Final Words

At one point, Muhammad lost the ability to speak. However, according to a hadith, in his final moments, he had the energy for one last act of hatred against those whom he perceived as his enemies: "As the Messenger of Allah was about to breathe his last, he drew his sheet upon his face and when he felt uneasy, he uncovered his face and said in that very state: 'Let there be curse upon the Jews and the Christians that they have taken the graves of their apostles as places of worship.' He in fact warned (his men) against what they (the Jews and the Christians) did."[95]

Another deathbed saying of Muhammad comes from a hadith that depicts Umar as recalling that his prophet also said: "If I live—if Allah wills—I will expel the Jews and the Christians from the Arabian Peninsula."[96] This is multiply attested, usually without the reference to whether or not Muhammad will survive long enough to fulfill his vow; in Muslim's version, Muhammad says simply: "I will expel the Jews and Christians from the Arabian Peninsula and will not leave any but Muslim."[97] The source for this is also given as Umar. Musa bin Uqba, however, writing as much as a century before the publication of the great hadith collections, states: "Umar used not to let Jews, Christians, and Magians remain more than three days in Medina to do their business, and he used to say 'Two religions cannot subsist together' and he exiled Jews and Christians from the peninsula of the Arabs."[98]

If Muhammad had said that he would expel the Jews and Christians from Arabia, and Umar had been right there to hear him, why does Umar not invoke Muhammad's words when saying that two religions cannot subsist together and expelling the "people of the book" from Arabia? Since he was doing exactly what Muhammad had allegedly

---

95 Sahih Muslim, book 5, no. 531.
96 Jami at-Tirmidhi, book 21, no. 1606.
97 Sahih Muslim, book 32, no. 1767a.
98 Ibn Ishaq, op. cit., xlv.

commanded, why did he make no reference to the words of his master? Musa bin Uqba was, after all, recording the words and deeds of Muhammad, and here was a tradition in which Umar did something that coincided exactly with what Muhammad had commanded. Is it possible, then, that the tradition about expelling Jews and Christians from Arabia began as something attributed to Umar and then became, in later versions of Muhammad's life, a statement and aspiration of Muhammad that Umar recounted?

The Death of Muhammad

According to Ibn Hisham, Muhammad went to the mosque one more time. One of the Muslims is depicted as recalling: "The curtain was lifted and the door opened and out came the apostle and stood at Aisha's door. The Muslims were almost seduced from their prayers for joy at seeing him, and he motioned to them [Tabari adds here "with his hand"] that they should continue their prayers. The apostle smiled with joy when he marked their mien in prayer, and I never saw him with a nobler expression than he had that day. Then he went back and the people went away thinking that the apostle had recovered from his illness."[99]

Ibn Hisham also includes a tradition in which Muhammad's last act is to clean his teeth. Aisha states:

> The apostle came back to me from the mosque that day and lay in my bosom. A man of Abu Bakr's family came in to me with a toothpick in his hand and the apostle looked at it in such a way that I knew he wanted it, and when I asked him if he wanted me to give it him he said Yes; so I took it and chewed it for him to soften it and gave it to him. He rubbed his teeth with it more energetically than I had ever seen him rub before; then he laid it down. I found him heavy in my bosom and as I looked into his face, lo his eyes were fixed and he was saying, "Nay, the most Exalted Companion is of paradise." I said, "You were given the choice and you have chosen, by Him Who sent you with the truth!" And so the apostle was taken.[100]

In one tradition, Aisha states: "It is one of God's blessings to me that the Messenger of God died on the day of my turn, in my house,

---

99 Ibid., 681.
100 Ibid., 682.

between my chest and my neck, and that he mixed my saliva with his at his death."[101] She is also depicted as saying defensively: "The apostle died in my bosom during my turn: I had wronged none in regard to him."[102] This was apparently meant to respond to, or to head off, complaints that she had monopolized his time when he should have been dividing it equally among his various wives, as he had done when he was healthy. Aisha adds: "It was due to my ignorance and extreme youth that the apostle died in my arms. Then I laid his head on a pillow and got up beating my breast and slapping my face along with the other women."[103]

Aisha was at this time around eighteen years old; to her, however, are ascribed numerous traditions of Muhammad's words and deeds. Because of the respect accorded Aisha in Sunni Islam as the "mother of the believers," Islamic scholars have remained generally untroubled by the fact that the primary witness to many of the most important events in their prophet's life was a teenage girl or even a preteen girl. For Sunnis, her reliability in relating events, even ones that did not involve her and may have been difficult for someone so young to understand, is unquestioned.

A hadith offers a slightly different picture of Muhammad's final moments: it has as one of his last acts not cleaning his teeth, but washing his face. Both traditions appear designed to give a picture of a noble death in which Muhammad is intent on purifying himself as he is about to meet the deity who was so very concerned for his welfare. Aisha is also the narrator of this tradition: "There was a leather or wood container full of water in front of Allah's Messenger. He would put his hand into the water and rub his face with it, saying, 'None has the right to be worshipped but Allah! No doubt, death has its stupors.' Then he raised his hand and started saying, 'with the highest companions,' till he expired and his hand dropped."[104]

Another hadith clarifies Muhammad's oblique statement about "the highest companions." Aisha is depicted as saying: "When Allah's Messenger was healthy, he used to say, 'No prophet dies till he is shown his place in Paradise, and then he is given the option (to live or die).' So when death approached him, and while his head was on my thigh, he

---

101 Ibn Kathir, *The Life of Prophet Muhammad*, op. cit., 4, 343.
102 Ibn Ishaq, op. cit.
103 Ibid.
104 Sahih Bukhari, vol. 8, book 81, no. 6510.

became unconscious for a while, and when he recovered, he fixed his eyes on the ceiling and said, 'O Allah! The Highest Companions,' I said, 'So, he does not choose us.' Then I realized that it was the application of the statement he used to relate to us when he was healthy. So that was his last utterance, i.e. 'O Allah! The Highest Companions.'"[105] The Qur'an says: "Whoever obeys Allah and the messenger, they are with those to whom Allah has shown favor, the prophets and the saints and the martyrs and the righteous. They are the highest companions" (4:69).

When he learned of Muhammad's death, Umar refused to believe it. He stood up in the mosque and said to those present: "Some of the disaffected will allege that the apostle is dead, but by God he is not dead: he has gone to his Lord as Moses the son of Imran went and was hidden from his people for forty days, returning to them after it was said that he had died. By God, the apostle will return as Moses returned and will cut off the hands and feet of men who allege that the apostle is dead."[106] Abu Bakr, on the other hand, paid his respects to the deceased: he went to Aisha's house, uncovered Muhammad's face, kissed it, and said: "You are dearer than my father and mother. You have tasted the death which God had decreed: a second death will never overtake you."[107]

Then Abu Bakr returned to the mosque and found Umar still speaking. "Gently, Umar, be quiet," he said, but Umar ignored him and continued to speak.[108] Finally, says Ibn Hisham, Abu Bakr "went forward to the people who, when they heard his words, came to him and left Umar."[109] Abu Bakr began with thanks and praise for Allah and then proclaimed: "O men, if anyone worships Muhammad, Muhammad is dead: if anyone worships God, God is alive, immortal."[110] Then, Ibn Hisham adds, Abu Bakr recited a Qur'anic verse: "Muhammad is only a messenger, messengers have passed away before him. Will it be that when he dies or is killed, you will turn back on your heels? He who turns back on his heels does no harm to Allah, and Allah will reward the thankful" (3:144).

---

105 Sahih Bukhari, vol. 8, book 80, no. 6348.
106 Ibn Ishaq, op. cit., 682–3.
107 Ibid., 683.
108 Ibid.
109 Ibid.
110 Ibid.

The Muslim who was the source of Ibn Hisham's account states: "By God, it was as though the people did not know that this verse had come down until Abu Bakr recited it that day."[111] Maybe it hadn't come down until that day.

Tabari notes that while most authorities stated that Muhammad was sixty-three years old when he died, "others state that he was sixty-five," and "yet others state that he was sixty years old."[112] Ibn Kathir, centuries later, also records traditions that state Muhammad was sixty-five years old at his death, along with others stating that he was sixty-three.[113] He died, Tabari adds, on June 7, 632, although other authorities say it was June 8.[114]

However old Muhammad was when he died, or if he ever actually lived and died at all, Abu Bakr was right: Islam would live on.

111 Ibid.
112 Abu Ja'far Muhammad bin Jarir al-Tabari, *The History of al-Tabari*, Volume IX, *The Last Years of the Prophet*, Ismail K. Poonawalla, trans. (Albany: State University of New York Press, 1990), 207.
113 Ibn Kathir, *The Life of Prophet Muhammad*, op. cit., 4, 369–70.
114 Al-Tabari, *The History of al-Tabari*, IX, op. cit., 209.

CHAPTER FOURTEEN

Muhammad's Character

History or Fable?

That, then, is the story of Muhammad as the early Islamic sources tell it. And despite all the variations, in the main, the primary elements of the story are the same across all the various traditions: Muhammad was born in Mecca, was called to be a prophet by the angel Gabriel, emigrated to Medina with his followers after a period of persecution, smashed a larger force of his enemies at the battle of Badr and gradually overcame their strength after a series of other battles, and died just before his people swept out of Arabia and conquered a huge expanse of the known world.

The similarity of the accounts of the general outline of Muhammad's life could be an indication that this material has a historical core, however much it may be obscured by legend. On the other hand, there is a certain programmatic similarity between the outline of Muhammad's life and that of Moses. There are numerous similarities in the broad outlines of the careers of both prophets. An angel calls both of them to assume their prophetic role. Both lead the believers to emerge victorious against stronger, more formidable foes. Both lead their persecuted people out of a land in which they face hostility and danger and into a new land where they face new challenges. Both are religious leaders but with a pronounced political and military role that flows from their religious status.

The seventh-century mentions of Muhammad affirm that he, or "the praiseworthy one," was a warrior and a prophet; all the other details come later. It is possible that the general outline of Muhammad's story was fashioned after that of Moses and then overlaid with various other traditions reflecting the concerns and priorities of the various factions that developed the hadith and sira literature. Often, these concerns and priorities were conflicting, giving rise to the contradictory elements of this literature. The compilers of the great hadith collections and the composers of the earliest biographies of Muhammad were attempting to bring some standardization to this huge mass of material, and they likely played a large role in developing this outline of Muhammad's life and career that has become familiar to Muslims and non-Muslims alike.

The scholar Robert Kerr, meanwhile, suggests that the life of Muhammad is patterned after a figure closer to hand than Moses: the Roman emperor Heraclius. Heraclius became emperor in 610, the year that Muhammad was supposed to have received his first visit from the angel Gabriel. Then, in 622, Heraclius left Constantinople in order to pursue his war against the Persians; this is traditionally the year in which Muhammad is said to have left Mecca in order to settle in Medina, where he first became a political and military leader. Then, in December 627, Heraclius's forces defeated the Persians in the Battle of Nineveh, roughly corresponding in time to Muhammad's decisive victory over the Quraysh in the Battle of the Trench. In 630, Heraclius triumphantly returned the True Cross to Jerusalem, as Muhammad triumphantly performed his farewell pilgrimage to Mecca after conquering the city.[1]

Whether or not Moses or Heraclius or someone else served as a template for the life of Muhammad, the absence of this often arresting and compelling figure from any remotely contemporary literature, and the abundance of contradictory material, leads to the inevitable conclusion that in the hadith and sira literature, we are dealing with a collection of fables with apologetic intent, not scrupulously remembered and carefully compiled history. The wealth of detail we encounter is designed to give the reader the impression that he is dealing with a carefully compiled and faithful historical account, but this is merely a literary artifice, not a reality.

In the stories about Muhammad, the details that give the impression of being part of a detailed, sober history are presented cheek-by-jowl with obviously legendary material that depicts Muhammad not only as a miracle worker, but as a kind of superman, a man with abilities that are far beyond those of ordinary mortals.

---

1 Robert Kerr, email to the author, September 15, 2023.

Ibn Sa'd, for example, knows so much about Muhammad that he even knows what foods he liked and disliked. His favorite food was "al-tharid of bread and al-tharid of dates, i.e. al-hays."[2] Al-tharid was "bread broken into pieces and soaked in soup."[3] This humble man of the people rejects the refined foods of the rich: "Fine flour of almonds was brought to the Prophet, may Allah bless him. The Apostle of Allah, may Allah bless him, said: Keep it away from me, it is the drink of the wealthy people."[4] On another occasion, Muhammad is served "butter, cheese and a spiny-tailed lizard."[5] Ibn Abbas is depicted as recounting that Muhammad "ate from butter and cheese," but did not touch the lizard.[6] Muhammad explains: "This is a thing that I have never eaten. He who likes may eat it."[7]

Ibn Sa'd then offers another version of this tradition in which, when Muhammad is presented with the spiny-tailed lizard," exclaims: "Transformed people! Allah knows best."[8] A hadith elucidates his words. One of Muhammad's companions is depicted as recounting: "We were in an army with the Messenger of Allah. We got some lizards. I roasted one lizard and brought it to the Messenger of Allah and placed it before him. He took a stick and counted its fingers. He then said: A group from the children of Israel was transformed into an animal of the land, and I do not know which animal it was. He did not eat it nor did he forbid (its eating)."[9]

Another tradition has Muhammad suspecting that the Jews were transformed into a different animal. Abu Huraira recounts that Muhammad said: "A group of Israelites were lost. Nobody knows what they did. But I do not see them except that they were cursed and changed into rats, for if you put the milk of a she-camel in front of a rat, it will not drink it, but if the milk of a sheep is put in front of it, it will drink it."[10] This hadith contains an insistence that Muhammad really did make this statement, in the form of a Jew asking Abu Huraira if Muhammad

---

2 Ibn Sa'd, op. cit, I, 463.
3 Ibid.
4 Ibid., I, 465.
5 Ibid.
6 Ibid.
7 Ibid., 466.
8 Ibid.
9 Sunan Abi Dawud, book 28, no. 3795.
10 Sahih Bukhari, vol. 4, book 59, no. 3305.

actually said this. Abu Huraira says: "I told this to Ka'b who asked me, 'Did you hear it from the Prophet?' I said, 'Yes.' Ka'b asked me the same question several times; I said to Ka'b: 'Do I read the Torah? (i.e. I tell you this from the Prophet.)"[11]

This recalls the notorious passages of the Qur'an in which Allah curses the disobedient Jews and turns them into animals, albeit neither lizards nor rats (2:63–5; 5:59–60; 7:166). One of these passages refers to "he whom Allah has cursed, on whom his wrath has fallen, and of whose sort, Allah has turned some into apes and pigs" (5:60). In the hadith, Muhammad isn't sure what animal the Jews were transformed into but refrains from eating a lizard in case it might be a Jew. Then, in the tradition included in Ibn Sa'd's collection, he rejects his lizard dinner because it is a meal of "transformed people." And he knows that the rats are Jews based on which milk they will drink and which they will reject.

Muhammad also displays supernatural knowledge in a tradition in which one woman states: "I slaughtered a she-goat for the Prophet."[12] During the meal, she recounts that Muhammad called out to her: "'O Abu Rafi! Let me have the forearm.' I passed it on to him. Then he said: 'Let me have the forearm.' I passed it on to him. Then he said: 'Let me have the forearm.'"[13] She then exclaimed: "O Apostle of Allah! Has a goat more than two forearms?"[14] Muhammad replied: "If you had kept quiet, you would have given me what I asked for."[15]

So in the midst of telling his devoted followers what foods the prophet of Islam liked and disliked, information that would necessarily have come from his closest companions, the Islamic traditions add that Muhammad had the ability to discern that an animal set before him for eating was actually a human being, a Jew who had been transformed, presumably for disobedience to Allah. Muhammad is also able to compel a goat to have three forearms when he is particularly hungry.

There are numerous other aspects of these traditions that emphasize that Muhammad was no ordinary man and which account for the near-worship he is accorded to this day, despite the protestations of Islamic apologists that he is a mere man.

---

11 Ibid.
12 Ibn Sa'd, op. cit., I, 463.
13 Ibid.
14 Ibid.
15 Ibid.

Muhammad's Appearance and Character

It is not surprising that the hadith and sira literature contain a great deal of information about Muhammad's physical appearance. It should also not be surprising at this point that this material is just as stylized as the rest of this literature, composed in order to emphasize certain points, above all, that Muhammad is no ordinary man but is the last prophet of Allah, the seal of the prophets. One Muslim describes him in this way: "The Apostle of Allah, may Allah bless him, is neither too short nor too tall. His hairs are neither curly nor straight but a mixture of two. He is a man of black hair and large skull. His complexion has a tinge of redness."[16] Another Muslim says: "I saw Allah's Messenger that he had white complexion and had some white hair."[17] Some framers of the Muhammad myth apparently believed that aging men should conceal the graying of their hair, for a hadith notes that Muhammad "dyed his beard with henna."[18]

His hair was, according to these traditions, neither curly nor straight, and he had a white complexion with a tinge of redness. These could be authentic biographical details, but in another hadith, Muhammad describes the appearances of the prophets whom he met on his night journey to Jerusalem. He says that Jesus was "a medium-statured man with white and red complexion and crisp hair."[19] In another tradition, Muhammad is depicted as saying: "I was shown in a dream in the night that near the Ka'bah there was a man fair-complexioned, fine amongst the white-complexioned men that you ever saw, his locks of hair were falling on his shoulders. He was a man whose hair were neither too curly nor too straight, and water trickled down from his head. He was placing his bands on the shoulders of two persons and amidst them was making a circuit around the Ka'bah. I said: Who is he? They replied: Al-Masih son of Mary."[20] In contrast, the Dajjal, the Antichrist figure in Islam who will appear in the end times, has "intensely curly hair."[21]

So Muhammad, with his white complexion and tinge of redness, and his hair that was neither curly nor straight, resembles Jesus, thereby

---

16 Ibn Sa'd, op. cit., I, 484.
17 Sahih Muslim, book 43, no. 2343a.
18 Sunan al-Nasai, vol. 6, book 48, no. 5083.
19 Sahih Muslim, book 1, no. 165b.
20 Sahih Muslim, book 1, no. 169b.
21 Ibid.

buttressing his own prophetic claim and status. He is also sharply different in appearance from the curly-haired Antichrist. Muhammad also describes Moses as "light brown in complexion."[22] This is to suggest that Muhammad is even purer and holier than Moses (which would be in keeping with the thoroughgoing and relentless antisemitism of the hadith and sira literature): the Qur'an says that "on the day when faces will be whitened and faces will be blackened, and as for those whose faces have been blackened, it will be said to them, Did you disbelieve after your belief? Then taste the punishment for disbelieving" (3:106). The faces of those who have done the will of Allah will be whitened, while those of miscreants will be blackened.

Ibn Sa'd depicts Aisha recording a homespun detail about Muhammad's character: "He was the best of mankind in manners. He was not indecent in deeds or words. He was not making noise in the markets, nor did he return evil for evil, but he excused and pardoned."[23] The phrase "he was not making noise in the markets" is striking: it is a vivid way for Aisha to express that Muhammad was dignified and composed, not boisterous or rude, and is one of the innumerable small details that give this literature the appearance of being a collection of the fresh recollections of Muhammad's companions.

Yet this little detail is actually presented as the fulfillment of a prophecy. Ibn Sa'd also asserts that one of the Muslims is asked to explain how Muhammad is described in the Torah (tawrah), presumably before the Jews corrupted the text to remove mention of the coming of the prophet of Islam: "We find in al-Tawrah, Muhammad is the chosen Prophet neither rough nor harsh, nor noisy in the market. He does not return evil for evil but forgives and pardons."[24]

In another version of this tradition, the same prophecy is located in the Gospel (injil) instead. Aisha is made to say: "Truly the Apostle of Allah is described in al-Injil as one not harsh or coarse or making noise in the market and that he does not return evil for evil but excuses and pardons."[25] In a certain sense, these traditions are both correct. Isaiah 41:1–3 states: "Behold my servant, whom I uphold, my chosen, in whom my soul delights; I have put my Spirit upon him, he will bring

22 Sahih Muslim, book 1, no. 165b.
23 Ibn Sa'd, op. cit., I, 428.
24 Ibid., I, 422.
25 Ibid., I, 425.

forth justice to the nations. He will not cry or lift up his voice, or make it heard in the street; a bruised reed he will not break, and a dimly burning wick he will not quench; he will faithfully bring forth justice." In Matthew 12:18–20, this is applied to Jesus, so the small detail Aisha offers about Muhammad not making noise in the markets is actually another element of the effort to depict Muhammad as the latest prophet in the line of Moses and Jesus.

Meanwhile, regarding Muhammad not being rough or harsh, the traditions entangle themselves in another contradiction. Ibn Sa'd relates a tradition in which Aisha says that Muhammad "did not beat his servant or a woman. He did not strike anything with his hand except when fighting in the path of Allah."[26] However, in a hadith that Muslim records, Aisha recounts that Muhammad "struck me on the chest which caused me pain."[27] At the online hadith compendium Sunnah.com, that was the initial translation, but after this passage garnered unwelcome attention from online critics of Islam, the translation was changed to "he gave me a nudge on the chest which I felt."[28] Sunnah.com offers this translation of a cognate of this tradition: "He gave me a shove in the chest that hurt me."[29]

So is Muhammad depicted as striking Aisha in a way that caused her physical pain, or was this a mistranslation? Edward William Lane's magisterial Arabic lexicon explains that the key word in the passage, lahadat (لَهَدَةً), means "He pushed, pushed away, or repelled, him: or pushed him violently upon the chest," or "he pushed him, pushed him away, or repelled him, on account of his baseness, or despicableness," or even "he struck him in the breasts," or "in the bases of the breasts," or "in the bases of the shoulder blades."[30] Thus, it appears that the translation rendering this as a painless "nudge" is more apologetic in intent than motivated by a concern for strict accuracy.

A desire to burnish Muhammad's image clearly motivated those who revised the translation at Sunnah.com, but they need not have bothered, as the Qur'an itself sanctions Muhammad's treatment of Aisha as depicted in this hadith. The Islamic holy book states: "Men have

---

26 Ibn Sa'd, op. cit., I, 431.
27 Sahih Muslim, book 11, no. 974b.
28 Ibid.
29 Sunan al-Nasai, vol. 4, book 36, no. 3964.
30 Edward William Lane, *An Arabic-English Lexicon* (London: Williams and Norgate), I, 6, 2676.

authority over women because Allah has made the one superior to the other, and because they spend their wealth to maintain them. Good women are obedient. They guard their unseen parts because Allah has guarded them. As for those from whom you fear disobedience, admonish them and send them to beds apart and beat them" (4:34).

The hadith in which Muhammad strikes Aisha does, however, contradict the testimony of the other tradition that states that Muhammad never struck a woman. Here again, it is likely that differing factions had differing views of how women should be treated, which in turn were transferred to their image of the Islamic prophet.

Not only are there traditions that depict Muhammad striking Aisha, but there are also traditions in which this man, who is depicted as being "not harsh or coarse," excoriates his enemies in language that can only be described as harsh and coarse. One hadith states: "Ubayy b. Ka'b told that he heard Allah's messenger say, 'If anyone proudly asserts his descent in the manner of the pre-Islamic people, tell him to bite his father's penis, and do not use a euphemism.' It is transmitted in Sarah [sic] as sunna," that is, as a reliable tradition.[31]

The fourteenth-century Sunni jurist Ibn Qayyim al-Jawziyyah justified speaking coarsely on the basis of this tradition and Abu Bakr's harsh rejoinder to Urwa around the time of the Treaty of Hudaybiyya: "And in the words of Abu Bakr As-Sideeq to 'Urwah: 'Suck Al-Lat's clitoris!'—there is a permissibility of speaking plainly the name of the private parts if there is some benefit to be gained thereby, just as he [Muhammad] permitted a plain response to the one who made the claims of the Jahiliyyah (i.e. claims of tribal superiority), by saying: 'Bite your father's penis!' And for every situation there is a (fitting) saying."[32]

Sexual and Prophetic Prowess

Many of the Islamic traditions about Muhammad are not situated at specific points of his career. Some of these are also extremely problematic,

---

31 *Mishkat Al Masabih*, James Robson, trans. (Lahore: Sh. Muhammad Ashraf Publishers, Booksellers & Exporters, Lahore, Pakistan, 1994), vol. II, book XXIV, ch. XIII, 1021. I am indebted to Sam Shamoun for this reference.

32 Ibn Qayyim al-Jawziyyah, *Provisions for the Hereafter (Mukhtasar Zad al-Ma'ad)*, summarized by Imam Muhammad Ibn Abdul Wahhab At-Tamimi (Riyadh: Darussalam, 2003), 383. I am indebted to Sam Shamoun for this reference.

not only from the standpoint of modern mores and sensibilities but even from the perspective of Islamic tradition.

Numerous traditions, as we have seen, endeavor to portray Muhammad as much greater than an ordinary man. These include accounts of his sexual prowess. Bukhari records a hadith that states: "Anas bin Malik said, 'The Prophet used to visit all his wives in a round, during the day and night and they were eleven in number.' I asked Anas, 'Had the Prophet the strength for it?' Anas replied, 'We used to say that the Prophet was given the strength of thirty (men).' And Sa'id said on the authority of Qatada that Anas had told him about nine wives only (not eleven)."[33] Why, amid literature that knows so much about Muhammad and in such precise detail, would there be uncertainty about something as public as the number of his wives?

It is noteworthy that Bukhari would include in his *sahih* (reliable) hadith collection an account that reflects uncertainty about the number of Muhammad's wives. Ibn Sa'd adds to the uncertainty by enhancing Muhammad's prowess even beyond the outlandish claim in the hadith Bukhari records, depicting the prophet of Islam as saying: "Gabriel brought a kettle from which I ate and I was given the power of sexual intercourse equal to forty men."[34]

When Muhammad was engaging in sexual intercourse with all of his wives in one night, he would only bother to wash once: "Anas said that the Prophet used to have intercourse with his wives, with only a single washing."[35] Another tradition adds that "she," who is unidentified in this tradition but is apparently Aisha, "also said that the Prophet used to wash his head with marshmallow when sexually defiled, contenting himself with that and not pouring water over it."[36] Such traditions were apparently invented either to discount the need to wash in between engaging in sexual intercourse with successive wives or slave women or to indicate that Muhammad was so exceptionally pure that he was exempt from what was required of most men in order to purify themselves.

Traditions of this kind were obviously constructed in order to inspire awe of Muhammad and reverence for Allah, that he would favor

---

33 Sahih Bukhari, vol. 1, book 5, no. 268.
34 Ibn Sa'd, op. cit., I, 438–9.
35 Mishkat al-Masabih, book 3, no. 455.
36 Mishkat al-Masabih, book 3, no. 446.

his prophet in this way. His superhuman prowess was not intended to depict a man overwhelmed with lust, but a man who was extraordinary in every way, a man who surpassed other men in truly every detail, and particularly in ways that rough ninth-century warriors would understand and respect. Those who constructed the Muhammad myth were not ascetics and were not interested in self-denial, and neither was their prophet. If he had the sexual strength of thirty or forty men, this did not signify to those who devised and disseminated this legend that the prophet of Islam was not in control of his sexual faculties; it meant that he was a larger-than-life figure, worthy of all the reverence Muslims could offer him without veering into outright idolatry.

Some of the stories constructed to illustrate this strike contemporary readers as exceedingly strange at best. Bukhari records a hadith in which Aisha is depicted as saying: "I used to wash the semen off the clothes of the Prophet and even then I used to notice one or more spots on them."[37] Muslim, on the other hand, records a variant version in which Muhammad, not Aisha, did the washing: "Amr b. Maimun said: 'I asked Sulaiman b. Yasar whether the semen that gets on to the garment of a person should be washed or not.' He replied: 'Aisha told me: "The Messenger of Allah washed the semen, and then went out for prayer in that very garment and I saw the mark of washing on it."'"[38]

Semen on the clothes of the prophet of Islam? On a repeated basis? While this story suggests to modern readers nothing more than an exceedingly lustful figure who can barely control his sexual urges, if he can be said to control them all, for those who fabricated these traditions, they were likely meant to convey that Muhammad was veritably bursting with virility. If anyone could be said to have been a man's man, it was Muhammad.

Muhammad and Hasan and Hussein

Numerous traditions record the great love Muhammad had for two sons of Ali ibn Abi Talib, Hasan and Hussein. One tradition has the prophet of Islam kissing one of the boys (the storyteller himself isn't sure which) after directing the boy to open his mouth: "Abu Hurayra said, 'These two ears of mine have heard and these two eyes of mine have seen the

---

37 Sahih Bukhari, vol. 1, book 4, no. 232.
38 Sahih Muslim, vol. 2, no. 289a.

Messenger of Allah take the palms of al-Hasan—or al-Husayn—in both his hands. His feet were on the feet of the Messenger of Allah. The Messenger of Allah said, 'Climb up.' The boy climbed until his feet reached the chest of the Messenger of Allah, and then the Messenger of Allah, said, 'Open your mouth.' Then he kissed him and said, 'O Allah, love him, for I love him!'"[39] When Muhammad died, according to the most common traditional reckoning, Hasan was seven years old, and Hussein was six.

Sulayman ibn Ahmad al-Tabarani was a Sunni hadith scholar who died in 971 AD; he records a startling tradition, complete with a detailed isnad chain: "Al-Hasan ibn Ali Al-Fasawi reported from Khalid ibn Yazid Al-Urani who reported from Jarir ibn Abd Al-Hamid who reported from Qabus ibn Abi Zabyan who reported from his father Husain ibn Jundub that Abdullah ibn Abbas said: 'I saw the Prophet Muhammad spreading apart the thighs of Al-Hasan and kissing his penis.'"[40]

This hadith is not in the major ninth-century hadith collections. Nevertheless, al-Hakim al-Nishapuri, a Persian Sunni who died in 1014, states that "the tradition is authentic (Sahih) according to its chain." But he adds that "the two did not publish it," referring to the two hadith collections Sunnis consider most reliable, Sahih Bukhari and Sahih Muslim.[41] Despite this omission, however, nearly three hundred years after al-Tabarani's death, some still considered this story to be factual. A thirteenth-century Islamic jurist, Yahya ibn Sharaf al-Nawawi (1233–1277), wrote:

> Some of the people of knowledge say: "The ablution is broken by touching one's own penis excluding the other." And I reply to these people with the proof of the tradition of Talq Ibn Ali, may God be pleased with him, that the Messenger was asked about touching from the penis in prayer, whereupon he said: "Should it be something other than a piece of you?" And through Abu Lailah, who said: "We were with the Prophet Muhammad, whereupon Al-Hasan came

---

39 Al-Adab al-Mufrad, book 12, no. 249. See also Al-Adab al-Mufrad, book 48, no. 1183.
40 Sulayman ibn Ahmad al-Tabarani, Al-Mu'jam-ul-Kabir, vol. 12, no. 12615. Quoted in "Opponents about kissing the intimate area," AhlulBeitOne, January 20, 2021, https://en.ahlulbait.one/2021/01/20/opponents-about-kissing-the-intimate-area/.
41 Al-Hakim al-Nishapuri, Al-Mustadrak Ala As-Sahihain, Hadith 6995, in "Opponents about kissing the intimate area," op. cit.

rolling on him. Then he removed his shirt and kissed his penis." And because he touched a part of his body, the ablution was not broken like the rest of the body parts and our companions prove it with the narration of Busrah and it is authentic (Sahih) just as we have submitted its explanation and in a narration Umm Habibah said: "I heard the Prophet Muhammad say: "Whoever touches his own private parts should perform the ablution." Al-Baihaqi commented that At-Tirmidhi said: "I asked Abu Zur'ah about the narration of Umm Habibah, whereupon he considered it good (Hasan)." He said: "I saw him considering it as being preserved."[42]

Even the renowned Islamic jurist and theologian Ibn Taymiyyah (1263–1328) regarded this tradition as authentic, stating flatly: "Prophet Muhammad used to kiss the penis of Al-Hasan."[43]

The hadith scholar al-Dhahabi (1274–1348) wrote a *History of Islam* in which he first carefully records the chain of transmitters: "Jarir bin Abdul Hamid said, on the authority of Qaboos, on the authority of his father, on the authority of Ibn Abbas."[44] Then he relates the tradition itself: "The Messenger of God parted Al-Hasan's thighs and kissed his penis."[45] He adds that Qaboos gave his approval to this transmission, saying: "Well spoken."[46]

A variant version comes from the slightly later hadith scholar Nur al-Din al-Haythami (1335–1405), who states that it was not Hasan but his younger brother Hussein who was the object of Muhammad's lewd affections: "I saw the Messenger of Allah parting Hussein's thighs and

---

42 Yahya ibn Sharaf al-Nawawi, *Al-Majmu*, II, 46–47, in "Opponents about kissing the intimate area," ibid. See also
https://web.archive.org/web/20210428141554/https://i2.wp.com/ahlulbayt.one/wp-content/uploads/2021/01/majmu3-e-nawawi-b-2-s-46-47.jpg?ssl=1.

43 Ibn Taymiyyah, *Majmu'-ul-Fatawa*, vol. 21, 522, in "Opponents about kissing the intimate area," ibid.

44 Al-Dhahabi, تاريخ الإسلام, (History of Islam), part 4, 36, https://web.archive.org/web/20220818084128/http://shiaonlinelibrary.com/%D8%A7%D9%84%D9%83%D8%AA%D8%A8/3515_%D8%AA%D8%A7%D8%B1%D9%8A%D8%AE-%D8%A7%D9%84%D8%A5%D8%B3%D9%84%D8%A7%D9%85-%D8%A7%D9%84%D8%B0%D9%87%D8%A8%D9%8A-%D8%AC%D9%A4/%D8%A7%D9%84%D8%B5%D9%81%D8%AD%D8%A9_32. See "Prophet Muhammad used to kiss the PENIS of small boys Hassan and Hussain," Atheism vs. Islam, n.d., https://atheism-vs-islam.com/index.php/islam-general/144-prophet-muhammad-used-to-kiss-the-penis-of-small-boys-hassan-and-hussain.

45 Ibid.
46 Ibid.

kissing his penis."[47] Al-Haythami adds that this tradition was "narrated by Al-Tabarani and its chain of transmission is good."[48]

Even as late as the fifteenth century, the Egyptian Islamic scholar Ibn Hajar al-Asqalani (1372–1449) took its authenticity for granted, writing: "Abdullah Ibn Abbas said: 'I saw Prophet Muhammad spreading apart the thighs of Al-Hasan and kissing his penis.' At-Tabarani reported it and it is a proof that a small child has no nakedness to cover."[49]

Still, as al-Nishapuri noted, this arresting account doesn't appear in any of the ninth-century hadith collections. Islamic scholars have tended to dismiss stories that appear after the publication of the primary hadith collections as obvious forgeries, not worthy of taking a place alongside the accounts of Muhammad's exploits at Badr, Khaybar, Tabuk, and the like. Yet as we have seen, those accounts don't have any stronger historical foundation than this tradition does, and the uncomfortable question must be asked: Why would anyone go to the trouble of fabricating such a hadith in the first place? Why would any stories have ever circulated among Muslims of Muhammad kissing the genitals of a boy who could not have been older than seven years old?

What's more, this story was considered sufficiently authentic to play a role in Islamic jurisprudence. The thirteenth-century jurist Ibn Qudamah legislates on its basis, declaring: "Whoever touches the male organ should perform the ablution of prayer and there is no difference whether it is a male organ of a child or adult, and this was expressed by Ata and Ash-Shafi'i. It is reported from Az-Zuhri and Al-Awza'i: 'Someone who touches the male organ of a child is not obligated to perform the ablution of prayer because it is permissible to touch and look at it and it has been reported from the Messenger of God that he kissed and touched the male organ of Hasan and did not perform the ablution of prayer."[50]

47 Nur al-Din Ali bin Abi Bakr al-Haythami, امجمع الزوائد ومنبع الفوائد (The Complex of Excesses and the Source of Benefits), (Beirut: Dar al-Fikr, 1991), 15108. https://web.archive.org/web/20111227003927/http://islamport.com/d/1/krj/1/81/1290.html. See "Prophet Muhammad used to kiss the PENIS of small boys Hassan and Hussain," op. cit.

48 Ibid.

49 Ibn Hajar al-Asqalani, Ad-Dirayah Fi Takhrij Ahadith al-Hidayah, 123–124, in "Opponents about kissing the intimate area," op. cit.

50 Ibn Qudamah, Al-Mughni, Book of Purity, I, 252–3, quoted in "The Kiss of the Prophet," Ahlul-BaitOne, December 20, 2020, https://en.ahlulbait.one/2020/12/20/the-kiss-of-the-prophet/. See also https://ar.wikisource.org/wiki/%D8%A7%D9%84%D9%85%D8%BA%D9%86%D9%8A_-_%D9%83%D8%AA%D8%A7%D8%A8_%D8%A7%D9%84%D8%B7%D9%87%D8%A7%D8%B1%D8%A9_2 and See "Prophet Muhammad used to kiss the PENIS of small boys Hassan and Hussain," op. cit.

The answer to the question of why such traditions would have circulated and been considered to be authentic in at least some Islamic circles is the same as for other problematic hadiths, both those considered authentic in mainstream Islam and those that are rejected: stories of Muhammad circulated because those who fabricated and distributed them benefited from them in some way. The words they put in Muhammad's mouth, or the deeds they attributed to him, were positions on controverted issues for which they wanted to show the support of the highest authority of all in Islam. If a hadith depicts Muhammad as doing something, some of the early Muslims wanted to do it as well and to justify the practice by wrapping it in Muhammad's mantle. In this case, quite simply, the fabricators of this hadith apparently wanted to justify sexual contact with young boys. Because they didn't see anything wrong with such contact, although they were aware that others did, they attributed it to Muhammad, whose status as the "excellent example" (Qur'an 33:21) for Muslims, always to be emulated, could not be questioned.

These traditions are never mentioned today in connection with the widespread Afghan practice of *bacha bazi* ("boy play"), in which an older male takes a young boy as a sexual companion. This practice is sometimes linked to the Qur'anic passage about the boys of paradise, who are mentioned in a passage that is strongly redolent of other passages describing the *houris*, the heavenly virgins who will pleasure the Muslim men in paradise for all eternity: "There wait on them immortal youths, whom, when you see them, you would take them for scattered pearls" (76:19) comes in a description of the joys of the blessed, which also include "enclosed gardens and vineyards, and large-breasted women of equal age" (78:32–3). However, if the example of Muhammad, which is considerably more explicit than the Qur'anic passage about the pearl-like boys, has had a role in the perpetuation of this practice, it would explain why it has persisted and remained so widespread in a nation that is otherwise renowned for the scrupulousness of its Islamic observance.

Homosexuality

Other Islamic traditions record Muhammad's conduct with adult males that doesn't accord with the hadith in which the prophet of Islam prescribes the death penalty for homosexuality: "If you find anyone doing as Lot's people did, kill the one who does it, and the one to whom it is done."[51] Lot is the figure from Genesis whose house in the city of Sodom is surrounded by a mob demanding that he send out the men who are visiting him "that we may know them" (Genesis 19:5). This is the foundation of Islam's death penalty for homosexuality. Yet numerous observers in Islamic lands have noted that the prohibition of homosexuality is often ignored, and this, too, may have justification in Muhammad's behavior as recorded in various traditions.

Sunan Abi Dawud, the same hadith collection in which Muhammad's prescription of the death penalty for homosexuality appears, also contains this curious story: "Narrated Usayd ibn Hudayr: AbdurRahman ibn Abu Layla, quoting Usayd ibn Hudayr, a man of the Ansar, said that while he was given to jesting and was talking to the people and making them laugh, the Prophet poked him under the ribs with a stick. He said: 'Let me take retaliation.' He said: 'Take retaliation.' He said: 'You are wearing a shirt but I am not.' The Prophet then raised his shirt and the man embraced him and began to kiss his side. Then he said: 'This is what I wanted, Messenger of Allah!'"[52]

Nearly half a millennium later, Ibn Kathir records a fuller variant of this tradition, ascribing it to much earlier authorities and featuring a different companion of Muhammad:

> Ibn Ishaq stated, "Habban b. Wasi b. Habban related to me, from sheikhs of his tribe, that when the Messenger of God Habban lined up his forces at the battle of Badr, he held an arrow which he used to indicate how they should adjust their position. He passed by Sawwad b. Ghaziyya, an ally of the Banu Adi b. al-Najjar, and a little ahead of the line. He poked him in the belly with the arrow, saying, 'Straighten up, Sawwad!'
>
> "He replied, 'O Messenger of God, I swear by Him who sent you with the truth and justice that you hurt me! So let me retaliate!'
>
> "The Messenger of God promptly uncovered his stomach and said, 'Retaliate then!' Sawwad hugged him and then kissed his stomach. The Messenger of God asked, 'Why did you do that, Sawwad?' He replied, 'O Messenger of God, you can see what is about to happen; I wanted my last contact with you to be my skin touching yours.'"[53]

---

51 Sunan Abi Dawud, book 40, no. 4462.
52 Sunan Abi Dawud, book 43, no. 5224.
53 Ibn Kathir, The Life of Prophet Muhammad, op. cit., 2, 272.

This is not, of course, overt homosexual activity. But nevertheless, the prospect of the prophet of Islam raising his shirt so that another man could kiss his side certainly does nothing to discourage homoeroticism in Islam.

Inappropriate Behavior with His Daughter

The story of Aisha is well known and discussed in chapter five. Less well-known is a tradition depicting Muhammad behaving extremely inappropriately toward his own daughter, Fatima. The Sunni hadith scholar and historian al-Khatib al-Baghdadi (1002–1071) recorded this hadith:

> Urwah Ibn Az-Zubair reported that Aishah said: "O Messenger of God, what is it with you that when Fatimah comes to you, you kiss her until you put your tongue all the way into her mouth as if you want to lick honey off her?" The Messenger of God replied: "Yes, O Aishah! When I was made to take the night journey, Gabriel took me to Paradise and presented me with an apple from it. So I ate it and it became a drop in my loins. After I descended, I performed intercourse with Khadijah and hence Fatimah is from this drop and she is the woman of Paradise. Whenever I long for paradise, I kiss her."[54]

The seventeenth-century Shi'ite hadith collection *Bihar al-Anwar* contains this:

> Hudhaifah is reported to have said: "The Messenger of God used not to go to sleep before kissing the area of the cheeks or above (*baina*) the breasts of Fatimah." And Ja'far Ibn Muhammad is reported to have said: "The Messenger of God used not to go to sleep until he put his noble face on the area above (*baina*) the breasts of Fatimah."[55]

A Shi'ite site where this hadith is recorded states: "The word 'baina' [بين] in the context means the area above (neck, forehead, etc.) and not 'in between.' This way of speaking can also be found in the works of the followers of Umar," that is, Sunnis. However, this explanation has more than a tinge of apologetic intent; the word "baina" is most commonly

---

54 Al-Khatib al-Baghdadi, *Tarikh Baghdad*, no. 1739, in "The Kiss of the Prophet," op. cit.
55 Mohammad-Baqer Majlesi, *Bihar-ul-Anwar*, vol. 43, 78, in "The Kiss of the Prophet," ibid.

translated precisely as "in between."[56] The Shi'ite site feels the need to present evidence for its translation of this word and offers, among other passages, a hadith from Sunan Abi Dawud: "The Messenger of God welcomed Ja'far Ibn Abi Talib, embraced him and kissed him on the area above (*baina*) his eyes (forehead)."[57] At the Sunni site Sunnah.com, this is translated as "The Prophet received Ja'far ibn Abu Talib, embraced him and kissed him between both of his eyes (forehead)."[58]

Regarding the hadith about Muhammad kissing Fatima, the precise meaning of the word *baina* doesn't actually make an immense difference. Either Muhammad kissed his daughter between her breasts or above them, around her neck and shoulders. Whichever one prefers, this is not the way a father should be kissing his child. Yet this tradition also became the basis of Islamic jurisprudence: al-Asqalani's massive commentary on Sahih Bukhari, *Fath al-Bari fi Sharh Sahih al-Bukhari*, directs: "The father is allowed to kiss any part of the body of the child and just so is the case with the adult child according to the majority of scholars, as long as it is not on the nakedness that is to be covered, and about the merits of Fatimah there emerged that the Messenger of God used to kiss her and in the same way Abu Bakr used to kiss his daughter Aishah."[59] The exclusion of the "nakedness that is to be covered" is fine, but there is plenty of room left for inappropriate behavior, including, as in the above hadith regarding Fatima, tongue kissing.

Cross-Dressing

A series of hadiths depict Muhammad on several occasions wearing Aisha's clothing. While it may seem initially that a man in his fifties could not even fit into the clothes of a preteen or young teenage girl, the clothing in question consisted of free-flowing garments such as robes. They were, however, distinctively designed for women, and the hadiths make note of this.

There has been some embarrassment among Islamic apologists regarding these passages, and so, in some cases, their meaning has been obscured. Sahih Muslim includes this story:

56 *Concise Oxford English-Arabic Dictionary of Current Usage*, N. S. Doniach, ed. (Oxford: Oxford University Press, 1982), 36.
57 "The Kiss of the Prophet," op. cit.
58 Sunan Abi Dawud, book 43, no. 5220.
59 Ibn Hajar al-Asqalani, *Fath al-Bari Fi Sharh Sahih al-Bukhari*, vol. 10, 357, in "The Kiss of the Prophet," op. cit.

Aisha, the wife of Allah's Apostle and Uthman both reported that Abu Bakr sought permission from Allah's Messenger for entrance (in his apartment) as he had been lying on his bed covered with the bedsheet of Aisha, and he gave permission to Abu Bakr in that very state and he, having his need fulfilled, went back. Then Umar sought permission and it was given to him in that very state and, after having his need fulfilled, he went back.

And Uthman reported: "Then I sought permission from him and he got up and said to Aisha: 'Wrap yourself well with your cloth,' then I got my need fulfilled and came back." And Aisha said: "Allah's Messenger, why is it that I did not see you feeling any anxiety in case of dressing properly in the presence of Abu Bakr and Umar as you showed in case of Uthman?" Thereupon Allah's Messenger said: "Verily Uthman is a person who is very modest and I was afraid that if I permitted him to enter in this very state he would not inform me of his need."[60]

The story is odd in a number of ways. Muhammad receives Abu Bakr and Umar, apparently while covered only with Aisha's bedsheet. When Uthman comes in, however, Muhammad "got up" and tells Aisha to cover herself well. Then he explains that he treated Uthman differently from how he dealt with Abu Bakr and Umar because he was very modest. This raises a number of questions. Was the problem that Aisha was in a state of undress? That is suggested by the fact that Muhammad tells her to wrap herself well, but nothing is said when Abu Bakr and Umar come in about Aisha being not fully dressed. And Aisha asks Muhammad about his not dressing properly, without saying anything about she herself not being properly dressed. Yet when Uthman comes in, we're told only that Muhammad got up, not that he got dressed.

Also, was the "cloth" that Muhammad told Aisha to wrap herself in the same as the "bedsheet of Aisha" in which Muhammad was covered when Abu Bakr and Umar came in? It could have been, as the word here translated as bedsheet is *mirt* (مِرْط), which is more commonly translated as a woman's garment. So was Muhammad dressed in Aisha's robe, which was apparently fine with Abu Bakr and Umar, but he told her to put it on before Uthman came in because Uthman would have looked askance at such behavior?

---

60 Sahih Muslim book 44, no. 2402a.

The advantage of this explanation is that it makes sense of the story's apparently disjointed elements. It explains why he tells Aisha to dress, rather than dressing himself when Uthman is about to come in; he may have had his own clothes underneath Aisha's, but to avoid scandalizing one of his closest companions, he took off Aisha's garment and told her to put it on before Uthman came in.

Supporting the idea that Muhammad wore Aisha's clothes is another hadith, which Muslim also records, in which *mirt* is translated as "mantle," that is, a loose sleeveless cloak. Aisha is depicted as recounting that Muhammad's wives sent his daughter Fatima to see Muhammad and settle an unspecified dispute regarding "the daughter of Abu Quhafa," Abu Bakr's father. It is clear from a variant version of this story that Bukhari records that the woman in question is Aisha; she was actually the granddaughter of Abu Quhafa, and Muhammad's other wives were annoyed that Muhammad favored her.

Fatima "sought permission to get in as he had been lying with me in my mantle [*mirt*]."[61] Fatima then says to Muhammad, "Verily, your wives have sent me to you in order to ask you to observe equity in case of the daughter of Abu Quhafa."[62] Muhammad replies: "O daughter, don't you love whom I love?"[63] Fatima reports this to Muhammad's wives, who ask her to return, but she refuses. The wives then send Zaynab bint Jahsh on the same mission. Muhammad "permitted her to enter as she (Aisha) was along with Allah's Messenger in her mantle, in the same very state when Fatima had entered."[64] Zaynab makes the same appeal to Muhammad that Fatima had made and insults Aisha in the process. Annoyed, Aisha recounts: "Then I exchanged hot words until I made her quiet."[65] This makes Muhammad smile, and he remarks: "She is the daughter of Abu Bakr."[66]

In Bukhari's version, the cause of the dispute is fully spelled out: "The Muslims knew that Allah's Messenger loved Aisha, so if any of them had a gift and wished to give to Allah's Messenger, he would delay it till Allah's Messenger had come to Aisha's home, and then he would

---

61 Sahih Muslim book 44, no. 2442a.
62 Ibid.
63 Ibid.
64 Ibid.
65 Ibid.
66 Ibid.

send his gift to Allah's Messenger in her home."[67] Before Fatima or Zaynab get involved, Muhammad's wives deputize Umm Salama, whom Muhammad had married after the Battle of Uhud, to handle this issue with Muhammad. The other wives tell Umm Salama that she "should request Allah's Messenger to tell the people to send their gifts to him in whatever wife's house he was."[68] Umm Salama does so, but Muhammad repeatedly refuses to reply. Finally, "when it was her turn, she talked to him again. He then said to her, 'Do not hurt me regarding Aisha, as the Divine Inspirations do not come to me on any of the beds except that of Aisha.'"[69]

This is once again a highly questionable translation. The passage here translated as "on any of the beds" is more literally "in any other garment," for the word translated as "beds" is *thawb* (ثُوْب), which is also a flowing robe. If, however, Muhammad is wearing Aisha's *thawb*, that would be a woman's garment.

Otherwise, Bukhari's story is much the same as Muslim's version. It continues by noting that the wives then sent Fatima to Muhammad and that she said to him: "Your wives request to treat them and the daughter of Abu Bakr on equal terms."[70] Muhammad replies: "O my daughter! Don't you love whom I love?"[71] In this version also, Fatima reports this to the wives, who ask her to go back and ask her again, but she refuses, and so Zaynab bint Jahsh goes instead. Zaynab insults Aisha, whereupon Aisha "started replying to Zainab till she silenced her," and Muhammad happily remarks: "She is really the daughter of Abu Bakr."[72]

Many have argued that if Muhammad really did like to dress in Aisha's clothing, this must be evidence of the historical accuracy of the accounts of his life, for such a bizarre story would never have been invented. However, the differences between the stories are more indication that these are not historical accounts. While they're quite similar, Muslim doesn't seem to know why the other wives are angry with Aisha beyond the fact that Muhammad is behaving inequitably toward them and favoring Aisha. Nor does he appear aware of Umm Salama's role in the entire

---

67 Sahih Bukhari, vol. 3, book 51, no. 2581.
68 Ibid.
69 Ibid.
70 Ibid.
71 Ibid.
72 Ibid.

dispute. This suggests once again that the sira material consists of legends that were elaborated in different ways by different factions or by Muslims at different places and times. But why fabricate stories in which Muhammad is wearing Aisha's clothing? The explanation may simply be that this indicates how close Aisha was to Muhammad, contrary to Shi'ite polemics that exalted Ali ibn Abi Talib and denigrated Aisha. Another possible reason why such an arresting detail as a cross-dressing prophet would have been included is that such traditions could only have been composed by people who wanted to engage in such practices themselves, and so ascribed them to the prophet of Islam.

Necrophilia

Bukhari records a strange hadith attributed to Anas bin Malik: "We were (in the funeral procession) of one of the daughters of the Prophet and he was sitting by the side of the grave. I saw his eyes shedding tears. He said, 'Is there anyone among you who did not have sexual relations with his wife last night?' Abu Talha replied in the affirmative. And so the Prophet told him to get down in the grave. And so he got down in her grave."[73]

According to Islamic tradition, three of Muhammad's four daughters died before him; this story does not specify at which daughter's funeral this supposedly occurred. None of the three were married to Abu Talha, so Muhammad was not inviting the grieving widower to pay his last respects to the deceased. Bukhari also offers another version of the same story in which Muhammad asks the same question; this version concludes: "And so Allah's Apostle told him to get down in her grave and he got down in her grave and buried her."[74] If burial is all this story is about, however, why does Muhammad ask the men with him which of them did not have sexual relations with his wife the previous night? It does appear as if he is inviting Abu Talha to have sexual relations with his deceased daughter in her grave.

Supporting this interpretation is another tradition in which Muhammad appears to engage in the practice himself: "The prophet of Allah took off his gown and put it on Umm Ali and slept with her in her grave and they kicked dirt on him, saying: 'Oh messenger of Allah, we saw you

---

73 Sahih Bukhari, vol. 2, book 23, no. 1285.
74 Sahih Bukhari, vol. 2, book 23, no. 1342.

do something no one else has ever done.' He said: 'I dressed her in my gown, so she can wear the gowns of paradise and I slept with her in her grave to relieve her of the torments of the grave.'"[75]

"Slept" is *id'tajat*, an Arabic word that has the same double meaning as the same phrase in English. If one person sleeps with another, they may be literally sleeping, or they may be having sexual relations. Muhammad's own comment, however, favors the idea that he had sexual relations with her. He says that because he slept with her, she will be relieved of the torments of the grave; this only makes sense if she will now be accorded the treatment reserved for the wives of Muhammad, the "mothers of the believers," rather than being judged like an ordinary woman. But she could only have become a wife of Muhammad if their marriage had been consummated.

Also giving credence to the idea that Muhammad engaged in necrophilia is the fact that some Islamic authorities teach that the practice is permissible. The sixteenth-century jurist Mohammad al-Sherbini al-Khateeb ruled that "there is no restriction against sex with a dead woman or an animal."[76] This idea has lingered even into modern times. The twentieth-century jurist Abd al-Hameed al-Sharawani wrote: "There is no need to rewash a dead woman if her husband has sex with her after she dies.... And there is no punishment for anyone who has sex with a dead woman or limits sex to sex with a dead woman."[77]

In March 2012, a Moroccan Muslim cleric, Abd al-Bari al-Zamzami, stated that necrophilia is "not to be expected from a normal, balanced person."[78] However, he added: "I do not have the right to prohibit that act merely because I consider it deplorable.... It is perfectly clear that marital relations are not severed by a wife's death. She remains her husband's wife. This being the case, the husband has the right to do whatever he wants with her. For instance, he may kiss her. It is

75 *Kanz al-Ummal* in *Sunan al Aqwal wa al-Af'al*, vol. 16, 158, quoted in Zakaria Botros, *The Reality of Islam According to Islamic Sources* (Buffalo Grove, Illinois: Hope of All Nations Association, 2018), 212.

76 Mohammad al-Sherbini al-Khateeb, *Al-Iqna3 fi Hal al-Faz: Abu Shoja'a* (Beirut: Dar al-Fikr, 1994), vol. 2, 521, quoted in Botros, ibid.

77 Abd al-Hameed al-Sharawani, *Howashi al-Sharwani* (Al-Qubra, Egypt: Al-Maktabah Al-Tojariah, 1983) vol. 1, 263, quoted in Botros, ibid.

78 "Moroccan Cleric Abd al-Bari al-Zamzami: Husbands May Have Sex with Dead Wife's Corpse; Women May Use Carrots as Vibrators," MEMRI, March 24, 2012, https://www.memri.org/tv/moroccan-cleric-abd-al-bari-al-zamzami-husbands-may-have-sex-dead-wifes-corpse-women-may-use.

common for a husband to kiss his wife after her death, out of love and sorrow. This is something that is done, and there is nothing wrong with it.... Having sex with your wife's corpse is permitted but not commendable."[79]

Then, in 2017, the Egyptian Sheikh Sabri Abdel-Raouf ignited a firestorm by issuing a fatwa discussing the permissibility of a Muslim having sexual relations with his dead wife. In his defense, the Egyptian daily *Youm 7* published a series of extracts from rulings justifying the practice. It quoted a book of Maliki jurisprudence stating: "As for the husband, if he has intercourse with his wife after her death, before or after her, then there is no punishment for him."[80] And from the Shafi'i school: "There is no restriction upon sexual intercourse with a dead person, according to the more correct view, because this is something that is alienated from nature, and the perpetrator shall be reprimanded or punished."[81]

Other Muslims, of course, argue that the hadiths upon which these justifications are based are weak and cannot legitimately be attributed to Muhammad. But here again, these traditions are on scarcely shakier ground than the rest of the hadith and sira literature. And so the real question is: Why were these traditions fabricated in the first place? The traditions depicting Muhammad allowing for the practice and possibly engaging in it himself likely spring from the same wellsprings as these jurisprudential rulings: some Muslims wanted to practice necrophilia, and so they composed traditions showing Muhammad involved in the practice.

Prostitution

Muhammad's jihads caused some of his men a particular kind of distress. Bukhari relates words attributed to Abdullah, one of Muhammad's companions: "We used to participate in the holy wars carried on by the Prophet and we had no women (wives) with us. So we said, 'Shall we castrate ourselves?' But the Prophet forbade us to do that and thenceforth he allowed us to marry a woman (temporarily) by giving her even

---

79 Ibid.
80 "كتب الشافعية والحنابلة والأحناف تكشف: نكاح الزوجة الميتة "ليس زنا" Youm 7, September 21, 2017.
81 Ibid.

a garment, and then he recited: 'O you who believe! Do not make unlawful the good things which Allah has made lawful for you.'"[82]

From this permission arose the idea of temporary marriage (*nikah mut'ah*, or pleasure marriage), which is marriage for a specified period of time. Generally in exchange for a sum of money, a woman marries a man for a night, a weekend, or some other specified period; then, the two go their separate ways. Sahih Muslim also includes a tradition stating that Muhammad later reversed his permission for this practice: "Ali b. Abi Talib reported that Allah's Messenger prohibited on the Day of Khaybar the contracting of temporary marriage with women and the eating of the flesh of domestic asses."[83]

Shi'ites, however, insist that the practice is still permissible and justified in a passage of the Qur'an: "And all married women except those whom your right hands possess. It is a decree of Allah for you. Lawful to you are all beyond those mentioned, so that you may seek them with your wealth in honest wedlock, not debauchery. And those whom you enjoy, give them their shares as a duty. And there is no sin for you in what you do by mutual agreement after the duty. Indeed, Allah is ever-knower, wise" (4:24). The section about there being "no sin for you in what you do by mutual agreement" is supposed to refer to the arrangement of a temporary marriage.

Clearly, this issue was controversial in the ninth century, for Muslim records a hadith in which two companions of Muhammad, Abdullah ibn Zubair and Ibn Abbas, have a heated dispute over the matter. Abdullah says: "Allah has made blind the hearts of some people as He has deprived them of eyesight that they give religious verdict in favor of temporary marriage," and the hadith specifies that he was referring to Ibn Abbas.[84] Ibn Abbas responds furiously: "You are an uncouth person, devoid of sense. By my life, Mut'a was practiced during the lifetime of the leader of the pious," that is, Muhammad.[85] Abdullah responds that if Ibn Abbas engages in the practice, "I will stone you with your stones."[86] Another tries to calm the situation, saying: "Be gentle. It was permitted in the early days of Islam, (for one) who was driven to it under the stress

---

82 Sahih Bukhari, vol. 6, book 65, no. 4615.
83 Sahih Muslim, book 16, no. 1407a.
84 Sahih Muslim, book 16, no. 1406k.
85 Ibid.
86 Ibid.

of necessity just as (the eating of) carrion and the blood and flesh of swine and then Allah intensified (the commands of) His religion and prohibited it (altogether)."[87]

Shi'ites, meanwhile, point out that hadiths permitting the practice remain in canonical Sunni hadith collections. This one is also from Sahih Muslim: "There came to us the proclaimer of Allah's Messenger and said: 'Allah's Messenger has granted you permission to benefit yourselves, i.e. to contract temporary marriage with women.'"[88] The fact that these were not removed despite their flat and open contradiction of traditions recording Muhammad's prohibition of the practice could indicate that, as some of these traditions state, he allowed the practice and later forbade it. It more likely indicates that in the ninth century, the controversy over this issue was intense, with both sides fabricating hadiths attributing their position to Muhammad.

Whatever the relative merits of each side of this argument may be, there is no doubt that no Muslims would be defending this practice, which amounts to prostitution, today were it not for the traditions stating that Muhammad himself permitted it.

Delusion

On top of all this, Bukhari records a tradition in which Muhammad suffers from a curious delusion: he thought he had had sexual intercourse when he had not. Aisha is depicted as saying: "Magic was worked on Allah's Messenger so that he used to think that he had had sexual relations with his wives while he actually had not."[89] One of the Muslims remarks: "That is the hardest kind of magic, as it has such an effect."[90] Muhammad eventually tells Aisha that the practitioner of this black magic was Labid bin al-Asam, "a man from Bani Zuraiq who was an ally of the Jews and was a hypocrite."[91] Muhammad concludes: "Allah has cured me; I dislike to let evil spread among my people."[92]

While it might be difficult to imagine why anyone who was trying to establish that Muhammad was the greatest of Allah's prophets would

---

87 Ibid.
88 Sahih Muslim, book 16, no. 1405a.
89 Sahih Bukhari, vol. 7, book 76, no. 5765.
90 Ibid.
91 Ibid.
92 Ibid.

depict him as susceptible to magic spells, the point is in Muhammad's conclusion: "Allah has cured me." The lesson that such stories were designed to teach was that Allah protects Muhammad from all the most potent dangers that people fear the most, including curses and other dark arts that the Jews, the worst enemies of the Muslims (cf. Qur'an 5:82) and their allies practice. Thus, this story is not intended to show Muhammad's weakness, but his strength as always enjoying Allah's protection, which presumably is also offered to the loyal believers as well.

CHAPTER FIFTEEN

Muhammad's Wisdom

The hadith literature supplements the teaching of strict monotheism, the primary message of the Qur'an, with folk wisdom that likely predates Islam but is attributed to Muhammad. This is done so as to enhance his aura as a man of more than ordinary knowledge and insight. These teachings generally have little or nothing to do with the central teachings of Islam and seem designed only to reinforce the notion that Muhammad sees more than the average man and that believers would be foolish to disregard his words.

Advice for the Wary

Some of these traditions amount to little more than superstitions, if that. Bukhari depicts Abu Huraira relating this statement from Muhammad: "If anyone of you rouses from sleep and performs the ablution, he should wash his nose by putting water in it and then blowing it out thrice, because Satan has stayed in the upper part of his nose all the night."[1]

Bukhari also includes this saying of Muhammad, supposedly transmitted by Ibn Abbas: "When you eat, do not wipe your hands till you have licked it, or had it licked by somebody else."[2] It is hard to envision how such a tradition could ever have arisen in the first place; perhaps it has to do with a desire to keep one's clothing free from stains in days long before paper napkins existed, much less were plentiful. In any case, here, as in other cases, attributing this recommendation to Muhammad gave it the imprimatur of the highest possible authority.

One odd hadith has Muhammad saying, according to Ali ibn Abi Talib: "The eyes are the leather strap of the anus, so one who sleeps

---

1 Sahih Bukhari, vol. 4, book 59, no. 3295.
2 Sahih Bukhari, vol. 7, book 70, no. 5456.

should perform ablution."[3] In another version of this story, Ali's later rival for the caliphate, Muawiya, makes clearer what Muhammad is supposed to be saying: "The eyes are the leather strap of the anus, and when the eye sleeps the leather strap is loosened."[4] Leather straps were used to open and shut the pouches in which the Muslims carried water; thus, the saying is explaining that when one's eyes are closed in sleep, he is liable to lose control of his anus and may break wind or even defecate, requiring ablution upon waking before prayers could be said. This is, however, a reflection of a primitive and prescientific view of biology; a connection between the eyes and sphincter control has never been established.

Folk Medicine

Muhammad is also depicted as having extraordinary insights into how to avoid various illnesses or get healed from them. Bukhari also has Abu Huraira relate that Muhammad said: "If a house fly falls in the drink of anyone of you, he should dip it (in the drink) and take it out, for one of its wings has a disease and the other has the cure for the disease."[5]

Another tradition has Muhammad telling believers not to be concerned about dirty water. One of the Muslims asks Muhammad: "Water is brought for you from the well of Buda'ah. It is a well in which dead dogs, menstrual clothes and excrement of people are thrown."[6] Muhammad is unconcerned: "Verily water is pure and is not defiled by anything."[7]

This foul water was not for drinking, but for ablutions, as the purity involved was ritual, not hygienic. Another version of this hadith states that clearly: "It was said, 'O Allah's Messenger! Shall we use the water of Buda'ah well to perform ablution while it is a well in which menstruation rags, flesh of dogs and the putrid are dumped?' Allah's Messenger said: 'Indeed water is pure, nothing makes it impure.'"[8]

That foul water may not have been for drinking, but in another hadith, Muhammad allows that as well: "We came to a pond in which there

---

3 Sunan Abi Dawud, vol. 1, no. 203.
4 Mishkat al-Masabih, book 3, no. 315.
5 Sahih Bukhari, vol. 4, book 59, no. 3320.
6 Sunan Abi Dawud, book 1, no. 67.
7 Ibid.
8 Jami at-Tirmidhi, vol. 1, book 1, no. 66.

was the carcass of a donkey, so we refrained from using the water until the Messenger of Allah came to us and said: 'Water is not made impure by anything.' Then we drank from it and gave it to our animals to drink, and we carried some with us."[9]

In other traditions, however, Muhammad contradicts this blanket permission to use all water by warning against impurities in water: "You should not pass urine in stagnant water which is not flowing then (you may need to) wash in it."[10] And: "None of you should take a bath in stagnant water when he is sexually impure."[11]

Modern-day commentators generally attempt to resolve this contradiction by asserting that the hadiths about it being impossible for water to be impure refer to flowing water, not stagnant water, and so whatever impurities may have been present would be carried away. Others argue that the difference lies in the amount of water in question.[12] These are perfectly reasonable explanations; it may also be that in an environment in which water was scarce, one faction among the Muslims wanted to emphasize that even water that wasn't in the best condition could still be used, while another faction differed.

Whether or not water was always pure, one must never drink it while standing up, as a tradition depicts Muhammad saying: "None of you should drink while standing; and if anyone forgets, he must vomit."[13]

In another tradition, Muhammad makes a recommendation to some newcomers to Medina who embraced Islam, but the story does not have a happy ending. Bukhari depicts Muhammad's companion Anas as recounting:

> Some people from the tribe of Ukl came to the Prophet and embraced Islam. The climate of Medina did not suit them, so the Prophet ordered them to go to the (herd of milch) camels of charity and to drink, their milk and urine (as a medicine). They did so, and after they had recovered from their ailment (became healthy) they

---

9 Sunan Ibn Majah, vol. 1, book 1, no. 520.
10 Sahih Bukhari, vol. 1, book 4, no. 239.
11 Bulugh al-Maram, book 1, no. 6.
12 See, for example, Abu Khadeejah Abdul-Wahid, "Water Is Pure and Nothing Can Make It Impure Except if an Impurity Is Added Which Changes Its Smell, Taste or Colour: Purification and the Types of Water," Islamic Studies Courses, February 13, 2022, https://abukhadeejah. com/water-is-pure-and-nothing-can-make-it-impure-purification-and-the-types-of-water/.
13 Sahih Muslim, book 36, no. 2026.

turned renegades (reverted from Islam) and killed the shepherd of the camels and took the camels away. The Prophet sent (some people) in their pursuit and so they were (caught and) brought, and the Prophets ordered that their hands and legs should be cut off and that their eyes should be branded with heated pieces of iron, and that their cut hands and legs should not be cauterized, till they die.[14]

This establishes camel urine as a remedy for ailments; some Muslims take this with the utmost seriousness to this day and justify Muhammad's recommendation with scholarly studies, thereby demonstrating that academic scholarship is hardly the neutral and disinterested pursuit of truth that many still assume it to be.[15]

Meanwhile, two Qur'anic passages make the punishment of the renegade Ukl tribesmen exemplary and to be emulated. One establishes that those who embrace Islam, emigrate to join the Muslims, and then turn away from it are to be hunted down and killed: "They wish that you would disbelieve even as they disbelieve, that you may be on the same level. So do not choose friends from them until they migrate in the way of Allah, if they turn back, then take them and kill them wherever you find them, and choose no friend or helper from among them" (4:89). The other establishes the punishment the Ukl received as to be meted out to others who set themselves against the Muslims' deity and prophet: "The only reward for those who make war upon Allah and his messenger and struggle to sow corruption on earth will be that they will be killed or crucified, or have their hands and feet cut off on opposite sides, or be expelled from the land. Such will be their degradation in this world, and in the hereafter, theirs will be an awful doom" (5:33).

Miraculous Bodily Fluids

Even Muhammad's bodily fluids, meanwhile, were beneficial for the believers. One hadith recounts that "the Prophet asked for a tumbler containing water and washed both his hands and face in it and then threw a mouthful of water in the tumbler and said to both of us (Abu

---

14 Sahih Bukhari, vol. 8, book 86, no. 6802.
15 See, for example, Norizam Salamt, Ruszymah Binti Haji Idrus, Mohd Izhar Ariff Mohd Kashim, and Mohd Helmy Mokhtar, "Anticancer, antiplatelet, gastroprotective and hepatoprotective effects of camel urine: A scoping review," *Saudi Pharmaceutical Journal*, v. 29(7), July 2021.

Musa and Bilal), 'Drink from the tumbler and pour some of its water on your faces and chests.'"[16]

In another hadith, a Muslim woman recounts: "I set out (for migration to Medina) as I was in the advanced stage of pregnancy. I came to Medina and got down at the place known as Quba and gave birth to a child there. Then I came to Allah's Messenger. He placed him (the child) in his lap and then commanded for the dates to be brought. He chewed them and then put the saliva in his mouth. The first thing which went into his stomach was the saliva of Allah's Messenger. He then rubbed his palate with dates and then invoked blessings for him and blessed him. He was the first child who was born in Islam (after Migration)."[17]

All the Muslims benefited from the wonderful powers of Muhammad's saliva. A tradition depicts one of Muhammad's companions, Jabir ibn Abdullah, recalling an occasion during the time of the siege of Medina when his wife made a meal for Muhammad, and the prophet of Islam proceeded to invite all the Muslims to partake of it. Jabir's wife was not happy, as apparently, she did not have enough food for all the Muslims, but she brought Muhammad "the dough, and he spat in it and invoked for Allah's Blessings in it. Then he proceeded towards our earthenware meat-pot and spat in it and invoked for Allah's Blessings in it. Then he said (to my wife): 'Call a lady-baker to bake along with you and keep on taking out scoops from your earthenware meat-pot, and do not put it down from its fireplace.' They were one thousand (who took their meals), and by Allah they all ate, and when they left the food and went away, our earthenware pot was still bubbling (full of meat) as if it had not decreased, and our dough was still being baked as if nothing had been taken from it."[18]

The resonances with Jesus' miraculous feeding of five thousand people with five loaves of bread and two fish (Matthew 14:14–21) are obvious, along with the added implication that the food was multiplied by the miraculous power of the prophetic saliva.

Ibn Kathir records two traditions in which the faithful also benefit from Muhammad's urine:

---

16 Sahih Bukhari, vol. 1, book 4, no. 188.
17 Sahih Muslim, book 38, no. 2146b.
18 Sahih Bukhari, vol. 5, book 64, no. 4102.

The Messenger of God had a pottery bowl into which he would urinate. When morning came, he would call out, "Umm Ayman, pour out the contents of the pot." One night I got up feeling thirsty and drank what it contained. And when the Messenger of God called out, "Umm Ayman, pour out the contents of the pot," I replied, "Messenger of God, I got up feeling thirsty and drank what was in it!" He commented, "You'll never suffer from your stomach!"[19]

And he depicts another woman as recounting:

The Prophet had a wooden bowl into which he would urinate and then place beneath his bed. A woman named Baraka came one day and drank it. He asked where it was, being unable to find it, and he was told, "Baraka drank it!" He stated, "She is kept out of hell-fire by a screen!"[20]

Supernatural Knowledge

Throughout the sira literature, as we have seen, Muhammad often displays knowledge of events far beyond ordinary human insight. He supposedly perceived when he had been poisoned because the poisoned food let him know, foresaw the Islamic conquest of the Middle East, perceived that various meats offered to him as food were actually transformed Jews, and much more. A series of hadiths also depict him warning that the last day was coming soon, within the lifetime of his hearers.

In one such tradition, Muhammad states that the day of judgment will come soon after his own ministry is completed: "I and the Last Hour are (close to each other) like this (and he, in order to explain it) pointed (by joining his) forefinger, (one) next to the thumb and the middle finger (together)."[21]

In another, Muhammad is asked: "When would the Last Hour come?"[22] The story continues: "Thereupon Allah's Messenger kept quiet for a while. Then looked at a young boy in his presence belonging to the tribe of Azd Shanua and he said: 'If this boy lives he would not

---

19 Ibn Kathir, The Life of Prophet Muhammad, 4, 462.
20 Ibid.
21 Sahih Muslim, book 54, no. 2950.
22 Sahih Muslim, book 54, no. 2953b.

grow very old till the Last Hour would come to you.' Anas said that this young boy was of our age during those days."[23]

A variant of this tradition, however, seems to mitigate this prediction, as Muhammad equates "the last hour" not with the end of the world and the divine judgment, but with the death of each individual: "Aisha reported that when the desert Arabs came to Allah's Messenger they asked about the Last Hour as to when that would come. And he looked towards the youngest amongst them and said: 'If he lives, he would not grow very old that he would find your Last Hour coming to you (he would see you dying)."[24]

The mitigating traditions are understandable, as it defies explanation that ninth-century Muslims would compose traditions depicting Muhammad making a prediction that turned out to be so resoundingly false. Either these are extremely early traditions that were preserved faithfully by word of mouth and written down two hundred years after Muhammad's death by tradition-minded Muslims who wanted to preserve every word the prophet of Islam uttered, even if it depicted him unfavorably, or else there was an expectation in the eighth or ninth century when these traditions were composed that the world would end soon, and it was considered useful in this case, as in so many others, to ascribe this idea to Muhammad. The youngest among the Muslims not long before Muhammad's death could conceivably have been a hundred years old in the 730s, and perhaps these traditions began circulating around that time.

Another possibility is that these traditions were designed to mimic the statement of Jesus: "Truly, I say to you, there are some standing here who will not taste death before they see the Son of man coming in his kingdom" (Matthew 16:28). If Christianity had its founding figure making what appeared to be a prediction of the end times being imminent, in words that were then interpreted in innumerable ways to mitigate the possibility that he had made a prediction that turned out to be wrong, then the founding figure of Islam would be made to do so as well. This would buttress the prophetic claim of the Muhammad figure, as he, like Jesus and others, would be depicted making enigmatic statements that

---

23 Ibid.
24 Sahih Muslim, book 54, no. 2952.

seemed false when taken in a literal manner but could mean any number of other things.

Other traditions depict Muhammad as having knowledge of other prophets beyond what is recorded in the Qur'an: "While Job was naked, taking a bath, a swarm of gold locusts fell on him and he started collecting them in his garment. His Lord called him, 'O Job! Have I not made you rich enough to need what you see?' He said, 'Yes, O Lord! But I cannot dispense with your Blessing.'"[25]

Other hadiths heap yet more opprobrium upon the Jews. In one, Muhammad is depicted as saying: "Were it not for Bani Israel, meat would not decay; and were it not for Eve, no woman would ever betray her husband."[26] Another has Muhammad excoriating the Jews' pride and contempt for divine commands: "It was said to Bani Israel, Enter the gate (of the town) with humility (prostrating yourselves) and saying: 'Repentance,' but they changed the word and entered the town crawling on their buttocks and saying: 'A wheat grain in the hair.'"[27]

Muhammad is also made to have particular knowledge of the end times and the last judgment. In one tradition, he says that Jews and Christians will replace Muslims in hell: "No Muslim would die but Allah would admit in his stead a Jew or a Christian in Hell-Fire. Umar b. Abd al-Aziz took an oath: By One besides Whom there is no god but He, thrice that his father had narrated that to him from Allah's Messenger."[28] In another swipe at Christianity, the Jesus of Christianity is depicted as faring the worst on the last day: "Narrated Abu Huraira: Allah's Messenger said, 'The most awful name in Allah's sight on the Day of Resurrection, will be (that of) a man calling himself Malik Al-Amlak (the king of kings)."[29] This appears to be a direct rebuke to the New Testament depictions of Jesus as the king of kings in the last days (Revelation 17:14, 19:16).

In another hadith, Muhammad is depicted as knowing that Jesus, not the Savior of Christianity but the prophet of Islam, as he is depicted in the Qur'an, will return and wreak vengeance upon the Christians for having twisted his message: "By Him in Whose Hands my soul is, surely

25 Sahih Bukhari, vol. 4, book 60, no. 3391.
26 Sahih Bukhari, vol. 4, book 60, no. 3399.
27 Sahih Bukhari, vol. 4, book 60, no. 3403.
28 Sahih Muslim, book 50, no. 2767b.
29 Sahih Bukhari, vol. 8, book 78, no. 6205.

the son of Maryam (Mary) Iesa (Jesus) will shortly descend amongst you people (Muslims) and will judge mankind justly by the Law of the Qur'an (as a just ruler) and will break the cross and kill the pig and abolish the *Jizya* (a tax taken from the non-Muslims, who are in the protection, of the Muslim government). This Jizya tax will not be accepted by Iesa (Jesus). Then there will be abundance of money and nobody will accept charitable gifts."[30]

The prophet of Islam also knows the joys that will await the blessed in paradise, beyond their descriptions in the Qur'an: "There is no one whom Allah will admit to Paradise but Allah will marry him to seventy-two wives, two from houris and seventy from his inheritance from the people of Hell, all of whom will have desirable front passages and he will have a male member that never becomes flaccid (i.e., soft and limp).'"[31] The "inheritance from the people of hell" are women who have been condemned to eternal torment and sentenced to serve their time by becoming sex slaves for the Muslim men in paradise.

There will be many such women, for in one tradition, Muhammad rebukes women as such, saying that they constitute the majority of those in hell: "O women! Give alms, as I have seen that the majority of the dwellers of Hell-fire were you (women).... You curse frequently and are ungrateful to your husbands. I have not seen anyone more deficient in intelligence and religion than you. A cautious sensible man could be led astray by some of you."[32]

Before the blessed can partake of these joys of paradise, however, their souls will remain for a time inside the bodies of green birds. One hadith depicts Muhammad being asked to explain this Qur'anic verse: "Do not think of those who are killed in the way of Allah as dead. No, they are living. With their Lord they have provision" (3:169).

Muhammad replies: "The souls of the martyrs live in the bodies of green birds who have their nests in chandeliers hung from the throne of the Almighty. They eat the fruits of Paradise from wherever they like and then nestle in these chandeliers. Once their Lord cast a glance at them and said: 'Do you want anything?' They said: 'What more shall we desire? We eat the fruit of Paradise from wherever we like.' Their

---

30 Sahih Bukhari, vol. 3, book 34, no. 2222.
31 Sunan Ibn Majah, vol. 5, book 37, no. 4337.
32 Sahih Bukhari, vol. 1, book 6, no. 304.

Lord asked them the same question thrice. When they saw that they will continue to be asked and not left (without answering the question), they said: 'O Lord, we wish that You would return our souls to our bodies so that we may be slain in Your way once again. When He (Allah) saw that they had no need, they were left (to their joy in heaven)."[33]

Along with women, meanwhile, murdered girls are also filling hell. Islamic apologists frequently claim that Islam represented a major moral advance over previous religions and societies and point to the Qur'an's prohibition of the killing of female children, which is implied in a passage about the day of judgment:

> When the sun is folded up,
> And when the stars fall,
> And when the hills are moved,
> And when the camels big with young are abandoned,
> And when the wild beasts are herded together,
> And when the seas rise,
> And when souls are reunited,
> And when the girl child who was buried alive is asked
> For what sin she was killed,
> And when the pages are laid open,
> And when the sky is torn away,
> And when the blaze is lit,
> And when the garden is brought near,
> Every soul will know what it has made ready. (81:1–14)

Less often invoked, however, is Muhammad's statement that female children thus murdered will suffer forever the tortures of hellfire: "Amir reported the Messenger of Allah as saying: 'The woman who buries alive her newborn girl and the girl who is buried alive both will go to Hell.' This tradition has also been transmitted by Ibn Mas'ud from the Prophet to the same effect through a different chain of narrators."[34]

Meanwhile, anyone who has waged jihad need not fear hell at all, for Muhammad is also quoted as saying that "anyone whose both feet get covered with dust in Allah's Cause will not be touched by the (Hell) fire."[35]

---

33 Sahih Muslim, book 33, no. 1887.
34 Sunan Abi Dawud, book 42, no. 4717.
35 Sahih Bukhari, vol. 4, book 56, no. 2811.

Those who have not waged jihad, on the other hand, may have little or nothing to fear either. Another tradition depicts Muhammad as saying: "Whoever believes in Allah and His Apostle, offers prayer perfectly and fasts the month of Ramadan, will rightfully be granted Paradise by Allah, no matter whether he fights in Allah's Cause or remains in the land where he is born."[36]

The jihadis, however, would go to a higher level of paradise, for which Muslims should strive: "Paradise has one-hundred grades which Allah has reserved for the Mujahidin who fight in His Cause, and the distance between each of two grades is like the distance between the Heaven and the Earth. So, when you ask Allah (for something), ask for Al-Firdaus which is the best and highest part of Paradise."[37] The hadith then adds a note of uncertainty: "The sub-narrator added, 'I think the Prophet also said, "Above it (i.e. Al-Firdaus) is the Throne of Beneficent (i.e. Allah), and from it originate the rivers of Paradise."'"[38] "I think"?

In another hadith, Muhammad reveals that Allah actually wants people to sin so that his mercy may abound: "By Him in Whose Hand is my life, if you were not to commit sin, Allah would sweep you out of existence and He would replace (you by) those people who would commit sin and seek forgiveness from Allah, and He would have pardoned them."[39]

Scientific Knowledge

Muhammad is also depicted as being aware of the workings of the physical world to a degree beyond the knowledge of his peers. In one hadith, he explains the seasons: "The (Hell) Fire complained to its Lord saying, 'O my Lord! My different parts eat up each other.' So, He allowed it to take two breaths, one in the winter and the other in summer, and this is the reason for the severe heat and the bitter cold you find (in weather)."[40]

The prophet of Islam likewise disclosed that those who suffered from fevers were experiencing the pains of hell prematurely: "Fever is from the heat of the (Hell) Fire; so abate fever with water."[41]

---

36 Sahih Bukhari, vol. 4, book 56, no. 2790.
37 Ibid.
38 Ibid.
39 Sahih Muslim, book 50, no. 2749.
40 Sahih Bukhari, vol. 4, book 59, no. 3260.
41 Sahih Bukhari, vol. 4, book 59, no. 3264.

Muhammad revealed that the anatomy of non-Muslims differed from that of Muslims: "Ibn Umar reported Allah's Messenger as saying that a non-Muslim eats in seven intestines whereas a Muslim eats in one intestine."[42] The translators of a cognate hadith explain this away with parenthetical glosses that make this curious statement into an observation that non-Muslims are gluttons, while Muslims are not: "Narrated Ibn Umar: Allah's Messenger said, 'A believer eats in one intestine (is satisfied with a little food), and a kafir (unbeliever) or a hypocrite eats in seven intestines (eats too much).'"[43]

As we saw in the story of the former rabbi Abdullah, Muhammad explained that a child resembled his mother or his father depending upon whose orgasm was first: "If a man's discharge proceeded that of the woman, then the child resembles the father, and if the woman's discharge proceeded that of the man, then the child resembles the mother."[44]

Further Prohibitions

The hadith literature also depicts Muhammad giving the Muslims new prohibitions that aren't found in the Qur'an. The Qur'an states: "O you who believe, strong drink and games of chance and idols and divining arrows are only an abomination of Satan's handiwork. Leave it aside so that you may succeed" (5:90).

A hadith has Muhammad supplementing this with a prohibition of a Persian game that was unlikely to have been known or played in seventh-century Arabia: "He who played *Nardashir* is like one who dyed his hand with the flesh and blood of swine."[45]

Another hadith depicts Aisha recounting that Muhammad acquiesced to Abu Bakr's denunciation of musical instruments while making an exception for a festive day: "Abu Bakr came to my house while two small Ansari girls were singing beside me the stories of the Ansar concerning the Day of Buath. And they were not singers. Abu Bakr said protestingly, 'Musical instruments of Satan in the house of Allah's Messenger!' It happened on the Eid day and Allah's Messenger said, 'O Abu Bakr! There is an Eid for every nation and this is our Eid.'"[46]

42 Sahih Muslim, book 36, no. 2060a.
43 Sahih Bukhari, vol. 7, book 70, no. 5394.
44 Sahih Bukhari, vol. 6, book 65, no. 4480.
45 Sahih Muslim, book 41, no. 2260.
46 Sahih Bukhari, vol. 2, book 13, no. 952.

Other traditions depict Muhammad as taking the dimmest possible view of musical instruments and "singing slave girls." In one, he is depicted as making a dark prediction: "In this Ummah there shall be collapsing of the earth, transformation and Qadhf," that is, false accusations of adultery and sodomy.[47] One of the Muslims asks him when this will be, and Muhammad responds: "When singing slave-girls, music, and drinking intoxicants spread."[48]

In another, Muhammad makes a similar prediction about the days when evil will be widespread: "People among my nation will drink wine, calling it by another name, and musical instruments will be played for them and singing girls (will sing for them). Allah will cause the earth to swallow them up, and will turn them into monkeys and pigs," a fate that was all the more ignominious for having been shared by the Jews.[49]

It would be even if these errant Muslims were drinking their wine out of silver drinking vessels, for Muhammad is also depicted as saying: "He who drinks in a silver utensil is only swallowing Hell-fire in his stomach."[50] These miscreants would fare worse still if their clothing fell below their ankles, for "Abu Huraira reported God's messenger as saying, 'The part of the lower garment which goes below the ankles is in hell.' Bukhari transmitted it."[51]

Dreams and Nightmares

Bukhari records a tradition in which one of Muhammad's companions recounts that one day, the prophet of Islam "asked us whether anyone of us had seen a dream. We replied in the negative. The Prophet said, 'But I had seen (a dream) last night that two men came to me, caught hold of my hands, and took me to the Sacred Land (Jerusalem). There, I saw a person sitting and another standing with an iron hook in his hand pushing it inside the mouth of the former till it reached the jawbone, and then tore off one side of his cheek, and then did the same with the other side; in the meantime the first side of his cheek became normal again and then he repeated the same operation again. I said, 'What is

---

47 Jami at-Tirmidhi, vol. 4, book 33, no. 2212.
48 Ibid.
49 Sunan Ibn Majah, vol. 5, book 36, no. 4020.
50 Bulugh al-Maram, book 1, no. 17.
51 Miskat al-Masabih, book 22, no. 4314.

this?'"[52] He related some more dreams and then explained: "As for the one whose cheek you saw being torn away, he was a liar and he used to tell lies, and the people would report those lies on his authority till they spread all over the world. So, he will be punished like that till the Day of Resurrection."[53]

His community did not take heed. It fabricated literally thousands of lies about what he said and did, and these did indeed spread all over the world. Like the poison Muhammad ingested at Khaybar, their ill effects are still being felt.

---

52 Sahih Bukhari, vol. 2, book 23, no. 1386.
53 Ibid.

CHAPTER SIXTEEN

The Legend Continues

Even Less Reliable Than Has Been Assumed

We have now seen that virtually nothing is written about Muhammad in the seventh century when he is supposed to have flourished. A great deal is written about him in the eighth century, although most of it is lost. And then, in the ninth century, there is a veritable explosion of written material about Muhammad. While there are numerous contradictions in this material, the broad outlines of the story are generally stable.

This does not, however, necessarily mean that the broad outline of the story is historically accurate; in the absence of any attestation of Muhammad's existence dating from the time he is supposed to have lived, the overarching unity in the traditions on the general outline of his life could indicate only that the core elements of the legend were agreed upon before most of it was committed to writing.

The ninth-century traditions are too far removed from what they describe, and there is far too much opportunity for additions, deletions, and other alterations for them to be taken at face value. This fact is becoming widely known, as is indicated in Islamic scholar Eric Ormsby's review of the contemporary Islamic apologist Lesley Hazleton's hagiographical biography of Muhammad, *The First Muslim: The Story of Muhammad*. Ormsby observes:

> Hazleton accepts the traditional Muslim account of Muhammad's life and mission pretty much as it stands in the sources. She relies heavily, indeed almost exclusively, on the standard English translation of the classical biography by the ninth-century Egyptian author Ibn Hisham (whose *sira* incorporates and completes an earlier eighth-century account), as well as on the monumental

work of the great tenth-century historian and Koran commentator al-Tabari. I note these dates not out of pedantry but to indicate a glaring problem with these sources: the earliest was composed a century after the Prophet's death in 632 and the latest almost three hundred years after that (al-Tabari died in 923). Even allowing for the fabled tenacity of memory in traditional Muslim culture, not to mention the exemplary critical rigour of both Ibn Hisham and al-Tabari, it seems improbable that either of these narratives could be considered factually accurate in all or even most of their details. Occasionally Hazleton acknowledges this, as when she notes of one episode that 'all of this is on the side of too good to be true', but in general she is content to reproduce the traditional and well-hallowed sequence of events.[1]

So is virtually everyone else who writes about the life of Muhammad today, whether they are believers, skeptics, or something in between. Without Ibn Hisham, Tabari, Ibn Sa'd, and al-Waqidi, as well as the biographical hadiths, none of which date from anywhere close to the time Muhammad is supposed to have lived, there is simply nothing to go on.

Nor is the picture substantially improved by any subsequent effort to sort out history from legend and pious fabrication.

Ibn Kathir

In the fourteenth century, the Islamic scholar Ibn Kathir, whose massive commentary on the Qur'an is still read and revered today, composed a biography of Muhammad of imposing length as part of *al-Bidaya wa-l-Nihaya* (The Beginning and the End), an even larger work on the history of the earlier prophets, Muhammad, and the Umayyad period.

This sira contains extensive quotations from Ibn Hisham's work and other earlier biographical material on the prophet of Islam; also, at numerous points, the author carefully evaluates various traditions and presents an explanation of why one tradition is to be accepted and another rejected. Despite appearances, however, this biographical work cannot be said to be any more of a scrupulously accurate history than its antecedents were. It bears numerous unmistakable signs of the fact

---

1 Eric Ormsby, "Making a Prophet," op. cit.

that in the centuries that had passed since Ibn Hisham wrote his sira, the elaboration and enhancement of the Muhammad legend had not been reevaluated or rejected.

Yusuf al-Hajj Ahmad, a modern-day scholar who helped prepare an edition of *al-Bidayah* that was published early in the twenty-first century, included several notes that suggest that his edition was not necessarily a scrupulously accurate edition of what Ibn Kathir actually wrote: "We relied on a number of printed and handwritten copies of the book and in cases where any contradiction or omission was found, we succeeded in establishing the most accurate and authentic text."[2] Ahmad added: "We left out the ahadeeth which proved to be baseless or weak and confined ourselves to the ahadeeth which are authentic or hasan and those which are acceptable due to the existence of other supporting narrations. On rare occasions, when it was found that there were no other ahadeeth in the chapter, we included some weak ahadeeth whose weakness was not of an extreme nature."[3]

Once again, the provenance of these weak hadiths, and the reasons why they may have been invented, was not discussed.

Ninth Century? Actually, No

What's more, the glimmer of hope that this material contains some kernels of historically accurate information, although these are virtually impossible to distinguish from the rest of the material, becomes even dimmer in light of the fact that *the ninth-century literature as we have it today does not date from the ninth century*. It only comes to us from later manuscripts, allowing even more possibility for alteration.

Throughout this book, I have referred to the sira of Ibn Hisham. As I explained in chapter two, Ibn Hisham reproduced much of the eighth-century sira of Ibn Ishaq, with Tabari preserving other portions. I've referred to it as the work of Ibn Hisham rather than as that of Ibn Ishaq because it is impossible to know how much Ibn Ishaq's text was altered when Ibn Hisham reproduced it.

Further complicating the situation is that Ibn Ishaq had two prominent students: Ziyad ibn Abdallah al-Bakkai and Yunus ibn Bukayr. According to the twenty-first-century Russian Islamic scholar Alexander

---

2 Ibid., 6.
3 Ibid.

Kudelin, al-Bakkai "considerably abridged the work of Ibn Ishaq."[4] Ibn Bukayr "assured his listeners that he communicated Ibn Ishaq's work 'word for word,'" but actually, "the medieval biographical literature tells us that 'he took the work of Ibn Ishaq, and then combined it with other ahadith.'"[5]

This represents just a small part of a much larger problem: Kudelin adds that "the work of Ibn Ishaq exists in more than 15 various editions."[6] The renowned contemporary ex-Muslim Islamic scholar Ibn Warraq concurs, noting: "The lost original of Ibn Ishaq's work has to be restored or recovered from at least fifteen different versions, excluding that of Ibn Hisham."[7] Kudelin points out that the Iraqi researcher S. M. al-Samuk has identified fifty different "transmitters" of Ibn Ishaq's sira, with "considerable differences between the texts."[8]

Ibn Kathir reflects this in his own biographical material on Muhammad. At one point, he relates this story:

> Ibn Hisham stated, "And when al-Asha was in Mecca or near thereto, some Quraysh polytheists stopped him and asked what business he had there. He told them that he had come seeking the Messenger of God.
>
> "One of the Quraysh commented, 'But Abu Basr, he is forbidding sex!' Al-Asha responded, 'I swear, that's no desire of mine.'
>
> "'But he's also forbidding wine,' the man objected.
>
> "'Well, that's something I do hold dear; I'll go off and have my fill of it for a year, then I'll come back and accept Islam!'
>
> "And leave he did. But he died that same year without returning to the Messenger of God.'
>
> Thus does Ibn Hisham tell this story here. He extracts a great deal from Muhammad Ibn Ishaq, and this is one thing added to his account by Ibn Hisham.[9]

Yet in Alfred Guillaume's magisterial 1955 edition of the work of Ibn Hisham/Ibn Ishaq, this story does not appear.

---

4 Alexander Kudelin, "Al-Sira al-Nabawiyya by Ibn Ishaq—Ibn Hisham: The History of the Texts and the Problem of Authorship," *Manuscripta Orientalia*, vol. 16, no. 1, 2010, 7.
5 Ibid.
6 Ibid., 8.
7 Ibn Warraq, Quest for the Historical Muhammad, op. cit., 27.
8 Kudelin, op. cit.
9 Ibn Kathir, *The Life of Prophet Muhammad*, op. cit., 2, 53.

Speaking about Ibn Ishaq's sira, Kudelin also notes that "the first publication of this monument" was "wonderfully prepared by F. Wüstenfeld."[10] Ferdinand Wüstenfeld (1808–1899) was a German scholar who published an edition of Ibn Ishaq's work in the 1860s. Wüstenfeld compiled his edition from Arabic manuscripts of varying reliability; Robert Kerr observes that "what was then considered to be a critical edition does not pass as such now."[11]

Kerr explains that the manuscripts of the sira literature "all mediaeval, from Spain," as well as from the fifteenth-century Ottoman Empire, "which would seem to strongly suggest that Muslims historically speaking did not add much significance to the work, excepting in twelfth century Spain and the early Ottoman period."[12] He added the striking detail that "there are only about ten or so manuscripts extant."[13]

It was Wüstenfeld's work that sparked interest in the early accounts of Muhammad's life even among Muslims. "After Wüstenfeld's edition of the Arabic text," Kerr stated, "we start finding Western translations, *biography* being a Western literary genre. These editions were then taken up by Muslims. You see that the first Arabic (pseudo)-critical editions only commenced in the 1960s as a reaction to this."[14] He concluded that "Islamic interest in the Sirah is derived from Western curiosity and has no long-standing tradition in Islam."[15]

Kerr also noted the development in the literature: "If we accept the general Islamic premise that Ibn Hisham transmitted content which he received orally and indirectly from students of Ibn Ishaq (certainly not from a written text if there ever was one, which I doubt, since Arabic was still in its infancy as a literary language in his days), then thereafter with al-Waqidi (*Kitab al-Maghazi*), and especially the latter's scribe and student Ibn Sa'd (*Kitab at-Tabaqat al-Kabir*), we see that blanks left by the previous author are filled in by those that continue the work, so too other later commentaries on al-Waqidi—suddenly dates, names of participants, geography and topography are mentioned in great detail, which prior authors seem not to have known."[16]

---

10 Kudelin, op. cit., 6.
11 Robert Kerr, email to the author, September 14, 2023.
12 Ibid.
13 Ibid.
14 Ibid.
15 Ibid.
16 Robert Kerr, email to the author, September 15, 2023.

Beyond the Ninth Century

Given the general lack of interest among Muslims in this literature, it is possible that this development continued even beyond the ninth-century and that the medieval manuscripts from which Wüstenfeld worked to compile his critical edition of Ibn Ishaq contain even more alterations from whatever the original work may have been. Thus, the ninth-century literature cannot even be assumed with confidence to have existed at that time in the form we have it today.

Robert Kerr accordingly noted that the contemporary Islamic scholar Mohammed Ali Amir Moezzi "adheres to the notion of an historical Muhammad but said, roughly translated, that despite all the sources, all we know about him fits on one piece of paper."[17]

That roughly corresponds to what is said about Muhammad in the seventh-century mentions of this name or title: a man arose from Arabia who was a warrior and a prophet. The rest is legend or history so mixed with legend that it is impossible to separate the two.

If there was a historical Muhammad, what he said and did and who he really was is thus even more thoroughly lost in the mists of time than was already clear from the lateness of the biographical material about him. Yet millions of Muslims today nevertheless believe fervently in the Muhammad who is depicted in the hadith and sira literature. The overwhelming majority of these people aren't even aware that the records of their prophet are open to question.

As a result of this dichotomy, the reported words and deeds of this peculiar and vexing figure will remain a matter of concern both for those who love the prophet of Islam and for those who are concerned about what some of his more ardent followers have done and will continue to do to those who remain outside the fold. "The evil that men do lives after them," says Marc Antony in Shakespeare's *Julius Caesar*, and in the case of Muhammad, whether he was an actual man who did the things that are ascribed to him or a legend constructed in order to justify and sanctify such behavior, the effect is the same: man or legend, Muhammad is one of the most consequential figures of world history, and the full story of the pain and human misery he has caused, and the blood he has spilled, has not yet been written.[18]

---

17 Robert Kerr, email to the author, September 14, 2023.
18 William Shakespeare, *Julius Caesar*, Act III, Scene II.

Acknowledgments

Even more than some of my others, this is just the sort of book for which there are numerous people to thank, and yet the very motion of gratitude can carry with it, thanks to those who may take umbrage at the thrust of this book, the whiff of a threat. That threat, of course, would not come from me.

I stand on the shoulders of the giants who blazed these trials, made these discoveries, and published them, often at immense personal cost. Special thanks to Ibn Warraq and Robert Kerr, and to all their colleagues who are pioneers in this field.

Thus, while I remain everlastingly grateful to the team at Bombardier Books for their ongoing interest in my work, and to those who have looked over this manuscript and made suggestions that vastly improved it, they shall remain nameless. May the unhappy necessity for this soon come to an end, and may the Western world recover some of the courage and determination to defend free thought and free expression that once made it great.